ADVANCED
C STRUCT
PROGRAMMING

ADVANCED C STRUCT PROGRAMMING

Data Structure Design and Implementation in C

John W. L. Ogilvie

John Wiley & Sons, Inc.
NEW YORK / CHICHESTER / BRISBANE / TORONTO / SINGAPORE

Copyright © 1990 by John Wiley & Sons, Inc.

All rights reserved. Published simultaneously in Canada.

Reproduction or translation of any part of this work beyond that permitted by Section 107 or 108
of the 1976 United States Copyright Act without the permission of the copyright owner is
unlawful. Requests for permission or further information should be addressed to the Permis-
sions Department, John Wiley & Sons, Inc.

Library of Congress Cataloging in Publication Data:

Ogilvie, John W. L.
    Advanced C struct programming: data structure design and implementation in C / John
W.L. Ogilvie.
        p.   cm.
    Includes bibliographical references.
    1. C (Computer program language) I. Title.
QA76.73.C15035 1990
005. 13'3—dc20   90-34645
ISBN 0-471-51943-X   CIP

Printed in the United States of America

10 9 8 7 6 5 4 3 2 1

To Genie

CONTENTS

Section Two   Examples

Section Three   The Framework

PREFACE

I wrote *Advanced C Struct Programming* because there are so few books on data structures for working programmers. Yes, there are introductory texts. But their data structures are inadequate for most professional programming. When you're wrestling with the complex structures at the heart of an interpreter or an operating system or a renderer, for instance, most data structure texts read like children's stories: "See the stack. See Jill *push()*. See Jill *pop()*. Push. Pop. Stacks are fun." The data structure books that aren't too simple are usually irrelevant. Sometimes they describe structures that are mathematically interesting, but impractical. More often, it's just too painful to adapt their particular structures for use in different programs to solve different problems.

Advanced C Struct Programming presents a practical method for designing and implementing complex data structures in C. The method consists of two parts: the Framework and the Plan. The Framework is a structure for organizing knowledge about data structures. It consists of four parts: Top-Level Goals, Abstract Data Type Descriptions, Struct Design Guidelines, and Struct Tricks. The Plan is an algorithm for using (and modifying) the Framework's resources to design and implement data structures.

The Plan and the Framework are designed for growth. They are not substitutes for programming expertise—there is no substitute. Use the Plan and the Framework as a lens to focus your programming efforts. I devised the Framework to organize programming folklore and expertise. Then I stuffed it with useful tricks and guidelines and techniques I've come across during the past seven years. Now I expect you to add your own insights to the Framework as you work. I don't believe you'll need to modify the Plan, or the Framework's organizational structure (as opposed to its current contents), but you're certainly free to.

I've been using the Plan and the Framework in different versions for five years. They have been very helpful. If you make the effort, they can provide you with the following benefits:

a way to bridge the gulf between the essential but simple data structures taught in most texts and the complex structures required in production code

a flexible framework for organizing programming tips, guidelines, and techniques
a plan of attack for large programming projects
an awareness of the tradeoffs being made in a program
checklists to be certain important functionalities aren't overlooked
a common ground for discussions between programmers and managers
insight into programmer motivation

Advanced C Struct Programming is different from other programming books in two ways: subject matter and approach. I've already spoken about the subject matter a bit, but allow me to continue by telling you where this book fits into the world of programming books.

If you survey the landscape of programming books, most works can be easily placed in one of just a few subject categories. There are books devoted to a single application program, usually a spreadsheet or a word processor. There are mathematical treatises stuffed with definitions, theorems, and proofs. There are introductions to programming in a particular language; these books are heavily (or lightly) commented language reference manuals. There are "cookbooks" that provide numerous algorithms and tested code for use in a particular area like graphics or networking. And there are introductory texts on data structures.

Advanced C Struct Programming does not fit into any of these subject categories. As I mentioned earlier, this is not an introduction to data structures. If you don't believe me, look at the Contents. You don't see a chapter on sorted lists, a chapter on stacks, a chapter on trees, and so forth. *Advanced C Struct Programming* picks up where introductory data structure texts leave off.

Likewise, *Advanced C Struct Programming* is not a "cookbook" of C networking code, or graphics routines, or any other particular application area. I chose a variety of examples to make it clear that the Plan and the Framework will work with a wide range of programs. The examples include code from interpreters, word processors, string pattern matchers, simulators, window managers, games, and database editing libraries.

If you thumb through the book, you'll see that it contains several thousand lines of C code. It's all debugged, and it's all useful. In fact, several of the examples are improvements on code that's currently in use in commercial products. But there are no "complete" applications or libraries; all the examples are pieces of larger programs. If you can use an example in one of your own programs, fine. But if you can't, please remember that the examples were chosen to illustrate the Plan, not to provide a complete implementation of anything in particular.

Finally, *Advanced C Struct Programming* is not an introduction to C. You should already know C syntax. The examples are all in C, because that happens to be my favorite programming language right now and because it's the language that will let me reach the greatest audience. But the code might just as easily have been written in Ada, Pascal, Modula-2, or C++, for instance. The Plan and the Framework are useful to programmers working in any of these languages.

The first section of *Advanced C Struct Programming* describes the Plan, that is, the algorithm for designing and implementing complex data structures in C. This is also where I set out the Framework, which will be used to organize our programming expertise. The middle section of the book contains examples of the Plan in action. This is where all the coding actually happens. The last section of the book is for reference. It contains the Framework of resources the examples rely on and is followed by a Glossary and Indexes.

So much for the difference in subject matter between *Advanced C Struct Programming* and other books. Now let's consider this book's unique approach to writing about programming. If you want to know how to improve the process of programming, you have to look at where code came from, and why, not just read the "final" code.

For this reason, I've written the examples in a "let's try this, oops, OK, let's try that" style. I've shown you the Plan in action (good and bad), instead of just showing you the results and waiting for applause.

Let me explain why by way of an analogy. Suppose I'm fluent in a foreign language, and a friend wants to learn the same language. Let's consider two teaching methods:

1. I lock my friend in a room with a thousand books, magazines, and newspapers written in the foreign language. I get television and radio broadcasts in the language piped into the room as well. Then I come back in six months to see what's been learned.

2. I give my friend a list of vocabulary words with English translations and a list of grammar rules for the language—how to conjugate verbs, how to form negatives, and so forth. I sit down with my friend, and we discuss the rules as we work through some examples. I explain why things that appeared correct won't work, I pass on little tricks I've learned, and so on.

With my friends, at least, the second method gives much better results in the long run. So that's the approach I've taken in *Advanced C Struct Programming*. I don't just present you with polished code and no discussion of how it came to be. Instead, I give you the Plan for designing and implementing good data structures, much as I'd give my friend above some grammar rules. I also give you the Framework of resources to build on, as I'd give my friend some basic vocabulary. Then I take you along as the code is designed and implemented, because there's a lot to be learned from the mistakes made along the way.

The point of the examples is to show the Plan in action, not simply to add to the world's sum total of debugged C code. I show you my mistakes, my debugging and testbed code, my consideration of earlier versions and why I didn't keep them, and so on. Thousands of decisions and assumptions are made along the way toward any "final" piece of code, but very few of these can be divined directly from the code itself. If you want to know why the code is the way it is, you have to take part in its creation, so that's what I try to let you do.

By the way, *Advanced C Struct Programming* is not just for programmers. If you manage programmers, the Plan and the Framework can help you get the results you want. As a manager, you should be certain your programmers know exactly which top-level goals are most important. You should be certain you and your programmers agree on the examples that are used to guide development. You should be able to distinguish the inevitable programming details from critical issues like which operations are/will be supported, what hardware is optional, and what assumptions have been made about error recovery. There are hundreds of such issues at stake in any commercial software development effort.

This book will help you manage all these problems, because the Plan and the Framework provide you and your programmers with a way to make these issues explicit. In my professional experience, the biggest problems arose not because people couldn't have discussed certain issues in time, but because the issues slipped through the cracks. They were overlooked until the damage was done. *Advanced C Struct Programming* can help you and your programmers ask these important questions in time, so the answers can guide the development effort to a successful conclusion.

I owe much of my programming expertise to the opportunities I've had to work with excellent programmers and managers on difficult projects. I can't list everyone here, but I would like to thank the following people for reviewing drafts of this book or otherwise sharing their expertise: Genie Ogilvie, Dr. Phil Lucht, Hyo Jong Lee, Gershon Elber, Bryan Trussel, Tom Wood, John Lowder, Scott Curtis, Kent Putnam, Scott Pritchett, Mike Dahl, Scott Young, Mark Ostlund, Lee Christensen, and Alan Crawford. Thanks are also due to Diane Cerra, Terri Hudson, Fran Bartlett, and the other excellent people at John Wiley & Sons and at G&H Soho for their assistance.

Pronoun gender alternates throughout the book; "he" and "she" appear in roughly equal numbers. Where it's not too awkward, I have simply avoided words that imply a gender, preferring instead terms like "programmer" and "manager," which refer to competence, not sex.

Any mistakes in *Advanced C Struct Programming* are solely my own. I would be pleased to know what you think of my work; I can be reached through Diane Cerra at John Wiley & Sons, Inc., 605 Third Avenue, New York, NY 10158-0012.

JOHN W.L. OGILVIE
June 1990
Salt Lake City, Utah

SECTION ONE

The Plan

CHAPTER 1
Introduction

If you haven't read the Preface yet, please do so now.

Our Plan for designing and implementing complex data structures in C is diagrammed in Figure 1-1. The Plan is a way to focus our expertise. It encourages us to make the most general, subtle, and far-reaching decisions first. Then we make increasingly specific decisions until we're at the point of choosing names for functions and variables and deciding what to put in each comment in the code.

The Plan is a top-down approach, but later decisions may feed back to change earlier

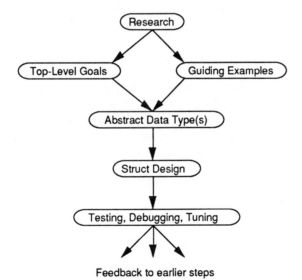

Feedback to earlier steps

FIGURE 1-1: The Plan for designing and implementing complex data structures.

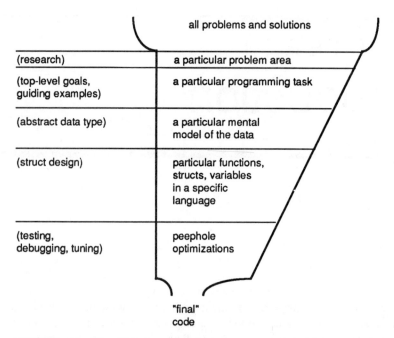

all problems and solutions

(research)	a particular problem area
(top-level goals, guiding examples)	a particular programming task
(abstract data type)	a particular mental model of the data
(struct design)	particular functions, structs, variables in a specific language
(testing, debugging, tuning)	peephole optimizations

"final" code

FIGURE 1-2: The Plan is a top-down approach in which we make increasingly specific decisions until we reach satisfactory code.

ones, as Figure 1-1 suggests. Figure 1-2 shows a slightly different model of the Plan. The narrowing funnel suggests that each major step in the Plan focuses our attention. At each step, we discard unwanted possibilities and specify in greater detail the possibilities that remain. When we choose to favor the top-level goal of portability over efficiency, for instance, we are discarding potential versions of the program that are very efficient but also very hard to port.

In practice, we may return to earlier steps in the Plan many times to make changes because of trouble encountered in later steps; we don't always fall straight through Figure 1-2 to the final code. Similarly, we may breeze right through some of the steps if the problem and program are simple enough. The Plan is a guideline, not an inflexible demand on our efforts. We must adapt it to different circumstances by spending more or less time on particular steps as appropriate.

Now let's discuss each of the steps in the Plan. Every step but the first will be examined in greater depth later in the book.

RESEARCH

The first step in solving any programming problem is to learn as much as possible about the problem area. If you're writing a compiler, you need to know something about language grammars and the target instruction set. If you're writing a renderer, you need a solid understanding of matrix transformations and scan-conversion, and so on.

However, *Advanced C Struct Programming* was not written to teach you how to do research. It will be taken for granted that you do what you can to learn about the problem areas you're programming in; research techniques are not discussed in this book. Each chapter in the Examples section (Section 2) shows how the problem at hand arises; none of the examples requires an extensive background in a particular problem area.

TOP-LEVEL GOALS

The purpose of this step is to define the main goals of the program and of the programming effort. Certain goals are often understood or assumed at the beginning of a project. When they are not made explicit, however, they are more often misunderstood than understood. Different people make different assumptions. If a programmer's assumptions don't match a manager's, or a marketer's, the results can be very painful.

What kind of assumptions are we talking about? What are some of the top-level goals we want to reach explicit decisions about? Three goals are described in detail in the Framework section of the book (Section 3), and each chapter in the Examples section has its own top-level goals. For now, just think of questions you could ask about any program or any programming task, and you'll have a list of possibilities for top-level goals:

How long does the program take to run?
How much memory does it need?
How long did it take to write the program?
Was it fun to write?
How hard is it for a novice to use the program? For an expert?
How hard would it be to use some of that code in another program?
What standard data formats does the program use?
How soon do you need a working version?
How reliable do you want the program to be?
What other environments might the program need to run in?
How do you split up the fame and fortune this program creates?
How do you pay for the mistakes this program makes?

You get the idea. Notice the wide variety of issues involved. Some top-level goals relate to human motivations and attitudes. Some require business or aesthetic judgments. Some require programming experience. Some top-level goals address program functionality, but only insofar as it is common to many programs—execution speed and memory requirements, for instance. We're not ready yet for specific examples of what we want the program to do; we'll get to that in the next section, "Guiding Examples."

We need to make our priorities clear because these goals can conflict with each other in many different ways. Sometimes the conflicts are obvious. If you want a compiler written from scratch, and you want it finished and totally reliable in three weeks, there's definitely a conflict between the time allotted and the reliability required.

Sometimes the conflict is more subtle. Consider the tradeoffs between writing a tool in-house and buying one off the shelf. If flexibility is the goal, writing it in-house might be better. If, on the other hand, quick implementation is the goal, buying something that's already written is the best choice. And if reliability, low cost, and happy programmers are goals, the choice depends on the circumstances. The point is, we want to be aware of the tradeoffs, so we must make the goals explicit.

GUIDING EXAMPLES

Where do programs come from? Someone thinks of something for a program to do, and someone writes the program. Then someone thinks of something else the program could do, and it's modified, or a new program is written. Of course, it's never this simple in practice, but the fact remains that programs come from examples. Specific examples drive all specifications of program functionality.

So how do we choose good examples? We can certainly come up with many specific examples of what we want our program to do. We can carefully sketch typical user sessions, we can list the features of competing products, and so on. But we need to filter the results of all this brainstorming if we want to make the best use of our time.

In Chapter 3, "Choosing Good Guiding Examples," we'll see how to use the Fundamental Characteristics of our preliminary set of examples to choose Guiding Examples. Guiding Examples overlap very little and summarize the functionality we want. They keep us on the right track as we design and implement our data structures, and they'll serve nicely as the core of a testbed or test suite. Sometimes they even wind up in a marketing brochure. Each chapter in the Examples section has its own Guiding Examples.

ABSTRACT DATA TYPES

We've researched our problem area. We've defined top-level goals and guiding examples so we can steer through the vast space of alternative programs. Now we're ready to start coding, right? Wrong. First we need an abstract description of our data types. Why? Because we need a solid understanding of the data organization and the operations that are relevant to the problem. For many programs, it's just too big a jump from the guiding examples to specific typedefs and functions. Programmers have traditionally bridged this gap with Abstract Data Types.

An abstract data type description (ADTD) basically consists of two parts: geometry and operators. The Geometry is basically the little diagram of boxes and arrows you sketch when you're trying to show someone a stack or a tree or whatever. The Operators are basically function specifications. I keep saying "basically" because there are some subtleties, but we'll take those up in Chapter 4, "Creating an Abstract Data Type," when we write our first ADTD.

Three ADTDs are also provided in the Framework section, and each chapter in the Examples section contains at least one ADTD. For now, just think of an ADTD this way: An

ADTD is the most specific description of data structures and their associated functions you can have without committing yourself to a particular programming language.

STRUCT DESIGN

This is the main coding step. We choose a specific programming language (C, in all the examples in this book). We decide between doubly linked and singly linked lists, between lists and arrays, and so forth—we have to define the data types in a way the compiler can understand. This is also when we flesh out the functions; their calling sequences are defined in the ADTD we wrote earlier.

This is the only step in the Plan that's not optional. We'll never have satisfactory final code if no code is written. So every chapter in the Examples section illustrates struct design and implementation; the Framework section also contains a collection of Struct Design Guidelines.

TESTING, DEBUGGING, AND TUNING

This is a separate step from Struct Design because my programming philosophy has always been "Make it readable, make it run, and then make it run fast if you need to." This is the step to "make it run fast, make it run in less memory, make it handle errors, and so on"; Struct Design is the step to "make it readable and make it run." It's true that some testing, debugging, and tuning occur during struct design, but I've emphasized these activities here for two reasons. First, doing so puts more emphasis on design during the Struct Design step. Second, testing and debugging are not nearly as popular with some programmers as tuning is, but they deserve to be.

Testing, debugging, and tuning are illustrated in each chapter in the Examples section; the Framework section also contains several "struct tricks" to help tune code for better performance.

THE FRAMEWORK

To put the Plan into action, we need certain resources that are not immediately obvious. Each step in the Plan represents a level of programming expertise in the range from the very general to the very specific. The resources for the Plan are organized the same way. The Framework divides resources according to their level of generality by providing a template description at each of four levels.

Figure 1-3 shows the four kinds of templates and examples provided in the Framework section. The correlation between these resources and the Plan is straightforward. Framework Top-Level Goals arise during the Top-Level Goals step in the plan, ADTDs are used during the Abstract Data Type(s) step, Struct Design Guidelines are used during Struct

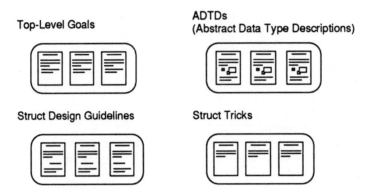

Top-Level Goals

ADTDs
(Abstract Data Type Descriptions)

Struct Design Guidelines

Struct Tricks

FIGURE 1-3: The Framework section provides templates for organizing different kinds of programming expertise.

Design, and the Struct Tricks can be helpful during the Testing, Debugging, and Tuning step of the Plan. No collection of resources is given for the Research step or the Guiding Examples step because these steps are so problem- and program-specific.

Resources in the Framework should be distillations of programming techniques or expertise. Much of the information in a typical introduction to data structures, for instance, can be summarized neatly by a collection of ADTDs. The main thing you get from such an introduction, after all, is a small repertoire of familiar data structures. This doesn't mean introductions are useless; far from it. It just means we have a way to summarize what we've learned from them. Likewise, the templates for Struct Design Guidelines and Struct Tricks provide a way to keep track of other good ideas without digging through the books or files we first saw them in.

The Framework section's examples are not meant to be either complete or perfect for your needs. They are provided as a starting point, to give you some examples of the Framework's advantages and limitations. It's up to you to expand the Framework by adding new resources to meet your own needs.

Now that you have an overview of the Plan and its resource Framework, we'll look at the Plan's steps in more detail. Then we'll work through a number of examples to watch the Plan in action.

CHAPTER 2
Setting Top-Level Goals

Different views of programming emphasize different goals for programs and programmers. When these goals conflict with one another, we have to make decisions that change the way we design and implement programs.

Our goal in this chapter is to build as complete a list of top-level goals as possible. Detailed descriptions of a few goals are also given in the Framework section at the end of the book, and each chapter in the Examples section sets its own top-level goals. We want to list as many goals as we can because the biggest problem with top-level goals is making them explicit. People tend to ignore them, and that causes trouble.

For instance, suppose you thought the boss wanted your program up and running as fast as possible, but the most important task turns out to be porting the code to a machine that has much less memory than the one you developed the program on. Chances are good you'll have to recode the whole program using very different structs. The extra work could have been avoided by recognizing the conflicting goals and making the boss prioritize them.

The classic tradeoff is between the top-level goals of minimizing memory requirements and minimizing execution time, but there are many other top-level goals as well: good error recovery, ease of use, having fun programming, using a library you're familiar with, writing clear code, getting something running right away, and so on. In fact, any question that can be asked about programming or programs in general implies a top-level goal: Is it reusable? Is it extendible? Is it portable? You get the idea.

So how do we identify these different goals? How about just sitting down and starting a list? We could do that (in fact, we've already started to), but there's a problem. There are many ways to view programming because programming is very complicated. If we just start listing goals, we'll get a list that reflects our view of the world: Programmers will get a list of goals programmers are concerned with, managers will get a list of things managers worry about, and some customer plucked from the relative safety of the street will make a list of things customers worry about.

These three lists are not necessarily identical. In fact, they might not overlap at all! As an extreme example, the programmer might list code reusability as a goal, while the manager wants the program working in one week and the customer wants a program that's easy to use. To make our collection of top-level programming goals as complete as possible, we need to use different people's views of programming. We'll look at programming from the point of view of three different groups of people:

1. Customers—people who have no grasp at all of programming
2. Contributors—people who have some idea of what's involved in programming
3. Programmers—people who know a lot about programming

We'll try to put ourselves inside the mind of each type of person, and then list the goals that emerge from that view. After that, we'll close the chapter by considering a simple algorithm for using top-level goals to make good programming decisions.

THINKING LIKE A CUSTOMER

OK, I'm a customer. I'm sitting here in front of a program I've never used before. I want to use it now. Do I care what language it's written in, or how well commented the code is, or whether the programmer enjoyed writing it? No. I'm not a programmer. Nor am I a manager responsible for the program's development or marketing. So I don't care how many programmer-years went into the program, or what projects were stuck on the back burner so this program could reach the market.

All I want to know is what the program can do for me and how much I'll enjoy it. More precisely, here are some questions I want answers to:

Is the manual clear, concise, and complete?
How much of the manual do I have to read before I can get some good work done?
How good is the technical support when I call in with a question?
Can I back up if I make a mistake while using the program?
How much fun is the program to use?
Will the program do something to keep me informed of its progress during long calculations, so I know it hasn't died?
Will people be impressed when they see me using the program?
Can I "test-drive" the program before I have to pay for it?
How much does the program cost? How much are upgrades?
Will the program run on my machine?
Will it get along with my other programs?
Does the program do what the marketing brochures claim it does?
Does the program make mistakes or crash when I use it?
Can I make a spare copy of the program as a precaution?

THINKING LIKE A CONTRIBUTOR

Now let's try to describe programming goals from a point of view one step closer to programmers. How does programming look to product managers, customer support people, managers of programmers, user group members, and technical writers? These people often have some kind of technical background and use programs of one kind or another regularly. They may even have done some programming, but not on the program in question. Instead, their contributions come in the form of suggestions, complaints, and supporting material like manuals and marketing brochures.

Managers of programmers, of course, must be able to follow the programming task in enough detail to track progress and problems. But it's not always easy to know how much detail is enough. Programmers and programming are different in important ways from other workers and tasks. Licker (1985) discusses these factors from a manager's point of view. They are also a topic of interest in the many works available on software engineering.

Here, however, we'll content ourselves with trying briefly to state goals for contributors and programmers. Most contributors (managers included) are not particularly interested in day-to-day programming details. They're interested in the results—in the program—just as customers are. So contributors ask many of the questions already presented under "Thinking Like a Customer." However, contributors are also interested in how the programming task affects their jobs. Contributors want answers to these questions:

Does the program fill a niche in the market?
How long will it take to write, and which programmers should do it?
What resources are needed for program development? For maintenance?
How strongly is the company pushing this program, and why?
Is the programmer who wrote this thing available to answer questions about it? Can I understand the answers when I get them?
Can I get some small changes made to the program? Some big ones?

THINKING LIKE A PROGRAMMER

Now it's time for those of you who are contributors and customers to try thinking like a programmer. Managers can certainly learn something valuable about programmer motivation by imagining what it's like to program. Anyway, it's fun. Those of you who already know how to think like a programmer can skip this section.

All right then. What is programming, anyway? I could answer by flooding you with technical jargon:

I implemented and maintain an extended subset BASIC interpreter that's the principal interface to our renderer, virtual memory handler, and VTR machine control code. It's 36,000 lines of C running on a proprietary 68020/microcoded expandable parallel architecture that's the hottest thing going in high-quality animated graphics.

But a response like this just leaves you wishing you hadn't asked. At best, I might hope you'll assume you didn't understand my answer because programming is really complicated but useful nonetheless. At worst, you'll decide that my answer proves what you've always suspected: A programmer is really nothing but an unpredictable extension of the computer. In either case, I haven't really answered your question.

Another way to learn about programming is to talk to programmers, or to read interviews with programmers. Lammers (1986) provides an excellent set of interviews with programmers on topics that are related to programming rather than to particular programs. This allows nonprogrammers to learn something worthwhile about programmers' perspectives, and thus, about their top-level goals, without becoming programmers themselves.

The method we'll use here, however, is to describe programming in terms of metaphors. That is, I'll describe programming concepts in terms of ideas you're already familiar with. Four metaphors for programming are given below, along with some of the top-level goals they suggest. Each metaphor captures several of the essential characteristics of what programmers do, and they're all fun. Notice how the different metaphors give rise to very different programming goals. OK, crank up the power to your imagination and dive in!

1. *Programs are oceans.* Programming is like swimming deep in the ocean, subject to unseen currents that can tumble you into a beautiful hidden garden or a jagged cliff. Diving down from the top of a program to go through some deeply nested function is like leaving the daylight behind and forcing yourself down, down to the depths to watch some self-fluorescing misshapen fish gape its huge mouth of razors at you.

When the writing is going well, it's like swimming effortlessly through clean water, creating the ocean as you swim, watching as the eels and kelp and sharks and dolphins and everything else pops into existence to either side, above and below. The other good programmers are fellow sea people down there with you, the same strong Atlantean race, but usually seen hazily through the currents that cross between you. The programmers that couldn't hack it are down there too—the haunted bodies of drowned sailors.

Your goals in this world are to keep swimming, keep creating clean ocean (i.e., code) in front of you, enjoy the odd majestic scenes you've created, and not get eaten alive or flung into sharp rocks because you weren't paying attention.

2. *Programs are spider webs.* Programs are like webs because there are so many possible paths from any given point. But programming is like walking a web in other ways, too. Some of the threads are relatively safe if you keep your balance, but others are sticky, dangerous traps. Some threads in programs are triggers—if you touch them at all, a large nasty spider comes rushing out, moving very quickly in ways you don't understand, and then SPLAT! You're paralyzed and hung upside-down to ferment.

Also, some threads are more important than others. If you cut too many of these anchors, the whole program will tumble down into a sticky mess, and you may be caught inside! A mess like that can never be untangled; it can only be rebuilt, and then only if you kept track of everything.

Your basic goal is to memorize the web (that is, learn the code) so you can move where you want in it. Stay away from nastiness triggers, don't cut too many anchors, and don't get stuck to the thing if it starts to collapse.

3. *Programs are magic spells.* Programming is much like living in a fantasy world where magic really works. Programmers create something from nothing every day. But it's not easy to work this magic; these code creatures are as slippery as they are intangible. Programmers have to master arcane languages and instruments. They work long hours in front of glowing objects that are either barely under control, working surreptitious evil, or raging in open rebellion. Programmers tend to work in isolation, as magicians do. Their sense of isolation is magnified by a pulsing dangerous thrill, a sense that at any instant they might be sucked permanently into an alternate dimension that bears little resemblance to the "real" world.

The basic goal for these programmers is to keep learning. They want to spend infinity mastering new arcana without getting sucked too far out of (or back into) reality.

4. *Programs are buildings.* Programming is like building a house. You have to plan things ahead of time or you probably won't like the results. Also, work on a house proceeds both in layers (foundation, walls, plumbing, electrical, sheetrock, paint, carpeting, furnishings) and in modules (bathroom, bedroom, patio, kitchen, and so on). Similarly, work on a program proceeds both in layers (idea or need, user interface, functional spec, data structures, calling sequences, various levels of abstraction in the coding) and in modules (functionally related sets of files, e.g., I/O, lexical analysis, parsing, symbol table, and so on).

The interfaces between the modules are important whether you're building a house or a program: Mismatched calling sequences are a bit like the bedroom thinking this spot in the wall gets a door and the bathroom thinking the same spot is where the sink goes.

Writing a program is also like building a house because both are a mixture of engineering and aesthetics. Aesthetic opinions shouldn't be ignored because most houses and most programs are built for habitation. Programmers live inside code. Different programmers prefer different styles of code, just as most people prefer one color scheme or floor plan over another.

Your goals are to build a solid, pleasant, well-organized house (i.e., program), and to plan ahead for later additions and changes to it.

These metaphors don't tell the whole story, of course. As programmers, our list of top-level goals includes everything mentioned so far and some other things as well. We also ask questions that are directly related to the task of programming:

How easy is the source to read?
How easy is the program to debug?
How easy is it to monitor the program's performance?
How flexible is the program?
How easy is it to verify the program?
How easy is the source to port?
Did I learn something useful writing this program?
Was the program fun to write?
Is the program powerful and clean, something to be proud of?
Does it require minimal hardware but support maximal hardware?
What industry or company standards does the program comply with?

And the opinions don't stop there. Programmers also have strong preferences where hardware, tools, schedules, tasks, and people are concerned. But that's enough for now.

Between thinking like a customer, thinking like a contributor, thinking like a programmer, and describing programming to nonprogrammers, we've come up with quite a list of top-level goals. As mentioned, a few goals are documented in the Framework section; others are listed in this chapter and in the chapters in the Examples section. Between all these sources, we have quite a checklist of possible goals, but you are also encouraged to add your own descriptions. Remember, we want to make the goals explicit.

CHOOSING BETWEEN CONFLICTING GOALS

So how do we use this list of explicit top-level goals in our daily programming? I would like to present a wonderful algorithm that lets programmers and managers choose correctly between conflicting goals in any situation. The algorithm would detect and resolve all conflicts. I would like to, but I can't. Every situation is different.

All is not lost, however. To simplify things, assume every goal either contributes to or conflicts with every other goal. This is a reasonable approximation to the truth, because meeting one goal takes time and other resources that could have been spent meeting another, and program changes can have unintended side effects. With this assumption we can describe in very general terms a method to identify the goals and act on them accordingly.

Goal Resolution Algorithm

```
while the program is not done {
    for each person P the program will interact with in any way {
        try to see the program from P's point of view (ask questions,
        read specs, etc.);
        list the goals P might have for the program, together with any
        related assumptions P might make;
        list the criteria P could use to decide if the goals have been
        met;
    } /* for each contributor */
    for each goal the program might need to meet {
        decide how important the goal is in relation to other goals;
        decide what needs to be done to meet the goal;
        take appropriate action, including starting over if necessary;
    } /* for each goal */
} /* while the code lives on */
```

We need some method like this because top-level goals conflict with each other regularly. The classic tradeoff is between price (tied to the implementation effort required) and performance (ease of use, completeness, accuracy, and so on). But there are other tradeoffs as well, since time spent on one goal is time not spent on another. If time is short, for instance, a programmer might be able to implement useful error messages or an effective data security system but not both. Of course, any change to a program puts efficiency and correctness at risk, since changes may have unintended effects.

To make things even worse, each top-level goal apparently conflicts with itself at times. That is, one person's idea of ease of use need not match someone else's. We can improve things a bit by breaking "ease of use" into "easy to learn," "easy to operate once you're familiar with it," "forgiving of unexpected inputs," "gives output that's easy to interpret," and so forth, but the expectations for each of these need not match either.

The only working solution is to get the people involved to understand each other so that their expectations match. Formal specifications, informal discussions, wish lists, prototypes, pseudocode, references to existing programs, and any other kind of communication are all legal here.

Use whatever works, because informed agreement between programmer and contributor is more critical, and harder to produce, than understanding between programmers. It is harder to produce because there is less common ground and because programmers and contributors often have different goals. But shared expectations are critical because months or years of programming time may be spent before misunderstanding surfaces; programmers see most aspects of a program in detail long before contributors do.

If a fellow programmer misunderstands something about a program you're both working on, you have enough common ground to explain the problem. Also, you have a decent chance of realizing that there's a problem after only hours or days of work, because programmers talk to each other daily about their work.

Programmers and contributors, on the other hand, tend to discuss programs less frequently and in less depth, because contributors have too little time, and programmers have too much detail. Contributors such as product managers have little time to spend on any one program because they are typically involved with several different programming efforts and have other duties as well.

Programmers have a mass of technical detail to manage. By its very nature, programming something useful means concerning yourself with many details so that other people can ignore them. When the contributor has too little time or the programmer has too much detail, programmers either flood the harried contributor with technical questions the contributor can't answer or make what they hope is the right choice and follow through on it rather than waiting to get the contributor's ideas. In either case, programmer and contributor expectations and efforts may be out of alignment with each other for a long time.

By employing the goal resolution algorithm above, programmers, managers, and customers can minimize the anger and wasted effort that is all too common in programming tasks. At best, everybody will agree on the top-level goals that guide the task. At worst, using the goal resolution algorithm will make the disagreements explicit.

CHAPTER 3
Choosing Good Guiding Examples

One of the things that distinguishes experts in any field from novices is the useful examples that experts can bring to bear on new problems. Through experience and insight, experts acquire a repertoire of sample problems and solutions and knowledge of the tradeoffs between alternate solutions. In fact, the hardest part of solving a problem often amounts to recognizing the similarities and differences between the problem at hand and the problems we already know how to solve.

The point of any book that teaches any subject should therefore be to expand the reader's repertoire of useful examples. Good examples provide an informal test suite, and they help us decide in greater detail which characteristics of possible solutions are most important to us. Let's try to decide just what it is that makes an example useful, and how we can generate useful examples.

WHAT MAKES AN EXAMPLE USEFUL?

Imagine we want to write a program. We have many questions to answer: When does it need to be finished? Who's going to use it? What hardware should it run on? and so on. But the biggest question is this: What's the program supposed to do? In other words, we want some examples.

But we don't want just any set of examples. We want useful examples. To be more precise, we want the smallest complete set of simple examples that illustrates the problem without forcing particular solutions on us. That is, we want a set of examples with the following qualities.

Desirable Qualities in a Set of Examples

1. Each example illustrates something important to our understanding of the problem. It might illustrate a typical aspect of the problem, or it might illustrate a less common but nonetheless critical aspect.
2. Every important aspect of the problem—typical or not—is covered by at least one example. The fundamental characteristics of each example are listed explicitly, so we know what's covered and what isn't. It's important to decide what variations in the examples are worth keeping, because we'll be getting rid of as many examples as possible to meet the requirements in goal 3.
3. The examples overlap as little as possible. In the ideal case, this means two things. First, each fundamental characteristic of the problem is illustrated by just one example. Second, the examples are independent of each other, so we can study each one separately. In practice, this ideal is rarely achieved, but we'll aim for it nevertheless because it helps keep the number of examples to a minimum.
4. The examples are simple and easy to understand. This ideal is also rarely achieved, but it's important to try.
5. The examples illustrate the problem without assuming particular solutions. This does not mean the examples don't suggest solutions; we hope they do. It means the examples are described in terms of their fundamental characteristics, rather than being presented as a set of implementations.

To illustrate these qualities, we'll start with a very simple problem. Then we'll consider a more realistic problem, to show that the qualities are even more desirable in solving hard problems than they are in solving easy ones.

SOME SIMPLE EXAMPLES

Suppose the problem is to keep track of people's movements in and out of a house. The first examples of movement that come to mind are these:

through a doorway
through a window
up or down the chimney
through a new hole cut in the wall, or through a broken door or a smashed window

Let's figure out the fundamental characteristics of these examples. What makes one example different from another? Well, the difference between going through a doorway and going down the chimney is that doorways are built for people to go through, and chimneys are not. We might call climbing down the chimney "unanticipated," whereas going through a doorway is "anticipated." This is our first fundamental characteristic: the degree to which the item's original purpose leads us to anticipate movement through the item.

What about the difference between using a doorway and going through a window? It's not unheard of to go through windows, so we don't want to call it "unanticipated." But it is rare. We can distinguish between the examples by adding a second fundamental characteristic: frequency.

If we consider the difference between using an existing doorway or window or chimney and creating a new hole by tunneling through the wall, a third fundamental characteristic emerges: destructiveness.

Of course, you can come up with your own set of fundamental characteristics if you don't like these. The choice of important characteristics will always be subjective. But the fact that you and I might choose differently doesn't mean it's useless to search for a good set of characteristics. The fundamental characteristics I choose will help me write a better program, just as your choices will help you with your programming.

Now let's list the examples again, along with their fundamental characteristics:

through a doorway—this is an anticipated use of doorways; it doesn't destroy anything; and it happens frequently

through a window—this is an anticipated use of windows; it doesn't destroy anything; and it happens rarely

up or down the chimney—this is an unanticipated use of chimneys (unless your name is Santa Claus); it doesn't destroy anything; and it happens rarely

through a new hole cut in the wall, or through a broken door or a smashed window— this is an unanticipated use of walls, windows, and doors; it involves destruction; and it happens rarely

This looks pretty good. Let's run through the list of desirable qualities and see how this set of example movements fares:

1. Each example illustrates the kind of movement we are interested in. For instance, motion through a doorway is typical, while cutting a hole in the wall is rare but worth noting as a possibility.

2. Every fundamental characteristic of movement—anticipatedness, destructiveness, frequency—is illustrated by at least one example. There are other ways in and out of

TABLE 3-1: Where the chosen examples fit in the space of combinations of fundamental characteristics.

Anticipated?	Destructive?	Frequent?	Example
no	no	no	up or down chimney
no	no	yes	
no	yes	no	through new hole in wall
no	yes	yes	
yes	no	no	through a window
yes	no	yes	through a doorway
yes	yes	no	
yes	yes	yes	

a house (tunnel through the floor, lift off the roof and fly, remove an entire wall), but they are suggested by our chosen examples. Tunneling through the floor, for instance, is unanticipated, destructive, and rare, just as cutting a hole in the wall is. There's no difference between the two in terms of their fundamental characteristics.

3. The examples overlap as little as possible. Each illustrates a different value for one of the three fundamental movement characteristics we decided on. In fact, since there are just three characteristics and each takes just two values (present/absent), we can list all possible combinations of characteristics explicitly. This is done in Table 3-1. All possible values of the characteristics are listed; the examples have been placed in the table according to the values they illustrate.

Table 3-2 shows one way to fill the blank entries in Table 3-1. Notice that we can fill the blanks either by marking certain combinations of fundamental characteristics as illegal or by including additional examples. In Table 3-2 we've done some of both.

For instance, we've expanded our examples to include ghosts who regularly float in and out without bothering to open the door. This is an unanticipated use of walls that is nondestructive and frequent (if you're a ghost). We've also added the example of a drunk who kicks down the door each night but feels enough remorse the next morning to fix it. This is an unanticipated use of doors that is both destructive and frequent.

By contrast, we've decided not to include anticipated destructive uses. If doors were made of spider webs, for instance, destroying them by walking through them would be an anticipated destructive use. Since we've outlawed examples requiring this combination of fundamental movement characteristics, the last two blanks in Table 3-1 are marked "ILLEGAL" in Table 3-2.

Suppose two of the examples had taken identical values for all three fundamental characteristics; this would be obvious from Table 3-1. We would either need to add a new

TABLE 3-2:   Table 3-1 completed by including new examples of valid movement and by outlawing invalid movements.

Anticipated?	Destructive?	Frequent?	Example
no	no	no	up or down chimney
no	no	yes	"ghost" through a wall or a closed door or window
no	yes	no	through new hole in wall
no	yes	yes	kick the door in each night, fix it each morning
yes	no	no	through a window
yes	no	yes	through a door
yes	yes	no	none—illegal—no anticipated uses are destructive
yes	yes	yes	none—illegal—no anticipated uses are destructive

characteristic that distinguished between the two examples or get rid of one of the examples. Filling in the table therefore helps eliminate duplicate examples and also makes us reconsider our choice of fundamental characteristics. Trying to fill in Table 3-1's blank spots also led us to add additional examples and to mark certain value combinations as illegal.

4. The examples are simple and easy to understand because they're based on ideas we are all familiar with and (for the most part) on common experiences.

5. The examples illustrate the problem without assuming particular solutions. We've made a few assumptions about sensing devices in the walls and chimneys, for instance, but none about data structures or algorithms.

SOME REALISTIC EXAMPLES

Let's consider a realistic programming problem. Later in the book, we consider the problem of getting from a selected piece of text or window or whatever to the corresponding struct. For instance, how does a word processor turn the (x, y) position of the cursor at the time the mouse button was pressed into the address of a particular text character in memory? We'll develop detailed examples of this screen-to-struct mapping problem in the Examples section. For now, we'll just do enough to illustrate our technique for choosing useful examples.

Thinking about programs in which displayed objects are selected leads to the following examples:

    games like chess, tic-tac-toe, othello, and go—find the internal struct that corresponds
        to the piece or square selected
    word processors—find the internal structs that match the character(s) or word(s)
        selected
    windows—find the internal struct representing the window or scroll bar or size box or
        other gadget selected
    menus—find the internal struct that corresponds to the menu item selected
    simulations—find the internal struct that corresponds to the vehicle, track section,
        load, or other item selected

The first step is to come up with a list of the fundamental characteristics of these examples. The easiest way to do this is to figure out what makes one example different from another. Certainly the displayed objects that can be selected are different in each case. In chess, playing pieces are selected, in word processors characters are selected, and so on. But this is not the kind of difference we're looking for.

Instead of dealing with the meaning or appearance of different selectable items, the fundamental characteristics should relate directly to our problem. The problem of mapping screen coordinates to corresponding structs is the same in chess, for instance, whether the knights look like horses or elephants; the problem is the same in a word processor whether the language displayed is English or French. The things that count are how selection regions are arranged on the screen, and how they interact. So we can tentatively list the following as our fundamental characteristics:

> whether or not the selection regions are all the same size (we'll assume they're always rectangular)
> whether the selection regions are arranged on the screen in regular rows and columns
> whether or not the selection regions overlap one another

Using these three characteristics to categorize our examples leads us to Table 3-3. Notice that we've already departed from the simple yes/no answers used in Tables 3-1 and 3-2. Chess pieces are arranged in regular rows and columns, so we can answer "yes" to "Regular?" in that case. Word processing text, however, is arranged in rows, but not lined up in columns. Answering "no" to "Regular?" in this case ignores the presence of rows, but we can't answer "yes" either, because that implies the presence of columns. So we answered "rows." Similarly, menu items have some regularity because they are arranged in columns, so the answer to "Regular?" is neither "no" nor "yes," but "columns."

In like manner, we've answered "containment" rather than "yes" to the question of whether or not the screen regions in a word processor overlap, because the overlap is not entirely arbitrary. The selection regions for a word and the characters it contains do overlap, but the character regions are always contained in the word's region. This is in contrast to the arbitrary overlap allowed between windows, for instance.

Being unable to use simple yes/no answers everywhere doesn't make Table 3-3 less useful; quite the opposite is true, since such simple answers often hide information. But it does mean an exhaustive list of all possible combinations of fundamental characteristics is much harder to create. Thus, points 2 and 3 in our list of desirable qualities emphasize a set of examples that is both small and complete.

Notice that windows and simulations take the same values for all three characteristics in Table 3-3. This means we either need to drop one of these examples or we need to add another fundamental characteristic that distinguishes between them. We'll do the latter.

The items displayed in a simulation move about on their own once the simulation starts, and they keep going in some hard-to-predict fashion until an external event stops them. We'll

TABLE 3-3: A first attempt to sort the screen-to-struct mapping examples according to fundamental characteristics. Notice that this set of characteristics does not distinguish between windows and simulations.

Same Size?	Regular?	Overlap?	Example
yes	yes	no	chess
no	rows	containment	word processors
no	no	yes	windows, simulations
yes	columns	no	menus

TABLE 3-4:   Table 3 expanded to include the new fundamental characteristic "Runs About?" which distinguishes between simulations and windows.

Same Size?	Regular?	Overlap?	Runs About?	Example
yes	yes	no	no	chess
no	rows	containment	no	word processors
no	no	yes	no	windows
no	no	yes	yes	simulations
yes	columns	no	no	menus

say that they "run about." Windows, on the other hand, do not run about. They move only in response to direct user action, and their movement is predictable and soon finished. Reorganizing our examples using this new fundamental characteristic leads to Table 3-4.

All right then. Let's run through the list of desirable qualities and see how the current set of examples and their fundamental characteristics holds up.

1. Each example illustrates something important to our understanding of the problem. For instance, it's certainly useful to know if the screen regions are all the same size and regularly arranged. Chess board regions are both, so it's possible to use a simple formula to decide which square on the chess board any point (x, y) is in: Subtract the offset of the board's corner and then divide x and y by the width and height of a square. Windows, on the other hand, are different sizes and may overlap, so we can't use a simple algebraic formula to decide which window an arbitrary point (x, y) lies in.

2. It's not true that every important aspect of the problem is covered by at least one example. When we develop these examples for actual use in implementing solutions, we'll see that other fundamental characteristics are also important.

   For instance, the number of items displayed affects the efficiency of using an exhaustive search to find all the selected structs. It might be possible to search all the displayed windows, for instance, to determine which one contains a selected point. But it's not reasonable to search every displayed character in a word processor, because there might be several thousand. So the number of items is a fundamental characteristic we've overlooked.

   However, even if we don't know for sure what the examples don't cover, at least we know what they do cover. This is one reason why we list the fundamental characteristics explicitly.

3. The examples overlap some, but they are independent enough for us to study each one separately. We would expect this to be the case because the screen-to-struct mapping problem has been solved differently in existing programs to do chess, word processing, and so on.

4. The examples are simple and easy to understand because they're based on existing programs we've all seen.

5. The examples illustrate the problem without assuming particular solutions. We did

suggest two possible solutions: an algebraic formula for use in the chess example and an exhaustive search for use with windows. Suggesting good solutions is much better than assuming a particular solution.

HOW TO CHOOSE GOOD EXAMPLES

Most people know how to think of examples, and in any case it's impossible to teach. So we'll assume people can come up with examples and concentrate on how to choose between examples and put the chosen examples to work. The previous examples illustrate the following process:

1. Decide in a general way where we're headed. For instance, "the problem is to track movement in and out of a house" or "the problem is to find all the structs that correspond to some region selected on the screen."
2. Think of many examples—brainstorm. Write down a very brief description of each example.
3. Extract the fundamental characteristics of the examples by deciding what makes one example different from another. Be sure the fundamental characteristics are pertinent to the problem being solved. Don't discard any examples yet.
4. Build a table listing the examples and the fundamental characteristic values for each. Don't restrict yourself to simple yes/no answers if doing so loses information about the ways fundamental characteristics apply to particular examples.
5. Rewrite the table, adding or removing fundamental characteristics and examples until a set of examples emerges that has the desired qualities listed at the first of this chapter.
6. Refer to the examples while solving the problem. Use them to decide when more than one implementation is needed by seeing how the fundamental characteristics of different examples compare (e.g., a chess game's formula-based implementation versus a window manager's search-based implementation).

You can also use the examples while creating abstract data type descriptions later in the Plan. Finally, use the examples to test proposed solutions for completeness and to devise test suites that exercise the typical as well as the less common but nevertheless critical aspects of the solutions.

Each chapter in the Examples section has its own guiding examples. We don't always use tables to summarize the examples; sometimes diagrams or (more often) prose is more appropriate. But we always look for examples whose fundamental characteristics are such that the examples have the desirable qualities we presented at the first of this chapter.

CHAPTER 4

Creating an Abstract Data Type

In this chapter we devote our attention to one of the most powerful general purpose programming tools: abstract data types. An abstract data type is a programming-language-independent group of rules for organizing and manipulating a collection of data elements. Once we have prioritized our top-level goals and chosen our guiding examples, the next step in the Plan is to create an abstract data type description (ADTD).

The main benefit of an ADTD is that writing it forces us to answer critical questions before we've committed a lot of effort to a particular implementation. If we don't answer the ADTD questions up front, we may need to change our code radically halfway through development when "new" requirements are discovered. These requirements may always have been there; we just didn't look hard enough for them. The ADTD will also help us generate alternate solutions and guide our implementation efforts.

FIRST EXAMPLE OF AN ADTD

Before we give a formal definition of an ADTD, let's look at an example. Following is an ADTD of our old friend the stack.

Stack ADTD

The stack is organized as a column of data elements; see Figure 4-1. Only the top of the column is accessible. None of the stack elements are side by side; any element is either under

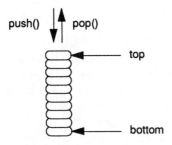

push() pop()

top

bottom

FIGURE 4-1: Sketch of a typical stack.

or over any other element. However, it is possible for the stack to be empty, or to contain just one element.

Different stack elements can have the same value or different values, but all the values in a regular stack are of the same type. Of course, different stacks can have elements with different types of value. For instance, one stack might contain integers, while another contains strings. A stack of structs is also possible, in which case the element type is defined by a typedef or similar type definition (in languages other than C).

If we're dealing with more than one stack at a time, we'll give each stack a name to distinguish it from all the other stacks.

The only way to add an element to the stack is to push it on top of all the elements currently in the stack:

```
int  push( mystack, value )
   stack  mystack; /* IN: stack to push value onto */
   int    value;   /* IN: new element's value */
/* returns status "OK" or "no such stack" */
```

The "IN" in the comments above means *mystack* and *value* are incoming parameters—whoever calls *push()* must supply appropriate values. The only way to take an element out of the stack is to pop it off the top of the stack:

```
int  pop( mystack, value )
   stack  mystack; /* IN: stack to pop value off of */
   int    *value;  /* OUT: value of element removed */
/* returns status "OK" or "empty stack" or "no such stack" */
```

This means the only way to rearrange the order of elements in a stack is to pop some off and then push them back in a different order than they were pushed in last time.

We will return to this stack ADTD later, to see how we can use it to generate alternative implementations. But first we want to see where this description came from.

FORMAL DEFINITION OF AN ADTD

A stack, or any other abstract data type, has many possible descriptions, and not just because it has many possible implementations. An ADTD is a summary of what is important, and (by its omissions) what is not important. Different descriptions of a particular abstract data type are inevitable, and useful, because different characteristics are important to different people, or even to the same person in different circumstances.

Do not think of ADTDs as eternal truth engraved in stone. You might not agree 100 percent with the suggestions presented here for writing abstract data type descriptions. That's fine. The main thing to get from this chapter and from the ADTDs throughout the book is the ability to create your own ADTDs to meet your own needs.

It's important, therefore, to understand how the ADTDs presented here were created. Abstract data types are not a new concept. A typical definition of abstract data types is given in Aho, Hopcroft, and Ullman (1983):

> We can think of an *abstract data type* (ADT) as a mathematical model with a collection of operations defined on that model.

The abstract data types described in *Advanced C Struct Programming* fit the following definition; although it uses different terminology, it's essentially the same as the one above:

> An *abstract data type* is an implementation-independent collection of data elements plus corresponding operations on the elements or on the collection as a whole.

However, neither of these definitions is specific enough. They leave too many questions unanswered when the time comes to begin coding. How we should go beyond this very general view of an ADT depends on what we want to do. Mathematicians, for instance, flesh out the general definition of an ADT in a way that meets their needs. But we're not mathematicians. Likewise, programming language designers discuss ADTs in ways that meet their goals; see Cleaveland (1986), for instance. Both these approaches are useful to programmers, as well as to mathematicians and language designers. But our main interest here is programming.

For that reason the abstract data types in *Advanced C Struct Programming* are described using a list of questions whose answers help us implement the type. Go ahead and look at the list of ADTD questions in Box 4-2 now to get a feel for them. Don't worry yet about learning all the terms used; there's an ADTD glossary in Chapter 5.

The ADTD questions were generated using the method described in Chapter 3, "Choosing Good Guiding Examples." That is, I sat down and started listing different data structures and the fundamental characteristics I felt distinguished them from each other. Each fundamental characteristic generated an ADTD question. For instance, sets and bags differ in that bags allow duplicates. This led me to define "allows duplicates" as a fundamental characteristic, and that characteristic eventually led in turn to the ADTD question "Does membership depend on the values of current members of the collection?"

After the list of questions stabilized, I checked it by trying to write ADTDs for some data structures used in production code. This led to more changes in the ADTD questions. After the list stabilized a second time, I organized the questions into the outline shown in Box 4-1, and made the glossary of ADTD terms shown in Chapter 5.

BOX 4-1:   Outline of an abstract data type description (ADTD). The corresponding questions are in Box 4-2.

0. Name
I. Geometry
    A. Sketch
    B. Positions
        1. Properties with respect to other positions
        2. Properties with respect to operators
    C. Relations
        1. Orderings
           a. Partial versus total
        2. Reflexive, symmetric, transitive properties
           a. Partitions
        3. One-to-one, one-to-many, many-to-many
    D. Semantics
        1. Dependence on position
        2. Dependence on value
II. Operators
    A. Name
    B. Semantics
        1. Create collection
        2. Add elements to collection
        3. Change relations between elements
        4. Delete elements from a collection
        5. Traverse a collection
        6. Obtain collection characteristics
           a. Number of elements
        7. Delete collection
        8. Record collection
    C. Parameters, return values
        1. Type
        2. Mode
        3. Legal values
    D. Properties with respect to geometry positions
III. Collection as a whole
    A. Membership restrictions
        1. Types
        2. Values
           a. Prospective member
           b. Current members
        3. Number of elements
        4. Environmental
    B. Multiple collections
        1. Rule for distinguishing between collections
        2. Proper subsets versus collections

BOX 4-2:   Questions whose answers describe an abstract data type. The questions are organized according to the outline in Box 4-1.

0. What name does this particular collection of data elements and operators go by, that is, what abstract data type are we concerned with?
I. What is the geometry of this abstract data type?
   A. Sketch a picture of the data type. Indicate special positions such as the top of a stack or root of a tree; also indicate positions at which elements can be added or removed. Show whether or not the elements are linked, as tree nodes or linked list elements are.
   B. What positions in the geometry are different from others, and how? For instance, ordered lists have three kinds of position: first element, last element, and somewhere in the middle.
      1. What are the properties of each position with respect to other positions? For instance, the first element of an ordered list precedes every other element.
      2. What are the properties of each position with respect to the operators? For instance, deleting the root of a tree is different from deleting a leaf node.
   C. What relations hold between the elements of the collection? Answer the following three questions for each relation, if they are applicable.
      1. Are the elements ordered by this relation?
         a. Is the ordering partial or total? For instance, trees and graphs are usually partially ordered, while linear lists are totally ordered.
      2. Is the relation reflexive? Is it symmetric? Is it transitive?
         a. Is the relation reflexive, symmetric, and transitive? That is, does the relation partition the collection? For instance, "is the same month as" partitions the collection of days. This relation is reflexive, since every day is in the same month as itself. It is symmetric, since day one is in the same month as day two if and only if day two is in the same month as day one. And it is a transitive relation, because day one in the same month as day two and day two in the same month as day three together imply that day one is in the same month as day three.
      3. Is the relation one-to-one, one-to-many, or many-to-many? For instance, the relation "is a child of" in a tree is one-to-many because it holds between one parent and many child nodes.
   D. What are the semantics of the elements? What does each element "mean"? In other words, how do we interpret particular snapshots of the collection as its elements change?
      1. How does the meaning of an element depend on its position in the collection? That is, what is the meaning of each position? For instance, the element at the front of a queue to some process is always the next element to be processed.
      2. How does the meaning of an element depend on its value? For instance, is there a special null value?
II. What are the operators?
   A. What is the name of each operator?
   B. What are the semantics of each operator?
      1. Is there an operator for creating a new collection, or is that creation somehow automatic? If the code supports only one collection, there may be no need for

a distinct creation operator. For instance, creating an empty list might involve nothing more than initializing a static pointer to NULL.

2. Is there an operator to add elements to the collection?
3. Are there any operators that change the relations between elements?
4. Is there an operator to delete elements from the collection?
5. Is there an operator to traverse a collection, and do something at each element (update a timestamp or pretty-print the values, for instance)?
6. Is there an operator to obtain collection characteristics? For instance, how can we find the number of elements in the collection?
7. Is there an operator to delete the collection? Do all the elements have to be deleted individually first?
8. Is there an operator to archive or display the collection's current geometry and values at any given point in time? This sort of operator is often essential for debugging.

C. What are the parameters and return values, if any, of each operator? These are most easily described by a commented calling sequence like the ones for *push()* and *pop()* in the stack ADTD shown earlier.

1. What is the data type of each parameter? We don't need compilable type declarations, since ADTDs are language-independent, but we do need the type's name and its range of possible values.
2. What is the mode of each parameter? That is, is the parameter used to carry a value in, to carry a value out, or both?
3. What are the legal values for the parameter (as opposed to the legal values for the parameter's data type)?

D. What are the properties of each operator with respect to positions in the geometry? This is question I.B.2., repeated here because it concerns operators.

III. What are the properties of the collection of data elements as a group? For instance, what are the properties of the stack as a whole, as opposed to the properties of individual stack elements or positions or operators?

A. What are the restrictions on membership in the collection?

1. Can only certain types of values be added to the collection? If so, what types are legal? For instance, we might specify that a stack can contain only integers, or that it can contain integers and character strings.
2. Can only certain values be added to the collection?
   a. Does membership depend on the value of the prospective member? For instance, we might fail on attempts to *push()* negative numbers onto a particular integer stack.
   b. Does membership depend on the values of current members of the collection? For instance, we might admit at most five elements with the same employee ID to an ordered list of vacation requests.
3. Is membership restricted according to the number of elements already in the collection? For instance, we might put a limit on the height of a stack or the depth of a tree. We also need to know whether it's legal for the collection to be empty.
4. Is membership restricted by some factor in the collection's environment? For instance, we might need a "bank door" stack which only allows *push()* calls to succeed between 9 AM and 5 PM New York time.

B. What are the rules governing multiple collections? A collection and an abstract data type are not necessarily identical. For instance, we might have an abstract stack type that allows an arbitrary number of actual stacks. Each stack is a collection; all the stacks together form the abstract data type.

1. If multiple collections are allowed, how do we distinguish between them? There are many possibilities. Each collection could have a name or a unique ID (a pointer will do nicely). Or perhaps we can access only the collection that was created most recently.
2. Can a proper subset of a collection be viewed as a collection in its own right? For instance, recursive tree operations usually view different nodes as the root of the tree, depending on the current depth of the recursion. Proper subsets of trees are therefore often regarded as trees. By contrast, it is uncommon to think of a subset of a stack as a stack in its own right.

The list of questions in Box 4-2 is our formal definition of an ADTD. We don't always need every one of these questions answered. ADTDs should be tailored to fit the task at hand, just like any other tool.

Notice that an ADTD is a combination of English and pseudocode. Pseudocode is used to specify operator calling sequences, but this doesn't mean we should describe an abstract data type with listings. Listings hide too much of what we want to know just now. They also impose a particular implementation on us. The whole point of an ADTD is to answer more general (but still vital) questions than the ones we are concerned with while actually coding.

Some flavor of the programmer's favorite languages inevitably creeps into the ADTD pseudocode, but the description should be independent of any particular programming language. The ADTD should be written to allow implementation in C or any other reasonably powerful language.

Notice that the stack ADTD does not specify the typedefs and defines needed to implement the stack in C. We are free to use a linked list, a list of integer arrays, or even a disk file if we wish! We can define the "OK" status as zero or one or any positive integer, or in any other way that allows *push()* and *pop()* to return an integer status.

In fact, the closest thing to a direct restriction on the stack's implementation is in the calling sequences for *push()* and *pop()*. We could use them just the way they are in actual code, but we are not required to. An ADTD specifies operator semantics and parameters, but function names and calling sequences may be changed slightly in the actual implementation, as long as they maintain the spirit of the ADTD. For instance, our function might wind up as:

```
#define STK_OK0
#define STK_NOT_FOUND    1
void   int_push(value, name, status)
   int  value;    /* IN: new element's value */
   char *name;    /* IN: stack's name */
   int  *status;  /* OUT: STK_OK or STK_NOT_FOUND */
```

instead of being identical to the ADTD *push()*:

```
int  push( mystack, value )
   stack  mystack; /* IN: which stack */
   int    value;   /* IN: new element's value */
/* returns status "OK" or "no such stack" */
```

But *int_push()* should still behave like the ADTD's *push()* operator in spirit.

GENERATING ALTERNATE SOLUTIONS WITH ADTDS

The ADTD is normally written while solving a data structure design problem for the first time. But even if we already have a solution implemented, we can use an ADTD to generate new solutions. All we do is change the answers to the ADTD questions. There are many possibilities, and judgment is required to choose between them; the ADTD simply provides a way to generate them. To illustrate the possibilities, let's generate some new stacks by changing the answers to three of the ADTD questions.

Alternative 1: A Lumpy Stack

In a conventional stack ADTD, we answer the question "What relations hold between the data elements in the collection?" with "is above." That is, there's a total ordering relation "is above" which tells whether one element is above or below another in the stack. Now suppose we add a new relation "is beside" and allow "is above" to be a partial ordering instead of a total one. This gives us a "lumpy" stack in which elements can be side by side as well as below or above other elements. A typical lumpy stack is shown in Figure 4-2.

Lumpy stack *push()* accepts a set of elements, and lumpy *pop()* returns a set. The classical stack we chose to introduce ADTDs with is the special case of a lumpy stack in which *push()* and *pop()* always use sets containing exactly one element. In other words, a lumpy stack is simply a stack of sets, while a conventional stack is a stack of individual elements.

Of course, we are not restricted to stacks of sets. We can make stacks of sorted lists, stacks of stacks, stacks of graphs, and so on. Whether or not these beasts are useful as well as fun is not important right now. Right now we're in a brainstorming phase, trying to generate alternatives that we'll evaluate later.

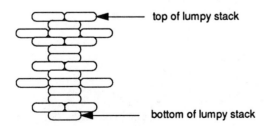
top of lumpy stack

bottom of lumpy stack

FIGURE 4-2: Sketch of a lumpy stack.

Alternative 2: Biased Stacks

The first answer to "What are the restrictions on membership in the stack?" is "any integer value can be pushed." Our original stack operators are "unbiased"; *push()* will accept any integer value. We can change this in any number of ways. For instance, we could insist that *push()* accept only an integer element greater than the current top-of-stack. Or we could make *push()* reject all negative values. Either biased *push()* would sometimes return "unacceptable value" as a status.

A different way to bias *push()* would be to base the bias not on the value of the prospective and current members, but on some other condition. For instance, the original stack ADTD placed no upper limit on a stack's size. In practice, programmers often define a maximum stack size and require *push()* to return "stack full" as a status.

Alternative 3: Additional Operators

The original answer to "What are the operators?" is "*push()* and *pop()*." But there are many other potentially useful operators, including these:

```
/*==============================================================*/
int  peek( mystack, down, value )
   stack  mystack; /* IN */
   int    down;    /* IN */
   int    *value;  /* OUT */
/*----------------------------------------------
Peek() copies into value  the element down  positions from the top of
mystack  without popping anything; it returns status "OK" or "invalid
down parameter."
-------------------------------------------------*/


/*==============================================================*/
int  size( mystack, elements )
   stack  mytstack;   /* IN */
   int    *elements;  /* OUT */
/*----------------------------------------------
Size() sets elements  to the number of elements in mystack; size()
returns a status of "OK" or "no such stack."
-------------------------------------------------*/


/*==============================================================*/
stack  create( stackname, status )
   char *stackname; /* IN */
   int *status;     /* OUT */
/*----------------------------------------------
Creates an empty stack named stackname. Without create(), push() must
create a new stack the first time it is called with a given name, or the
```

```
creation must be hidden in some initialization code. Create returns a
stack ID, and sets status to "OK," "name already in use" or "no memory."
If create() is available, push() might return "no such stack" in
addition to the other status possibilities already mentioned.
---------------------------------------------*/
```

GUIDING IMPLEMENTATION WITH ADTDS

We can make a few observations here about using ADTDs to guide implementation and testing. Checking the code against an ADTD can't tell us that we are done, because we may need bug fixes or performance tweaks that aren't mentioned in any ADTD. But the ADTD can tell us that we're not done. For instance, if the ADTD lists an operator that isn't coded, or a restriction on membership that isn't implemented, we're not done yet.

ADTDs can help with testing by highlighting likely trouble spots. Special positions in the ADTD geometry correspond to boundary conditions we should pay close attention to while testing. For instance, an empty stack means no element occupies the top-of-stack or bottom-of-stack position; a stack with one element means the same element occupies those two special positions. And it's certainly worthwhile to see what our *pop()* code does when the stack is empty, or when it has just one element.

Our code should also preserve the relations between elements, the distinction between different collections (e.g., different stacks of integers distinguished by name), any membership restrictions, and so on. ADTDs contain a great deal of semantic information we should verify before we decide we're done coding.

Sometimes an ADTD suggests that one implementation be used instead of another. We'll see some examples of this useful loop in the Example chapters:

```
while (not satisfied with the implementation) {
   examine alternative ADTDs
   consider alternative implementations
   change the ADTD and the implementation as needed
}
```

For instance, suppose we have decided to implement our abstract stack data type as a linked list:

```
typedef struct int_list {
   int             value; /* actual value */
   struct int_list *down, /* points to element underneath */
                   *up;   /* points to element above */
} int_list;
```

Our first attempt at a list header might be a simple pointer:

```
static int_list    *stack = NULL;  /* points to stack base */
```

Now suppose we're looking over the ADTD and notice that there's a *size()* operator that people can call to see how many elements are in the stack. We know we don't want to run the list every time *size()* is called—that's too slow. We can make *push()* and *pop()* increment and decrement some variable, but where do we put the variable?

The answer depends on the answer to another question: How many stacks will there be? In other words, do *push()* and *pop()* in the ADTD take a stack's name (or some other identifier) as a parameter? If they don't, the cleanest solution is probably to add another static:

```
static int   size = 0;  /* number of elements in stack */
```

If, on the other hand, there are going to be many stacks, we'll go with an arrangement something like the following, so that the list of elements in each stack and the element count for that stack are together:

```
typedef struct {
   struct int_list *elements;  /* list of stack elements */
   int             count;      /* number of stack elements */
} int_head;
#define MAX_STACKS 10 /* maximum number of stacks */
static int_head   all_stacks[MAX_STACKS];
```

In summary, we've seen that ADTDs are simply the answers to a list of questions about how the data is organized and what operations can be performed on it. We've seen an example of an ADTD and several variations on it, obtained by changing our answers to the ADTD questions. We've also begun to see how ADTDs can be used to guide our implementation efforts; ADTDs will be at the heart of each chapter in the Examples section.

CHAPTER 5
Glossary of ADTD Terms

This glossary defines terms (shown in bold) that arise in abstract data type descriptions (ADTDs). A more general glossary is provided at the end of the book.

abstract data type (ADT): An implementation-independent set of rules that describe a **collection** of **data elements** and various **operators** that can be used on the elements or on the collection as a whole. There are many ways to describe ADTs; we use a list of questions and answers known as an abstract data type description (ADTD).

calling sequence: The calling sequence of an **operator** is the list of parameters it expects. Each parameter has a name, a **type of value**, and a **mode**.

collection: Each **abstract data type** contains one or more collections of **data elements**. In general, code that supports only one collection hides the initializations needed to create an empty collection. By contrast, code that supports multiple collections normally supplies an **operator** for creating new empty collections. The code in Chapter 16, "Matching String Patterns," provides examples of each; graph.c supports one collection, while stringsets.c supports many.

data elements: Each **abstract data type** contains one or more **collections** of data elements. Abstract data types can be viewed as data (data elements), along with rules for organizing the data (**geometry, relations**) and rules for manipulating the data (**operators**). The data elements in a collection are all of one **type of value**.

geometry: A geometry is a general description of how the data elements are **positioned** within a collection. Familiar geometries include the stack, list, circular list, and tree. The geometry is what you're modeling when you sketch a collection; sketches typically use boxes to represent data elements, arrows to mark places elements can be inserted or removed, more arrows to indicate the elements' relative order, a line around the boxes to show what elements are in the collection, and similar conventions. However, other figures can be useful, too; see, for instance, Chapter 13, "Playing a Grammar Game."

mode: Possible **operator** parameter modes are *in*, *in-out*, and *out*. *In* parameters are those whose value may be used by the operator but not changed by it. *Out* parameters may be given valid values by the operator; their incoming value is ignored. *In-out* parameters are those whose values may be used or changed or both.

one-to-one, one-to-many, many-to-many: These three kinds of relation are illustrated in Figure 5-1. A relation R is one-to-one if, for every element x, there is just one y such that $R(x, y)$ holds. In other words, the relation is really a function or *mapping*. For instance, if the collection is the integers, and the relation R is the group of all (x, y) such that $y = 2x$, we clearly have a function.

We can generalize this a bit, in two ways. First, we can speak of one-to-one relations even if not every element is mapped. For instance, in a program, there is a one-to-one mapping between a subset of the string tokens ("int," "typedef," "if," "find_average," "total," etc.) present and the case-sensitive language's reserved words. Every string that maps to a reserved word maps to exactly one reserved word, and every reserved word is represented by exactly one string, but not every string maps to a reserved word.

The second generalization involves one-to-many and many-to-many mappings. The mapping between a typical tree and its nodes is one-to-many. That is, many child nodes map to one parent node in a tree, and one parent may have many children, whether it does at present or not. Similarly, the mapping between stack elements under the relation "is above" is many-to-many. A particular element might be above many other elements and might have many elements above it.

operator: An operator is a function that alters or examines a collection of data elements. By definition, operators are the only way to alter or examine collections.

ordering relation: An ordering relation between the members of a collection imposes an order on them according to their values. For instance, "integer less than" and

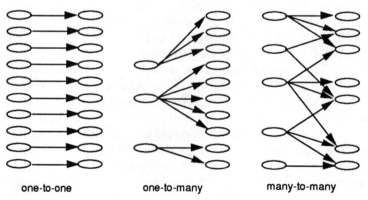

one-to-one   one-to-many   many-to-many

FIGURE 5-1: Three kinds of relation.

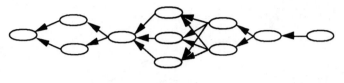

partial order

total order

FIGURE 5-2: Different kinds of orderings.

"alphabetical order" are ordering relationships, while "these integers leave the same remainder when divided by six" and "these nodes in a graph are neighbors" are not ordering relations. Ordering relations are either **partial** or **total**.

partial order: A partial order is illustrated in Figure 5-2. An **ordering relation** is called "partial" if there is any pair of different values x and y for which x does not precede y and y does not precede x. For instance, the **relation** "is a prerequisite of" is a partial order on the set of college courses. Some courses must precede others, but it is not true that, given any two courses, one is a prerequisite of the other. Consider calculus and creative writing, for example—neither has to precede the other, so "prerequisite" is only a partial order. By way of contrast, see **total order**.

partition: A **relation** is said to "partition" a collection if the relation divides the collection into subsets such that (a) every element is in one of the subsets, and (b) no element is in more than one subset. Relations that are **reflexive, symmetric,** and **transitive** always partition a collection.

For instance, the relation "gives the same remainder when divided by six" is illustrated in Figure 5-3. Since every integer gives some remainder upon division by six, and no integer gives more than one remainder, this relation partitions the integers into six subsets.

position: A position is a location within a **geometry** that may be occupied by one or more data elements. Examples include the top of a stack, the root of a tree, and the end of a list. **Operators** often treat a **data element** differently when it occupies different positions in a geometry. For instance, only the element at the top of a stack can be popped off the stack; elements in other positions are not accessible.

proper subset: A subset of a collection is called "proper" if it does not contain the entire collection. The set of even integers is a proper subset of the set of all integers. Viewing an interior tree node as a root gives rise to a proper subtree, that is, a tree whose nodes form a proper subset of the set of nodes contained in the entire tree.

reflexive: A binary **relation** R is called "reflexive" if $R(x, x)$ is true for every element x in a collection. For instance, the relation "integer equals" is reflexive since $x = x$ for every integer x. The relation "integer less than" is not reflexive, since no integer is less than itself.

{..0, 6,12,...}, {...1, 7, 13,...}, {...2, 8, 14,...},
{..3, 9,15,...}, {...4, 10, 16,...}, {...5, 11, 17,...}

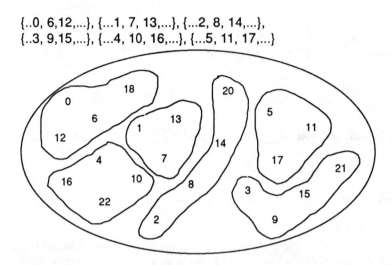

FIGURE 5-3: A collection of integers partitioned by the relation "gives the same remainder when divided by six."

relation: A relation R is a boolean function whose parameters are elements of a given collection. The function need not be implemented, but it must be implementable. The order of the parameters is important; $R(x, y)$ need not be the same as $R(y, x)$ if x and y are distinct (see **symmetric**). Incidentally, the notation $R(x, y)$ suggests a binary relation, but relations may be **one-to-one**, **one-to-many**, or **many-to-many**.

semantics: An **operator's** semantics is its meaning, namely, its effect on the collection and the parameters it was called with.

status code: Each **operator** reports on the success or failure of the requested operation by setting a status variable. Status codes come in two flavors; either "everything is fine" or "error such-and-such occurred."

symmetric: A binary **relation** R is called "symmetric" if, for all elements x, y in a collection, $R(x, y)$ true implies $R(y, x)$ is true. For instance, the tree relation "is a sibling of" is symmetric since y is a sibling (child of the same parent) of x whenever x is a sibling of y. The relation "integer less than" is not symmetric, since $x < y$ certainly does not imply $y < x$ for all integers x and y.

total order: A total order is illustrated in Figure 5-2. An **ordering relation** is called "total" if $((x$ precedes $y)$ or $(y$ precedes $x))$ is true for all distinct x, y. For instance, alphabetical order is total; given any two distinct strings of alphabetic characters, one is always alphabetically before the other. By way of contrast, see **partial order**.

transitive: A **relation** R is called "transitive" if, for all elements x, y, and z in a collection, $R(x, y)$ and $R(y, z)$ together imply $R(x, z)$ is true. For instance, the stack relation "under" is transitive since x under y and y under z implies x is under z for any choice of x, y, and z in the stack. The relation "is a friend of" among people is unfortunately not transitive; even if x gets along fine with y and y and z are the best of friends, x and z might still hate each other.

type of value: Every element of a collection has one or more associated values. These values fall into data types such as integer, real, string, boolean, pixel, social security number, mass, and so on. A data type is implemented either directly with one of a language's elemental types (e.g., integer) or indirectly with some combination of elemental types (e.g., by using a C struct or Pascal RECORD).

CHAPTER 6
Summary

In this chapter, we need to do three things. First, we'll describe which parts of *Advanced C Struct Programming* you can turn to for help with each step of the Plan. Second, we'll show why *Advanced C Struct Programming* is justified in focusing on data structures—after all, many programmers would argue that data structures and algorithms are inseparable. Third, we'll see how the Plan relates to object-oriented programming in general, and to programming in C++ in particular.

WHERE TO GO FOR HELP

Recall that the Plan consists of six steps, performed more or less in order (we may return to earlier steps, or skip steps, as we choose):

1. Research the problem area.
2. Formulate top-level goals.
3. Select guiding examples.
4. Create an ADTD.
5. Put together a "Struct Design"—write typedefs, #defines, and global variable declarations that implement the ADTD geometry; write functions that implement the ADTD operators.
6. Test, debug, and tune the code.

This next list tells which portions of *Advanced C Struct Programming* are helpful during each step of the Plan:

1. Research: You're on your own. Well, not entirely. There are always libraries, coworkers, experts, luck, and guesses. But *Advanced C Struct Programming* is not a guide to research methods.

2. Top-Level Goals:
   "Goal Resolution Algorithm" (see page 14) and discussion in Chapter 2, "Setting Top-Level Goals"
   "Top-Level Goals" in each of the Examples chapters
3. Guiding Examples:
   "How to Choose Good Examples" (see page 23), "Desirable Qualities in a Set of Examples" (see page 17), and discussion in Chapter 3, "Choosing Good Guiding Examples"
   "Guiding Examples" in each of the Examples chapters
4. ADTD:
   ADTD questions and discussion in Chapter 4, "Creating an Abstract Data Type"
   Chapter 5, "Glossary of ADTD Terms"
   "Abstract Data Type Description" in each of the Examples chapters
   ADTD template and examples in the Framework section
5. Struct Design:
   "Generating Alternate Solutions with ADTDs" (see page 31) and "Guiding Implementation with ADTDs" (see page 33) in Chapter 4, "Creating an Abstract Data Type"
   "Attempt One," "Attempt Two," and so forth in each of the Examples chapters
   C code in each of the Examples chapters
   "Application to C Structs" in each of the top-level goals in the Framework section
   Struct design guideline template and examples in the Framework section
6. Testing, Debugging, and Tuning:
   "Attempt One," "Attempt Two," and so forth in each of the Examples chapters
   C code in each of the Examples chapters
   Struct trick template and examples in the Framework section

DATA STRUCTURES VERSUS ALGORITHMS

Advanced C Struct Programming is a book about data structure design and implementation. It is not about algorithms. But how can we separate data structures from algorithms? Wirth (1976) sums up a common point of view among programmers in the preface to his book *Algorithms + Data Structures = Programs*:

> [It became] clear that decisions about structuring data cannot be made without knowledge of the algorithms applied to the data and that, vice versa, the structure and choice of algorithms often strongly depend on the structure of the underlying data.

How, then, can *Advanced C Struct Programming* presume to study data structures in isolation from algorithms? The answer is, "it does and it doesn't."

As you'll see in the Examples section, *Advanced C Struct Programming* ignores certain kinds of algorithms. We don't do any wind-tunnel simulations, for instance, or matrix multiplications, or Fourier transforms. In programs whose main purpose is cranking through mathematical calculations, algorithms reign supreme, and data structures are often simply arrays of real numbers. Pointers are rarely employed. In this sort of program, there's no need to bring in "heavy machinery" like ADTDs to assist in data structure design and implementation.

In *Advanced C Struct Programming*, by contrast, we concentrate on problems where data organization is more important than mathematical formulae. We ignore problems that require numerical analysis or other solutions that are perhaps very intensive computationally but that employ simple data structures. In other words, we have separated data structures from certain types of algorithms by concentrating on problems that require something more complex than a few arrays to hold the data.

However, data structures should never be designed or implemented separately from certain other algorithms, namely, their associated operators. The functions that create, traverse, delete, update, and display data structures depend very strongly on the model used to organize the data and on the way that model is implemented.

A data structure should be designed and implemented from the start as an organized collection of data elements plus a group of operators that manipulate the elements or the entire collection. It just doesn't do to leave the operators for later. In other words, data structure design and implementation should be guided by an ADTD!

Now we see how *Advanced C Struct Programming* both does and does not isolate data structures from algorithms. It ignores some algorithms (those that require only simple data structures), but it pays close attention to others (the abstract data type's operators).

In a sense, *Advanced C Struct Programming* is the complement of books that provide many algorithms (often numerical) but leave the choice of data structures (often arrays or something equally simple) to the reader. *Advanced C Struct Programming* provides many abstract data types (and tools for crafting them) but leaves it up to the reader to employ these or other ADTs in complete programs.

OBJECT-ORIENTED PROGRAMMING AND THE PLAN

The Plan fits very neatly into the object-oriented approach to programming. First of all, research and top-level goals and guiding examples are clearly important no matter what programming paradigm or language is used. You'll have just as much trouble working in Smalltalk or C++ or any other object-oriented language as you will working in C if you don't understand the problem area, or if you don't agree on top-level goals with the rest of the contributors, or if you choose bad guiding examples.

But the correlation between object-oriented programming (OOP) and the Plan is much closer than that. Abstract data types (ADTs) are an essential part of OOP. To see why, consider what OOP actually consists of. A number of definitions have been advanced, but they're generally similar to the one in Stroustrup (1987):

> ...operations applied in a uniform manner to objects on heterogeneous lists.

For instance, suppose our objects are spheres, cubes, line segments, and combinations thereof. The combinations are obtained by using our operators: creation, scaling, positioning, intersection, and union. If we take an OOP approach, the same scaling operator, for

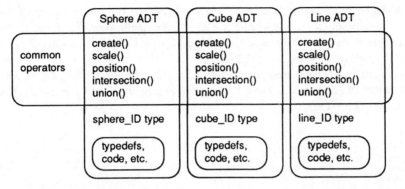

FIGURE 6-1: Object-oriented programming means coordinating abstract data types to provide a common group of operators.

instance, can be applied to spheres, cubes, line segments, or any combination of the three. The other operators can also be "applied in a uniform manner" to the objects in our heterogeneous (i.e., "mixture of types") group.

In other words, OOP simply means we coordinate a group of ADTs so that each provides certain operators. This definition is illustrated in Figure 6-1. Incidentally, each ADT in Figure 6-1 provides only the "common" operators. Every operator provided by the sphere ADT, for instance, is also provided by the other two ADTs. This is not necessary, but it is desirable if we want to follow an object-oriented paradigm. The main goal of OOP is the ability to apply any given operator in the same way to every object. The more exceptions there are, the harder programming is.

How a group of ADTs is implemented is a separate question from whether or not those ADTs are coordinated to provide common operators. If the ADTs provide the same operators, we're following an OOP paradigm; to the extent that they don't, we're not.

Different languages provide different features for implementing ADTs and OOP. For instance, C++ supports classes (see Stroustrup, 1987), Ada provides packages (Booch, 1983), and Modula-2 programs are divided into modules (Ogilvie, 1985).

All these solutions have one thing in common—a functional interface to data. Object-oriented programs do not simply pass around pointers to structs, at least not in a way that lets any piece of code anywhere in the program use the pointer directly in a statement like "foo–>count++;." Instead, the data structure implementation details (the typedef, for instance) are hidden. The ADT's structs can be created, traversed, deleted, updated, or displayed only by way of functions that are somehow "exported" by the class or package or module. These exported functions implement the operators specified in the ADTD.

C does not provide nearly the support for OOP that these other languages do. In fact, according to Stroustrup (1987), that is one of the main reasons C++ was invented. It's not too far off the mark to say that C++ is C plus OOP. Using object-oriented programming and abstract data types in C (or even in C++) requires self-discipline. So C's shortcomings simply make the Plan in general, and ADTDs in particular, that much more important.

All right. We have the Plan firmly in hand, and we know which parts of *Advanced C Struct Programming* to turn to when the Plan starts wriggling out of our grasp. We know we can safely study data structures apart from algorithms as long as we pay attention to the ADT operators. And we've seen that the Plan fits neatly into the world of OOP, so that much of what we learn from the examples can be carried with us to new languages such as C++. After a brief introduction to the examples in the next chapter, we'll start putting the Plan to work on real-world problems.

SECTION TWO

Examples

CHAPTER 7
Introduction

Before looking at our first example of the Plan in action, let's review the reasons these particular examples were chosen. We'll also discuss the reasons the examples are presented as ongoing processes rather than final results. Then we'll finish this brief introduction by summarizing the coding style used in the examples.

Some of the examples might make you wonder "Why bother? The operating system (or window manager, or some other existing tool) will do that for me. I'll never need to write an X, so why should I study this example of writing an X?" There are two answers to this.

First, professional programmers do sometimes need to "roll their own" versions of existing programs. For instance, you might need to implement a bare-bones operating system on new proprietary hardware. Or you might want to reimplement a program so you'll have access to source code you can modify and/or claim the rights to. In any case, it seems unlikely that you can predict accurately and completely what programming problems you'll be handed to work on during the next five years.

More importantly, however, you must realize that the particular pieces of C code presented are not the point of *Advanced C Struct Programming*. The examples are there to show how the Plan works. A wide variety of examples is included to demonstrate how the Plan can be used to design and implement data structures in a wide variety of programs. You can learn something about writing good data structures from example X even if you never do need to write an X.

The examples present programming as a craft in progress, instead of simply listing the code that results from the process. This means that you will probably know the code as well as you would if you had written it yourself, before you've even read it! You should know the code (aside from stylistic concerns like the choice of variable names) because you've seen it designed, and you've watched as different attempts were made to write its critical typedefs and functions.

Each example begins with a problem description and then works through the steps in the Plan. You are there for each step, from the selection of top-level goals and guiding examples all the way through ADTD creation to the various attempts at coding. And I do mean "various attempts."

For three good reasons, I have included most of the dead ends and faulty solutions I encountered along the way to each "final" piece of code. The C code presented at the end of each Examples chapter also contains a testbed and debugging aids, for these same three reasons:

1. By watching mistakes happen and afterward determining what went wrong, you greatly improve your chances of avoiding similar errors. There is a big difference between knowing intellectually that a certain problem might occur and running into that problem head-on. Head-on collisions are both more painful and more instructive.
2. Some dead ends lead to struct tricks or struct design guidelines that aren't useful in the current program but might be helpful in another piece of code. We accumulate these goodies in the Framework section as they arise.
3. Code you've written yourself is easier to understand than code written by someone else. It's also more interesting. Interesting code is more likely to be correct and also more likely to be used as a model for other code. However, I haven't figured out yet how to publish a book in which all the code was written by whoever happens to be reading the book (at least, not in a way that generates royalties for me). The next best thing to having you write the code is to put you "inside my head" while I'm writing the code, so that's what I've done.

Each chapter in the Examples section contains two parts:

1. An English discussion, mixed with figures and code fragments, that explains why the code is the way it is.
2. A complete listing of the "final" C program.

Since we devote so much effort to designing the code and to experimenting with different implementations of its most critical parts, there is no line-by-line analysis of the code at the end.

Incidentally, you'll notice that I referred above to "final" code; "final" is in quotes because I don't believe in final code. Code that is useful is always changing. Code becomes set in a final fixed form only after people stop using it or companies refuse to support it further (in which case people will generally stop using it). The code in *Advanced C Struct Programming* is no exception to this rule. It is not meant to be final. You're welcome to build on it, as long as you don't violate copyright law.

And now, here are a few words about coding style: "Everybody's is different." Actually, we need a few more words than that. The list below summarizes the C coding style used in *Advanced C Struct Programming*:

Each function is preceded by a comment which describes the function's purpose, its parameters, its return value, which global variables it uses, and similar useful facts.
Function parameter modes (from ADTDs, remember?) are marked by comments: /* IN */, /* OUT */, and /* IN, OUT */.

Functions are static whenever possible.

Functions return void (i.e., no return value) whenever possible.

#defines are in all uppercase, except for macros, that is, #defines that take parameters. Macros are closer in spirit to functions than they are to constants, so their names resemble function names.

The names of functions that are not static contain either a prefix or some keyword (e.g., "rsv" in Chapter 8, "Building a Collection of Reserved Words"); when two functions are both named "foo," for instance, some very nasty headaches can be caused by linking the code for this *foo()* to a call intended for that *foo()*, and some linkers don't even emit a warning message.

In keeping with ANSI C, *malloc()* is declared as "void *malloc();" instead of as "char *malloc();".

Many files refer to the header file "boolean.h"; here it is:

```
/*---------------------------------------------

        boolean.h
-----------------------------------------------*/


/*=============================================

Purpose:
  Provides a typedef and defines that make code easier to read.
==============================================*/
#ifndef _BOOLEAN_H_
#define _BOOLEAN_H_

typedef int     boolean;
#define true    1
#define false   0


#endif  _BOOLEAN_H_
```

Some files also refer to the function strsave(); here it is:

```
/*=============================================*/
char    *strsave( str )
  char    *str;   /* IN */
/*---------------------------------------------
Purpose:
  Allocates new memory and copies a string into it; terminates
  the new copy with a '\0' character.
Parameters:
  str     string to copy
  Returns pointer to new null-terminated copy of string, or
  NULL on failure.
-----------------------------------------------*/
{
```

```
char    *new;
void    *malloc();

if (!str)
    return (NULL);
if (!(new = (char *)malloc(strlen(str) + 1)))
    return (NULL);
strcpy(new, str);
return (new);
} /* strsave */
```

Boolean.h and the other header files use #ifdef guards; see the struct trick "Nesting Include Files" (page 397) in the Framework section.

Testbeds are also surrounded by #ifdefs so they can be in the same file as the functions they test without increasing the object code's size unnecessarily.

So much for style. Let's summarize. *Advanced C Struct Programming* is not a "cookbook" whose purpose is providing a great deal of code for you to type in and run gleefully for hours on end. The examples were chosen to illustrate the Plan in action. Accordingly, they are presented as processes, complete with dead ends and testbeds. The Plan is not a substitute for programming expertise; it's a way to focus and enhance that expertise. If you're like me, you believe we can all use a little focused enhancement from time to time, so let's get started.

CHAPTER 8
Building a Collection of Reserved Words

Suppose we're writing an interpreter or compiler and want a good way to represent the programming language's reserved words. Our language is based on one that's in common use, but we are implementing an "extended subset" that is tailored to a particular application. This means that we do not support everything other implementations support, but we do support some extensions not seen in other implementations. We expect the definition of the language to change somewhat over the next year or two as we refine our ideas about what language features are useful for our application area.

TOP-LEVEL GOALS

We want to minimize execution time and maximize portability, at the expense of increased implementation time and increased memory requirements if necessary. However, memory requirements are unlikely to increase much, because the total data is just a few hundred reserved words plus some overhead to organize them. Even if we tried to be inefficient, it would be hard to chew up megabytes instead of a kilobyte or two.

The main cost will probably be increased implementation time to ensure portability and speedy execution. Implementation time will also increase because we want to sharpen our judgment by considering different solutions instead of settling for the first one that appears to work.

GUIDING EXAMPLES

Looking for examples of different kinds of reserved words yields the following list:

> data types like "int," "char," and "float"
> statements or parts thereof, like "return," "if," and "while"
> operators like "and," "not," and "mod" (these are from Pascal, not C)
> standard functions like "abs"

The rest of the strings are user-defined identifiers, not reserved words. We could add a fifth category—"strings that aren't reserved"—to remind ourselves that not every string fits into one of the four categories above.

The single fundamental characteristic of a reserved word is its kind. Since operators can be thought of as standard functions that have an unusual syntax, we'll allow three values for this fundamental characteristic: data type, statement, and standard function.

ABSTRACT DATA TYPE DESCRIPTION

Now we'll create an ADTD of our solution. The most productive ADTD questions are often those related to the geometry and the operators, so that's where we'll start.

What is the geometry of the collection?   Let's start by saying what the geometry is not. It's not a stack, a queue, a ring, a graph, or a tree. In fact, there doesn't seem to be any need at all for special positions like "tree root" or "top of stack." At first glance, the collection of reserved words is simply a set of strings.

On the other hand, since we're dealing with strings, the possibility of listing them in alphabetical order comes to mind. But what good does that do us? If we're going to arrange the strings in some order, it ought to be in order of decreasing frequency of use, not in alphabetical order. Then we could test the most likely possibilities first and cut down the search time when we check to see if a string is reserved.

OK, it's decided. Our geometry is a list of strings, with the most frequently used reserved words at the front. When we say "list," remember that we're talking abstract data type "list," not "linked list" or "array." We haven't committed ourselves to an implementation yet; all we've done is restrict ourselves to implementations of lists.

What relations hold between the elements of the collection?   The main relation is the total ordering "is used more often than." This ranking may be arrived at subjectively, or by sampling existing source code, but it will be needed to speed up access to the reserved words. In ADTD terms, particular positions have no special properties, but they do have an implicit priority. We want the most commonly used words at the front of the list.

We also need a relation that partitions the elements according to the kind of reserved word they represent. During parsing, we will want to distinguish, for instance, between reserved words like "for" that appear in statements and reserved words like "char" that denote types. We'll call this partitioning relation "is same kind of reserved word."

What are the operators? We'll need to add strings to our list of reserved words, but we won't need to delete them. Whether or not a word is reserved does not change during runtime. Imagine the chaos if "for" and "char" were reserved at one point during compilation but not at another!

We'll also need a way to test any given string for membership in the list, that is, to determine whether or not the string is a reserved word. If the string is reserved, we need some way to tell what "kind" of word it is—which of the guiding examples it matches—as well as exactly which reserved word it is.

We can combine the operators that answer "is this a reserved word?" and "which reserved word is this?" into one by having the "which reserved word is this?" operator return a null ID if a word is not reserved and a valid ID if it is.

We could do away with the need for a "what kind of reserved word is this?" operator by making the ID that comes from "which reserved word is this?" be a pointer. Then the application could just use the pointer to access all the information associated with the reserved word. However, we won't do this. It's safer to copy the information than it is to give out pointers. A corrupt reserved word list would be fatal.

In summary, we'll need a set of operators something like this:

```
/*================================================================*/
int      init_reserved_words()
/*----------------------------------------------------
Does whatever initialization is needed, so it has to be called before
any of the other operators; it returns "OK" or we quit.
-------------------------------------------------------*/


/*================================================================*/
int      add_reserved_word( new, freq, info )
   char *new;     /* IN */
   int  freq;     /* IN */
   ??   info;     /* IN */
/*----------------------------------------------------------
Adds new  to the list if it's not already there; returns "OK," "already
there," or "internal screw-up (e.g., not initialized yet)."  Freq tells
us where to put the word in the list—higher frequency words go at the
front of the list.  We'll need some way to resolve things if different
new  values are passed with the same freq;  but that can wait until
implementation time.  Info  answers "what kind of reserved word is
this?" and any similar questions.
-------------------------------------------------*/


/*================================================================*/
int      get_reserved_id( test_me, my_id )
   char *test_me;    /* IN */
   int  *my_id;      /* OUT */
/*-------------------------------------------------------
If test_me  is a reserved word, set my_id  to its nonzero ID and return
```

```
"OK".  If test_me  is not reserved, set my_id  to zero and return "OK".
Return "internal screw-up" if init_reserved_words() has not been called.
------------------------------------------------*/


/*============================================================*/
int     get_reserved_info( id, info )
  int id;     /* IN */
  ??    *info; /* OUT */
/*-------------------------------------------------
If id  is a valid reserved word ID, copy the info (e.g., what kind of
reserved word - statement, data type or standard function) into info and
return "OK."  We don't know yet what all the info is, so we haven't
specified a type for info.  Return "bad ID" if id  is not valid, and
return "internal screw-up" if init_reserved_words() has not been called.
------------------------------------------------*/
```

No traversal operators were defined, but we might add a debugging operator called *print_reserved_words()* that dumps the list in order, showing each reserved word's spelling, its kind, and any other useful information. No deletion operator was defined because the list of reserved words disappears when the interpreter or compiler exits, passing control back to the shell or whoever invoked it.

What are the restrictions on membership in the collection? The only restriction that's obvious is "no duplicates." But we need to be perfectly clear about this. What makes a duplicate? Are "if" and "IF" the same? How about "int" the data type and "int" the standard function? OK, we'll say that our language is not case-sensitive, so yes, "if" and "IF" represent the same reserved word. We'll assume further that input is forced to uppercase by the time it reaches us.

Also, we're going to flex our design muscles and say that a reserved word can appear in the list only once, even if it can be used in more than one way in the language. We'll make the info that's associated with each reserved word represent a set of valid possibilities instead of just one. Thus, "int" will go into the reserved word list with information that says it can be used as a data type or as a standard function, but not as a keyword in a flow-of-control statement. "If," on the other hand, can be used in statements, but not in variable declarations or where a function call is expected.

So the allowable data types are strings with associated flags to indicate the kind(s) of reserved word the string denotes.

We expect the set of reserved words for the language to change, but the range of possibilities is not vast. We have a rough idea how many reserved words to expect in the next six months or so; if we have 100 reserved words now, maybe we'll have 300 after six months. In any case, there's a limit on the number of reserved words.

How many collections are allowed by this ADT? There is just one list of reserved words per compiler or interpreter.

Can a proper subset of a collection be operated upon as a collection in its own right?
No. The *add_reserved_word()* operator must have access to the entire list to avoid duplicates. The *get_reserved_id()* and *get_reserved_info()* operators must also have access to the entire list so they don't miss a valid reserved word.

ATTEMPT ONE

The ADTD gives us a good framework to guide our implementation, but there are plenty of questions left. For starters, how should we implement the list? The two obvious choices are (1) as a linked list whose elements are allocated at run-time; or (2) as elements in an array that is allocated at program load-time. The design guidelines rule out the use of a linked list of arrays; see the design guideline "Avoid Sorted Lists of Arrays" (page 360).

A linked list is easier to make insertions in, but it requires extra memory for its pointers. An array is reasonable since we know the number of reserved words at compile-time. But insertion into arrays is expensive because we sometimes need to "slide" entries to new positions to make space for a new value in the middle of the list.

Ah, but wait a minute! Maybe we can get the best of both approaches. Operations on the list occur in two distinct phases: building and accessing. After the list of reserved words is built during the compiler or interpreter's initialization, it won't be changed. The list will only be read; that's why there is no *delete_reserved_word()* operator in the ADTD. Nobody says data has to stay in the same kind of variables for the duration of the program. The design guideline "Consider Copying Data to a Better Format" (page 365) suggests we consider building the list in a dynamic structure and then copy it to a more rigid structure.

So suppose we go ahead and use a linked list during creation of our list of reserved words and then copy the results to a static array. After all, we know exactly how many reserved words there are, so we can size the array precisely and save the memory used by all the list pointers. The code that builds the list will then look something like this:

```
if (init_reserved_words() != OK) {
  fprintf(stderr,
      "couldn't initialize list of reserved words\n");
  exit(1);
}
if (add_reserved_word("FOR", 100, STATEMENT_WORD) != OK) {
  fprintf(stderr, "couldn't add reserved word FOR\n");
  exit(1);
}
if (add_reserved_word("CHAR", 110, TYPE_WORD) != OK) {
  fprintf(stderr, "couldn't add reserved word CHAR\n");
  exit(1);
}
if (add_reserved_word("ABS", 70, FUNCTION_WORD) != OK) {
  fprintf(stderr, "couldn't add reserved word ABS\n");
  exit(1);
```

```
    }
    /* and so forth, for the other reserved words */
```

ATTEMPT TWO

But wait a minute. We are providing frequencies to *add_reserved_word()* to make sure the most commonly used words end up at the front of the list. These frequencies are known at compile-time, which means we can get rid of the *freq* parameter in *add_reserved_words()*. Instead of passing the frequency to indicate where the word should be inserted, we'll simply build the list in order. The first call to *add_reserved_word()* puts in the first word of the list, the second call puts in the second most frequently used word, and so on, up to the last call that adds the rarest reserved word.

A nice result of making the *add_reserved_word()* calls in order is that we can do away with the linked list entirely, since the only reason we wanted to use a linked list was to make insertion easier. We'll put the list of reserved words directly in an array instead. Our C code looks like this now:

```
/* bitflags that define possible kinds of reserved words: */
#define RSV_STATEMENT   1
#define RSV_DATA_TYPE   2
#define RSV_FUNCTION    4
typedef struct {
   char *text;   /* points to "FOR", etc. */
   int  kinds;   /* see RSV_xxx defines */
} rsv_word_info;

#define TOTAL_RSV_WORDS    100
static rsv_word_info       rsv_words[TOTAL_RSV_WORDS];

if (init_reserved_words() != OK) {
   fprintf(stderr,
       "couldn't initialize list of reserved words\n");
   exit(1);
}
/* add_reserved_word() calls in order—most frequently
   used words are added first: */
if (add_reserved_word("CHAR", RSV_DATA_TYPE) != OK) {
   fprintf(stderr, "couldn't add reserved word CHAR\n");
   exit(1);
}
if (add_reserved_word("FOR", RSV_STATEMENT) != OK) {
   fprintf(stderr, "couldn't add reserved word FOR\n");
   exit(1);
}
if (add_reserved_word("ABS", RSV_FUNCTION) != OK) {
```

```
      fprintf(stderr, "couldn't add reserved word ABS\n");
      exit(1);
}
/* and so on for the other reserved words */
```

ATTEMPT THREE

We improved our first solution by looking at the *add_reserved_word()* operator. We can improve our second solution by considering the other operators, *get_reserved_id()* and *get_reserved_info()*.

Recall that *get_reserved_id()* takes a string *test_me* and searches the list of reserved words to see if *test_me* is in it somewhere. We expect to do a lot of searches. Except for identifiers that lie inside string constants or comments, every identifier in the source program has to be compared against the list of reserved words.

The way we do things now, each search will involve numerous calls on *strcmp()* or some similar string comparison function. This is not good, because a typical implementation of *strcmp()* looks like this:

```
strcmp( a, b )
   char *a,
        *b;
{
   for ( ; *a == *b; a++, b++ ) {
      if (*a == '\0') {
         return (0);
      }
   }
   return (*a - *b);
} /* strcmp */
```

In other words, a typical *strcmp()* is most efficient at distinguishing strings that differ near their beginnings. For instance, *strcmp("for," "statistics")* is relatively fast, but *strcmp("static," "statistics")* is not. What's more, any *strcmp()* call at all makes us pay the price of a function call—we must allocate a stack frame, set up the parameters, and so forth.

What we need is a string representation that allows fast comparisons. The best we can hope for is to turn each string into an integer. Then each of our character-by-character string comparisons turns into a single test for equality between integers, and we've eliminated the function call overhead.

So how do we turn a string into an integer? We could do this:

```
int     encode_1( str )
   char *str;   /* IN */
{
   /* The encoding is the first character, cast as an int. */
```

```
    return ((int)(str[0]));
} /* encode_1 */
```

But this is a bad solution—*encode_1()* maps "struct," "switch," and "silly" all to 115 (assuming ASCII). As much as possible, we want different strings to go to different integers. OK, how about this one?

```
int     encode_2( str )
  char *str;    /* IN */
{
  int  sum = 0;

  /* The encoding is sum of chars in string, cast as ints. */
  if (str) {
    for ( ; *str; str++) {
      sum += (int)(*str);
    }
  }
  return (sum);
} /* encode_2 */
```

This is a little better. We catch null string pointers, and we map "struct," "switch," and "silly" to different values (677, 658, and 557). But we can do better. *Encode_2()* still maps all of "int," "tin," and "nit," not to mention "hot," to 331. We need to take into account each letter's position in the string:

```
int  encode_3( str )
  char *str;    /* IN */
{
  int  sum = 0,
    i;

  /* The encoding is a weighted sum of the chars in the */
  /* string, cast as ints. There are many other ways to */
  /* weight the sum besides the one used here. */
  if (str) {
    for (i = 0; str[i]; i++) {
      sum += (i+1)*(int)(str[i]);
    }
  }
  return (sum);
} /* encode_3 */
```

Encode_3() fixes the "int," "tin," "nit" problem, but we still get collisions: "ord" and "adr" both go to 639, "go" and "in" both map to 325, and so on. We could look for a better encoding function, but can we ever hope to eliminate all collisions? Is there a perfect encoding function lurking out there somewhere in a mathematical jungle? Probably not, because there seem to be so many more strings than there are integers.

But let's not just guess that there are more strings than integers, let's find out for sure. Be kind and suppose the maximum length of a string is seven characters. If strings contain only alphabetic characters and we ignore case, there are 26^7 different strings possible—that's 8,031,810,176. On a system that uses 32-bit integers, the largest unsigned integer is $2^{32} =$ 4,294,967,295, so there are roughly twice as many strings as integers.

Hmmm. What do you say we go talk to the Hardware Engineering Department Manager about adding one more bit? That would give us 8,589,934,591 as the largest unsigned integer, which means we would have more integers than seven-character alphabetic strings and our reserved word list search would be incredibly fast. Think she'll go for it? Probably not. In practice, there really are many more strings than integers.

So we need some way to handle collisions. What happens when two reserved words have the same encoding? We could try to find a different encoding function that doesn't map any reserved words to the same integer. This is not as bad as it sounds, because there are so few reserved words relative to the number of integer values, and because there are many ways to do the encoding. For instance, here's one more:

```
int     encode_4( str )
  char *str;   /* IN */
{
  int  sum = 0,
       i,
       off; /* character's offset from blank ' ' */

  if (str) {
    for (i = 0; str[i]; i++) {
      off = ((int)str[i]) - ((int)' ');
      sum += i*off*off;
    }
    sum -= (int)str[0];
  }
  return (sum);
} /* encode_4 */
```

However, this makes it harder to add new reserved words because we might have to fiddle around with the encoding function. Another possibility is to change the reserved words to avoid duplicate encodings; if we're designing the language extensions, we get to decide between "write" and "print" or "float" and "real."

However, the cleanest solution is to go ahead and put both words in the table, as illustrated in Figure 8-1. We encode the new string and then compare it to the encodings of the reserved words already in the table. If the encodings don't match, there's no way the strings could match. On the few occasions in which the encodings do match, we go ahead and do the *strcmp()*, comparing the strings character-by-character to see if they actually match.

Text	Encoding
FOR	34
WHILE	212
ABS	711
SWITCH	212
CHAR	4123
IF	334

FIGURE 8-1: A table in which two reserved words have the same encoding.

This approach is much faster than calling *strcmp()* for every comparison, and we only "err" on the side of safety. Sometimes the encodings will match when the strings do not, but that won't be often, and we won't give out any "false positives" because we always confirm an encoding match with an actual *strcmp()*.

In summary, we use an array of reserved word structs, each of which has a spelling, an encoded form of that spelling, and a set of flags that tell us how the reserved word can be used legally in a program. The array implements an ordered list in which the most frequently used words are nearest the front, to speed searches. The encodings also allow us to speed up the searches by cutting way down on the number of character-by-character string comparisons we have to do.

LISTING: rsv_words.c

```
/*--------------------------------------------
                    rsv_words.c
-------------------------------------------*/

/*=================================================================
Purpose:
    Provide code that builds a list of reserved words for a
    compiler or interpreter. This file includes the testbed
    (main()), the builder functions (init_rsv_words(),
    add_rsv_word()), access functions (get_rsv_id(),
    get_rsv_info()), and supporting defines, typedefs, static
    variables and functions (encode()).

    It was compiled under LightspeedC (TM) on a Macintosh SE.
-------------------------------------------*/
#include "stdio.h"
#include <boolean.h>
/*--------------------------------------------
    Error codes returned by reserved word functions:
*/
#define RSV_OK              0
```

```
#define RSV_NOT_INITED    1
#define RSV_BAD_ID        2
#define RSV_NO_MEMORY     3
#define RSV_TOO_MANY      4
#define RSV_UNEXP_NULL    5
#define RSV_DUPLICATE     6


/*-------------------------------------------
    Internal form of reserved words:
*/
typedef struct{
    char *text;        /* spelling: "FOR", "IF", etc. */
    int  code;         /* text encoded for fast compares */
    int  kinds;        /* legal uses of this word; see defines */
} rsv_word_info;

/* These define the legal uses of reserved words; they are flag values
used in the rsv_word_info.kinds field: */
#define RSV_NOT_IN_USE    0
#define RSV_STATEMENT     1
#define RSV_DATA_TYPE     2
#define RSV_FUNCTION      4

/* The list of reserved words is kept in an array: */
#define RSV_MAX_WORDS     100
static rsv_word_info      rsv_words[RSV_MAX_WORDS];

static int    rsv_inited = false; /* see init_rsv_words() */

extern char   *strsave();

#define _RSV_TESTBED_
#ifdef  _RSV_TESTBED_
/*===============================================================*/
main()
/*-------------------------------------------
Purpose:
    Testbed to make sure the rest of the functions in this file
    work.
Parameters:
    none
------------------------------------------------*/
{
    int i, j;

    if (init_rsv_words() != RSV_OK) {
        fprintf(stderr,
                "couldn't initialize list of reserved words\n");
```

```
                exit(1);
        }
        print_rsv_words();
        if (get_rsv_id("FOR", &i) != RSV_OK) {
            fprintf(stderr, "couldn't get ID of reserved word FOR\n");
        }
        if (get_rsv_info(i, &j) != RSV_OK) {
            fprintf(stderr,
                    "couldn't get info of reserved word FOR\n");
        }
        printf("FOR id %d info %d\n", i, j);
        if (get_rsv_id("CHAR", &i) != RSV_OK) {
            fprintf(stderr, "couldn't get ID of reserved word CHAR\n");
        }
        if (get_rsv_info(i, &j) != RSV_OK) {
            fprintf(stderr,
                    "couldn't get info of reserved word CHAR\n");
        }
        printf("CHAR id %d info %d\n", i, j);
        if (get_rsv_id("ABS", &i) != RSV_OK) {
            fprintf(stderr, "couldn't get ID of reserved word ABS\n");
        }
        if (get_rsv_info(i, &j) != RSV_OK) {
            fprintf(stderr,
                    "couldn't get info of reserved word ABS\n");
        }
        printf("ABS id %d info %d\n", i, j);
        if (get_rsv_id("BOGUS", &i) != RSV_OK) {
            fprintf(stderr,
                    "couldn't get ID of reserved word BOGUS\n");
        }
        if (get_rsv_info(i, &j) != RSV_OK) {
            fprintf(stderr,
                    "couldn't get info of reserved word BOGUS\n");
        }
        printf("BOGUS id %d info %d\n", i, j);
        if (get_rsv_id("INT", &i) != RSV_OK) {
            fprintf(stderr, "couldn't get ID of reserved word INT\n");
        }
        if (get_rsv_info(i, &j) != RSV_OK) {
            fprintf(stderr,
                    "couldn't get info of reserved word INT\n");
        }
    printf("INT id %d info %d\n", i, j);
} /* main */
#endif _RSV_TESTBED_

/*==============================================================*/
```

```
int     init_rsv_words()
/*------------------------------------------
Purpose:
    Builds the list of reserved words, putting the most frequently
    used ones at the front of the list by calling add_rsv_words()
    first with them.
Parameters:
    rsv_inited  static global; if we init OK, this is set "true" to
                allow later calls to get_rsv_id() and
                get_rsv_info()
    Returns status.
------------------------------------------*/
{
    int i, res;

    for (i = 0; i < RSV_MAX_WORDS; i++) {
        rsv_words[i].text = NULL;
        rsv_words[i].code = 0;
        rsv_words[i].kinds = RSV_NOT_IN_USE;
    }
    if ((res = add_rsv_word("INT",
                    RSV_FUNCTION | RSV_DATA_TYPE)) != RSV_OK)
        return (res);
    if ((res = add_rsv_word("CHAR", RSV_DATA_TYPE)) != RSV_OK)
        return (res);
    if ((res = add_rsv_word("FOR", RSV_STATEMENT)) != RSV_OK)
        return (res);
    if ((res = add_rsv_word("ABS", RSV_FUNCTION)) != RSV_OK)
        return (res);
    /***** uncomment to be sure we catch duplicates:
    if ((res = add_rsv_word("FOR", RSV_STATEMENT)) != RSV_OK)
        return (res);
    ******/
    rsv_inited = true;
    return (RSV_OK);
} /* init_rsv_words */


/*==============================================================*/
static int     add_rsv_word( txt, flgs )
    char *txt; /* IN */
    int  flgs; /* IN */
/*------------------------------------------
Purpose:
    Adds a word to the end of the list of reserved words; the most
    frequently used words should be at the front of the list to
    speed searches.
Parameters:
    txt         the reserved word's spelling
```

```
    flgs          the reserved word's allowable uses:
                      RSV_NOT_IN_USE        (no word here yet)
                      RSV_STATEMENT
                      RSV_DATA_TYPE
                      RSV_FUNCTION
    rsv_words     static global; this holds the list of reserved
                  words
    Returns status.
-------------------------------------------------*/
{
    int  cod, i;
    char *strsave();

    if (!txt)
        return (RSV_UNEXP_NULL);
    cod = encode(txt);
    for ( i = 0;
        ((i < RSV_MAX_WORDS) &&
         (rsv_words[i].kinds != RSV_NOT_IN_USE));
         i++  ) {
        if ((rsv_words[i].code == cod) &&
            (!strcmp(rsv_words[i].text, txt))) {
            fprintf(stderr,
                    "reserved word %s is already in list\n",
                    txt);
            return (RSV_DUPLICATE);
        }
    }
    if (i >= RSV_MAX_WORDS) {
        fprintf(stderr,
                "can't add reserved word %s; too many words\n",
                txt);
        return (RSV_TOO_MANY);
    }
    if (!(rsv_words[i].text = strsave(txt))) {
        fprintf(stderr,
                "can't add reserved word %s; out of memory\n",
                txt);
        return (RSV_NO_MEMORY);
    }
    rsv_words[i].code  = cod;
    rsv_words[i].kinds = flgs;
    return (RSV_OK);
} /* add_rsv_word */


/*===============================================================*/
static int  encode( str )
    char *str; /* IN */
```

```
/*-------------------------------------------
Purpose:
    Convert a string to a more-or-less unique integer.
Parameters:
    str     string to be encoded; this should never be NULL
    Returns the encoding.
-------------------------------------------*/
{
    int sum, i;

    for (sum = i = 0; str[i]; i++) {
        sum += (i+1)*(int)(str[i]);
    }
    return (sum);
} /* encode */


/*===============================================================*/
static int  print_rsv_words()
/*-------------------------------------------
Purpose:
    Help debugging by printing the list of reserved words in their
    internal form.
Parameters:
    rsv_words  static global; this holds the list of reserved words
  Returns status.
-------------------------------------------*/
{
    int  i;
    char kind[40];

    for ( i = 0;
         ((i < RSV_MAX_WORDS) &&
          (rsv_words[i].kinds != RSV_NOT_IN_USE));
         i++  ) {
        strcpy(kind, " ");
        if (rsv_words[i].kinds & RSV_STATEMENT)
            strcat(kind, "STATEMENT ");
        if (rsv_words[i].kinds & RSV_DATA_TYPE)
            strcat(kind, "DATA TYPE ");
        if (rsv_words[i].kinds & RSV_FUNCTION)
           strcat(kind, "FUNCTION ");
        fprintf(stdout,
                "reserved word #%d: %s:%s (%d)\n",
                i,
                rsv_words[i].text,
                kind,
                rsv_words[i].kinds);
    }
```

```
        return (RSV_OK);
} /* print_rsv_words */


/*================================================================*/
int        get_rsv_id( tst, id )
    char *tst; /* IN */
    int  *id;  /* OUT */
/*----------------------------------------
Purpose:
    Check to see if a string is reserved. If it is, get its ID for
    use by get_rsv_info(); if it's not reserved, set id parameter
    to zero.
Parameters:
    tst     string to search reserved word list for
    id      tst's ID if tst is reserved; otherwise zero
    Returns status.
----------------------------------------*/
{
    int   cod, i;

    *id = 0;
    if (!rsv_inited)
        return (RSV_NOT_INITED);
    cod = encode(tst);
    for ( i = 0;
        ((i < RSV_MAX_WORDS) &&
         (rsv_words[i].kinds != RSV_NOT_IN_USE));
        i++  ) {
        if ((rsv_words[i].code == cod) &&
            (!strcmp(rsv_words[i].text, tst))) {
            *id = i+1; /* convert array index to ID */
            return (RSV_OK);
        }
    }
    return (RSV_OK);
} /* get_rsv_id */


/*================================================================*/
int        get_rsv_info( id, info )
    int  id;    /* IN */
    int  *info; /* OUT */
/*----------------------------------------
Purpose:
    Get the info associated with a given reserved word; right now,
    that means getting the set of flags that specifies legal uses
    of the word.
Parameters:
    id      this better have been obtained by an earlier call to
```

```
            get_rsv_id()
    info    if ID is valid, this gets the flag(s) that were passed
            into add_rsv_word()
    Returns status.
-----------------------------------------*/
{
    *info = 0;
    if (!rsv_inited)
        return (RSV_NOT_INITED);
    id--;  /* convert ID to array index */
    if ((id < 0) ||
        (id >= RSV_MAX_WORDS) ||
        (rsv_words[id].kinds == RSV_NOT_IN_USE))
        return (RSV_BAD_ID);
    *info = rsv_words[id].kinds;
    return (RSV_OK);
} /* get_rsv_info */
```

CHAPTER 9

Protecting a Database During Editing

We are writing a library that applications will use to safely access some database. By "database" we mean any collection of structures that point to each other; this may or may not be a database in the narrow sense (relational, network, etc.). By "access" we mean create new structures, delete structures, and change the contents of structures. Pointers are changed as side effects of creation and deletion, but the application does not and should not know the details. "Safe access" means we will do as much as possible to preserve database integrity, whether the application runs correctly or not.

TOP-LEVEL GOALS

We're writing a library for use by applications that don't exist yet. This means the database is sure to change as the application programmers discover what they really need, as opposed to what they now think they'll need. So we want to insulate applications from changes in library and database implementation details as much as possible. This means a clean interface is a priority; the less the application programmer needs to know about the database internals, the better.

However, our main goal is to preserve the database's integrity. This is particularly important if the database is shared by more than one program. If program A damages the database, program B might well come tumbling down. Many painful hours might be spent trying to understand why program B failed before it is determined that program A actually caused the problem. What's more, if program A and program B were written by different people, the emotional costs of not knowing which program caused the problem could also be very high.

If you've ever tried to write an application that relies on a buggy compiler or operating system, you know how frustrating it can be when your attention is split between the problem you were assigned and bugs in somebody else's code. Even if the database is used by only one program, we want the access library free of bugs so the application programmer using it can concentrate on the application instead of chasing bugs in our code.

Flexible code and structures are also priorities. That is, we'd like to be able to change the database structs without changing calling sequences in the applications. But the most important top-level goal is maintaining database integrity. We need some useful examples of the ways the database might be damaged.

GUIDING EXAMPLES

Notice that we're not interested in examples of different databases, except insofar as their implementations might conflict with our efforts to maintain database integrity. We don't care if the database contents represent employee records or polygons or photon torpedoes. Whatever the data, we must protect it.

What we want, then, are useful examples of the ways the application might damage the database. Following the method in Chapter 3, "Choosing Good Guiding Examples," yields the list shown in Table 9-1.

Notice that we've listed only application bugs. We're writing the library, so we'll assume it doesn't do any damage by failing to check for NULLs after allocating memory, overrunning array bounds, and so on. It's not that we think the application programmers are idiots, while the library programmers are not. It's just that the library must be debugged before the application. Knowing that the library is robust will be an enormous help in debugging the application, since the application's main purpose is to build and edit the database.

The fundamental characteristic that the examples in Table 9-1 share is pointer abuse. Each example is different from the others because the pointer into the database is

---

TABLE 9-1: The most common ways an application bug could damage a database.

1. "Out of bounds." The application gets a pointer to a database struct and overruns an array or otherwise writes outside the part of the struct it was supposed to use.
2. "Dangling pointer." After a deletion, the application uses a dangling pointer to reference a database struct that is no longer there.
3. "Type mismatch." The application gets a pointer to a database struct of type *foo*, miscasts it as a pointer to type *baloo*, and writes database memory through this pointer.
4. "Damaged pointer." The application gets a pointer to a database struct, hammers the pointer, and then references the database through this bad pointer.
5. "Berserker code." The application runs wild in memory, overwriting itself, other programs, the database, and whatever else gets in its way. (In Scandinavian lore, a "berserker" is a furious warrior who attacks everyone in sight without any concern for his own safety. I have seen programs do this, and lived to tell the tale.)

---

abused in a different way. If we did away with pointers entirely, we'd also avoid these nasty bugs. But coding C without pointers is like coding FORTRAN; why punish ourselves for no good reason? Anyway, we're not ready yet to start implementing any solution, much less such a radical one.

ABSTRACT DATA TYPE DESCRIPTION

What name does this particular collection of data elements and operators go by, that is, what abstract data type are we concerned with? We're really dealing with two collections. The first collection is the database structures. We know nothing about these, and we really don't want to learn any details, because we're looking for solutions that preserve the integrity of all kinds of databases. And we certainly don't want our data integrity to disappear when we change the database implementation by adding new struct types or fiddling with the current typedefs.

The second collection is the one we're trying to devise. This is the collection of structures used to preserve the integrity of the database collection. We'll call this the database interface structure collection, or "interface collection" for short.

What is the geometry of the collection? We don't care what the geometry of the database collection is. The interface collection geometry depends on how we protect against the application bugs listed earlier while still maintaining flexibility and hiding details from the application programmer.

When a C function needs access to a struct, we usually pass it the struct's address. But our list of application bugs makes it clear that passing database struct addresses to the application program is unacceptable. Accessing structs directly through a pointer is certainly faster than using some scheme involving validated IDs or handles. But speed is not the main goal—data integrity is. There's just no way to ensure database integrity if the application has pointers into the database. Well, almost no way. We could splatter the database with checksums and verify them after every library call, but that would be very expensive, and it would only detect errors, not prevent them. We're looking for something better.

If we don't give the application pointers into the database, it needs some other way to identify different structures. Perhaps it knows by context which structure is being operated on. But that's possible only if there is just one struct of any given type. We can't make such a restrictive assumption about our databases, so forget that idea.

Instead of identifying structs by address or by what's being done to the database, we will associate a "handle" with each struct. A handle is an ID whose internal format is immaterial to the application; the application refers directly to database objects only by way of handles. The interface collection is the collection of handles the application uses to identify database structs to the library. By using handles instead of addresses, we also hide the details of database structures from the application and gain the chance to change database typedefs somewhat without changing the application source.

Getting back to the original question about geometry, it's clear that we don't want a tree of handles, or a stack or a list or any other arrangement. The interface collection's geometry is simply a set. In ADTD terms, this means there are no distinguished positions in the geometry—each position is just like every other position.

What relations hold between the data elements in the collection? Any relations between interface collection elements would only be needed to reflect relations between database collection structs. But we're trying to use the handles to hide database implementation details from the application, not to propagate them upward. So there should be no relations at all between the different handles.

What relations hold between this collection and other collections? At first glance, it seems like there should be a one-to-one correspondence between handles and database structs. But we should allow for the possibility that some database structs are only there to support the structs the application deals with directly. So what we really have is a one-to-one correspondence between interface handles and the database structs created by the application. We'll call this correspondence the "handle-to-struct mapping."

What rules does each relation follow? The handle-to-struct mapping is one-to-one. Given a particular database struct, we can either find its unique handle or ignore it; given a particular handle, we can find the unique database struct it refers to. The database structs we ignore are the ones we use only to support structs the application creates. These "support" structs have no handles because the application never refers to them directly.

What are the operators? At first glance, the operators are these two:

```
/*==================================================================*/
void *handle_to_address( hnd )
    database_handle hnd;    /* IN */


/*==================================================================*/
database_handle address_to_handle( adr )
    void *adr;   /* IN */
```

But this is too simple to work. If *database_handle* values are built only from the address of a struct, we can't protect against the "dangling pointer" application bug. We have no way to tell that the pointer we just converted from a handle points to where a struct used to be. Perhaps we could maintain a list of all currently valid pointers, updating it as we create and delete database structs. This would protect against the "dangling pointer" bug, and against the "damaged pointer" bug as well. As long as we knew that a bogus handle never maps to a valid address, we'd have a way to tell if the application told us to convert a bogus handle.

But we're getting into implementation decisions now, and the ADTD is not the place to do that (unless there's some doubt whether the ADTD can even be implemented, and there isn't). So let's just say for now that something else is needed to create a usable *database_handle*—the struct address alone is not enough. Our operators look like this for now:

```
/*=====================================================================*/
void *handle_to_address( hnd )
  database_handle hnd;     /* IN */


/*=====================================================================*/
database_handle address_to_handle( adr, ??? )
  void *adr;   /* IN */
  ??? ???;     /* IN, but as yet unknown */
```

What are the restrictions on membership in the collection? To be converted into a handle, a pointer must point to a database struct created by the application through the library. There is no hard limit on the number of handles.

How many collections are allowed by this ADT? There is just one set of handles, that is, one collection in the ADT. Since there are no operators that take the entire collection of handles as input (as opposed to taking individual handles as input), proper subsets are irrelevant.

What is the meaning of each element in the collection? Each handle corresponds to one database struct created by the application. There is no relation between the value of a particular handle and the value of other handles in the collection, except that there are no duplicates. The value of the handle clearly depends on the position of the database struct in memory, since the handle must convert to a pointer. Its value must also depend on other factors, which we don't yet know, so we can avoid damage from the application bugs listed earlier. These other factors will probably be represented somehow as parameters of the *address_to_handle()* operator.

ATTEMPT ONE

We need a mapping from database structs created by the application to handles, so we can insulate the application from database implementation details and protect the database from application bugs. The easiest starting point is the list of application bugs to protect against. We'll repeat the bugs as we deal with them (or fail to!), starting with the easiest one first:

> 4. "Damaged pointer." The application gets a pointer to a database struct, hammers the pointer, and then references the database through this bad pointer.

If we give the application a handle that contains both a pointer and a checksum on that pointer, we can tell with reasonable certainty whether or not the application has hammered the handle. So our first attempt looks like this:

```
typedef struct {
  void *address;  /* pointer to database struct */
  int  checksum;
} database_handle;
```

```
/* "bad" handle passed to application when any library function call to create a database
entity fails; this handle can never be generated from a valid database
struct address: */

database_handle  NULL_handle = {0, -1};

/*================================================================*/
void    *handle_to_address( hnd )
  database_handle hnd;  /* IN */
/*----------------------------------------
Purpose:
  Verify that a database handle used in an application points to
  a database struct created by the application. If the handle is
  good, translate it into a pointer to the struct and return that
  pointer; otherwise, return NULL.
Parameters:
  hnd  handle to verify and translate to address; this
    function is called by every library function the
    application uses to create, write, or delete a database
    entity
  Returns valid pointer or NULL.
----------------------------------------*/
{
  if (hnd.checksum == get_checksum(hnd.address)) {
    return (hnd.address);
  }
  else {
    return (NULL);
  }
} /* handle_to_address */

/* number of bits in a checksum; should be less than the number of bits
in an int: */
#define CHECKSUM_BITS     4
/* other defines for get_checksum(): */
#define CHECKSUM_MASK     0x0000000F /* CHECKSUM_BITS low bits on */
#define BITS_PER_BYTE     8
/*================================================================*/
static int  get_checksum( adr )
  void *adr;  /* IN */
/*----------------------------------------
Purpose:
  Compute checksum on an address; called by handle_to_address().
  -1 returned means "bad checksum."
  Assumes sizeof(long) == sizeof(void *).
Parameters:
  adr  address; if this is NULL, checksum is -1
  Returns checksum; valid checksums never equal -1.
```

```
                      -------------------------------------*/
{
  int  i, sum;
  long long_adr; /* longs, pointers same size */

  if (!adr) {
    return (-1);
  }
  long_adr = (long)adr;
  sum = 0;
  for  (i = 0;
       i < (BITS_PER_BYTE*sizeof(char *)/CHECKSUM_BITS);
       i++) {
    sum += (int)(long_adr & CHECKSUM_MASK);
    long_adr >> CHECKSUM_BITS;
  }
  return (sum & CHECKSUM_MASK);
} /* get_checksum */


/*================================================================*/
database_handle address_to_handle( adr )
  void *adr;   /* IN */
/*----------------------------------------
Purpose:
  Translate an address into a handle which will be given to the
  application; the address is never seen by the application.
Parameters:
  adr  address of database struct; this function is called by
     every routine the application calls to create database
     entities
  Returns handle, or NULL_handle if adr is NULL - the application
  must test for NULL_handle using handle_is_NULL(). The
  application must copy the handle to a database_handle variable
  it allocated.
                      -------------------------------------*/
{
  database_handle res;

  if (!adr) {
    return (NULL_handle);
  }
  if ((res.checksum = get_checksum(adr)) == -1) {
    return (NULL_handle);
  }
  res.address = adr;
  return (res);
} /* address_to_handle */
```

Notice how we had to devise a "NULL" handle to pass back to the application to indicate failure. Generalizing NULL like this is very common; reserving one value of any particular type as "bad" makes error detection much easier.

But where should *NULL_handle* be declared? *NULL_handle* must be visible both to the library and to the application. Placing this in a header file ("database.h," say) will not work because space for the variable is never allocated or initialized:

```
extern database_handle    NULL_handle;
```

But if we place this in database.h, we're allocating and initializing one *NULL_handle* per include:

```
database_handle NULL_handle = {0, -1};
```

The linker will yell about multiple definitions in the application if more than one of its files includes database.h, because we're using the same name to refer to multiple memory locations. Suppose we're ridiculous and allow the application and library to include database.h in only one file each. We must still link in the library, so *NULL_handle* will refer to two memory locations and the link will still fail.

A nice way to get around this problem is described in the Framework section in struct trick "Variables in Header Files" (see page 390). The solution is to put the following in database.h, and define *DATABASE_GLOBALS* just once, in one of the library files right before it includes database.h:

```
#ifdef DATABASE_GLOBALS
database_handle NULL_handle = {0, -1};
#else
extern database_handle    NULL_handle;
#endif DATABASE_GLOBALS
```

This allocates the space for the *NULL_handle* struct just once, in the library file that defines *DATABASE_GLOBALS*. Every other file that includes database.h sees *NULL_handle* as an extern.

This attempt at a solution looks like it won't be too hard to implement. But how well does it satisfy our goals? With the checksum, we can tell if the application overwrites a *database_handle* and prevents a "damaged pointer" application bug from destroying the database. Bad handles will not be translated into bad pointers, and the evil attempt to overwrite some innocent section of the database will be thwarted.

But what about the other bugs in the list? If we rephrase the first bug using "handle" instead of "pointer" (the application never gets a pointer into the database!), it looks like this:

1. "Out of bounds." The application gets a handle to a database struct and overruns an array or otherwise writes outside the part of the struct it was supposed to use.

This can't happen now either. Since we are not giving out pointers, any library call to put values in a database struct must have the values listed explicitly as parameters. The library copies the parameters into the database, not the application. So they might be the wrong values, but they will never be written to a spot outside the appropriate struct member:

```
/* foo represents all the database typedefs used by the library to
represent entities created by the application; these typedefs are hidden
from the application: */
typedef struct foo {
  struct foo  *next;
  int         flags;
  glurp       data;
  char        *name;
} foo;
/* possible errors; we'll put these in database.h: */
#define DATABASE_STAT_OK          0
#define DATABASE_STAT_BAD_HANDLE  1
#define DATABASE_STAT_BAD_STRING  2
#define DATABASE_STAT_NO_MEMORY   3
/* The calling sequence for write_database_foo() is known to the
application, but this function's source is not, because we may want to
change foo or glurp, for instance: */
/*===============================================================*/
int write_database_foo( foo_handle, val_1, val_2, val_3 )
  database_handle foo_handle;    /* IN */
  int             val_1;         /* IN */
  glurp           val_2;         /* IN */
  char            *val_3;        /* IN */
/*----------------------------------------

Purpose:
  Safely write some values into a database foo entity. Other
  database entities have corresponding functions, e.g.,
  write_database_baloo().
Parameters:
  foo_handle  handle to a foo entity; from create_database_foo()
  val_1,
  val_2,
  val_3       some values to copy to the database foo struct
              identified by foo_handle
  Returns DATABASE_STAT_xxx, with xxx an appropriate error status
---------------------------------------------------*/
{
  foo *dest;
  char *strsave(), *tmp;
  void *handle_to_address();

  /* validate the handle */
  if (!(dest = handle_to_address(foo_handle))) {
    return (DATABASE_STAT_BAD_HANDLE);
```

```
  }
  /* copy the new values in, but let yourself undo the write if
  anything goes wrong */
  if (!val_3) {
    return (DATABASE_STAT_BAD_STRING);
  }
  tmp = dest->name;
  if (!(dest->name = strsave(val_3))) {
    dest->name = tmp;
    return (DATABASE_STAT_NO_MEMORY);
  }
  free(tmp);
  dest->flags = val_1;
  dest->data = val_2;
  return (DATABASE_STAT_OK);
} /* write_database_foo */
```

So far so good. We are protected against the "out of bounds" and "damaged pointer" application bugs. Moving down the list of bugs, we come to this one:

2. "Dangling pointer." After a deletion, the application uses a dangling pointer to reference a database struct that is no longer there.

Even if we replace "pointer" with "handle," we have a problem. Something like this could happen in the application under our current solution:

```
foo_handle = create_database_foo(...);
...
delete_database_foo(foo_handle);
...
write_database_foo(foo_handle, ...);
```

After the delete, the *foo* struct is gone but the *write_database_foo()* call has no way to know this. The memory the struct previously occupied might now be unused, or it could be taken in part or whole by another database struct. It could even be occupied by a different *foo* struct, that is, by a struct that was created by another call to *create_database_foo()*:

```
foo_handle = create_database_foo(...);
...
delete_database_foo(foo_handle);
...
/* this next create happens to reuse memory just freed: */
foo_handle_2 = create_database_foo(...);
...
/* writes to foo_handle_2 struct! */
write_database_foo(foo_handle_foo, ...);
```

This means we need to rethink our definition of type *database_handle*.

ATTEMPT TWO

We need a better connection between each handle and the struct it represents. The handle has to "know" somehow when its struct has been deleted. Right now the only connection between handle and struct is the struct's address. What if we put matching timestamps in the struct and its handle? The typedefs would look like this:

```
typedef struct {
    void *address;  /* pointer to database struct */
    int  checksum;
    int  timestamp;
} database_handle;

/* foo represents all the database typedefs used by the library to
represent entities created by the application: */
typedef struct foo {
    struct foo  *next;
    int         timestamp;  /* used by handle_to_address() */
    int         flags;
    glurp       data;
    char        *name;
} foo;
```

The typical library creation function now looks something like this:

```
/*=============================================================*/
database_handle create_database_foo(..., stat )
    ... /* whatever is needed to initialize the new foo */
    int *stat;  /* OUT */
/*---------------------------------------------
Purpose:
    Create and initialize a new database foo entity.
Parameters:
    Whatever is appropriate.  Remember, we're not designing the
    database or its library of functions.  We're designing the
    handle interface between the application and the database
    structs. If the create_xxx() calls want parameters to
    initialize newly created structs, that's fine. If the library
    wants separate create_xxx() and write_xxx() calls, that's fine
    too. Our focus is what happens inside create_xxx() to convert
    the new database struct's address into a handle for the
    application to use.
    stat   error code if NULL_handle is returned, or
           DATABASE_STAT_OK
    Returns valid handle on success, NULL_handle on failure, sets
    stat
    ----------------------------------------------*/
```

```
{
  foo  *new;
  database_handle address_to_handle(), res;
  void *malloc();

  *stat = DATABASE_STAT_OK;
  /* validate the incoming parameters if there are any */
  ...
  /* create the new struct */
  if (!(new = (foo *)malloc(sizeof(foo)))) {
    *stat = DATABASE_STAT_NO_MEMORY;
    return (NULL_handle);
  }
  /* convert from address to handle for application */
  res = address_to_handle(new);
  if (res == NULL_handle) {
    free(new);
    *stat = DATABASE_STAT_BAD_HANDLE;
    return (NULL_handle);
  }
  /* initialize the new struct, link it to other structs */
  ...
  /* return handle to application */
  return (res);
} /* create_database_foo */
```

The *address_to_handle()* and *handle_to_address()* functions must be changed slightly, in order to set and check for matching timestamps in the new database struct and its handle:

```
/*================================================================*/
database_handle  address_to_handle( adr )
  void *adr;  /* IN */
/*------------------------------------------
Purpose:
  Translate an address into a handle that will be given to the
  application; the address is never seen by the application.
Parameters:
  adr address of database struct application created; this
      function is called by every routine the application
      calls to create database entities
  Returns handle, or NULL_handle if adr is NULL—the application
  must test for NULL_handle using handle_is_NULL(). The
  application must copy the handle to a database_handle variable
  it allocated.
  ------------------------------------------*/
{
  database_handle  res;
```

```
    if (!adr) {
      return (NULL_handle);
    }
    if ((res.checksum = get_checksum(adr)) == -1) {
      return (NULL_handle);
    }
    res.timestamp = get_timestamp();
    adr->timestamp = res.timestamp;
    res.address = adr;
    return (res);
} /* address_to_handle */


/*================================================================*/
void *handle_to_address( hnd )
  database_handle  hnd;  /* IN */
/*-----------------------------------------------
Purpose:
  Verify that a database handle used in an application points to
  a database struct created by the application. If the handle is
  good, translate it into a pointer to the struct and return that
  pointer; otherwise, return NULL.
Parameters:
  hnd  handle to verify and translate to address; this
       function is called by every library function the
       application uses to create, write, or delete a database
       entity
  Returns valid pointer or NULL.
-----------------------------------------------*/
{
    if (hnd.checksum != get_checksum(hnd.address)) {
      return (NULL);
    }
    if (hnd.timestamp != hnd.address->timestamp) {
      return (NULL);
    }
    return (hnd.address);
} /* handle_to_address */
```

If there's only a negligible chance of the application finding a matching value where the struct timestamp was, we're looking pretty good. We can make the chance negligible by doing two things. First, every struct should get a different timestamp. Second, the *delete_database_foo()* function should put an invalid timestamp in the struct before it's freed, in case other data has not been written there by the time the application mistakenly uses the handle of the deleted struct.

If this code ran, it would take care of the "dangling pointer" application bug. But there's a serious problem. In *handle_to_address()*, we refer to *hnd.address->timestamp*; in *address_to_handle()*, we refer to *adr->timestamp*. But *hnd.address* and *adr* are void pointers. That is, they can point to anything as far as the C compiler is concerned. Since they are not pointers to structs that contain timestamp members, the code won't compile.

We made *database_handle.address* a void pointer because we wanted to allow handles for more than one type of database struct. But the compiler can't generate code for timestamp members in different types of structs unless we cast *hnd.address* to the appropriate type. So we need to change our *database_handle* typedef yet again.

ATTEMPT THREE

Now we need to use the type of a given struct, as well as its address and timestamp, when converting an address to a handle. If we do this, we will not only be able to use the timestamp to avoid damage from the "dangling pointer" application bug, we will also be able to avoid the "type mismatch" bug entirely. Replacing "pointer" with "handle," these are the bugs we're trying to nullify:

2. "Dangling handle." After a deletion, the application uses a dangling handle to reference a database struct that is no longer there.
3. "Type mismatch." The application gets a handle to a database struct of type *foo*, miscasts it as a handle to type *baloo*, and writes database memory through this handle.

To implement type checking on handles, we need something like the following:

```
/* database_handle.type values: */
#define DATABASE_TYPE_TRASH     0   /* illegal type */
#define DATABASE_TYPE_FOO       1
#define DATABASE_TYPE_BALOO     2
/* and so on for all the other database entities the application can
create */

typedef struct {
  void *address;    /* pointer to database struct */
  int  checksum;
  int  timestamp;
  int  type;        /* see DATABASE_TYPE_xxx defines */
} database_handle;

typedef struct foo {
  struct foo  *next;
  int         timestamp;  /* used by address_to_handle() */
  int         type;       /* used by address_to_handle() */
  int         flags;
  glurp       data;
  char        *name;
} foo;
```

```
type def struct baloo {
  struct baloo  *next,
                *prev;
  double        data[12];
  int           timestamp;  /* used by address_to_handle() */
  int           type;       /* used by address_to_handle() */
} baloo;

/*==================================================================*/
database_handle  address_to_handle( adr, typ )
  void *adr;  /* IN */
  int typ;    /* IN */
/*--------------------------------------------
Purpose:
  Translate an address into a handle which will be given to the
  application; the address is never seen by the application.
Parameters:
  adr  address of database struct application created; this
       function is called by every routine the application
       calls to create database entities
  typ  DATABASE_TYPE_xxx value that tells what type of struct
       adr points to
  Returns handle, or NULL_handle if adr is NULL - the application
  must test for NULL_handle using handle_is_NULL(). The
  application must copy the handle to a database_handle variable
  it allocated.
--------------------------------------------*/
{
  database_handle  res;

  if (!adr) {
    return (NULL_handle);
  }
  if ((res.checksum = get_checksum(adr)) == -1) {
    return (NULL_handle);
  }
  res.timestamp = get_timestamp();
  switch (typ) {
    case DATABASE_TYPE_FOO:
      ((foo *)adr)->type = typ;
      ((foo *)adr)->timestamp = res.timestamp;
      break;
    case DATABASE_TYPE_BALOO:
      ((baloo *)adr)->type = typ;
      ((baloo *)adr)->timestamp = res.timestamp;
      break;
    default:
      return (NULL_handle);
  }
```

```
    res.type = typ;
    res.address = adr;
    return (res);
} /* address_to_handle */


/*===============================================================*/
void *handle_to_address( hnd )
    database_handle  hnd;  /* IN */
/*---------------------------------------
Purpose:
    Verify that a database handle used in an application points to
    a database struct created by the application. If the handle is
    good, translate it into a pointer to the struct and return that
    pointer; otherwise, return NULL.
Parameters:
    hnd  handle to verify and translate to address
    Returns valid pointer or NULL.
---------------------------------------------*/
{
    if (!hnd.address ||
        (hnd.checksum != get_checksum(hnd.address))) {
        return (NULL);
    }
    switch (hnd.type) {
      case DATABASE_TYPE_FOO:
        if (((foo *)hnd.address)->type != hnd.type)
            return (NULL);
        if (((foo *)hnd.address)->timestamp != hnd.timestamp)
            return (NULL);
        break;
      case DATABASE_TYPE_BALOO:
        if (((baloo *)hnd.address)->type != hnd.type)
            return (NULL);
        if (((baloo *)hnd.address)->timestamp != hnd.timestamp)
            return (NULL);
        break;
      default:
        return (NULL);
    }
    return (hnd.address);
} /* handle_to_address */


/*===============================================================*/
database_handle  create_database_foo(..., stat )
    ... /* whatever is needed to initialize the new foo */
    int *stat;  /* OUT */
/*---------------------------------------
```

Same as before, but the calling sequence of address_to_handle() has a
new parameter called "type."

```
      -----------------------------------------*/
{
   ...
   res = address_to_handle(new, DATABASE_TYPE_FOO);
   ...
} /* create_database_foo */

/*================================================================*/
int  delete_database_foo( foo_handle )
   database_handle  foo_handle;  /* IN */
/*-------------------------------------------
Purpose:
   Safely delete a foo entity from the database. Other database
   entities have corresponding functions, e.g.,
   delete_database_baloo().
Parameters:
   foo_handle  handle of entity to delete; from
               create_database_foo()
   Returns appropriate DATABASE_STAT_xxx value.
      -----------------------------------------*/
{
   void *handle_to_address();
   foo  *was;

   if (!(was = (foo *)handle_to_address(foo_handle))) {
      return (DATABASE_STAT_BAD_HANDLE);
   }
   /* unlink struct from other structs (no code shown here) */
   ...
   /* make sure type and timestamp are no longer valid, in case
   the application tries to write via this foo_handle after
   deletion */
   foo->type = DATABASE_TYPE_TRASH;
   foo->timestamp = DATABASE_TIMESTAMP_TRASH;
   free(was);
   return (DATABASE_STAT_OK);
 } /* delete_database_foo */
```

The last thing to do is to implement *get_timestamp()*, keeping in mind the need for a value we can use as *DATABASE_NULL_TIMESTAMP*. We've been thinking "timestamp" all along, that is, make a system call to get the current time and use that. But time in a computer is discrete. What time unit do we use? We'll start with something big, work our way down to something small, and see if we find a fit along the way.

Suppose we measure time in years. There's a problem whenever the application does something like this:

```
handle_1 = create_database_foo(...);
```

```
...
handle_2 = create_database_foo(...);
```
Handle_1 and *handle_2* get the same timestamp (unless the system is
really incredibly overloaded!). Worse yet, suppose the application did
this kind of thing:
```
handle_1 = create_database_foo(...);
...
delete_database_foo(handle_1);
...
handle_2 = create_database_foo(...);
```

Then the *handle_1* and *handle_2* database structs might occupy the same memory over
different periods of time. But this means the address, type, and timestamp are all the same—
handle_1 and *handle_2* are identical, even though they refer to different database entities!
This is definitely not good. We've exaggerated by using a timestamp that changes only once
a year. But the same problem could happen if we use seconds or even milliseconds.

OK, suppose we use the smallest possible time unit. We still have a problem. We don't
have an infinite number of bits to represent the timestamp. All timestamps are modulo some
number (probably whatever the largest integer value is). The smaller the unit, the more
often timestamps will roll over past zero and start repeating. So smaller time units also
increase the chance of getting the same timestamp more than once while the application
runs.

Maybe there's an appropriate time unit, and maybe there isn't. Either way, there's no
obvious choice for the timestamp null value *DATABASE_TIMESTAMP_TRASH*, since zero
is a valid timestamp. But that doesn't matter, because we don't really need a timestamp. We
don't need a correlation between the value put in a handle and the clock on the wall; we don't
need creation dates on database structs. It just isn't worth using a real timestamp.

All we really need is a unique integer for each struct the application creates. So we'll
replace the notion of a timestamp by that of a struct number:

```
static int  database_struct_number = 1;
#define DATABASE_NO_STRUCT_NUMBER        0

/*================================================================*/
int  get_struct_number()
/*------------------------------------------------

Purpose:
   Provide a unique struct number for each database struct the
   application creates via library calls.
Parameters:
   Returns a struct number that never equals
   DATABASE_NO_STRUCT_NUMBER
------------------------------------------------*/
{
   if (database_struct_number == DATABASE_NO_STRUCT_NUMBER)
     database_struct_number++;
```

```
        return (database_struct_number++);
} /* get_struct_number */
```

ATTEMPT FOUR

Our final solution is essentially what we arrived at after our third attempt, using *struct_number* instead of timestamp. While writing the testbed, however, it became clear that *handle_to_address()* needs the type passed in. This is so we can verify that the type in the struct, the type in the handle, and the type expected by the database function (e.g., *delete_database_foo()* versus *delete_database_baloo()*) are all the same.

So how did we do? We can protect the database against damage from four of the five application bugs we worried about:

1. "Out of bounds." The application gets a handle to a database struct and overruns an array or otherwise writes outside the part of the struct it was supposed to use.

Protection: The application never writes directly to database structs, because it never has a struct's address. Well, it does, since the address is in the handle and the application has the handle, but it is strictly forbidden to use that address. All values to be written to a database struct are passed as separate parameters to library functions which then modify the database. If an array is overrun, it's because of a bug in the library, not one in the application.

2. "Dangling handle." After a deletion, the application uses a dangling handle to reference a database struct that is no longer there.

Protection: Whenever a struct is deleted, the memory location that held its type and *struct_number* is reset to illegal values, so subsequent *handle_to_address()* calls will not validate the handle of any deleted struct.

3. "Type mismatch." The application gets a handle to a database struct of type *foo*, miscasts it as a handle to type *baloo*, and writes database memory through this handle.

Protection: Passing a foo handle to a library function that expects a baloo handle will cause an error because the function verifies that the type in the handle, in the database struct, and in the library routine are all the same. When this verification fails, database access is denied.

4. "Damaged handle." The application gets a handle to a database struct, hammers the handle, and then references the database through this bad handle.

Protection: Chances are virtually zero that an overwritten handle will pass *handle_to_address()*'s validation. The type member will probably no longer match the type stored in the struct, and the checksum will almost certainly not match the checksum of whatever garbage was put in the handle's address member.

Unfortunately, we are still not protected against the fifth bug:

5. "Berserker code." The application runs wild in memory, overwriting itself, other programs, the database, and whatever else gets in its way.

In extreme cases, we could fill the database with checksums and verify them all after each and every library call. We could also put the access library and the application in different logical memory spaces by making them separate processes and then rely on the hardware memory protection (MMU chip) to trap illegal database accesses. But there's no simple way to prevent damage if the application just runs wild. The best protection is to have someone who's both good and motivated write the application, so it won't run wild.

LISTING: database.h

```
/*---------------------------------------
                    database.h
---------------------------------------*/

/*==================================================================
Purpose:
    Provides typedefs, defines, globals for the database library and
    for the handle library; see handle_test.c.
==================================================================*/
#ifndef _DATABASE_H_
#define _DATABASE_H_

#include <boolean.h> /* for convenience */

/* database_handle values are what the application gets back from the
database library—the handle library is used by the database library to
convert between the addresses it uses internally and the handles it
gives applications. */
/* Applications should NEVER reference database_handle struct members
directly! */
typedef struct {
    void    *address;        /* pointer to database struct */
    int     checksum;
    int     struct_number;
    int     type;            /* see DATABASE_TYPE_xxx defines */
} database_handle;

/* database_handle.type values: */
#define DATABASE_TYPE_TRASH        0 /* illegal type */
#define DATABASE_TYPE_FOO          1
#define DATABASE_TYPE_BALOO        2
/* and so on for all other database entities the application can create.
*/

/* This is the illegal value for database_handle.struct_number used
internally by the handle library: */
#define DATABASE_NO_STRUCT_NUMBER  0

/* This "bad" handle is passed to the application when any library
function call to create a database entity fails; this handle can never
be generated from a valid database struct address: */
```

```
#ifdef DATABASE_GLOBALS
database_handle NULL_handle = { NULL,
                                -1,
                                DATABASE_NO_STRUCT_NUMBER,
                                DATABASE_TYPE_TRASH };
#else
extern database_handle      NULL_handle;
#endif DATABASE_GLOBALS

/* possible status after any database routine: */
#define DATABASE_STAT_OK            0
#define DATABASE_STAT_BAD_HANDLE    1
#define DATABASE_STAT_BAD_STRING    2
#define DATABASE_STAT_NO_MEMORY     3

/* example database types: */
typedef float       glurp;
typedef struct foo {
    struct foo  *next;
    int         struct_number; /* used by address_to_handle() */
    int         type;          /* used by address_to_handle() */
    int         flags;
    glurp       data;
    char        *name;
} foo;

typedef struct baloo {
    struct baloo    *next,
                    *prev;
    double          data[12];
    int             struct_number; /* used by address_to_handle() */
    int             type;          /* used by address_to_handle() */
} baloo;

#endif _DATABASE_H_
```

LISTING: handle.c

```
/*----------------------------------------
                        handle.c
----------------------------------------*/

/*================================================================
Purpose:
    This is the handle-address conversion routines library; see
    handle_test.c.
```

```
===============================================================*/
#define DATABASE_GLOBALS     /* allocate & init NULL_handle */
#include <stdio.h>
#include "database.h"

static int database_struct_number = 1; /* see get_struct_number() */

/*===============================================================*/
database_handle     address_to_handle( adr, typ )
    void    *adr; /* IN */
    int     typ;  /* IN */
/*--------------------------------------------------
Purpose:
    Translate an address into a handle that will be given to the
    application; the address is never seen by the application.
Parameters:
    adr     address of database struct application created; this
            function is called by every routine the application
            calls to create database entities
    typ     DATABASE_TYPE_xxx value that tells what type of struct
            adr points to
    Returns handle, or NULL_handle if adr is NULL—the application
    must test for NULL_handle using handle_is_null(). The
    application must copy the handle to a database_handle variable
    it allocated.
--------------------------------------------------*/
{
    database_handle    res;

    if (!adr) {
        return (NULL_handle);
    }
    if ((res.checksum = get_checksum(adr)) == -1) {
        return (NULL_handle);
    }
    res.struct_number = get_struct_number();
    switch (typ) {
        case DATABASE_TYPE_FOO:
            ((foo *)adr)->type = typ;
            ((foo *)adr)->struct_number = res.struct_number;
            break;
        case DATABASE_TYPE_BALOO:
            ((baloo *)adr)->type = typ;
            ((baloo *)adr)->struct_number = res.struct_number;
            break;
        default:
            return (NULL_handle);
    }
```

```
        res.type    = typ;
        res.address = adr;
        return (res);
} /* address_to_handle */

/*===============================================================*/
void    *handle_to_address( hnd, typ )
    database_handle hnd;  /* IN */
    int             typ;  /* IN */
/*- - - - - - - - - - - - - - - - - - - - - - - - - - - - - - - -
Purpose:
    Verify that a database handle used in an application points to
    a database struct created by the application. If the handle is
    good, translate it into a pointer to the struct and return that
    pointer; otherwise, return NULL.
Parameters:
    hnd     handle to verify and translate to address
    typ     DATABASE_TYPE_xxx value that tells what type of struct
            hnd is supposedly the handle to
    Returns valid pointer or NULL.
- - - - - - - - - - - - - - - - - - - - - - - - - - - - - - - -*/
{
    if (!hnd.address) {
        return (NULL);
    }
    if (hnd.checksum != get_checksum(hnd.address)) {
        return (NULL);
    }
    if (hnd.type != typ) {
        return (NULL);
    }
    switch (hnd.type) {
        case DATABASE_TYPE_FOO:
            if (((foo *)hnd.address)->type != hnd.type) {
                return (NULL);
            }
            if (((foo *)hnd.address)->struct_number !=
                                        hnd.struct_number) {
                return (NULL);
            }
            break;
        case DATABASE_TYPE_BALOO:
            if (((baloo *)hnd.address)->type != hnd.type) {
                return (NULL);
            }
            if (((baloo *)hnd.address)->struct_number !=
                                        hnd.struct_number) {
                return (NULL);
```

```
                }
                break;
            default:
                return (NULL);
        }
    return (hnd.address);
} /* handle_to_address */


/*===============================================================*/
boolean     handle_is_null( hnd )
    database_handle    hnd;  /* IN */
/*------------------------------------------
Purpose:
    Check whether a database handle equals NULL_handle. This
    function is provided for two reasons:

    (a) some C compilers do not allow struct comparison—only
    struct members can be compared (as shown below);

    (b) the application shouldn't need to worry about any changes
    in database_handle or details of implementation—every
    operation on a handle is provided by the library
Parameters:
    hnd       handle to check
    Returns true if handle is null, false otherwise.
------------------------------------------*/
{
    return ((hnd.address == NULL_handle.address) &&
            (hnd.checksum == NULL_handle.checksum) &&
            (hnd.type == NULL_handle.type) &&
            (hnd.struct_number == NULL_handle.struct_number));
} /* handle_is_null */


/* This defines the number of bits in a checksum; this should be less
than the number of bits in an int: */
#define CHECKSUM_BITS     4
/* other defines for get_checksum(): */
#define CHECKSUM_MASK     0x0000000F /* CHECKSUM_BITS low bits on */
#define BITS_PER_BYTE     8
/*===============================================================*/
static int  get_checksum( adr )
    void    *adr;  /* IN */
/*------------------------------------------
Purpose:
    Compute checksum on an address; called by handle_to_address().
    -1 returned means "bad checksum."
    Assumes sizeof(long) == sizeof(void *).
Parameters:
```

```
    adr     address; if this is NULL, checksum is -1
    Returns checksum; valid checksums never equal -1.
-------------------------------------------------*/
{
    int     i, sum;
    long    long_adr; /* long, pointers are same size */

    if (!adr) {
        return (-1);
    }
    long_adr = (long)adr;
    sum = 0;
    for (i = 0;
        i < (BITS_PER_BYTE*sizeof(char *)/CHECKSUM_BITS);
        i++) {
        sum += (int)(long_adr & CHECKSUM_MASK);
        long_adr >> CHECKSUM_BITS;
    }
    return (sum & CHECKSUM_MASK);
} /* get_checksum */


/*===============================================================*/
static int  get_struct_number()
/*-----------------------------------------------
Purpose:
    Provide a unique struct number for each database struct the
    application creates via library calls.
Parameters:
    Returns a struct number that never equals
    DATABASE_NO_STRUCT_NUMBER
-------------------------------------------------*/
{
    if (database_struct_number == DATABASE_NO_STRUCT_NUMBER)
        database_struct_number++;
    return (database_struct_number++);
} /* get_struct_number */
```

LISTING: handle_test.c

```
/*-----------------------------------------------
                    handle_test.c
-------------------------------------------------*/


/*===============================================================
Purpose:
```

Our environment contains three components: a library that
provides routines to build and edit some database, an
application that uses this library, and a "handle" library that
protects the database structures from certain application bugs
by providing routines to convert between structure addresses
and handles. Only handles are used in the application—the
application never directly uses a pointer into the database.

This file provides a testbed that exercises the handle library.
To do this, it was necessary to create some database structures
and routines, but these are just examples. The handle library
may be used with any database.

The testbed driver is main(); the sample database structures are
foo and baloo; the sample database access routines are
create_database_foo(), write_database_foo(), and
delete_database_foo(). All these are in this file.
The handle library is in handle.h and handle.c.

This code was compiled under LightspeedC (TM) on a Macintosh SE.

```
-------------------------------------------------*/
#include <stdio.h>
#include <Storage.h>
#include "database.h"


/*===============================================================*/
main()
/*-------------------------------------------------
Purpose:
```
    Test the handle library to make sure it protects the database
    against the following application bugs:

    1. "Out of bounds." The application gets a handle to a database
    struct and overruns an array or otherwise writes outside the
    part of the struct it was supposed to use.
    2. "Dangling handle." After a deletion, the application uses a
    dangling handle to reference a database struct that is no
    longer there.
    3. "Type mismatch." The application gets a handle to a database
    struct of type foo, miscasts it as a handle to type baloo, and
    writes database memory using this handle.
    4. "Damaged handle." The application gets a handle to a
    database struct, hammers the handle, and then references the
    database through this bad handle.

    This testbed also checks briefly to make sure the handle-to-
    struct mapping is really 1-to-1.

Each test is independent of the others, so their order can be changed.
Parameters:
none
---*/
```
{
    database_handle foo_handle, foo_handle_copy,
                    handle_1, handle_2,
                    create_database_foo();
    int             stat, *int_array;

    printf("Testing database handle library...\n");
    /* We protect against "out of bounds" bug by never passing out
    pointers; only the database library routines can write directly
    to foo structs.*/

    /* Test protection against "dangling handle" bug: */
    foo_handle = create_database_foo(&stat);
    if (stat != DATABASE_STAT_OK) {
        printf( "(dangling handle) foo create failed, stat = %d\n",
                stat);
        exit (-1);
    }
    stat = delete_database_foo(foo_handle);
    if (stat != DATABASE_STAT_OK) {
        printf( "(dangling handle) foo delete failed, stat = %d\n",
                stat);
        exit (-1);
    }
    /* try to use the handle whose structure was just deleted: */
    stat = write_database_foo(foo_handle, 77, 1.2345, "yowzah");
    if (stat == DATABASE_STAT_OK) {
        printf("NOT protected against dangling handles!\n");
    }

    /* Test protection against "type mismatch" bug: */
    foo_handle = create_database_foo(&stat);
    if (stat != DATABASE_STAT_OK) {
        printf( "(type mismatch) foo creation failed, stat = %d\n",
                stat);
        exit (-1);
    }
    /* try to use handle and function whose types don't match: */
    stat = delete_database_baloo(foo_handle);
    if (stat == DATABASE_STAT_OK) {
        printf("NOT protected against miscast handles!\n");
    }
    /* now use correct deletion function: */
```

```
stat = delete_database_foo(foo_handle);
if (stat != DATABASE_STAT_OK) {
    printf( "(type mismatch) foo deletion failed, stat = %d\n",
            stat);
    exit (-1);
}


/* Test protection against "damaged handle" bug: */
foo_handle = create_database_foo(&stat);
if (stat != DATABASE_STAT_OK) {
    printf( "(damaged handle) foo creation failed, stat = %d\n",
            stat);
    exit (-1);
}
/* save the good handle and then hammer it: */
foo_handle_copy = foo_handle;
int_array = (int *)(&foo_handle);
int_array[0]++;
/* try to use the hammered handle: */
stat = delete_database_baloo(foo_handle);
if (stat == DATABASE_STAT_OK) {
    printf("NOT protected against hammered handles!\n");
}
/* now use the good handle: */
stat = delete_database_foo(foo_handle_copy);
if (stat != DATABASE_STAT_OK) {
    printf( "(damaged handle) foo deletion failed, stat = %d\n",
            stat);
    exit (-1);
}


/* verify that handles are unique (this could be done in much
more depth—we're relying on having thought the problem through
rather than proving the solution is correct by testing every
case): */
handle_1 = create_database_foo(&stat);
if (stat != DATABASE_STAT_OK) {
    printf("(unique) foo creation 1 failed, stat = %d\n", stat);
    exit (-1);
}
/* delete first struct to increase the chance the next create
will use the same memory: */
stat = delete_database_foo(handle_1);
if (stat != DATABASE_STAT_OK) {
    printf("(unique) foo deletion 1 failed, stat = %d\n", stat);
    exit (-1);
}
handle_2 = create_database_foo(&stat);
```

```
        if (stat != DATABASE_STAT_OK) {
            printf("(unique) foo creation 2 failed, stat = %d\n", stat);
            exit (-1);
        }
        if ((handle_1.address == handle_2.address) &&
            (handle_1.type == handle_2.type) &&
            (handle_1.struct_number == handle_2.struct_number)) {
            printf("Handle-struct mapping is NOT 1-to-1!\n");
            exit(-1);
        }
        stat = delete_database_foo(handle_2);
        if (stat != DATABASE_STAT_OK) {
        printf("(unique) foo deletion 2 failed, stat = %d\n", stat);
        exit (-1);
        }
        printf("Finished testing; no other messages means\n");
        printf("everything worked fine.\n");
} /* main */


/*==============================================================*/
database_handle    create_database_foo( stat )
    int  *stat;    /* OUT */
/*---------------------------------------------
Purpose:
    Create and initialize a new database foo entity.
Parameters:
    Whatever is appropriate. Remember, we're not designing the
    database or its library of functions. We're designing the handle
    interface between the application and the database structs. If
    the create_xxx() calls want parameters to initialize newly
    created structs, that's fine. If the library wants separate
    create_xxx() and write_xxx() calls, that's fine too. Our focus
    is what happens inside create_xxx() to convert the new database
    struct's address into a handle for the application to use.
    stat          error code if NULL_handle is returned, or
                  DATABASE_STAT_OK
    Returns valid handle on success, NULL_handle on failure, sets
    stat
---------------------------------------------*/
{
    foo            *new;
    database_handle address_to_handle(), res;
    void            *malloc();

    *stat = DATABASE_STAT_OK;
    /* validate the incoming parameters here if there are any */
    /* create the new struct */
    if (!(new = (foo *)malloc(sizeof(foo)))) {
```

```
        *stat = DATABASE_STAT_NO_MEMORY;
        return (NULL_handle);
    }
    /* convert from address to handle for application */
    res = address_to_handle(new, DATABASE_TYPE_FOO);
    if (handle_is_null(res)) {
        free(new);
        *stat = DATABASE_STAT_BAD_HANDLE;
        return (NULL_handle);
    }
    /* initialize the new struct as needed, link it to other
    structs */
    /* return handle to application */
    return (res);
} /* create_database_foo */
```

/* The calling sequence for write_database_foo() is known to the
application, but the source is not, in case we want to change foo or
glurp, for instance: */

```
/*================================================================*/
int     write_database_foo( foo_handle, val_1, val_2, val_3 )
    database_handle foo_handle;    /* IN */
    int             val_1;         /* IN */
    glurp           val_2;         /* IN */
    char            *val_3;        /* IN */
/*------------------------------------------
Purpose:
    Safely write some values into a database foo entity. Other
    database entities have corresponding functions, e.g.,
    write_database_baloo().
Parameters:
    foo_handle  handle to a foo entity; from create_database_foo()
    val_1,
    val_2,
    val_3       some values to copy to the database foo struct
                identified by foo_handle
    Returns DATABASE_STAT_xxx, with xxx an appropriate error status
------------------------------------------*/
{
    foo     *dest;
    char    *strsave(), *tmp;
    void    *handle_to_address();

    /* validate the handle */
    if (!(dest = (foo *)handle_to_address(
                            foo_handle, DATABASE_TYPE_FOO))) {
        return (DATABASE_STAT_BAD_HANDLE);
```

```
        }
        /* copy the new values in, but let yourself undo the write if
        anything goes wrong */
        if (!val_3) {
            return (DATABASE_STAT_BAD_STRING);
        }
        tmp = dest->name;
        if (!(dest->name = strsave(val_3))) {
            dest->name = tmp;
            return (DATABASE_STAT_NO_MEMORY);
        }
        free(tmp);
        dest->flags = val_1;
        dest->data = val_2;
        return (DATABASE_STAT_OK);
} /* write_database_foo */


/*================================================================*/
int     delete_database_foo( foo_handle )
    database_handle    foo_handle;          /* IN */
/*----------------------------------------
Purpose:
    Safely delete a foo entity from the database. Other database
    entities have corresponding functions, e.g.,
    delete_database_baloo().
Parameters:
    foo_handle  handle of entity to delete; from
                create_database_foo()
    Returns appropriate DATABASE_STAT_xxx value.
-------------------------------------------*/
{
    void    *handle_to_address();
    foo     *was;

    if (!(was = (foo *)handle_to_address(
                            foo_handle, DATABASE_TYPE_FOO))) {
        return (DATABASE_STAT_BAD_HANDLE);
    }
    /* unlink struct from other structs here if necessary */
    /* Now make sure type and struct_number are no longer valid, in
    case the application tries to write via this foo_handle after
    deletion */
    was->type = DATABASE_TYPE_TRASH;
    was->struct_number = DATABASE_NO_STRUCT_NUMBER;
    free(was);
    return (DATABASE_STAT_OK);
} /* delete_database_foo */
```

```
/*================================================================*/
int     delete_database_baloo( baloo_handle )
    database_handle    baloo_handle;   /* IN */
/*--------------------------------------------
Purpose:
    Safely delete a baloo entity from the database.
Parameters:
    baloo_handle      handle of entity to delete; from
                      create_database_baloo()
    Returns appropriate DATABASE_STAT_xxx value.
--------------------------------------------*/
{
    void    *handle_to_address();
    baloo   *was;

    if (!(was = (baloo *)handle_to_address(
                        baloo_handle, DATABASE_TYPE_BALOO))) {
        return (DATABASE_STAT_BAD_HANDLE);
    }
    /* unlink struct from other structs here if necessary */
    /* Now make sure type and struct_number are no longer valid, in
    case the application tries to write via this handle after
    deletion */
    was->type = DATABASE_TYPE_TRASH;
    was->struct_number = DATABASE_NO_STRUCT_NUMBER;
    free(was);
    return (DATABASE_STAT_OK);
} /* delete_database_baloo */
```

CHAPTER 10
Matching Structs to Screen Regions: Introduction

Suppose we're writing a program that accepts input from a pointing device (mouse, puck, light pen, or whatever). When the user selects a point on the screen with the device, the device driver sends our program the location of that point in screen coordinates. Then it's our problem to take that (x, y) pair and decide which struct was selected.

As we saw in Chapter 3, "Choosing Good Guiding Examples," this problem of matching structs to screen regions is actually a wide class of problems. It turns out that different solutions work best for different kinds of application. Therefore, our discussion of the problem is divided into three chapters. This introductory chapter describes the problem in general, sets top-level goals, and provides some guiding examples. We also start on an ADTD in this chapter, but different guiding examples suggest different ADTDs. So we pursue two of the guiding examples separately in the next two chapters; the other examples are left as exercises.

Following is a typical example of the process we're interested in:

1. A word processor's user moves the mouse to position the cursor over a particular character.
2. The user clicks the mouse button twice in rapid succession without moving the cursor.
3. The word processor notes that selections are being made, and assembles the information related to each selection—the (x, y) cursor position and the times for each click. The cursor positions and click times are close enough to regard the entire

sequence (position cursor, button down, button up, button down, button up) as a double click at (x, y).

4. The word processor determines that two selectable items are displayed at (x, y): a character and a word that contains the character.

5. The word processor knows that a double click means word selection, so it highlights the word to show it is selected. Then the word processor waits for the next operation, which the user presumably wants applied to the selected word.

Our problem is finding a good way to accomplish step 4, that is, to map any given screen position to the internal structures that correspond to the characters, icons, windows, and so forth the user sees on the screen.

Let's call the distinct user-selectable items on the screen the program's "visible choices." In a word processor, for instance, characters and words are visible choices. In a window manager, the visible choices include windows, buttons, and scroll bars. In a chess program, knights, bishops, and the other chess pieces are all visible choices.

Every visible choice occupies some region on the screen. When a user selects a point (x, y) on the screen, our problem is to find every visible choice whose region contains that point. There may be more than one visible choice associated with any given point on the screen. In word processors, for instance, documents contain paragraphs which contain words which contain characters. So a given point (x, y) might refer to a character or a word or a paragraph or even to the entire document.

More generally, suppose the user selects a region on the screen, not just a point (by dragging the mouse, for instance). We want to find all internal structs corresponding to the characters, words, lines, paragraphs, pages, or whatever whose screen regions intersect the selected region.

We know the user has some kind of pointing device to make the selection with, but we don't care whether it's a mouse, a tablet puck, a track ball, a light pen, a touch screen, or something else. Our solution has to work with all these devices and with any other device that lets users select a point or region on the screen. All these devices provide (x, y) coordinates.

Some devices also provide other information—mouse buttons, pen pressure, and so on. We also know there's almost certainly a keyboard out there, which might be used in combination with the pointing device. There is also always a history of previous selections. All these additional sources of information provide a context for the program to use in deciding what was actually selected. But we're interested only in the (x, y) portion of all this information. Our problem is restricted to finding all the internal structs associated with a selected point or region. After that, it's up to particular programs to use buttons, history, and other contextual information to choose between the structs we present as the only possibilities.

TOP-LEVEL GOALS

We've hinted at some top-level goals, but let's list them explicitly. Our screen-to-struct mapping method has to be independent of the type of pointing device used. It has to be fast, because it's part of a user interface. Also, it must be easy to add more visible choices, because user interfaces change. Good error recovery is important. For instance, a given screen point might not have an associated visible choice.

Finally, reliability and consistency are essential. The user interface is all most users have to go on when they're trying to build a mental model of how a program works. Users do not have source code to help them figure out what's happening, and they tend to ignore manuals whenever possible. A program whose user interface is inconsistent or unreliable is just too frustrating to be worth the effort if any other program will get the job done. (It's interesting to note, however, that people often enjoy briefly demonstrating such clearly unusable programs to their friends. We all enjoy brief encounters with oddities. My favorite is the computer that refused to boot until its self-test startup diagnostics were disabled— then it ran fine!)

GUIDING EXAMPLES

So far we have mentioned word processors, chess programs and window managers as examples of programs that need to map screen (x, y) coordinates to internal data structures. Let's create an explicit set of examples to guide our efforts, using the methods described in Chapter 3, "Choosing Good Guiding Examples." We want test cases that are different from each other in some important way and that represent problems we might actually encounter. Following is the result of brainstorming to think of examples; the descriptions are not brief, but we haven't extracted the fundamental characteristics yet.

Games Like Chess

We need windows and menus to play chess, but let's postpone our discussion of them so we can start with something simpler. The visible choices of interest right now are the game pieces—pawns, knights, and so forth—and the squares of the chessboard. The squares are arranged in regularly spaced rows and columns and the pieces are on the squares, with at most one piece per square. Every square's screen region is a rectangle of the same size. We might as well make the screen regions of the pieces the same size as the underlying squares' regions. Selectable pieces can come to rest only on the squares. The total number of squares and pieces varies widely, with chess at the low end and games like go and life that have many identical pieces at the high end. The squares never move and the pieces move only when the user or the computer takes a turn.

Word Processors

The visible choices of interest are characters, words, paragraphs, and so on. These are arranged in irregularly spaced rows and columns. Since proportional fonts and different font sizes are used, the screen regions are different sizes, but they are all rectangular. Regions may overlap, but the only type of overlap involved is containment—characters are contained in words, words are contained in lines, and so on. One word never partially overlaps another the way one window can overlap another.

We can't rule out any (x, y) values as possible locations for a character because different font sizes and proportional fonts are in use. However, placement on the screen is not entirely arbitrary either, since text is arranged in lines. If we give big screen regions to tabs and the last character in each line, the character regions taken together cover a single rectangular display area on the screen. The total number of visible choices varies, but it tends to be large, with values over 1,000 quite common. Text moves only as a direct result of user action.

Windows

The visible choices of interest in this case are windows and window components—slide bars, close boxes, buttons, and so on. These are not positioned in regular rows or columns. Position and region size vary with time, but regions are always rectangular. Overlap is not restricted to containment of one screen region strictly within another. There may be many screen (x, y) positions that lie in no window's region. The number of windows and components varies, but it tends to be small, with numbers over 100 quite rare. Changes in the position of a visible choice usually happen as a direct result of user action—the windows do not move about on their own.

Menus, Palettes

The visible choices of interest in this case are menu bars, menus, and menu options. Their position may be fixed, or they may "pop up" wherever the mouse or pen points. The regions are rectangular, of fixed size when present, and overlap only by way of containment (options are contained within menus). Most screen positions lie outside every visible choice's region—menus do not normally cover the screen. The number of choices varies, but it tends to be small, with numbers over 100 quite rare. Changes in the position of a visible choice usually happen as a direct result of user action.

Simulations, Animations

The visible choices in this case vary greatly, but there aren't as many as there appear to be. Keep in mind the definition of visible choices as "user-selectable." Even though most video games, for instance, contain many little bombs, starships, gorillas, and other items moving about the screen, these items are usually not selectable. Only the main character in such a game might be called a visible choice, and that's stretching the definition because the main character is always selected, whether the user wants it to be or not.

Suppose we consider a simulation of a factory floor, in which the visible choices are tracks, automated vehicles, and loads to carry. We can imagine ourselves selecting loads, moving them, moving track, deleting automatic vehicles, and so forth. Thinking about different things we might want to do with track makes it clear that the screen regions in this case are positioned arbitrarily, are of varying size, and are not necessarily rectangular. Overlap is not limited to containment. There may be many screen (x, y) positions that lie in no region. The number of visible choices varies greatly. Finally, it's clear that the region positions change constantly, whether the user is active or not, because things are supposed to move about on their own in a simulation.

Looking over this set of examples, we see many possibilities for fundamental characteristics. As shown in Table 10-1, however, we can distinguish between all five examples using just the two characteristics listed below. If we need additional characteristics, we can always go back to the brainstorming results above.

regular—whether the screen regions are arranged in regular rows and/or columns
run about—whether the program moves regions around on the screen for arbitrarily long times

ABSTRACT DATA TYPE DESCRIPTION

Now we're ready to create an ADTD. Since we're dealing with a mapping between two sets of things (screen coordinates and internal structs), we'll start by stating clearly what collections we're dealing with.

What name does this particular collection of data elements go by, that is, what abstract data type are we concerned with? The internal structs used to represent visible choices will vary from program to program, but what we're interested in will not change. We want to decide how to organize any program's structs to make the screen space-to-internal structs mapping most efficient. A long but correct name for our collection would therefore be "the screen-to-struct mapping portion of structs that is used to locate the structs that represent visible choices internally."

What is the geometry of the collection? In other words, what organization do we impose on our internal structs to make the screen-to-struct mapping efficient? It's clear we want to

TABLE 10-1:   Fundamental characteristic values of the chosen examples.

Regular?	Run About?	Example
yes	no	chess
rows	no	word processors
no	no	windows
columns	no	menus
no	yes	simulations

sort structs somehow according to their (x, y) screen coordinates. It's also clear that this sort won't be enough by itself, since visible choices occupy whole regions, not single points, and the regions can overlap. There might be zero, one, or many regions containing any particular (x, y) value.

There is another complication, too. How do we link the sorted structures together? Do we use one long list, or a list of lists, or some kind of tree, or something else? This is not just an implementation question, because the mental model of a tree geometry, for instance, is different from that of a list geometry no matter what language you're programming in.

The different examples above suggest different geometries. There's so much regularity to a chessboard's visible choices, for instance, that no list or tree is necessary. We can use a simple algebraic formula to decide which square on the chessboard a given (x, y) lies in. A chessboard-sized array of pieces (pawn, rook, knight, bishop, king, queen, and square_unoccupied) is the most natural geometry in this case.

The most natural geometry for a word processor is a list of lists. Each line of text is represented by a linked list of characters, and the document is a list of these character lists.

Windows pose a new problem we didn't have in the chess example: Regions can overlap in arbitrary ways. The easiest way to handle overlapping is to add depth and allow a window to be only at one depth. This prevents situations like the one illustrated in Figure 10-1. So our mental model of the geometry is a group of two-dimensional rectangles of different sizes floating parallel to each other in three-dimensional space.

Each rectangle represents a window. The rectangles are parallel to each other (the z-axis, say, is normal to each) because a window can only be at one depth. Whenever a selected point is in a region common to two overlapping windows, one window will be in front of the other, and the window in front will be the one selected.

These rectangles are ordered by the (x, y, z) coordinates of, say, their top left corners. The x- and y-components of a given point in any rectangle are just the point's screen coordinates. The z-component is something we generate to reflect the number of windows in front of the point. For instance, a visible point might belong to a window with $z = 0$ while a point underneath two windows has $z = -2$. How to actually keep track of a point's z-value is an implementation question, but it's clear we can store one z-value per window rather than one per point.

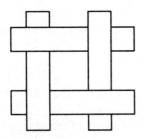

FIGURE 10-1:   If each window can be at more than one depth, it may be impossible to tell which window is in front.

TABLE 10-2: Table 10-1 updated by adding "Overlap" as a new fundamental characteristic.

Regular?	Run About?	Overlap?	Example
yes	no	exact or none	chess
rows	no	containment	word processors
no	no	arbitrary	windows
columns	no	none	menus
no	yes	arbitrary	simulations

For convenience, we'll call this whole mental model the "sheets-of-paper geometry." As a sketch of the geometry, all we need to do is imagine a tabletop that has some sheets of paper lying on top of it; each sheet represents a window. Even better, we could imagine a computer monitor showing a group of open windows.

It appears that overlapping is a more important characteristic than we originally thought, so we'll update our table of guiding examples accordingly; the results are in Table 10-2.

So far, the examples have suggested three geometries: array, list-of-lists, and sheets-of-paper. Menus and palettes suggest some mixture of the array and sheets-of-paper geometries. They suggest one-dimensional arrays because items occupy fixed size regions that don't move relative to each other. A simple calculation can determine which option's region a given (x, y) falls in once we know the size of each menu or palette option, their order, and the screen position of one corner of the menu or palette. However, a sheets-of-paper geometry also comes to mind because menus can sometimes overlap each other, especially if submenus are involved.

The last example is that of simulations. The array geometry won't work here because there's not enough regularity in the visible choices for a simple formula to map screen (x, y) to a particular struct. The list-of-lists fails because the visible choices in a simulation do not fall naturally into lines the way text does. However, we can use the sheets-of-paper geometry.

There are two differences between simulations and windows. First, as noted in Table 10-2, the visible choices in a simulation can move about without direct human intervention. Windows, on the other hand, don't normally rush about by themselves (frightening thought, isn't it?). Second, there are often many more visible choices in a simulation than there are visible windows, simply because windows must be big enough to hold some text or image if they are to be useful. But neither of these differences makes the sheets-of-paper geometry inappropriate.

So altogether we have just three geometries: array, list-of-lists, and sheets-of-paper. Which one should we choose? Since we're trying to solve the screen space-to-internal struct mapping problem for all the examples, the answer ought to be "All three, one at a time." However, the array geometry is too simple to learn much from, so the actual answer is "First, we'll get a list-of-lists solution. Then we'll solve the sheets-of-paper problem as well."

Using two geometries means basing our search for solutions on two ADTDs, so we'll break our effort into two chapters to avoid confusion. The next two chapters describe solutions based on the list-of-lists and sheets-of-paper geometry respectively. We refer back to the examples and top-level goals described in this chapter whenever doing so helps us solve the problem at hand.

It might or might not be the case that implementing one geometry helps us implement the other later on. But it is clear that starting with good examples, top-level goals, and an attempt at an ADTD will help both implementations. In particular, we see how ADTDs guide implementation.

We suspect, for instance, that similar code will work in both a simulation and a window manager because their ADTDs have the same sheets-of-paper geometry. That code is unlikely to be the best solution in a word processor or chess game, however. The visible choices in those two cases are arranged more regularly, reflecting their array and list-of-lists geometry, respectively. We could use the more general sheets-of-paper solution in a chess game or word processor, but it would be better to take advantage of their simpler geometries to speed up and simplify the screen-to-struct mapping code.

CHAPTER 11

Matching Structs to Screen Regions: A Word Processor Solution

In the previous chapter, one of the guiding examples we chose was a word processor. In this chapter, we'll write an ADTD for the list-of-lists geometry suggested by that example and then implement it. By the way, we'll refer to the previous chapter as the "introduction" throughout this chapter and the next chapter, meaning, of course, the "introduction to the screen-to-struct mapping problem."

TOP-LEVEL GOALS

We discussed these goals in the introduction, so we'll just recall them briefly here. The mapping from screen (x, y) values to internal structs must be fast. It must be easy to add more visible choices. Good error recovery is important, and reliability and consistency are essential.

GUIDING EXAMPLES

In the introduction, we characterized word processors as follows:

Regular?	Run About?	Overlap?	Example
rows	no	containment	word processors

This characterization was developed from the description of word processors in the introduction. "Regular?–rows" means that characters are arranged in regular rows but not in regular columns. "Run About?–no" means they do not move about on their own for arbitrarily long periods in ways that are hard to predict. "Overlap?–containment" means that the only way screen regions overlap is when one region is contained in another.

ABSTRACT DATA TYPE DESCRIPTION

Now let's complete the abstract data type description we started in the introduction. Again, we'll start by stating clearly what collections we're dealing with.

What name does this particular collection of data elements go by, that is, what abstract data type are we concerned with? The data elements are characters, words, and lines of text. We want to decide how to organize character, word, and line structs to make the screen-to-struct mapping most efficient. There are also other constraints on the organization of these structs, such as the need to support efficient string searches. So the abstract data type we're interested in is just one aspect of the program's data elements.

This was also the case in the example we discussed in Chapter 9, "Protecting a Database During Editing." In that example, we didn't care much what data was stored in the database; we just wanted a good mapping between database structs and the handles used by applications.

Unlike the database example, however, the separation between the mapping we're interested in and the rest of the struct organization is not always clear. In the database example, we mapped one handle to one struct address, and the mapping was constant over time for any given handle. The screen-to-struct mapping, however, is neither one-to-one nor constant. It's not one-to-one because one screen region may map to many character, word, and line structs. The screen-to-struct mapping is not constant because a given screen region maps to different structs if we scroll the text. So we must consider scrolling, searching, and other operations when organizing our structs, even though our main interest is the screen-to-struct mapping.

What is the geometry of the collection? In other words, what organization do we impose on our internal structs to make the screen-to-struct mapping efficient? The different examples in the introduction suggested different geometries; in this chapter, we concentrate on the list-of-lists geometry.

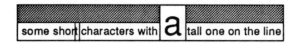

FIGURE 11-1: Selection region height matches individual character height, leading to unselectable areas between lines.

The most natural geometry for a word processor is a list of lists. Each line of text is represented by a linked list of characters (including white space). The document itself is a list of these character lists.

But why put each line of text in a separate list? Why not simply view the text as one long list of characters? We need to separate different lines of text because of an assumption we're making: We assume every character in a given line has the same y-values for its selection region. That is, it doesn't matter that some characters appear taller and some appear shorter, or don't appear at all, like blank and tab. The range of heights that the cursor's hot spot must be in to select a character is constant for any given line.

If we don't make this assumption, there are "dead regions" between the lines, where attempting a selection gives no result. Clicking over the "t" in Figure 11-1, for instance, does nothing if the cursor points to the dead region above the "t." This is not acceptable. There are no gaps horizontally between characters; why should we maintain vertical gaps? It's stupid to go out of our way when the only gain is a frustrated user.

We can fill these gaps by assuming a constant range of y-values for each line's selection regions; see Figure 11-2. Putting one tall character anywhere in a line of short characters effectively heightens the screen regions of all the short characters to match the tall character's region. Screen region heights are constant for each line, but they may differ from one line to the next. In short, we need to represent the geometry as a list of lines of character regions, that is, as a list-of-lists.

What relations hold between the data elements in the collection? What relations hold between this collection and other collections? The characters are ordered from left to right in each line on the screen, and the lines are ordered from top to bottom, according to a relation we'll call "precedes."

There's also another relation, which we'll call "contains." For now, we'll say that a line contains one or more words, and each word contains one or more characters (including white

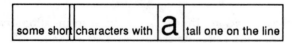

FIGURE 11-2: Selection region height matches the height of the largest character's region, eliminating unselectable areas between lines.

space). We can add the notion of an empty word or empty line later if we need it. We'll think of a word that's hyphenated and split over two lines as being two words:

    inter-
    national

These rules assume a language like English, which is written left to right, top to bottom, and which generally uses more than one character per word. Not every language matches this model. If we fail to localize our assumptions about "precedes" and "contains," our word processor will need a major overhaul to deal with Arabic or Chinese, or with chemical and mathematical equations.

What are the properties of each position in the geometry with respect to the operators and with respect to elements in other positions? The list-of-lists geometry has seven positions: "first character," "first word," "first line," "last character," "last word," "last line," and "somewhere in the middle." The first character precedes all other characters, and the last is preceded by all other characters. The first word precedes all other words, and so on. The first line contains the first word, which contains the first character, and the last line contains the last word, which in turn contains the last character. No surprises here.

What rules does each relation follow? The relation "precedes" is a total ordering on lines, words, and characters taken one at a time. That is, given any two distinct lines, one always precedes the other; the same is true for any two words or any two characters. But "precedes" is only a partial ordering if we mix element types. Given a line and a character, one does not necessarily precede the other. However, given any two data elements, either one precedes the other or one contains the other.

The "contains" relation is not reflexive; a word, for instance, cannot contain itself because words contain only characters. Contains is not symmetric, either. A word can contain a character, but a character cannot contain a word (another modification we'd need to support Chinese!). What about transitivity? If a line contains a word, and the word contains a character, it makes sense to say that the line contains the character. So contains is transitive, but transitivity is possible only when each of the three elements is of a particular type.

What are the operators? We don't need to list here all the operations possible in a word processor. We are interested only in operations that pertain directly to the mapping from screen space to internal structs. The most important of these is the mapping operation itself: given a screen region, find all character, word, and line structs whose regions intersect the screen region.

We also need a few additional operations: create an empty list-of-lists, add a struct and its associated region to a list-of-lists, delete a struct and its associated region. As a debugging tool, it would also be nice to print the entire list-of-lists, including, of course, all current screen region boundaries.

What are the restrictions on membership in the collection? A commercial word processor contains many types of structs. For instance, we might have structs to represent a word of text, to implement an undo option, and to keep track of the fonts available, among other things. But the only structs of interest are those that have an associated screen region. The structs representing words of text, for instance, correspond directly to user-selectable visible choices, so they belong in our data collection. None of the rest of the structs mentioned represent visible choices, so they are barred from membership.

The data types allowed are the structs used to represent characters, words, and lines of text. If paragraphs were selectable as units, we could add them, but characters, words, and lines give us a realistic enough example to work with. There's no hard limit on the number of elements in our list-of-lists. Membership is not based on the values of current or prospective members. Instead, membership is based on how a struct is used—if it represents a visible choice, it's in, if not, it's out.

How many collections are allowed by this ADT? We're thinking of one list-of-lists per file. Since a word processor might have multiple files open, multiple collections are allowed. However, there are no direct connections between elements in different collections; we'll ignore the transfer of text from one file to another, since it probably won't involve any screen-to-struct mapping capabilities beyond the ones needed for transferring text about within a single file.

Can a proper subset of a collection be viewed as a collection in its own right? It seems unlikely that we'd want to operate on a strict subset of a collection. Doing so has the effect of recognizing only some of the visible choices, even though all the choices are displayed to the user. For instance, imagine trying to use a word processor that lets you select a block of text for deletion but only deletes every other word, or every word that starts with "S," or every word not in the spelling dictionary, depending on the mode it's in!

What is the meaning of each element in the collection? Each element in the collection represents a user-selectable visible choice: characters, words, and lines of text. The structs that represent these visible choices are sorted according to their screen regions in some way that is still unclear.

ATTEMPT ONE

We have many questions left to answer before we start coding. What I'd like to do is to keep a dynamic list of unanswered questions, adding questions as new ones arise and removing them as we find answers. However, you're looking at a book, not at a computer monitor, so I can't update the text while you are reading it. What I'll do instead is sneak ahead and collect all the questions and put them in Box 11-1. This isn't entirely satisfactory, because it suggests all the questions arose at once. What actually happens, of course, is that the answer to one question often raises other questions. But collecting the questions in one place seems preferable to repeating them all each time the list changes.

BOX 11-1:   Unanswered questions.

1. Should we implement the list-of-lists geometry as a linked list of linked lists?
2. Should we make singly or doubly linked lists?
3. What type of elements are kept in each list—characters, words, lines, or something else?
4. Do we fold the list-of-lists into a single large list, or do we represent the hierarchy explicitly?
5. What are typical word processor operations whose implementation might conflict with efficient implementation of the screen-to-struct mapping?
6. Will using doubly linked lists require too much memory?
7. What exactly is in those line header structs shown at the bottom of Figure 11-7?
8. How should we represent the screen regions? We have to make it easy to change many screen regions all at once, because all our representative operations— scrolling, changing font size, string insertion, string deletion, and searching—can result in large (or small) pieces of text moving about on the screen. We'll need an offset somewhere in there.
9. How do we deal with screen regions for items that have been scrolled off the screen? What happens when they get scrolled back on again?
10. What happens when something is selected, then scrolled off the screen, then operated on? That is, what happens when no new selection is made after the first selection is scrolled out of sight?
11. Have we satisfied the ADTD?
12. How do we implement horizontal scrolling?

The first question is whether we should implement the list-of-lists geometry as a linked list of linked lists. It's true our geometry is called "list-of-lists." But that doesn't mean we have to use pointers. Lists can also be implemented with arrays, or with a mixture of pointers and arrays, as discussed in the design guideline "Avoid Sorted Lists of Arrays" (page 360). Thinking about linked lists leads to question 2.

Question 2 asks whether we should make singly or doubly linked lists. The difference in memory requirements between singly and doubly linked lists depends on the number of elements in the list. Adding one more pointer to each struct in a linked list of individual characters can easily double our memory requirements. But searching backward and editing are going to be much harder without that back-pointing link. If we keep a list of character arrays instead of individual characters, we could reduce the number of pointers needed. Before deciding between singly and doubly linked lists, however, we need to decide what the list elements are.

Question 3 asks what type of elements are kept in each list—characters, words, lines, or something else? Speaking of list elements recalls the phrase "list-of-lists." The most obvious implementation of a list-of-lists geometry is a hierarchy of lists like the one shown in Figure 11-3. But there are alternatives. Figure 11-4 shows an implementation that uses embedded sublists. In this case, we represent the data in a text file as one long list of

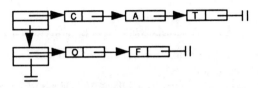

FIGURE 11-3:   A list-of-lists geometry implemented using a linked list of pointers to distinct linked lists.

characters. We have to choose between these two models, so we have yet another question to answer.

Question 4 asks whether we should fold the list-of-lists into a single large list or represent the hierarchy explicitly. Before we can answer, we need more information. In particular, we need more constraints. Luckily, there's an enormous constraint we haven't discussed yet. We've been trying to organize the word processor's structs to support the screen-to-struct mapping. But those same structs must also be organized to efficiently support typical word processor operations like insertion, deletion, and searching. So, let's consider what happens to the structs once they're selected. In order to do this, we have to ask question 5: What are the typical operations?

Now we can finally start answering questions! We'll start with question 5, because it's the one that causes the greatest pain if we go wrong. What word processor operations could the screen-to-struct mapping interfere with? We need some examples, so we'll apply the method from Chapter 3, "Choosing Good Guiding Examples." The first step is to get a general idea of what we're looking for; we have that. The next step is to brainstorm and think of many examples. However, we know we can ignore operations that have no possible effect on the screen regions of text. This leaves the following examples to consider:

> open an existing file
> create a new file
> exit without writing the file
> write the file and exit
> copy from one file to another
> search, or search and replace
> insert new text

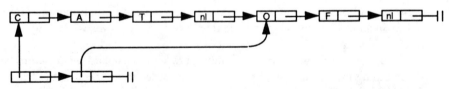

FIGURE 11-4:   A list-of-lists geometry implemented using a linked list of pointers to a single large linked list.

move a block of text
delete a block of text
change fonts
change font size
bold, italic, shadow, underline, superscript, subscript
center, justify left, justify right
change margins
change headers or footers
set tab stops
set a mark, go to a mark
scroll horizontally, scroll vertically, page in either direction

Defining keyboard macros, recovering a file, and undoing the previous command can also move characters about, but we won't consider these operations because each is simply a series of simpler operations that we are already considering.

The next step is to extract those fundamental characteristics of the examples that are pertinent to the screen-to-struct mapping problem.

Looking over these examples, we see file opening and closing of different sorts. This is when the data structures that represent screen regions will need to be either created and initialized, or freed, respectively. When a file is opened, we have to read the data from disk into whatever struct organization is chosen, building linked lists and so forth as we go. If the organization is too large or inflexible, we won't be able to fit the file in memory. If the organization is too complicated, it will take too long to get the structures built. We also have to reverse the operation when the file is closed. So one fundamental characteristic of any example operation is whether the entire set of regions is being created and initialized, freed, or just updated.

Moving on through our brainstorming results, we see several kinds of text movement—copying from one file to another, deleting text, inserting text, and so on. So another fundamental characteristic is whether the order of characters in the file is changed.

There are also several kinds of scrolling—vertically, horizontally, by pages, by changing the margins, by going to a mark, by searching. These operations all change which struct a region corresponds to without changing either the order of characters or the character display characteristics (font size, bold, italic, etc.). Speaking of which, there are also several ways to change display characteristics without changing the character sequence. These include changing fonts or font size, using bold or italics, sub- and superscripting, setting tab stops (change the width of a tab's display region), and centering text (change the width of the display regions of the line's first and last characters). So another fundamental characteristic is whether the display characteristics are changed.

We mentioned searching already in connection with scrolling, but searching is different from scrolling in that every character is tested until a match is found. Searches require struct-by-struct traversal of the character list in a way that scrolling does not. The character, word, and line structs must be organized well to make searching efficient, and that organization might affect the organization we choose for the screen-to-struct mapping. So yet another fundamental characteristic is whether we need to traverse the list of characters.

TABLE 11-1: The fundamental characteristics of word processor operations that affect screen regions.

Create?	Order?	Display?	Traverse?	Examples
create	no	no	no	open an existing file
create	no	no	no	create a new file
free	no	no	no	exit without writing the file
free	no	no	no	write the file and exit
no	yes	no	no	copy from one file to another
no	no	no	yes	search
no	yes	no	yes	search and replace
no	yes	no	no	insert new text
no	yes	no	no	move a block of text
no	yes	no	no	delete a block of text
no	no	yes	no	change fonts
no	no	yes	no	change font size
no	no	yes	no	bold, italic, shadow, underline, superscript
no	no	yes	no	center, justify left, justify right
no	no	yes	no	change margins
no	yes	no	no	change headers or footers
no	no	yes	no	set tab stops
no	no	no	no	set a mark, go to a mark
no	no	no	no	scroll, page (horizontally or vertically)

Typical word processor operations are summarized in Table 11-1 according to their fundamental characteristics. Table 11-2 shows the same information after duplicates have been removed.

We won't bother to verify here that the following set of examples has the desirable characteristics spelled out in Chapter 3, "Choosing Good Guiding Examples," but it does. As our representative operations, then, we have the following:

open or close a file
scroll (horizontally or vertically)

TABLE 11-2: Table 11-1 after duplicate operations have been removed.

Create?	Order?	Display?	Traverse?	Examples
yes	no	no	no	open or close a file
no	yes	no	no	insert or delete text
no	no	yes	no	change font size
no	no	no	yes	search for a string
no	no	no	no	scroll horizontally or vertically

change a string's font size
insert or delete a string
search for a string

So much for question 5. Our list of unanswered questions is finally getting smaller.

Now let's consider question 1 in connection with each of these representative operations. Should we use arrays, linked lists, or some mixture of the two to represent text internally? Reading a file from disk into memory is easier using arrays, since fewer links are involved. In fact, the simplest read is to allocate a single character array big enough for the entire file, and read into it. Likewise, running through memory to write to disk when the file is closed is easier with fewer links, and so is deallocating memory. So file open and file close prefer arrays to linked lists.

Scrolling, font size changes, and searches are made just as easily with an array of characters as with a linked list. Searches might be even faster with arrays than with lists. Insertion and deletion, however, are much easier with linked lists. What's more, insertion and deletion are also the most common operations, since they maintain the order of the character data that is manipulated by the other operations. So the fact that insertion and deletion favor linked lists overrides the earlier preference for arrays.

Nevertheless, suppose we did use arrays. The array elements must be individual characters, since that's the smallest unit that is inserted or deleted. But inserting and deleting characters arbitrarily in an array or even in a list of arrays is ugly at best; see the design guideline "Avoid Sorted Lists of Arrays" (page 360). So the answer to question 1 is that we'll use linked lists. We've also answered question 3—the smallest atomic elements in our lists must be characters. Or, to be precise, they must be character structs, since each character has display and other information (yet to be determined) associated with it, as well as an ASCII value.

On to question 2: Do we want singly or doubly linked lists? Doubly linked lists are a bit harder to create while reading a newly opened file because we have more links to establish, but the real difference is that they require more space than singly linked lists. When closing the file, on the other hand, there's no difference—it's just as easy to traverse and deallocate a doubly linked list as a singly linked one. Font size changes are made just as easily with either kind of list. When we scroll or search, however, we are as likely to move backward as forward.

Deletions are also easier to manage in doubly linked lists because the backward link makes it possible to avoid a lot of list traversal. For instance, suppose we want to delete "ucks" from the line "gently give a rucksack." As shown in Figures 11-5 and 11-6, the selection process gives us pointers to the structs that hold "u" and "s"—"u" starts the string "ucks," which was selected for deletion, and "s" ends it. To make the line into "gently give a rack," we need a pointer to the "r" so we can make it point to the "a" in "sack" instead of the "u" in "ucks."

In the singly linked list shown in Figure 11-5, we can't go back from the "u" to the "r"; we have to go forward from the front of the list until we find the struct that points to the "u," namely, the "r." In the doubly linked list in Figure 11-6, however, we avoid this traversal because "u" points back to "r." Since deletion is a very common operation, we'll go with

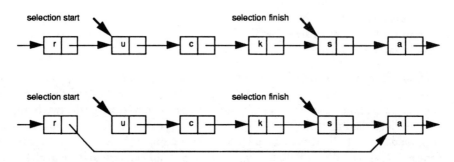

FIGURE 11-5: Part of a singly linked list before and after pointers are changed to delete a selected substring.

doubly linked lists for now, but we'll make a note (question 6) to consider the memory requirements in more detail before writing any code.

Question 4 asks whether we should implement the list-of-lists as a list of distinct lists, as a single long list with embedded sublists, or as something else. The two models illustrated in Figure 11-3 and Figure 11-4 are both of roughly equal complexity and require about the same memory, so opening and closing files is no harder in one case than in the other.

Both models also give us a struct at the head of each line of text. We can put the y-value range for the entire line in this line header struct. For instance, we could note in the line header that a given line's character regions run from $y = 12$ to $y = 24$ (we'll assume screen coordinates are in pixels). When we change font size, we update this y range in either case, so that's no help in choosing between Figure 11-3 and Figure 11-4. Scrolling is also just as easy (or hard) with either model.

Insertion, deletion, and searching, however, are easier with the sublist model because all the file's characters are in a single list. This is especially nice when searching for a substring that might span two lines. List traversal is complicated in the list of distinct lists shown in Figure 11-3 because the line header structs are directly involved. Overall, the embedded sublist model seems to be the best choice. Of course, we'll update it to use doubly linked lists as shown in Figure 11-7.

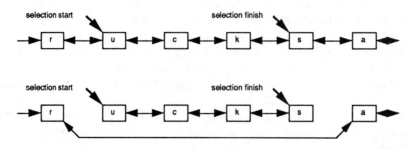

FIGURE 11-6: Part of a doubly linked list before and after pointers are changed to delete a selected substring.

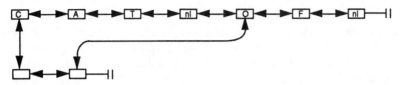

FIGURE 11-7:   A list-of-lists geometry implemented as a doubly linked list of line header structs that point into a doubly linked list of character structs.

On to question 6: Can we afford the memory needed to hold a doubly linked list? Well, we don't need to keep the entire file in the doubly linked list. Some of it could be cached in arrays, and some might even be on disk, depending on the amount of memory available and the size of the file and how fast disk accesses are. The only part of the text that absolutely must be in the doubly linked list organization is the part that's currently displayed and therefore selectable.

Not enough text is selectable at any point to worry about the difference between singly and doubly linked lists for currently displayed text. For instance, a window that is 50 lines by 120 characters holds at most $50*120 = 6{,}000$ list elements. Even if pointers are 4 bytes each, this is only an extra $4*6{,}000$, which is less than 24 Kbytes. On smaller systems where memory is more precious, pointers are only 2 bytes, and 12 Kbytes is probably not too high a price to pay to speed up deletions.

On the other hand, keeping only visible text in the doubly linked list means moving the text between the list and a RAM or disk cache. It's much simpler to keep the entire file in the doubly linked list than it is to change the list contents every time the user scrolls. But the simplicity has a price—it's no longer obvious whether doubly linked lists are worth the extra memory.

For discussion, let's take 60K characters as a typical file size. That means it will take 60K extra pointers to go from a singly to a doubly linked list. On the personal computer end of the scale where machines tend to have no more than 1 Mbyte of memory, pointers are 2 bytes, so we need an extra 120 Kbytes to move a typical file from singly to doubly linked. It may not be worth such a large percentage of the available memory just to speed up deletions. On a typical workstation, by contrast, we have 4-byte pointers, 4 Mbytes of physical memory, and 16 Mbytes of virtual memory. In this case, 240 Kbytes is easy to come by.

In other words, we need to specify a target environment to choose between singly and doubly linked lists. We'll take a Macintosh SE with 4 Mbytes of memory and 4-byte pointers as our environment (that's what the code in this book was written on). It's still a judgment call, since 240 Kbytes is roughly one-sixteenth of the total memory, but we'll implement doubly linked lists. Minimizing execution speed was one of our top-level goals, and minimizing memory requirements was not.

Incidentally, in practice, we'd probably want to keep more than just the selectable text in memory. To make scrolling reasonably fast, we might also keep in memory N pages (screenfuls of text) before and after the currently displayed page. N varies, but something like $N = 2$ might be useful. It depends on how long disk reads take and how much memory we have to work with.

Our list of unanswered questions is empty for the moment, and we're much closer to something we can code with some degree of confidence. But old questions always give rise to new questions. Putting them on the list, we get questions 7 through 11.

Let's tackle question 8 first, since it seems to be the central one among those left. One way to represent the screen region for a character, say, would be to list the corners explicitly:

```
typedef struct char_element {
   struct char_element   *next,
                         *prev;
   char                  value;
   int                   top_left_x,
                         top_left_y,
                         bottom_right_x,
                         bottom_right_y;
} char_element;
```

There are a couple of problems with this. First, it will be very painful to update the affected *char_element* structs each time we scroll or otherwise change the values in *char_element.top_left_x*, and so on. Second, we're wasting space. Half of character $N+1$'s coordinates are duplicates of the values stored in character N's struct whenever both characters are on the same line:

```
N_plus_1.top_left_x equals N.bottom_right_x
N_plus_1.top_left_y equals N.top_left_y
```

All we really need to store is the y-value range for the entire line of characters, the starting x-value for the leftmost character in the line, and each character's width. Although we've decided to keep y-value ranges in the line header structs, we never said how exactly to store them. We could keep y_top and y_bottom in each line header. But that wastes space; since there are no dead regions between lines, a given line's bottom is the next line's top.

So we'll keep the topmost y-value someplace and store a single height in each line header struct. Just as each line has a height, each character has a width associated with it; we're supporting proportional fonts and different font sizes. Just knowing the font isn't enough to know a character's width. The width of a character depends on the font, the font size, whether the character is bold, and perhaps on other factors as well. So we'll store a width in each character struct:

```
int    topmost_y;  /* assumes top of display area is horizontal */
int    leftmost_x; /* assumes vertical left margin of display */

typedef struct line_header {
   struct line_header   *next,
                        *prev;
   struct char_element  *first_char;
   int                  height; /* in pixels */
} line_header;
```

```
typedef struct char_element {
  struct char_element   *next,
                        *prev;
  char                  value;
  int                   width; /* in pixels */
  /* possibly other fields, related to display: bold, etc. */
} char_element;
```

These typedefs and globals give us enough information to implement a mapping function. This first version of *xy_to_char_struct()* maps only single screen points, not screen regions:

```
/*===============================================================*/
char_element    *xy_to_char_struct(x, y)
  int  x,   /* IN */
       y;   /* IN */
/*- - - - - - - - - - - - - - - - - - - - - - - - - - - - - - - -
Purpose:
  Finds the character struct whose region a given screen
  coordinate falls in.
Parameters:
  global line_header *first_line; this points to the first line
        currently displayed
  x, y    screen coordinate
  Returns pointer to character's struct, or NULL if given (x, y)
  doesn't fall in any character's screen region.
- - - - - - - - - - - - - - - - - - - - - - - - - - - - - - - -*/
{
  line_header     *line;
  char_element    *ch;
  int             cur_x, cur_y;

  if ((x < leftmost_x) || (y < topmost_y))
    return (NULL);
  for ( line = first_line, cur_y = topmost_y;
        line && (cur_y + line->height < y);
        line = line->next ) {
    cur_y += line->height;
  }
  if (!line)
    return (NULL);
  for ( ch = line->first_char, cur_x = leftmost_x;
        ch && (cur_x + ch->width < x);
        ch = ch->next ) {
    cur_x += ch->width;
  }
  return (ch);
} /* xy_to_char_struct */
```

Notice that we added a global, *first_line*, in order to implement *xy_to_char_struct()*.

This implementation of the screen-to-struct mapping has several problems. For instance, it doesn't deal correctly with partially filled lines or screens. If you click the cursor at the same height as the last character in a display line but far to the right of the character, that last character should be selected. In this version of *xy_to_char_struct()* it won't be, because the character's region isn't wide enough. The region for the last character in each line should extend all the way to the right edge of the display area. Similarly, the region for the last character in the file should extend to the bottom edge of the display area.

However, before we start tuning *xy_to_char_struct()*, let's finish what we started to do—answer question 8. How do we update our screen regions and internal structs when performing typical word processor operations?

When we open a file, we have to initialize the globals and then create the list of *line_headers* and their lists of *char_elements* as we read the file in. Similarly, we must write each *char_element.value* to disk and deallocate memory when the file is closed.

Scrolling vertically amounts to changing the global *first_line* so it points at a different *line_header* struct. Notice that this implies the "scrolling unit" is one line. That is, it's impossible to scroll so that the top edge of the window cuts through the center of a line. Scrolling horizontally isn't supported yet; we'll add that to our list as question 12.

Changing font size includes updating *line_header.height* to reflect the height of the tallest character in the line; we might also need to update some *char_element.width* values. String insertion and deletion update the screen regions involved automatically because we used width and height offsets from a known starting position instead of storing each character's position directly in its *char_element* struct.

Finally, consider searching. The actual scanning of the characters does not change the display. If we find the string, however, we'll want to display it with its surrounding text. But jumping to a new position without changing file contents is the same as vertical scrolling without intervening display updates—only the beginning and ending visible text is displayed.

In summary, there are no serious conflicts between the proposed screen-to-struct organization and typical word processor operations. That takes care of question 8.

The answer to question 9 is now clear. Items that are scrolled off the screen do not have screen regions. But we maintain their width, height, and relative position in the lists of *line_headers* and *char_element* structs, so we can recompute their screen regions when needed.

The answer to question 10 is that we have separate pointers to tell what is selected and what is visible. A string does not have to be visible to be selected. Assuming for the moment that a selected region is always contiguous, we can track selections by using two globals:

```
char_element     *first_sel_char;
char_element     *last_sel_char;
```

These two pointers get their values from calls to *xy_to_char_struct()*. We could expand this approach to support an arbitrary number of discontiguous selections by using a list of pairs of pointers. But this is good enough for now, since our implementation of the screen-to-struct mapping won't limit the user's ability to make selections.

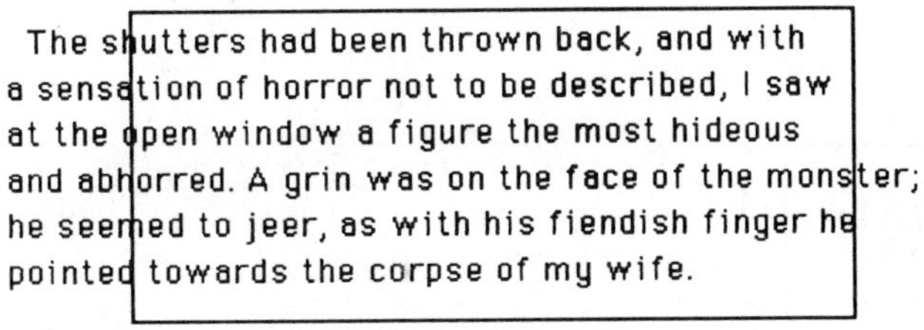

```
The shutters had been thrown back, and with
a sensation of horror not to be described, I saw
at the open window a figure the most hideous
and abhorred. A grin was on the face of the monster;
he seemed to jeer, as with his fiendish finger he
pointed towards the corpse of my wife.
```

FIGURE 11-8: A section of text from *Frankenstein*, by Mary Shelley. The portion potentially visible on the screen is outlined.

What about question 12 on horizontal scrolling? The only method our current typedefs suggest to implement horizontal scrolling is to change *line_header.first_char*, the pointer to the first (leftmost) character in the line. There are two problems with this. First, we lose our pointer to the first character in the display line. We need this pointer to pin scrolling that makes the text move right. In other words, a user can scroll text to the left as far as the window will allow, since there's no hard limit on line length. But it should not be possible to scroll text to the right past the beginning of the line.

The second problem in scrolling by changing *line_header.first_char* is the possibility of ragged left edges whenever different characters are different widths. In other words, what is the horizontal scrolling unit? Recall that the vertical scrolling unit was a line—entire lines appear or disappear during scrolling. We could make the horizontal scrolling unit a character. But characters may have different widths, and making the scrolling unit pixels instead of characters leads to a much cleaner left edge, as shown in Figures 11-8, 11-9, and 11-10.

We can implement horizontal scrolling by pixels if we add a global:

```
int     cur_leftmost_x;
```

We already keep the leftmost *x*-value of the display area in the global *leftmost_x*. The new global *cur_leftmost_x* is used to keep track of the left edge of the text as it is scrolled horizontally. For instance, suppose we have a situation like the one illustrated in Figure 11-11.

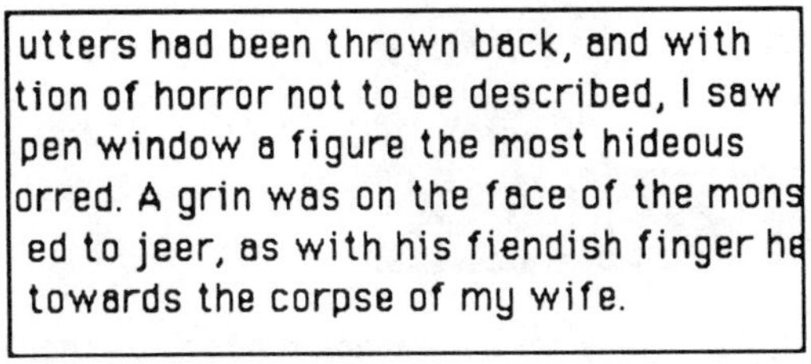

```
utters had been thrown back, and with
tion of horror not to be described, I saw
pen window a figure the most hideous
orred. A grin was on the face of the mons
ed to jeer, as with his fiendish finger he
towards the corpse of my wife.
```

FIGURE 11-9: The text from Figure 11-8 displayed with entire characters as the horizontal scrolling unit; notice the ragged left edge.

```
utters had been thrown back, and with
tion of horror not to be described, I saw
pen window a figure the most hideous
orred. A grin was on the face of the mons
hed to jeer, as with his fiendish finger he
 towards the corpse of my wife.
```

FIGURE 11-10: The text from Figure 11-8 displayed with pixels as the horizontal scrolling unit; the left edge is cleaner than in Figure 11-9.

The screen is pinned to an infinite plane, the display window is pinned to the screen, and the text moves about when we scroll. The top left corner of the screen is at (0, 0), and (*x, y*) values increase as we move right and down. The top left corner of the window is at (0, 10), with the top left corner of the text display area at (10, 20) because of the left margin and the window's title bar. This means *leftmost_x* = 10 and *topmost_y* = 20. Initially, *cur_leftmost_x* is also 10. As we scroll horizontally, moving text to the left, *cur_leftmost_x* decreases. If we scroll left 30 pixels, so that the leftmost pixel displayed is 30 pixels right of the first pixel in the line, *cur_left_most_x* will be 10 – 30 = –20.

Now we can recode *xy_to_char_struct()* to support horizontal scrolling. While we're at it, we'll make it more efficient by not computing *(cur_y + line–>height)* and *(cur_x + ch–>width)* twice. We'll also extend the idea of *leftmost_x* and *topmost_y* to check for coordinates to the right of or below the text's display region. Finally, we'll fix this version so it deals correctly with partially filled lines and partially filled screens. This is done by using a new global, *last_line*, which points to the last line being displayed, and by adding a *last_char* member to the *line_header* typedef.

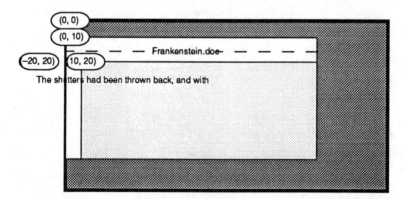

FIGURE 11-11: The relationship between text, the display area, the window, and the screen after scrolling text to the left.

```
/* screen region text is displayed in: */
int      topmost_y;
int      leftmost_x;
int      bottommost_y;
int      rightmost_x;

line_header *first_line;
line_header *last_line;

typedef struct line_header {
   struct line_header    *next,
                         *prev;
   struct char_element   *first_char,
                         *last_char;
   int                   height; /* in pixels */
} line_header;

typedef struct char_element {
   struct char_element   *next,
                         *prev;
   char                  value;
   int                   width; /* in pixels */
} char_element;

/*==============================================================*/
char_element    *xy_to_char_struct(x, y)
   int  x,   /* IN */
        y;   /* IN */
/*- - - - - - - - - - - - - - - - - - - - - - - - - - - - - - -
Purpose:
   Finds the character struct whose region a given screen
   coordinate falls in. Assumes screen coordinates are oriented
   like this:
        +- - - -> +x
        |
        |
     +y v
```

The screen region for a newline extends right from the
newline's first pixel to x = +infinity. Similarly, the screen
region for the last character in the file extends right and
downward to x = +infinity, y = +infinity. In practice, the
values passed in will always be finite, since they must lie in
some window on the screen. The reason for these big regions
is to make sure the screen regions fill the window the text is
displayed in—there should be no "dead" regions in the
displayed text.

Parameters:
    global line_header *first_line; this points to the first line
       currently displayed
    global line_header *last_line; this points to the last line
       currently displayed (might be cut horizontally by the
       bottom edge of the window)
    global ints topmost_y, bottommost_y, leftmost_x, rightmost_x;
       these delimit the display area
    global int cur_leftmost_x; this is the current left edge of
       the text, which is not necessarily inside the display
       area
    x, y   screen coordinate
    Returns pointer to character's struct, or NULL if given (x, y)
    doesn't fall in any character's screen region.

```
- - - - - - - - - - - - - - - - - - - - - - - - - - - - - - - - - - - - - - -*/
{
    line_header     *line;
    char_element    *ch;
    int             cur_x, cur_y;

    /* outside screen region text is displayed in? */
    if ((x < leftmost_x)  || (y < topmost_y) ||
       (x > rightmost_x)  || (y > bottommost_y) )
        return (NULL);
     for (   line = first_line, cur_y = topmost_y;
             (line &&
                    ((cur_y += line->height) < bottommost_y) &&
                    (cur_y < y));
                line = line->next ) {
        /* empty */
     }
     /* selected a point below the last line of a partially */
     /* filled text display region? */
     if (!line)
         line = last_line;
     for (   ch = line->first_char, cur_x = cur_leftmost_x;
             (ch &&
                 ((cur_x += ch->width) < rightmost_x) &&
                 (cur_x < x));
             ch = ch->next ) {
        /* empty */
     }
     /* selected a point to the right of last character in line? */
     if (!ch)
         ch = line->last_char;
     return (ch);
} /* xy_to_char_struct */
```

Only question 11 is left: Have we satisfied the ADTD? Well, we've decided how to organize characters to support the screen-to-struct mapping while still supporting typical word processor operations like insertion. We've also decided how to represent display lines of text.

We haven't said much about representing words, but there's not much to say. A word is a contiguous string of characters that contains no white space or punctuation. Given a pointer to a character, it's easy to chase the forward and backward links from that character until we find the first and last character of the surrounding word. So we can implement words as follows:

```
typedef struct {
   char_element  *first_char,
                 *last_char;
} word;
```

If we find we need lists of words, we can add the necessary pointers. This also effectively implements the "contains" operator. The "precedes" operator is implemented by the underlying list of *char_element* structs for words and characters, and by the list of *line_header* structs for lines. Implementing functions to create a new list-of-lists, insert and delete elements, and traverse the list will be straightforward. Finally, notice that there's no hard limit on the number of elements in the list-of-lists as implemented. So we have in fact implemented the ADTD, or at least the hardest parts thereof.

One final note before turning to the code. All this was just our first attempt! We could try other implementations, but instead, we'll just summarize the choices made along the way that could be made differently without changing the ADTD or causing problems with implementation of typical operations like deletion.

1. If memory is scarce, we could use singly linked lists.
2. If memory is scarce, we could use some caching scheme so that only the displayed text is actually in the doubly linked list. A compromise would be to keep N pages before and after the displayed text in memory, and leave the rest of the file on disk.

LISTING: s2s.c

```
/*- - - - - - - - - - - - - - - - - - - - - - - - - - - - - - - - - - -
                              s2s.c
- - - - - - - - - - - - - - - - - - - - - - - - - - - - - - - - - - -*/

/*===================================================================
Purpose:
   This file provides a testbed that exercises the screen-to-struct
   mapping function s2s_xy_to_char_struct(); the testbed driver is
   main().The "s2s" in this file's name stands for "screen-to-
   struct".
```

```
   This code was compiled under LightspeedC (TM) on a Macintosh SE.
- - - - - - - - - - - - - - - - - - - - - - - - - - - - - - - - - - - - - - - - -*/
#include <stdio.h>
#include <Storage.h>
#include <boolean.h>

/* Useful abbreviations:
   sel = selected
   cur = current
   da  = display area
*/

typedef struct line_header {
   struct line_header *next,
                *prev;
   struct char_element    *first_char,
               *last_char;
   int          height; /* in pixels */
} line_header;

typedef struct char_element {
    struct char_element   *next,
                *prev;
   char         value;
   int          width; /* in pixels */
} char_element;

typedef struct {
   char_element    *first_char,
            *last_char;
} word;

/* screen region text is displayed in: */
int     da_top;
int     da_left;
int     da_width;
int     da_height;

int     cur_leftmost_x;

char_element    *first_sel_char;
char_element    *last_sel_char;

line_header     *first_line;
line_header     *last_line;

#define _S2S_TESTBED_
#ifdef  _S2S_TESTBED_
```

```
/*=================================================================*/
main()
/*- - - - - - - - - - - - - - - - - - - - - - - - - - - - - - - -
Purpose:
   Test s2s_xy_to_char_struct().
Parameters:
   none, but test data is either read interactively or generated
   automatically
- - - - - - - - - - - - - - - - - - - - - - - - - - - - - - - -*/
{
   int          x, y, ch,
                display_area_top, display_area_left,
                display_area_width, display_area_height,
                chelm_width, chelm_height;
   char_element  *chelm_ptr,
                *s2s_append_char(),
                *s2s_xy_to_char_struct();
   char         chelm_value;
   boolean        s2s_inited();
   void         s2s_dump();
   FILE        *fopen(), *dump_fp;
   char         response[8]; /* "yes" or "no" */
   boolean        interactive;

   printf("Testing screen-to-structs mapping library...\n");
   printf("Do you want to enter test points interactively?\n");
   printf("Answering 'No' causes test data to be generated\n");
   printf("automatically. Enter points interactively? (y/n) ");
   scanf("%s", response);
   ch = getchar(); /* toss carriage return */
   if ((response[0] == 'y') || (response[0] == 'Y'))
      interactive = true;
   else
      interactive = false;
   if (interactive) {
      printf("Display area top, left, width, height> ");
      scanf( "%d %d %d %d",
           &display_area_top,
           &display_area_left,
           &display_area_width,
           &display_area_height);
      ch = getchar(); /* toss carriage return */
      if (!s2s_inited(display_area_top,
                  display_area_left,
                  display_area_width,
                  display_area_height)) {
         printf("Initialization failed\n");
         exit(-1);
```

```
          }
        printf("Enter characters and their screen sizes; set\n");
        printf("width or height to zero to terminate the list.\n");
        for (chelm_width = chelm_height = 1;
             ((chelm_width > 0) && (chelm_height > 0));
             ) {
          printf("\nnext char's value, width, height> ");
          scanf(  "%c %d %d",
                       &chelm_value, &chelm_width, &chelm_height);
          ch = getchar(); /* toss carriage return */
          if ((chelm_width > 0) && (chelm_height > 0) &&
              !s2s_append_char(
                           chelm_value, chelm_width, chelm_height)) {
              printf("Failed to append char_element struct\n");
              chelm_width = chelm_height = 0;
          }
        }
      }
      else { /* generate test data automatically */
          display_area_top    = 0;
          display_area_left   = 0;
          display_area_width  = 100;
          display_area_height = 200;
      if (!s2s_inited(display_area_top,
                  display_area_left,
                  display_area_width,
                  display_area_height)) {
          printf("Initialization failed\n");
          exit(-1);
        }
        if (!s2s_chars_appended()) {
          printf("Fill with test data failed\n");
          exit(-1);
        }
      } /* if interactive */
      printf("\n");
      printf("Now we have the test data, we can test the mapping.\n");
      printf("Enter (x, y) screen coordinates; to terminate\n");
      printf("the list, enter x = y = -1.\n");
      printf("After each coordinate is entered, the character it\n");
      printf("points to will be displayed, with its char_element\n");
      printf("address.\n");
      for (x = y = 0; ((x != -1) && (y != -1)); ) {
        printf("\nnext x, y> ");
        scanf("%d %d", &x, &y);
        ch = getchar(); /* toss carriage return */
        if ((x != -1) && (y != -1)) {
          if (!(chelm_ptr = s2s_xy_to_char_struct(x, y))) {
```

```
        printf("\nOutside screen display area.");
      }
      else {
        printf( "\nValue: %c", chelm_ptr->value);
      }
    }
  }
  if (!(dump_fp = fopen("s2s_dump", "w"))) {
    printf("fopen s2s_dump failed\n");
    exit(-1);
  }
  printf("\nDumping test data to file: s2s_dump.");
  s2s_dump(dump_fp, true);
  fclose(dump_fp);
  printf("\nDone testing for now.\n");
} /* main */
#endif _S2S_TESTBED_


/*===============================================================*/
boolean    s2s_inited(top, left, width, height)
   int top,      /* IN */
     left,       /* IN */
     width,      /* IN */
     height;     /* IN */
/*- - - - - - - - - - - - - - - - - - - - - - - - - - - - - - - -
Purpose:
  Initialize the screen-to-struct mapping globals.
Parameters:
  global line_header *first_line, *last_line; these are NULLed,
        global ints da_top, da_left, da_width, da_height;
  global ints da_top, da_left, da_width, da_height;
        these delimit the display area; they're set to the
        values passed in top, left, width, and height, if
        those values define a rectangle with area
  global int cur_leftmost_x; set to the left value passed in
- - - - - - - - - - - - - - - - - - - - - - - - - - - - - - - - -*/
{
  if ((width <= 0) || (height <= 0)) {
    printf("s2s_inited: display rectangle has no area\n");
    return (false);
  }
  da_top    = top;
  da_left   = left;
  da_width  = width;
  da_height = height;
  cur_leftmost_x = da_left;
  first_sel_char = NULL;
  last_sel_char  = NULL;
```

```
      first_line    = NULL;
      last_line     = NULL;
      return (true);
   } /* s2s_inited*/


   /*==============================================================*/
   char_element    *s2s_append_char(value, width, height)
      char    value;    /* IN */
      int      width,   /* IN */
               height;  /* IN */
   /*- - - - - - - - - - - - - - - - - - - - - - - - - - - - - - - -
   Purpose:
      Append new character at end of character list, that is, at end
      of text file. This function is used to build a collection of
      data to test s2s_xy_to_char_struct(); in a production word
      processor, of course, we'd need general insertion and deletion
      routines, not just one to append chars.
   Parameters:
      global line_header *first_line, *last_line; these are updated
      value    ASCII character value
      width,
      height   size of character's rectangular screen region in pixels
      Returns pointer to new char struct; returns NULL on failure
   - - - - - - - - - - - - - - - - - - - - - - - - - - - - - - - -*/
   {
      char_element    *new_chelm, *nxch;
      line_header    *new_line;
      int             total_width;
      void         *malloc();

      if (width > da_width) {
        printf("s2s_append_char: character is too wide\n");
        return (NULL);
      }
      if (height > da_height) {
        printf("s2s_append_char: character is too high\n");
        return (NULL);
      }
      if (!(new_chelm =
            (char_element *)malloc(sizeof(char_element)))) {
        printf("s2s_append_char: out of memory\n");
        return (NULL);
      }
      new_chelm->value = value;
      new_chelm->width = width;
      new_chelm->next  = NULL;  /* append at end of char list */
      if (!last_line) {
        /* this is the first s2s_append_char() call after init */
```

```
  if (!(last_line =
         (line_header *)malloc(sizeof(line_header))))) {
    printf("s2s_append_char: out of memory\n");
    free(new_chelm);
    return (NULL);
  }
  first_line = last_line;
  last_line->next = NULL;
  last_line->prev = NULL;
  last_line->height = height;
  last_line->first_char = new_chelm;
  last_line->last_char  = new_chelm;
  new_chelm->prev = NULL;
  return (new_chelm);
}
/* decide whether to add char to current last line or
   make new line: */
for (  nxch = last_line->first_char, total_width = 0;
     nxch && (total_width + width <= da_width);
     total_width += nxch->width, nxch = nxch->next ) {
  /* empty */
}
if (total_width + width <= da_width) {
  last_line->last_char->next = new_chelm;
  new_chelm->prev = last_line->last_char;
  last_line->last_char = new_chelm;
  if (last_line->height < height)
    last_line->height = height;
  return (new_chelm);
}
else {
if (!(new_line =
            (line_header *)malloc(sizeof(line_header)))) {
    printf("s2s_append_char: out of memory\n");
    free(new_chelm);
    return (NULL);
  }
  new_line->first_char = new_chelm;
  new_line->last_char  = new_chelm;
  new_line->next = NULL;
  new_line->prev = last_line;
  new_line->height = height;
  new_chelm->prev = last_line->last_char;
  last_line->last_char->next = new_chelm;
  last_line->next = new_line;
  last_line = new_line;
  return (new_chelm);
}
```

```
    } /* s2s_append_char */

    /*=================================================================*/
    static boolean    s2s_chars_appended()
    /*- - - - - - - - - - - - - - - - - - - - - - - - - - - - - - - - -
    Purpose:
        Fill the display area with test data so we can check the
        screen-to-struct mapping.
    Parameters:
        none, but of course which characters are on which lines
        depends on the da_* globals and the values hard-coded inside
        test function
    - - - - - - - - - - - - - - - - - - - - - - - - - - - - - - - - -*/
    {
        char_element     *new, *s2s_append_char();
        char             ch;

        ch = 'a';
        /* display is 100 wide by 200 high */
        /* line 1 is 10 high, 2 chars, each 50 wide */
        if (!(new = s2s_append_char(ch++,50,5)))  /* height will be 10 */
           return (false);
        if (!(new = s2s_append_char(ch++,50,10)))  /* force height=10 */
           return (false);
        /* line 2 is 10 high, 3 chars, each end character is
           narrow and center is wide: */
        if (!(new = s2s_append_char(ch++,1,1)))
           return (false);
        if (!(new = s2s_append_char(ch++,98,1)))
           return (false);
        if (!(new = s2s_append_char(ch++,1,10)))
           return (false);
        /* line 3 is just 1 high, 4 chars of width 25 each */
        if (!(new = s2s_append_char(ch++,25,1)))
           return (false);
        if (!(new = s2s_append_char(ch++,25,1)))
           return (false);
        if (!(new = s2s_append_char(ch++,25,1)))
           return (false);
        if (!(new = s2s_append_char(ch++,25,1)))
           return (false);
        /* line 4 is just 1 narrow char with height 10; region should be
           extended by s2s_xy_to_char_struct() all the way to the right
           edge as if the char were 100 wide, and down as if it were
           200 - 21 = 179 high: */
        if (!(new = s2s_append_char(ch++,1,10)))
           return (false);
        return (true);
```

```
} /* s2s_chars_appended*/

/*================================================================*/
static void        s2s_dump( fp, dump_chars )
    FILE    *fp;         /* IN */
    boolean dump_chars; /* IN */
/*- - - - - - - - - - - - - - - - - - - - - - - - - - - - - - - - - -
Purpose:
    Print the current screen-to-struct mapping info for debugging.
Parameters:
    fp          open stream to dump to; a stream is passed instead
                of a filename in case we want to dump to stdout or
                stderr
    dump_chars  if true, dump all screen-to-struct globals and
                whatever they lead to, including all char_element
                structs and line_header structs;
                if false, dump the globals and line header structs
- - - - - - - - - - - - - - - - - - - - - - - - - - - - - - - - - -*/
{
    line_header        *next_line;
    char_element       *next_chelm;
    int                top, left, bottom, right;

    fprintf(fp,
            "da: top = %d left = %d width = %d height = %d\n",
            da_top,
            da_left,
            da_width,
            da_height);
    fprintf(fp,
            "cur_leftmost_x = %d\n",
            cur_leftmost_x);
    top  = da_top;
    left = da_left;
    for (   next_line = first_line;
            next_line;
            top += next_line->height,
                left = da_left,
                next_line = next_line->next) {
        fprintf(fp,
                "LINE @ %08lx: height = %d ",
                next_line,
                next_line->height);
        fprintf(fp,
                "next = %08lx prev = %08lx\n",
                next_line->next,
                next_line->prev);
        fprintf(fp,
```

```
                        "    first_char = %08lx (%c) ",
                    next_line->first_char,
                    ((next_line->first_char) ?
                        next_line->first_char->value : ' '));
            fprintf(fp,
                    "last_char = %08lx (%c)\n",
                    next_line->last_char,
                    ((next_line->last_char) ?
                        next_line->last_char->value : ' '));
        if (dump_chars) {
            for (   next_chelm = next_line->first_char;
                    next_chelm &&
                        (next_chelm->prev != next_line->last_char);
                    left += next_chelm->width,
                        next_chelm = next_chelm->next) {
                fprintf(fp,
                        "CHAR (%c) @ %08lx: width = %d ",
                        next_chelm->value,
                        next_chelm,
                        next_chelm->width);
                fprintf(fp,
                        "next = %08lx prev = %08lx\n",
                        next_chelm->next,
                        next_chelm->prev);
                fprintf(fp,
                        "    region = (%d,%d) to (%d,%d)\n",
                        left,
                        top,
                        left + next_chelm->width,
                        top + next_line->height);
            } /* for each char in line */
        } /* if dump_chars */
    } /* for each line */
} /* s2s_dump */


/*=============================================================*/
char_element    *s2s_xy_to_char_struct(x, y)
    int x,  /* IN */
        y;  /* IN */
/*- - - - - - - - - - - - - - - - - - - - - - - - - - - - - - -
Purpose:
    Finds the character struct whose region a given screen
    coordinate falls in. Assumes screen coordinates are oriented
    like this:
                    +- - - -> +x
                    |
                    |
                +y  v
```

The screen region for a newline extends right from the
newline's first pixel to x = +infinity. Similarly, the screen
region for the last character in the file extends right and
downward to x = +infinity, y = +infinity. In practice, the
values passed in will always be finite, since they must lie in
some window on the screen. The reason for these big regions
is to make sure the screen regions fill the window the text is
displayed in—there should be no "dead" regions in the
displayed text.
Parameters:
      global line_header *first_line; this points to the first line
              currently displayed
      global line_header *last_line; this points to the last line
              currently displayed (might be cut horizontally by the
              bottom edge of the window)
      global ints da_top, da_left, da_width, da_height;
              these delimit the display area
      global int cur_leftmost_x; this is the current left edge of
              the text, which is not necessarily inside the display
              area
      x, y   screen coordinate
      Returns pointer to character's struct, or NULL if given (x, y)
      doesn't fall in any character's screen region.
--*/
{
    line_header   *line;
    char_element   *ch;
    int   cur_x, cur_y;

    /* outside screen region text is displayed in? */
    if ((x < da_left) || (y < da_top) ||
        (x >= da_left + da_width) || (y >= da_top + da_height))
        return (NULL);
    for (line = first_line, cur_y = da_top;
            (line &&
                ((cur_y += line->height) < da_top + da_height) &&
                (cur_y <= y));
            line = line->next) {
        /* empty */
    }
    /* selected a point below the last line of a partially */
    /* filled text display region? */
    if (!line)
        line = last_line;
    for (ch = line->first_char, cur_x = cur_leftmost_x;
            (ch &&
                ((cur_x += ch->width) < da_left + da_width) &&
                (cur_x <= x));
            ch = ch->next) {

```
            /* empty */
    }
    /* selected a point to the right of last character in line? */
    if (!ch)
        ch = line->last_char;
    return (ch);
} /* s2s_xy_to_char_struct */
```

CHAPTER 12

Matching Structs to Screen Regions: A Window Manager Solution

In the previous chapter, we implemented a screen-to-structs mapping for a word processor. In this chapter, we want to implement that mapping for a window manager. The first question is this: Is it "fair" to use insights gained from the word processor design and implementation during the window manager design and implementation?

After all, if our original goal had been nothing more than implementing the screen-to-struct mapping for a window manager, we wouldn't have done the work in the previous chapter. So in some sense, it's unfair to present a solution here that uses insights or code from the word processor chapter.

However, we did do that work, and it's foolish to ignore related problems that are already solved. So if you haven't read the previous chapter or the introduction to the screen-to-struct mapping, go read them before continuing, because we will use them in this chapter. We'll refer to them as the "word processor chapter" and "introduction," respectively.

In the introduction, we developed two guiding examples that suggested a "sheets-of-paper" geometry: windows and simulations. We'll focus here on windows. We need to write an ADTD for the sheets-of-paper geometry, but first let's recall the highlights of our example.

This is a typical instance of the screen-to-struct mapping process we're interested in, adapted very slightly from the introduction:

1. A window manager's user moves the mouse to position the cursor over a particular part of a particular window.
2. The user presses the mouse button down, moves the mouse, and then lets the button up.
3. The window manager notes that a selection is being made and assembles the information related to the selection—the (x, y) cursor positions and times for each button position. The cursor positions and times are far enough apart and in the right order (position cursor, button down, position cursor, button up) so that the entire sequence is interpreted as a drag from $(x1, y1)$ to $(x2, y2)$.
4. The window manager determines that four selectable items are partly or totally displayed in the drag region: a scroll box, a scroll bar the box can move in, the window the scroll bar and box are associated with, and a second window.
5. The window manager knows that the four selectable items are stacked, with the second window on the bottom, the first window on top of that, the first window's scroll bar on top of both windows, and the scroll box on top of the other three items. Since the scroll box is on top, the selection applies to it. A drag means "move the scroll box, if the starting and ending positions are in the box's scroll bar." Since $(x2, y2)$ is in the scroll bar, the box is moved, and the window manager sends a message to the application so it can do whatever is appropriate, such as scrolling text.

Our problem is finding a good way to accomplish step 4. That is, suppose the user sees an item at a particular position on the screen and selects that position somehow. How do we map that screen position to the internal structures that correspond to the item(s) displayed at that position? After we've found them, it's up to the window manager to choose between the structs we've presented as the only possible selections.

TOP-LEVEL GOALS

Our goals are the same as in the introduction and the word processor chapter. The mapping from screen (x, y) values to internal structs must be fast. It must be easy to add or remove visible choices. Good error recovery is important, and reliability and consistency are essential.

GUIDING EXAMPLES

In the introduction, we characterized windows as follows:

Regular?	Run About?	Overlap?	Example
no	no	arbitrary	windows

This characterization was developed from the description of windows in the introduction. "Regular?—no" means that we can't expect windows to be arranged in regular rows and columns. "Run About?–no" means they do not move about on their own for arbitrarily long periods in ways that are hard to predict. We're concentrating on windows, not simulations.

"Overlap?—arbitrary" means that windows' screen regions overlap in arbitrary ways. One region might contain another, they might each contain a corner of the other, they might not overlap at all, and so on.

ABSTRACT DATA TYPE DESCRIPTION

Now we're ready to complete the abstract data type description we started in the introduction. We'll start by stating clearly what collections we're dealing with.

What name does this particular collection of data elements go by, that is, what abstract data type are we concerned with? At first glance, the data elements are windows and all the various window components—slide bars, size boxes, title bars, close boxes, buttons, and so forth. But we don't care about the differences in functionality between these components. We care only about screen regions. This being the case, we can lump all these window components together and call them instances of a "sheet." Sheets are flat, can overlap each other (however, see Figure 10-1 in the introduction), and occupy rectangular screen regions. We want to decide how to organize our collection of sheet structs to make the screen-to-struct mapping most efficient.

What is the geometry of the collection? It is the sheets-of-paper geometry from the introduction. Recall that our mental model of this geometry is a group of two-dimensional rectangles of different sizes floating parallel to each other in three-dimensional space. Each rectangle represents a window or window component. The rectangles are parallel to each other because a window cannot be at once both half over and half under another window.

These rectangles are ordered by the (x, y, z) coordinates of, say, their top left corners. The x- and y-components of a given point in any rectangle are just the point's screen coordinates. The z-component is something we generate to reflect the number of windows in front of the point.

What relations hold between the data elements in the collection? The relations for the list-of-lists geometry were "precedes" and "contains." In the sheets-of-paper geometry, we can define a "precedes" relation even though sheets may overlap by considering just one corner of each sheet; we'll use the top left corner. Similarly, there is no "contains" relation, but there is an "overlaps" relation. Finally, we need a way to handle depths. We could add a relation "is in front of," but we can use "precedes" just as easily by specifying that $(x1, y1, z1)$ precedes $(x2, y2, z2)$ no matter what $x1$, $x2$, $y1$, and $y2$ are as long as $z1 > z2$.

Or can we? Suppose we have the following three sheets:

sheet A: top left corner at (10, 10), depth equal to 0 (it is on top of sheet B)
sheet B: top left corner at (10, 10), depth equal to –1 (it is below sheet A)
sheet C: top left corner at (110, 110), depth equal to 0

Which order is correct? More precisely, since we get to define the meaning of "precedes," which order do we want to be correct?

The definition of "precedes" given above to avoid adding "is in front of" would put the sheets in the order A, C, B. C precedes B because 0 > -1. But A and B are much more likely to be selected together than A and C. It seems likely that A and B, therefore, should be together according to "precedes." To get the order A, B, C, we will change our definition of "precedes" to the following:

> $(x1, y1, z1)$ precedes $(x2, y2, z2)$ if $(x1, y1)$ precedes $(x2, y2)$, that is, if $(x1, y1)$ is encountered before $(x2, y2)$ when we scan the screen from left to right and top to bottom beginning at the top left corner.

This makes "precedes" a partial ordering, so we should define "is in front of" after all. But we probably won't need to use "is in front of," because we'll return sheets at all depths as possible selections. To put it another way, the screen-to-structs mapping is just part of the selection process, and it is a part in which we only have to worry about (x, y) values; depth will be taken into account by another part of the selection process.

What relations hold between this collection and other collections? The relations between the collection of sheets and the other collections of structs in the window manager is similar to that between the list-of-lists collection and the other structs in a word processor. That is, sheet structs are actually portions of whatever window manager structs represent selectable items:

```
typedef struct selectable {
   /* fields related to screen-to-struct mapping */
   /* fields related to other operations */
} selectable;
```

The fields related to the screen-to-struct mapping do not vary from one window manager to another; only the other fields change. We saw something like this in Chapter 9, "Protecting a Database During Editing." As in the word processor chapter, we need to be sure that the screen-to-struct mapping is implemented in a way that does not interfere with other window manager operations.

What are the properties of each position in the geometry with respect to the operators and with respect to elements in other positions? Each sheet lies at some depth, so the "precedes" relation gives rise not only to "first" and "last" positions, but also to "first in layer" and "last in layer" for each layer, that is, for each z-value. In other words, given two windows in a layer at depth (say) –2, one of the windows is closer to the top left corner than the other.

What rules does each relation follow? As noted above, the "precedes" relation is a partial ordering. The "overlaps" relation is reflexive, since every sheet overlaps itself. "Overlaps" is symmetric if we agree that overlapping means intersection, not containment; x overlaps y if and only if y overlaps x. But "overlaps" is not transitive—x can overlap y and y overlap z without x overlapping z, as shown in Figure 12-1.

What are the operators? Taking a hint from the word processor chapter, we note that it isn't necessary to list here all the operations possible in a window manager. We are interested

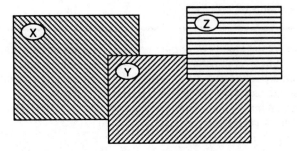

FIGURE 12-1: The "overlaps" relation is not transitive.

only in operations that pertain directly to the mapping from screen space to internal structs. The most important of these is the mapping operation: Given a screen region, find all sheet structs whose regions intersect the screen region.

We also need a few additional operations: create an empty collection of sheets, add a struct and its associated region to a collection of sheets, delete a struct and its associated region. As a debugging tool, it would also be nice to print the entire collection of sheets, including, of course, all current screen region boundaries.

What are the restrictions on membership in the collection? The only structs of interest are those that have an associated screen region. There's no hard limit on the number of elements in our collection of sheets. Membership is not based on the values of current or prospective members. Instead, membership is based on how a struct is used—if it represents a visible choice, it's in, if not, it's out.

How many collections are allowed by this ADT? We're envisioning one collection of sheets. A subset of the collection can be operated on as though it is the entire collection as long as every sheet overlapped by a sheet in the collection is also in the collection. This condition ensures that we'll get the same results for any screen point that is in the union of the subcollection's screen regions as we would for the entire collection. Adding the rest of the sheets to the subcollection won't add to the set of sheets which contain the selected point.

What is the meaning of each element in the collection? Each element in the collection represents a user-selectable visible choice: a window or some window component. Meaning for us has nothing to do with the difference between a slide bar and a close box, for instance. A sheet's "meaning" is its screen region, period.

ATTEMPT ONE

All the unanswered questions have been collected into Box 12-1. The questions were generated by adapting pertinent questions asked in the word processor chapter to the sheets-of-paper geometry we're using in this chapter.

BOX 12-1: Unanswered questions.

1. How should we implement the sheets-of-paper geometry as a linked data structure? We need to determine the overall scheme (list, tree, or something else), choose between singly and doubly linked structures after examining memory requirements and other tradeoffs, and decide how to represent screen regions.
2. What are typical window manager operations that might conflict with efficient implementation of the screen-to-struct mapping?
3. Have we satisfied the ADTD?

We'll start answering question 1 by finding some examples of the ways screen regions can overlap. A good set of examples and the representation of character screen regions in the word processor chapter might be all we need to devise a good representation of window screen regions.

There are two main differences between character regions and window regions: the typical number of regions active at one time and the restrictions on how regions can overlap. Thousands of characters are typically selectable at one time. Searching character regions exhaustively to find selected structs takes too long because there are too many regions. By contrast, only a small number of window components are selectable at any time—more than a few hundred is very rare, and there are probably ten components or less if one open window fills the screen. This means a simple exhaustive linear search can be used to find all the regions that intersect a selected screen area.

Figure 12-2 shows some examples of the different ways sheets can overlap. Even if we consider only two regions at a time, there are many possibilities. With characters, the only type of overlap was containment—word regions contain character regions. Window overlap is much more complicated.

The examples in Figure 12-2 were generated using the method described in Chapter 3, "Choosing Good Guiding Examples." This means that every example differs from every other with respect to at least one fundamental characteristic. The fundamental characteristics used to distinguish these examples are the following:

whether the regions differ in width, height, both, or neither
whether the intersection of the two regions is empty, a point, a line, a subset of the two regions, one of the regions, or both of the regions
whether the regions came together vertically, horizontally, both, or neither
which region is on top
whether the top left corners of the regions share the same x-value, the same y-value, both values, or neither

The first thing to notice about the examples in Figure 12-2 is that there are so many of them. Figure 12-2 suggests that overlap examples are hard to classify, and that many additional examples could be found.

In other words, we should keep our data structure as simple as possible, because there's a very good chance we will overlook important cases if we assume too much about the ways sheets can overlap. So we'll use a simple doubly linked list of *window_region* structs:

```
typedef struct window_region {
    struct window_region    *next,
                            *prev;
    int                     tlx,    /* top left corner (x, y) */
                            tly;
    int                     width,  /* width in pixels */
                            height, /* height in scanlines  */
                            depth;  /* 0 = on top, else < 0 */
    struct who_knows        *window_internals;
    /* whatever this particular window system needs to
       represent windows—this is probably one thing for
       a Macintosh and quite another for an IBM PC or a Sun,
       for instance */
} window_region;
```

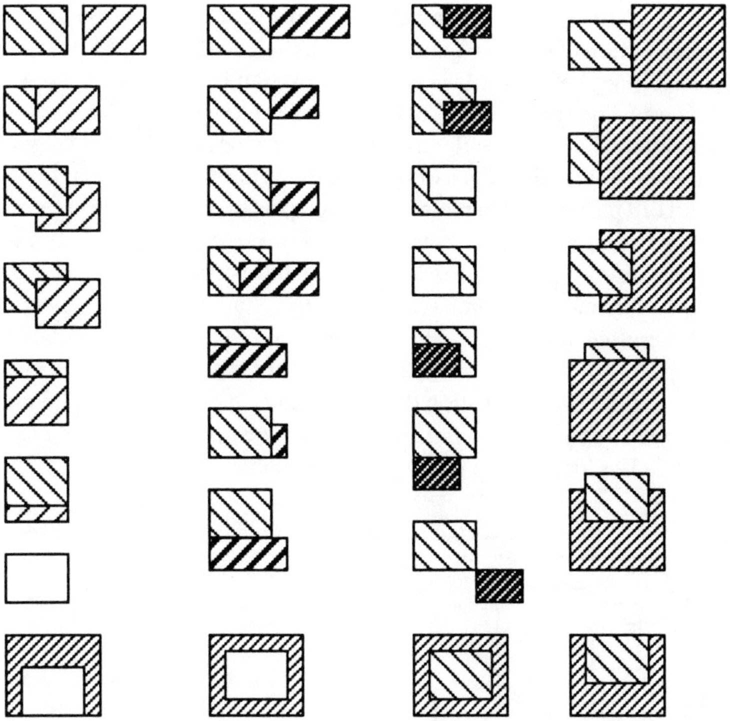

FIGURE 12-2: Some of the many ways two screen regions can overlap or abut each other. Patterns identify particular regions; all regions of a given size are filled with the same pattern. However, if one of the regions is completely under the other, it is shown filled with white space instead of its customary pattern. In all other cases, only that portion of a region which is not under the other region is shown.

Notice that we're using starting positions plus offsets instead of using absolute positions; we borrowed this idea from the word processor chapter.

We're relying in two ways on the fact that there aren't more than a few hundred of these *window_region* structs. First, we made the list doubly-linked instead of singly-linked without worrying about the memory required to hold those backward-pointing *window_region.prev* values. The backward links will be useful when the list order needs to be updated because a window was moved. Second, we used a simple list instead of a tree or a hashed list or some other fast access organization. If the list isn't more than a few hundred elements long, we can afford the time needed to search it exhaustively for regions that intersect the selected screen area.

Actually, the search doesn't have to be exhaustive. Now we'll see that our choice of "precedes" definitions was correct. We'll keep the *window_region* list ordered from screen top left to bottom right according to the coordinates of each region's top left corner. This means we can stop searching for more intersections after reaching a *window_region* whose top left corner is below the selected screen area. This is illustrated in Figure 12-3. Notice that we're comparing single points—top left window corners—against an entire region.

Notice from Figure 12-3 that we cannot stop our search after encountering a region that is to the right of the selected area but not below it. If we did stop at region B, we'd overlook the intersection of regions C and D with the selected area. We can eliminate B, but we can't stop searching the list until we encounter region E. Since E is below the selected area, and F follows E, neither E nor F can intersect the selected area.

We can eliminate B from consideration no matter what its width and height are because windows don't wrap around the edges of the screen. Windows don't wrap because we view the screen as part of a plane, not as a rectangular viewport on a cylinder or sphere. If windows wrapped, moving a window's top left corner to the bottom right corner of the screen would make part of the window appear at the screen's top left corner.

So much for *window_region.next*, *.prev*, *.tlx*, *.tly*, *.width*, and *.height*. What is *window_region.window_internals*? This is just a pointer to whatever data the window manager we're dealing with requires. This includes, but is not limited to, display characteristics, information about the application that is running inside a window, and pointers to the code and data structures needed to perform a window component's functions—the things that make it a slide bar instead of a close box, for instance.

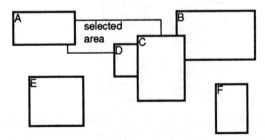

FIGURE 12-3: Six sheets and a selected screen area. The windows are ordered from top left to bottom right—A, B, C, D, E, F.

Remember, we're interested only in finding window components whose regions intersect a selected area of the screen. It's not our job to worry overmuch about what happens to those components once we tell the window manager they've been selected.

The only part of our structure left to explain is *window_region.depth*. Recall our scheme of setting *depth* to zero for the topmost window, and *depth* to minus *N* for a window that is under *N* other windows. But who keeps track of *depth*? We've been speaking all along of handing every possible selected region to the window manager and letting it decide what to do with them. In Figure 12-3, for instance, regions A, C, and D intersect the selected area, so they are the ones our screen-to-struct mapping function should return when we pass it the six regions and the selected area shown in that figure.

The window manager might decide to select all three regions, or to select none, or to select only the regions on top (A and C). In any case, only the window manager proper needs to read *window_region.depth*. What's more, only the window manager can set *window_region.depth*, because the screen-to-struct mapping function doesn't know (and shouldn't know) the rules for moving one window on top of another. In other words, we'll need something like *depth*, but it should be part of the data pointed to by *window_region.window_internals*.

The screen-to-struct mapping function will return a sublist of the list of all *window_regions*, but how? How can a function return a list or sublist of values? There are many possibilities. We could allocate an array of *window_region* pointers inside each call to the mapping function. We could set a flag in selected structs. We could allocate a linked list of pointers to selected regions inside the mapper. We could add more pointers to the *window_region* typedef and keep a list of selected regions within the list of all regions. We could make the mapping function return one selected *window_region* at a time and call it as many times as necessary.

The tradeoffs between these approaches are described in the design guideline "Returning a Sublist" (page 369). Bearing this guideline in mind, we'll add a new pointer to the *window_region* struct and use it to maintain a sublist of selected regions, as illustrated in Figure 12-4.

The answer to question 1, then, is that we'll use a doubly linked list of *window_region* structs that use top left corner plus width and height values to represent screen regions. The modified *window_region* typedef is shown below.

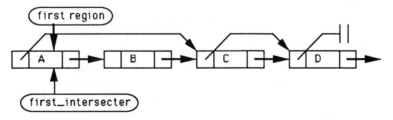

FIGURE 12-4:   A sublist of regions—A, C, and D—within the list of all window component regions.

```
typedef struct window_region {
    struct window_region     *next,
                             *prev,
                             *next_intersecter;
    int                      tlx,   /* top left corner (x, y) */
                             tly;
    int                      width, /* width in pixels */
                             height;/* height in scanlines  */
    struct who_knows         *window_internals;
} window_region;
```

Notice that we've moved the *depth* value into *window_internals*. We've also added the pointer *next_intersecter* to maintain a sublist of regions that intersect the selected screen area; the screen-to-struct mapper will return a pointer to the first *window_region* in this sublist.

To answer question 2, let's recall the answer to the corresponding question from the word processor chapter. We came up with the following typical word processor operations that might conflict with the screen-to-struct mapping:

open or close a file
scroll (horizontally or vertically)
change a string's font size
insert or delete a string
search for a string

The window operations suggested by these word processor operations are:

open or close a window
move all windows horizontally or vertically at once
resize a window
move one or more windows
(nothing corresponds to searching for a string)

Nothing in our planned implementation of a list of *window_regions* conflicts with any of these operations. The biggest concerns in the word processor chapter were memory requirements and search speed. Memory is not a concern with windows, because there are relatively few *window_region* structs. Search speed is not a concern because there's no concept of searching the list of structs for a particular sequence of *window_regions*. We are further insulated from affecting the rest of the window manager by using *window_region.window_internals* to explicitly separate the screen-to-struct mapping from the data used by a particular window manager.

This leaves question 3: Have we satisfied the ADTD? Yes, we have. The list of *window_regions* supports the "precedes" and "overlaps" operators, the sheets-of-paper geometry, and the rest of the ADTD. We're ready to write the screen-to-struct mapping function.

The essence of the mapping function is an intersection-finder. Given a selected area of the screen, we have to find all the intersections between the selected area and a given list of *window_regions*. From our look at different kinds of overlap in Figure 12-2, we know we need a way to classify the ways a *window_region* and a selected area can overlap. We don't want to miss any cases.

Suppose we imagine different placements of the *window_region* with respect to a selected area that is fixed in place. Figure 12-5 shows how the selected area divides the screen into nine sections. This will be true even if the selected area is a line or a point. Now imagine placing a *window_region* so its top left corner is in each of the sections. If the corner is inside the selected area, the *window_region* and selected area must intersect. Conversely, if the *window_region*'s top left corner is to the right of or below the selected area, the two cannot intersect.

This leaves Sections 1, 2, and 3. If the top left corner of the *window_region* is in Section 1, the region must extend both down and to the right if it is to intersect the selected area. In other words, suppose WR is a *window_region* whose top left corner is at *(WR.tlx, WR.tly)* and suppose the selected area is at (x, y) as shown in Figure 12-5. Then we have the following test:

```
if ((WR.tlx < x) && (WR.tly < y)) {
  if ((WR.tlx + WR.width >= x) && (WR.tly + WR.height >= y)) {
    /* WR intersects the selected area */
  }
  else {
    /* WR does not intersect the selected area */
  }
} /* if WR's top left corner is in Section 1 */
```

Similar tests can be used for Sections 2 and 3. However, the tests are simpler in these two cases. A *window_region* WR whose top left corner is in Section 2 need only extend down far enough to intersect the selected area—we need only to test *WR.tly + WR.height* against y. Likewise, if WR's top left corner is in Section 3, we need only test *WR.x + WR.width*

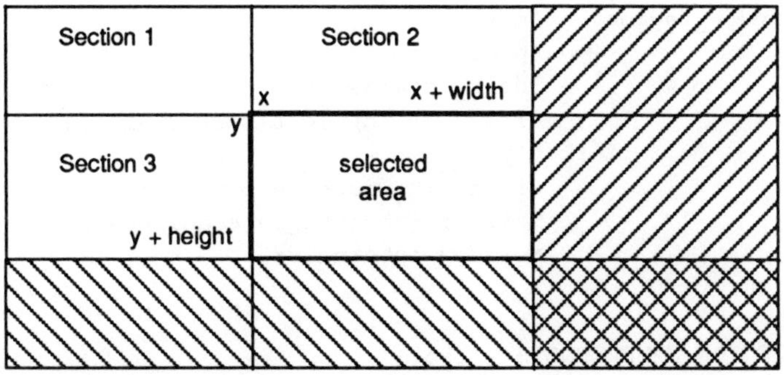

FIGURE 12-5:   Selecting a screen area divides the screen into nine sections. The selected screen area runs horizontally from *x* to *x* + width, and vertically from *y* to *y* + height.

against *x*. These tests are coded in the mapping function *intersecting_regions()* in our code at the end of the chapter.

We've answered the ADTD questions, and the questions that arose during our attempt at implementation, in sufficient detail to feel confident we haven't overlooked anything major. So we're ready to start coding.

LISTING: regions.c

```
/*- - - - - - - - - - - - - - - - - - - - - - - - - - - - - - - - - - - - - -
                              regions.c
- - - - - - - - - - - - - - - - - - - - - - - - - - - - - - - - - - - - - */

/*========================================================================
Purpose:
    This file provides a testbed that exercises the window manager
    screen-to-struct mapping function intersecting_regions(); the
    testbed driver is main().

    This code was compiled under LightspeedC (TM) on a Macintosh SE.
- - - - - - - - - - - - - - - - - - - - - - - - - - - - - - - - - - - - */
#include <stdio.h>
#include <Storage.h>
#include <boolean.h>

/* NOTE: window_region.window_internals is used in the testbed as
    the name of the region; in a real window manager, it would point
    to a structure that contained the window's name, display
    characteristics, or other information. We don't need any of that
    to test the screen-to-struct mapper, however, so we left it out.
*/
typedef struct window_region {
    struct window_region    *next,
                            *prev,
                            *next_intersecter;
    int                     tlx,    /* top left corner (x, y) */
                            tly;
    int                     width, /* width in pixels */
                            height;/* height in scanlines   */
    char                    *window_internals;
} window_region;

#define MAX_REGION_NAME_LENGTH    255

#define _REGIONS_TESTBED_
#ifdef  _REGIONS_TESTBED_
```

```
/*================================================================*/
main()
/*- - - - - - - - - - - - - - - - - - - - - - - - - - - - - - - -
Purpose:
    Test the screen-to-struct mapping function intersecting_regions().
Parameters:
    none—appended_regions() is used to build a test data set,
    and dump_region_lists() is used to determine the results, that
    is, to see if intersecting_regions() set up the correct list
    of regions that intersect the selected screen area.

    The test data is read from file "test_regions", which has the
    following syntax:

    <test_file>      = <selected area> <region list>
    <selected area> = <x> <y> <width> <height>
    <region list>   = (empty) | <region list> <region>
    <region>         = <name> <x> <y> <width> <height>
    <name>           = no more than MAX_REGION_NAME_LENGTH characters

    For instance, if this data is in "test_regions," all four
    regions shown should be on the intersecting regions list:

    30 30 40 40
    one   0   0   40 40
    two   60 0   40 40
    three 0   60 40 40
    four  60 60 40 40

    This set of test data corresponds to Figure 12-3 in the text; the
    list of intersecting regions contains A, C, and D:

    50 10 80 40
    A 0    0    60   40
    B 140  0    60   60
    C 110  30   40   80
    D 90   40   30   30
    E 20   70   50   50
    F 170  80   20   50

    Test results are printed to file "test_results."
- - - - - - - - - - - - - - - - - - - - - - - - - - - - - - - - - - */
{
    FILE            *fopen(), *fp;
    int             sel_x, sel_y, sel_w, sel_h,
                    reg_x, reg_y, reg_w, reg_h;
    char            reg_name[MAX_REGION_NAME_LENGTH + 1];
    void            dump_region_lists();
```

```
window_region    *appended_region(),
                 *first_reg = NULL,
                 *first_intersecter,
                 *new_reg = NULL,
                 *intersecting_regions();

printf("Testing screen-to-struct intersecting_regions()...\n");
if (!(fp = fopen("test_regions", "r"))) {
    printf("main: couldn't open file 'test_regions'\n");
    exit (-1);
}
if (fscanf( fp,
            "%d %d %d %d\n",
            &sel_x, &sel_y, &sel_w, &sel_h) != 4) {
    fclose(fp);
    printf("main: couldn't read selected area info\n");
    exit (-1);
}
printf( "selected area: %d %d %d %d\n",
        sel_x, sel_y, sel_w, sel_h);
while (fscanf( fp,
              "%s %d %d %d %d\n",
              reg_name, &reg_x, &reg_y, &reg_w, &reg_h) == 5) {
    printf( "appending region: %s %d %d %d %d\n",
            reg_name,
            reg_x,
            reg_y,
            reg_w,
            reg_h);
    if (!(new_reg = appended_region(new_reg,
                                    reg_x,
                                    reg_y,
                                    reg_w,
                                    reg_h,
                                    reg_name ))) {
        fclose(fp);
        printf("main: couldn't append region\n");
        exit (-1);
    }
    if (!first_reg)
        first_reg = new_reg;
}
fclose(fp);
first_intersecter = intersecting_regions(  first_reg,
                                           sel_x,
                                           sel_y,
                                           sel_w,
                                           sel_h );
```

```
    if (!(fp = fopen("test_results", "w"))) {
        printf("main: couldn't open file 'test_results'\n");
        printf("dumping test results to stdout:\n");
        dump_region_lists(stdout, first_reg, first_intersecter);
    }
    else {
        printf("Dumping test results to file: test_results\n");
        dump_region_lists(fp, first_reg, first_intersecter);
        fclose(fp);
    }
    printf("\nDone testing.\n");
} /* main */
#endif _REGIONS_TESTBED_


/*================================================================*/
void    dump_region_lists( fp, first, first_intersecter )
    FILE            *fp;                    /* IN */
    window_region   *first,                 /* IN */
                    *first_intersecter; /* IN */
/*- - - - - - - - - - - - - - - - - - - - - - - - - - - - - - - - -
Purpose:
    Dump the list of all window_regions and the sublist of
    intersecting regions, for debugging.
Parameters:
    fp                 open stream to dump to
    first              first window_region in main list
    first_intersecter  first window_region that intersects
                       selected screen area—this sublist is
                       dumped separately from first's list
- - - - - - - - - - - - - - - - - - - - - - - - - - - - - - - - -*/
{
    window_region   *nxt;

    if (!fp) {
        printf("dump_region_lists: NULL stream\n");
        return;
    }
    fprintf(fp, "\n*** All Window Regions: ***\n");
    for (nxt = first; nxt; nxt = nxt->next) {
        fprintf(fp, "window_region @ 0x%08lx: '%s'\n",
                nxt,
                nxt->window_internals);
        fprintf(fp, "  tlx=%d tly=%d width=%d height=%d\n",
                nxt->tlx,
                nxt->tly,
                nxt->width,
                nxt->height);
        fprintf(fp,
```

```
                        "  next=0x%081x prev=0x%081x ",
                    nxt->next,
                    nxt->prev);
            fprintf(fp,
                    "next_intersecter=0x%081x\n",
                    nxt->next_intersecter);
        }
        fprintf(fp,
                "\n*** Regions That Intersect Selected Area: ***\n");
        for (   nxt = first_intersecter;
                nxt;
                nxt = nxt->next_intersecter) {
            fprintf(fp, "window_region @ 0x%081x: '%s'\n",
                    nxt,
                    nxt->window_internals);
            fprintf(fp, "  tlx=%d tly=%d width=%d height=%d\n",
                    nxt->tlx,
                    nxt->tly,
                    nxt->width,
                    nxt->height);
        }
        return;
} /* dump_region_lists */


/*================================================================*/
window_region   *appended_region(prev, x, y, width, height, name)
    window_region   *prev;          /* IN */
    int             x,              /* IN */
                    y,              /* IN */
                    width,          /* IN */
                    height;         /* IN */
    char            *name;          /* IN */
/*- - - - - - - - - - - - - - - - - - - - - - - - - - - - - - - - -
Purpose:
    Create a list of window_regions to test intersecting_regions().
Parameters:
    prev    region to append to—if this is NULL, the new
            region's prev pointer gets NULL
    x, y    coordinates of the new region's top left corner
    width,
    height  size of the new region in pixels and scanlines
            respectively; zero is allowed, but negative values
            are not
    name    for debugging, the name of the region; in a real
            window manager, the window_internals would include
            much more than this
    Returns pointer to new window_region on success, NULL otherwise.
- - - - - - - - - - - - - - - - - - - - - - - - - - - - - - - - -*/
```

```
{
    char            *strsave();
    window_region   *new;
    void            *malloc();

    if ((width < 0) || (height < 0)) {
        printf("appended_region: negative width or height\n");
        return (NULL);
    }
    if (!(new = (window_region *)malloc(sizeof(window_region)))) {
        printf("appended_region: out of memory\n");
        return (NULL);
    }
    if (!(new->window_internals = strsave(name))) {
        free(new);
        printf("appended_region: out of memory\n");
        return (NULL);
    }
    new->next = NULL;
    if (prev)
        prev->next = new;
    new->prev = prev;
    new->next_intersecter = NULL;
    new->tlx = x;
    new->tly = y;
    new->width = width;
    new->height = height;
    return (new);
} /* appended_region */

/*============================================================*/
window_region   *intersecting_regions(regions, x, y, width, height)
    window_region   *regions;   /* IN */
    int             x,          /* IN */
                    y,          /* IN */
                    width,      /* IN */
                    height;     /* IN */
/*- - - - - - - - - - - - - - - - - - - - - - - - - - - - - - -
Purpose:
    Finds all members of the regions list that intersect the
    region defined by x, y, width, and height. Assumes screen
    coordinates are oriented like this:
                +- - - -> +x
                |
                |
         +y v

Parameters:
```

```
        regions the list of window component regions to check for
                intersections with the selected screen area; this
                list is linked by window_region.next and .prev
        x, y    coordinates of the selected screen area's top left
                corner
        width,
        height  size of the selected screen area in pixels and
                scanlines respectively; zero is allowed, but negative
                values are not
        Returns a pointer to the first window_region struct that
        intersects the selected screen area, or NULL if no region
        intersects selected area. All the intersecting regions are
        linked in a sublist using window_region.next_intersecter;
        the value returned by intersecting_regions() points to the
        head of this sublist.
------------------------------------------------------------*/
{
        window_region    *nxt,
                         *prev_intersecter  = NULL,
                         *first_intersecter = NULL;
        boolean          intersects;

        if (!regions || (width < 0) || (height < 0))
            return (NULL);
        for (nxt = regions; nxt; nxt = nxt->next) {
            /* first see if nxt region is below selected area */
            if (nxt->tly > y + height) {
                return (first_intersecter);
            }
            /* see if region is not to right of selected area */
            if (nxt->tlx <= x + width) {
                intersects = true;
                if ((nxt->tlx < x) && (nxt->tlx + nxt->width < x)) {
                    intersects = false;
                }
                if ((nxt->tly < y) && (nxt->tly + nxt->height < y)) {
                    intersects = false;
                }
                if (intersects) {
                    if (prev_intersecter) {
                        prev_intersecter->next_intersecter = nxt;
                        nxt->next_intersecter = NULL;
                        prev_intersecter = nxt;
                    }
                    else {
                        first_intersecter = nxt;
                        prev_intersecter = nxt;
                        nxt->next_intersecter = NULL;
```

```
                    }
              }
        }    /* if region is not too far right */
    }    /* for each region that's not too far down */
    return (first_intersecter);
} /* intersecting_regions */
```

CHAPTER 13

Playing a Grammar Game

In this chapter, we'll design and implement a simple game that reinforces grammar terminology. The game works as follows. Play starts with a sentence template, and a set of words that can be used to complete it. The template is a sentence in which some words have been replaced by grammatical terms:

A <adjective> <noun> <adverb> <verb> that my <noun> is <adjective>!

The object is to fill the template in a way that is grammatically correct but semantically silly. For instance, suppose our set of words included the following:

blue, fresh, monkey, jaguar, quickly, quietly, sings, laughs

Then we could complete the template above in any of the following ways:

A blue monkey quickly sings that my jaguar is fresh!
A fresh jaguar quietly laughs that my monkey is blue!
A fresh monkey quietly sings that my monkey is blue!

TOP-LEVEL GOALS

We're writing an interactive game, so the code has to execute quickly to avoid boring the players. Some sort of display mechanism will be needed, but we'll keep it simple and clearly separated from the rest of the game, so we can port the game more easily. Finally, the people using the game are most likely children or nonprogrammers, or both. So we want a simple interface, and we want code that runs reliably and is tolerant of unexpected input.

GUIDING EXAMPLES

Figure 13-1 shows our guiding example. The sentence template is the one presented at the beginning of the chapter; the words we choose from to complete the sentence are:

sings, monkey, blue, slowly, jaguar, laughs, eggnog, tired, fresh, quietly, quickly, smells

Since one of our top-level goals is to keep the display code simple and portable, we won't try to implement the interface shown in Figure 13-1. So why show a picture of something we aren't going to deliver? There are three things to keep in mind:

1. We haven't promised to deliver the interface in Figure 13-1. In fact, we've specifically said we won't implement it. So we're not misleading anyone.
2. Figure 13-1 gives us something to aim at as an ultimate goal. It's always worthwhile to imagine different versions of a program. Doing so can motivate you by reviving your interest, assist you by suggesting "hooks" for future enhancements, and warn of potential trouble spots.
3. Figure 13-1 suggests how the game is played—something we certainly need to understand before writing any code!

Let's use Figure 13-1 to play the grammar game mentally. First, we hit the "NEW GAME" button. This fills the wheel with a new set of nouns, verbs, adjectives, and adverbs. The "ROTATE" buttons make the wheel rotate about an imaginary axis that is perpendicular to the screen. The "INSERT" button tries to insert the word currently at the top of the wheel into the template above the wheel.

The template was generated when we pressed "NEW GAME." Unlike the word wheel, which rotates only while one of the "ROTATE" buttons is held down, the template rotates constantly, about an imaginary vertical axis that lies inside the screen. If you prefer, you can imagine the template scrolling to the left, with new copies of the template always appearing on the right. Either way, the template moves past the big arrow at the top of the word wheel.

The object of the game is to make a grammatically correct but semantically silly sentence as quickly as possible by inserting words from the wheel into the rotating template. When the "INSERT" button is pressed, the program checks the grammatical category of the word at the top of the wheel against the template word that is directly above the big arrow. If the categories match, the word from the wheel is copied over the template word.

If the template and word wheel grammatical categories don't match, the program makes a disappointed noise and the template is not changed. In Figure 13-1, for instance, the insertion would fail because "sings" is a verb, and the big arrow points to "<adjective>." Template words that are not grammatical categories never match the word wheel. In Figure 13-1, for instance, we can never replace "A," "that," "my," or "is." They are constants, so to speak, whereas words like "<adjective>" are variables.

A sequence of successful insertions might produce the following changes in Figure 13-1's template:

A <adjective> <noun> <adverb> <verb> that my <noun> is <adjective>!

A <adjective> <noun> quickly <verb> that my <noun> is <adjective>!
A <adjective> <noun> quickly <verb> that my jaguar is <adjective>!
A blue <noun> quickly <verb> that my jaguar is <adjective>!

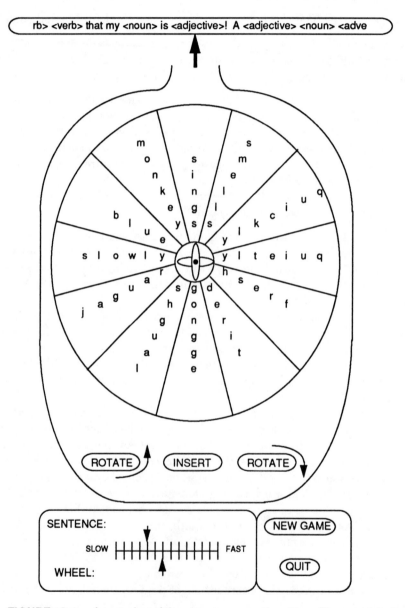

FIGURE 13-1: A snapshot of the grammar game in action. The user interface shown here is more sophisticated than the one we'll actually implement, but it provides a nice summary of how the game is played.

A blue <noun> quickly smells that my jaguar is <adjective>!
A blue <noun> quickly smells that my jaguar is fresh!
A blue eggnog quickly smells that my jaguar is fresh!

A number of variations on this basic version of the grammar game are possible. Figure 13-1 actually shows a variation in which users can control how fast the template sentence and the word wheel rotate. We could also add time limits or different levels of difficulty. We could require more sophisticated knowledge of grammar by distinguishing between singular and plural, for instance, or by using different languages. On the wheel, instead of replacing inserted words by a copy of themselves, we could replace them by new words in the same or different grammatical categories. The possibilities are not endless, but there are enough to fill a few rainy afternoons.

We'll stick with the simplest version of the game we can. But this talk of variations raises the possibility of using something other than Figure 13-1 as our guiding example. We should choose the fundamental characteristics we want in our guiding examples. Then we can see how well Figure 13-1 represents these characteristics and supplement it with additional figures if need be.

The number of different grammatical categories is an important characteristic of the game. There is a big difference between a game with just one category (<noun>, for instance) and a game with multiple categories. It would be a mistake to follow an example that had only one category when we want to write a game that supports multiple categories. Figure 13-1 is a good example in this respect, since it suggests four categories (<noun>, <verb>, <adjective>, and <adverb>).

Since we're replacing parts of the template, we want an example in which replacements appear next to each other, and another in which they are separated by "constant" text. Figure 13-1 is also a good example with respect to this fundamental characteristic. Its template contains adjacent replacements ("<adjective> <noun> <adverb> <verb>") as well as separated replacements ("my <noun> is <adjective>!").

It would also be useful to have an example template that begins and ends with a replacement. The template rotates in Figure 13-1, but in an actual implementation, there will be a beginning and an end to whatever structure(s) we use to represent the template internally. So we'll want a test case to make sure the insertion code correctly handles replacements at each end of the template. Figure 13-1 does not provide this, since it begins and ends with "constants" ("A" at the beginning and "!" at the end). So when the time comes to check the "INSERT" button code, we'll also use this as a guiding example:

<noun> quietly <verb>

Figure 13-1 also makes an assumption about the length of the template. It seems unrealistic to hope that every template will exactly fill the display box above the wheel. Even if all the templates were the right length, we would still have a problem, because insertions change the template's length. So we need an example of a string that is too long to fit in the box:

The <adjective> <noun> ran up and down and over and around, and finally came to rest at the foot of the <noun>, where it <verb> till I picked it up.

We don't need an example of a template that is too short to fit in the display box, because that would only be true of empty templates, and we'll make a rule right now that no template is empty. After all, an empty template provides a very boring game.

In summary, we have three example templates: the one in Figure 13-1, the short one that gets replacements at each end, and the one that's too long to fit in the display box. It seems unlikely that we'll need any more examples of replacement words than the ones shown on Figure 13-1's word wheel, so we're ready to write an ADTD.

ABSTRACT DATA TYPE DESCRIPTION

What is the geometry of this abstract data type? Figure 13-1 will serve for now as our sketch of the geometry. We may need to supplement it, but it's a good place to start. In ADTD terms, the top of the word wheel is a special position. The template character currently pointed to by the big arrow is also in a special position.

Show whether or not the elements are linked, as tree nodes or linked list elements are. This is an interesting task. Do we represent the template using an array or a linked list? Figure 13-1 doesn't show how the template elements are connected. But we can remedy this shortcoming by adding another figure.

Figure 13-2 shows two possible representations of a template string. My first impulse is to use an array like the one shown in Figure 13-2(b), just because strings always go in arrays in C. Besides, stretching a string into a linked list of individual characters like the one shown in Figure 13-2(a) seems too expensive. All those pointers occupy memory, and it will also take some time to chase them when we display the string. However, we can't tell for certain whether we need a linked list or not until we decide what operations will be performed on the data. So we'll skip ahead, answer the question about operators, and then return to the geometry portion of the ADTD.

What are the operators? We need an operator to generate new words for the wheel and one to generate new templates. The situation is improving, but programs are still pretty poor

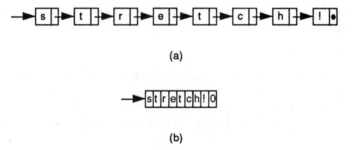

(a)

(b)

FIGURE 13-2: Two representations of strings. (a) shows a linked list of individual characters, terminated by a NULL pointer. (b) shows an array of chars, terminated by a NULL character.

at generating natural language of any sort. In a production version of the grammar game, we can simply read the templates and replacement words from a file, which might be provided by the user or by us. However, our current concern is data structure design, not file formats, so for now we'll just hard-code the template and word wheel.

We also need an insertion operator. This operator compares the grammatical category of the word at the top of the wheel with the category of the template character the big arrow points to. If the categories match, the word is inserted in the template, replacing one of the category markers like "<noun>" or "<verb>." The operator also fills the empty space in the word wheel; for now, we'll simply fill the blank with a copy of the word that was just inserted. If the categories do not match, the operator returns without changing the template.

We also need an operator to rotate the word wheel, an operator to rotate the template, an operator to display the word wheel, and an operator to display the template. Finally, we may want operators to pretty-print the internal structures so we can debug the program.

OK, back to the geometry. Looking at the operators, it's clear we'll prefer Figure 13-2(a) to Figure 13-2(b), because insertion is so much easier with linked lists than with arrays.

Before we write a lot of code, however, we should make sure an implementation based on Figure 13-2(a) is feasible. Just how much longer does it take to display a string one character at a time (Figure 13-2(a)) than it takes to display a conventional C string (Figure 13-2(b))? To find out, I wrote the following little test program:

```
typedef struct char_elem {
    struct char_elem *next;
    char             value;
} char_elem;

static char_elem *string = NULL;
#define MAX_LEN    1024
#define DISP_COUNT 3


/*===============================================================*/
main()
/*- - - - - - - - - - - - - - - - - - - - - - - - - - - - - - - -
Purpose:
    Test to see if it's practical to stretch a string into a
    linked list of individual characters—how long does it take
    to display such a stretched string?
Parameters:
    none, but sets global char *string
- - - - - - - - - - - - - - - - - - - - - - - - - - - - - - - -*/
{
    char      buf[MAX_LEN];
    void      *malloc();
    char_elem *new;
    int       i;

    printf("String to stretch (max of %d chars)> \n", MAX_LEN-1);
```

```
    scanf("%s", buf);
    /* build stretched string backwards so we always
       insert at the front of the list: */
    for (i = strlen(buf) - 1; i >= 0; i--) {
      if (!(new = (char_elem *)malloc(sizeof(char_elem)))) {
        printf("out of memory\n");
        return;
      }
      new->value = buf[i];
      new->next  = string;
      string = new;
    }
    printf( "Displaying string: %d stretched, %d compact:\n\n",
        DISP_COUNT, DISP_COUNT);
    for (i = 0; i < DISP_COUNT; i++) {
      for (new = string; new; new = new->next)
        printf("%c", new->value);
      printf("\n");
    }
    for (i = 0; i < DISP_COUNT; i++) {
      printf("%s\n", buf);
    }
} /* main */
```

The answer is that you have to look hard to notice the difference in display time between a linked list of characters and an array of characters. In terms of user-perceptible time, it just doesn't take that long to chase 100 or so pointers, or to make the extra 100 or so calls to *printf()*. We can get away with a linked list representation like the one in Figure 13-2(a) because our lists are always relatively short. So that's what we'll use, because it will make insertions much easier.

What relations hold between the elements of the collection? The characters in the template are totally ordered, as are the words on the wheel. In both cases, however, the elements are also linked in a ring, so there is no first element or last element. We want the elements to be circularly linked so that rotating them will be easier.

What are the restrictions on membership in the collection? Word wheel membership is restricted to words that belong to the grammatical categories that appear in the templates. For instance, if the templates contain only "<verb>" and "<noun>," then the word wheel shouldn't hold adjectives. (Actually, we could make the game harder by putting in some words that never match, but that's another variation we'll ignore for now.)

This restriction is enforced by users, not by the program. It has to be. Without human help, the program can't tell which category a word belongs to. Even with human assistance, there will always be difficult cases. No matter how precisely we describe the grammatical categories that appear in the template, some words will be found that meet the description but still aren't grammatically correct. For instance, "jump" won't work in the following template, even though it's a verb, because it matches the pronoun "I," not the pronoun "she":

She <verb> over the moon.

Now let's try to implement the word wheel and template.

ATTEMPT ONE

We'll start with the template. We need a linked list like the one in Figure 13-2(a). Or do we? That list allows characters to be inserted between characters, but we need only to insert words between words. So we actually need a linked list of words, not a list of characters. This brings us to the problem of representing each word. We could use a fixed-size array:

```
typedef struct array_word {
   struct array_word        *next;
   char                     value[MAX_WORD_LENGTH];
} array_word;
```

Or we could use a char pointer and allocate just enough space to hold each word:

```
typedef struct pointer_word {
   struct pointer word       *next;
   char                      *value;
} pointer_word;
```

The advantages and disadvantages of a list of arrays are discussed in the design guideline "Avoid Sorted Lists of Arrays" (page 360). In that discussion, however, the assumption is made that elements can be inserted within an array. This is not the case with the template we're trying to implement here, since we're inserting words between words, not inserting characters between characters. So even though that design guideline appears at first glance to be applicable, it is not.

The main tradeoff between the two typedefs above is that *array_word* imposes a maximum word length while *pointer_word* requires more memory management code. We'll use the array representation; we can afford large arrays because we don't need many of them. This will use more memory, but not so much that it would be worth the extra effort to use *pointer_words*.

Just how much more memory will *array_word* structs use than *pointer_word* structs? We can make an educated guess by considering our third guiding example, which was chosen because it is longer than typical templates:

The <adjective> <noun> ran up and down and over and around, and finally came to rest at the foot of the <noun>, where it <verb> till I picked it up.

This template contains 30 words and 148 characters. The longest word is "<adjective>," which contains 12 characters (counting the final '\0'). A conservative estimate, then, is that templates are 30 words long, with each word no more than 20 characters in length. This means an *array_word* representation with *MAX_WORD_LENGTH* = 20 would use 30*20 = 600 bytes to represent our long template. Using *pointer_word* structs would require

148 + 30°sizeof(char •) bytes. If pointers are two bytes long, this means pointer_words require 148 + 60 = 208 bytes. So we are wasting 600 – 208 = 392 bytes by using *array_words* instead of *pointer_words*. We can afford this much waste in exchange for the simpler memory management.

Notice that our template data structure has undergone some serious changes. At first, we were going to use a conventional array of chars, as shown in Figure 13-2(b). Then we decided insertions would be much easier if we represented the template string as a linked list of individual characters. We even wrote a little test code to make sure it wouldn't take too long to display the template a character at a time. Pleased with the test results, we dropped Figure 13-2(b)'s conventional array in favor of the linked list of characters in Figure 13-2(a).

Now we've decided that we need a linked list of words, not a list of characters. So we've abandoned Figure 13-2(a) in favor of the *array_word* typedef above. We're getting close, but we're not done yet.

The next step is to find a way to represent grammatical categories. We need an easy way to compare the word wheel's topmost word with the template word that is currently above the word wheel's big arrow. In Figure 13-1, for instance, we need to compare the grammatical categories of "sings" and "<adjective>." We do not want to do a string comparison between "<adjective>" and "sings." Aside from being slow, string comparison gives the wrong answer; "<adjective>" and "blue" are not equal as strings even though "blue" is an adjective.

So we need to add grammatical categories directly to our structure. While we're making changes, we'll also rename the type from *array_word* to *template_word*, because the choice between pointers and arrays has been made in favor of arrays:

```
#define IS_A_CONSTANT      0
#define IS_A_NOUN          1
#define IS_A_VERB          2
#define IS_A_ADJECTIVE     3
#define IS_A_ADVERB        4

typedef struct template_word {
  struct template_word    *next;
  char                    value[MAX_WORD_LENGTH];
  int                     category;
} template_word;

/* sample test to see if *next is a verb: */
template_word *next;
...
if (next->category == IS_A_VERB) {
  /* *next is a verb */
```

There is still one small problem. Some words fit in more than one grammatical category. Is "bump" a verb or a noun? It's both. We could require the people who create the templates and choose the words for the wheel to avoid such ambiguities. Or we could allow words to belong to more than one category. The second alternative is better.

To see why we should allow words to belong to several categories, look at Figure 13-1 again. A word's category is not visible on the word wheel. Someone who is trying to use "bump" as a noun when the program only recognizes "bump" as a verb will not be happy. So we should allow words to belong to several categories because we want happy users.

To put it another way, one of our top-level goals was to be tolerant of unexpected input. The easiest way to do that is to expect a wider range of input—let "bump" be a verb or a noun or both. Of course, it's still up to a human to tell us which categories "bump" and the other words belong to, but at least we can change the defines so they implement bitflags instead of mutually exclusive enumeration values:

```
#define IS_A_CONSTANT      0
#define IS_A_NOUN          1
#define IS_A_VERB          2
#define IS_A_ADJECTIVE     4
#define IS_A_ADVERB        8

/* sample test to see if *next is a verb: */
template_word *next;
...
if (next->category & IS_A_VERB) {
  /* *next is a verb */
```

This brings us to the question of comparing grammatical categories to determine if the selected word on the wheel can be inserted in the template at the chosen point. We need a typedef for the words on the wheel. We could use the *template_word* typedef, but for the fact that the wheel rotates in both directions. That means we need to be able to move both forward and backward along the wheel. And that, in turn, means we need a doubly linked list:

```
typedef struct wheel_word {
   struct wheel_word        *next,
                            *prev;
   char                     value[MAX_WORD_LENGTH];
   int                      category;
} wheel_word;
```

Now let's go back to Figure 13-1 and the ADTD and see what we've missed. The template will be implemented as a circular singly linked list of arrays and associated grammatical categories. That is, the template is a circular list of *template_word* structs. The word wheel will be a circular doubly linked list of *wheel_word* structs. The *wheel_word* list is circular and doubly linked so we can rotate the wheel in either direction; the *template_word* list is circular and singly linked so we can rotate the template in one direction.

We'll need some way to keep track of our current position in both these circular lists.

The word wheel rotates a word at a time, so a simple *wheel_word* pointer is all we need to keep track of which word is at the top of the wheel. The template, however, rotates a character at a time. So to know where we are in the template, we need to know at which word in the template we are, and at which character within that word we are. This means we'll need a *template_word* pointer and an integer array index.

Comparing the current word at the top of the wheel with the template to see if an insertion is legal is now quite easy:

```
/* current template, word wheel position: */
typedef struct template_position {
   struct template_word    *word; /* current word */
   int                     ch;    /* index into word->value */
} template_position;

static template_position  template_pos = {NULL,0};
static wheel_word         *wheel_pos    = NULL;

...

/* now the check to see if insertion is legal looks like this: */
if (wheel_pos->category & template_pos.word->category) {
   /* insertion is legal */
```

Figure 13-3 summarizes the implementation we've designed thus far. The structs at the current template and wheel positions have been magnified; the current positions were chosen to match Figure 13-1. For instance, Figure 13-1's big arrow points to the first 'e' in the template word "<adjective>." So *template_pos.word* points to the *template_word* struct that contains value "<adjective>," and *template_pos.ch* is 4 (4 is the array index of "e" in "<adjective>").

Notice also that Figure 13-3 shows the wasted space in the arrays. This is indicated by the garbage that follows the '\0' string terminators. Finally, notice that the values in the bitflag fields *template_pos.word->category* and *wheel_pos->category* are such that we get zero when we use bitwise and ("&" in C) on them to see if insertion is legal. This is right, because "sings" is a verb, and "<adjective>" matches only adjectives.

Continuing with our review of the ADTD to see what we've missed, we come to the operators. Are there any we don't yet know how to implement? The operator to generate new templates and word wheels builds new circular lists of *wheel_words* and *template_words* using hard-coded test values.

The heart of the insertion operator is a bitwise and ("&") between *wheel_pos->category* and *template_pos.word->category*. If insertion is legal, we must also set *template_pos.word->value* to *wheel_pos->value*, and *template_pos.word->category* to *IS_A_CONSTANT*.

The rotation operators for the template and the wheel amount to updating *template_pos* and *wheel_pos*. The struct dump routines are simply some *printf()* calls. None of these routines will be hard to write.

TEMPLATE:

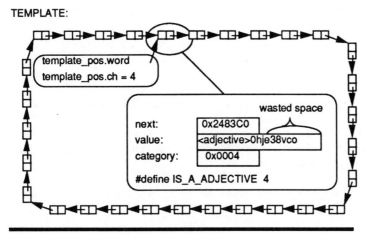

WORD WHEEL:

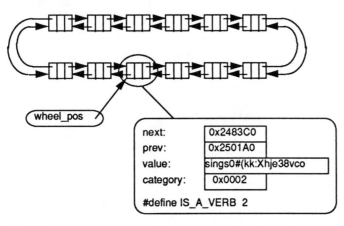

FIGURE 13-3: A summary of the grammar game's implementation. Current word wheel and template positions correspond directly to Figure 13-1.

The only routines we haven't devised an implementation strategy for are the display routines. Our main interest here is in data structures, not in graphics libraries or a finished commercial product, so we'll keep these display routines very simple. Our display will be much cruder than Figure 13-1. We'll need another static *template_position* variable, *display_pos. Display_pos* is used to keep track of the leftmost character being displayed, just as *template_pos* keeps track of the character currently selected by the big arrow at the top of the word wheel:

```
static template_position  display_pos = {NULL, 0};
```

Now we can write the program.

LISTING: grammar.c

```
/*- - - - - - - - - - - - - - - - - - - - - - - - - - - - - - - - - - - - -
                        grammar.c
- - - - - - - - - - - - - - - - - - - - - - - - - - - - - - - - - - - - -*/

/*===================================================================
Purpose:
    This is a simple game that reinforces grammar terminology
    by letting players construct sentences that are grammatically
    correct but semantically silly.

    This code was compiled under THINK's LightspeedC (TM) on a
    Macintosh SE. Code marked by "THINK" in comments is specific
    to the THINK compiler or libraries.
- - - - - - - - - - - - - - - - - - - - - - - - - - - - - - - - - - - - -*/
#include <stdio.h>
#include <boolean.h>

#define MAX_WORD_LENGTH      20  /* includes terminal '\0' */
/* MAX_WORD_LENGTH blanks (see display()): */
static char          blanks[] = "                    ";
#define CHARS_DISPLAYED      50

typedef int          bitflags;
#define IS_A_CONSTANT      0
#define IS_A_NOUN          1
#define IS_A_VERB          2
#define IS_A_ADJECTIVE     4
#define IS_A_ADVERB        8
#define IS_A_ALL (IS_A_NOUN | IS_A_VERB | IS_A_ADJECTIVE | IS_A_ADVERB)

typedef struct template_word {
    struct template_word      *next;
    char                      value[MAX_WORD_LENGTH];
    bitflags                  category;   /* 1 category per word */
} template_word;

typedef struct {
    struct template_word      *word; /* current word */
    int                       ch;    /* current char in word->value */
} template_position;

typedef struct wheel_word {
    struct wheel_word         *next,
                              *prev;
    char                      value[MAX_WORD_LENGTH];
```

```
    bitflags              categories;      /* multiple categories OK */
} wheel_word;

static template_position    template_pos = {NULL, 0};
static template_position    display_pos  = {NULL, 0};
static wheel_word           *wheel_pos   = NULL;

/* commands for crude user interface: */
#define CMD_QUIT           'q'
#define CMD_NEW_GAME       'n'
#define CMD_INSERT         ' '
#define CMD_CLOCK          'k'
#define CMD_COUNTERCLOCK   'j'

/*===============================================================*/
main()
/*- - - - - - - - - - - - - - - - - - - - - - - - - - - - - - - -
Purpose:
    Grammar game.
Parameters:
    none
- - - - - - - - - - - - - - - - - - - - - - - - - - - - - - - - -*/
{
    char    ch;
    boolean new_game();
    void    display(), insert(), rotate_wheel(), rotate_template();

    printf("Grammar Game\n");
    if (!new_game()) {
        printf("couldn't set up new game\n");
        return;
    }
    for ( ; ; ) {
        display();
        if (kbhit()) { /* THINK: char available from keyboard? */
            ch = getchar(); /* get ch from stdin w/out echoing */
            if (ch == CMD_QUIT) {
                printf("\n\nThanks for playing!\n");
                return;
            }
            else if (ch == CMD_NEW_GAME) {
                if (!new_game()) {
                    printf("couldn't set up new game\n");
                    return;
                }
            }
            else if (ch == CMD_INSERT) {
```

```
                insert();
            }
            else if (ch == CMD_CLOCK) {
                rotate_wheel(1);
            }
            else if (ch == CMD_COUNTERCLOCK) {
                rotate_wheel(-1);
            }
            else {
                /* ignore it */
            }
        } /* if user typed a command */
        rotate_template();
    }
} /* main */


/*================================================================*/
static void     rotate_template()
/*- - - - - - - - - - - - - - - - - - - - - - - - - - - - - - - - -
Purpose:
    Rotate the template by removing one character on the left and
    adding one on the right.
Parameters:
    none, but sets global template_position variables
    display_pos and template_pos
- - - - - - - - - - - - - - - - - - - - - - - - - - - - - - - - -*/
{
    display_pos.ch++;
    if (!(display_pos.word->value[display_pos.ch])) {
        display_pos.word = display_pos.word->next;
        display_pos.ch   = 0;
    }
    template_pos.ch++;
    if (!(template_pos.word->value[template_pos.ch])) {
        template_pos.word = template_pos.word->next;
        template_pos.ch   = 0;
    }
} /* rotate_template */


/*================================================================*/
static void     rotate_wheel( direction )
    int     direction;  /* IN */
/*- - - - - - - - - - - - - - - - - - - - - - - - - - - - - - - - -
Purpose:
    Rotate the word wheel one position.
Parameters:
    direction   -1 => rotate counterclockwise, 1 => rotate
                clockwise
```

```
        Sets global wheel_word *wheel_pos
------------------------------------------------------*/
{
    if (direction > 0)
        wheel_pos = wheel_pos->prev;
    else
        wheel_pos = wheel_pos->next;
} /* rotate_wheel */


/*================================================================*/
static void     insert()
/*- - - - - - - - - - - - - - - - - - - - - - - - - - - - - - - -
Purpose:
    Compare grammatical category of current template word with
    categories met by current wheel word. If wheel word can match
    template word, change template to a constant and overwrite
    "<adjective>" or whatever was in it by the wheel word.
Parameters:
    none, but uses global wheel_word *wheel_pos and global
    template_position template_pos.
------------------------------------------------------*/
{
    if (wheel_pos->categories & template_pos.word->category) {
        template_pos.word->category = IS_A_CONSTANT;
        strcpy(template_pos.word->value, wheel_pos->value);
    }
} /* insert */


/*================================================================*/
static boolean     new_game()
/*- - - - - - - - - - - - - - - - - - - - - - - - - - - - - - - -
Purpose:
    Remove the existing template and wheel circular lists, if
    any. Build new template and wheel lists. (NOTE: new lists
    are hard-coded at present; they should be read from a file
    or input by the user in a production-quality game).

    Initializes globals wheel_pos, template_pos, display_pos.
Parameters:
    none
------------------------------------------------------*/
{
    void    free_wheel(), free_template(), init_display();
    boolean add_to_wheel(), add_to_template();

    free_wheel();
    free_template();
    if (!add_to_template("!", IS_A_CONSTANT))
```

```
                    return (false);
        if (!add_to_template("", IS_A_ADJECTIVE))
                    return (false);
        if (!add_to_template(" is", IS_A_CONSTANT))
                    return (false);
        if (!add_to_template("", IS_A_NOUN))
                    return (false);
        if (!add_to_template(" my", IS_A_CONSTANT))
                    return (false);
        if (!add_to_template(" that", IS_A_CONSTANT))
                    return (false);
        if (!add_to_template("", IS_A_VERB))
                    return (false);
        if (!add_to_template("", IS_A_ADVERB))
                    return (false);
        if (!add_to_template("", IS_A_NOUN))
                    return (false);
        if (!add_to_template("", IS_A_ADJECTIVE))
                    return (false);
        if (!add_to_template(" A", IS_A_CONSTANT))
                    return (false);
        if (!add_to_wheel(" sings", IS_A_VERB))
                    return (false);
        if (!add_to_wheel(" monkey", IS_A_NOUN))
                    return (false);
        if (!add_to_wheel(" blue", IS_A_ADJECTIVE))
                    return (false);
        if (!add_to_wheel(" slowly", IS_A_ADVERB))
                    return (false);
        if (!add_to_wheel(" camaro", IS_A_NOUN))
                    return (false);
        if (!add_to_wheel(" laughs", IS_A_VERB))
                    return (false);
        if (!add_to_wheel(" eggnog", IS_A_NOUN))
                    return (false);
        if (!add_to_wheel(" tired", IS_A_ADJECTIVE))
                    return (false);
        if (!add_to_wheel(" fresh", IS_A_ADJECTIVE))
                    return (false);
        if (!add_to_wheel(" quietly", IS_A_ADVERB))
                    return (false);
        if (!add_to_wheel(" quickly", IS_A_ADVERB))
                    return (false);
        if (!add_to_wheel(" smells", IS_A_VERB))
                    return (false);
        init_display();
        return (true);
} /* new_game */
```

```
/*================================================================*/
static void     init_display()
/*----------------------------------------
Purpose:
    Initializes display. Should only be called after the template
    list has been built.
Parameters:
    none, but sets global template_position variables
    display_pos and template_pos
-----------------------------------------*/
{
    int     total;

    /* the starting template position should be offset from the
       starting display position by half the width of the template
       display: */
    display_pos.word = template_pos.word;
    display_pos.ch   = 0;
    for (total = 0; total < CHARS_DISPLAYED/2; total++) {
        template_pos.ch++;
        if (!(template_pos.word->value[template_pos.ch])) {
            template_pos.word = template_pos.word->next;
            template_pos.ch   = 0;
        }
    }
    return;
} /* init_display */


/*================================================================*/
static void     free_wheel()
/*----------------------------------------
Purpose:
    Remove the existing circular list of wheel words, if any.
Parameters:
    none, but sets global wheel_word *wheel_pos
-----------------------------------------*/
{
    wheel_word      *nxt, *victem;

    if (!wheel_pos)
        return;
    /* 'cut' list so it's not circular: */
    wheel_pos->prev->next = NULL;
    /* now delete elements from wheel_pos to end of list: */
    for (nxt = wheel_pos; nxt; ) {
        victem = nxt;
        nxt = nxt->next;
        free(victem);
```

```
        }
      wheel_pos = NULL;
} /* free_wheel */

/*===============================================================*/
static void      free_template()
/*- - - - - - - - - - - - - - - - - - - - - - - - - - - - - - - -
Purpose:
    Remove the existing circular list of template words, if any.
Parameters:
    none, but sets global template_position template_pos
- - - - - - - - - - - - - - - - - - - - - - - - - - - - - - - -*/
{
    template_word   *nxt, *victem;

    if (!template_pos.word)
        return;
    /* 'cut' list so it's not circular; unlike the doubly-linked
       wheel_word list, we can't go backwards, so we have to run
       forwards through the template_word list until we reach
       the element we want to make the end of the list: */
    for (   nxt = template_pos.word;
            nxt->next != template_pos.word;
            nxt = nxt->next )
        ;
    nxt->next = NULL;
    /* now delete elements from wheel_pos to end of list: */
    for (nxt = template_pos.word; nxt; ) {
        victem = nxt;
        nxt = nxt->next;
        free(victem);
    }
    template_pos.word = NULL;
    template_pos.ch   = 0;
} /* free_template */

/*===============================================================*/
static boolean  add_to_wheel( text, kinds )
    char    *text;  /* IN */
    int     kinds;  /* IN */
/*- - - - - - - - - - - - - - - - - - - - - - - - - - - - - - - -
Purpose:
    Add a word to the circular list of wheel words. Each word must
    belong to one or more of the following grammatical categories:

        <noun>
        <verb>
        <adjective>
```

```
        <adverb>

Parameters:
    text    text of word to add
    kinds   flags (combination of IS_A_xxx defines) that tell
            which grammatical categories this word belongs to;
            zero is illegal
    Sets global wheel_word *wheel_pos and updates pointers in
    the wheel list.
- - - - - - - - - - - - - - - - - - - - - - - - - - - - - - - - - - - - - - - - - -*/
{
    wheel_word      *new;
    void            *malloc();

    if (!(new = (wheel_word *)malloc(sizeof(wheel_word)))) {
        printf("out of memory\n");
        return (false);
    }
    if ((!kinds) || (kinds & ~IS_A_ALL)) {
        printf("unknown kind %d of wheel word: %s\n", kinds, text);
        free(new);
        return (false);
    }
    else {
        new->categories = kinds;
    }
    strcpy(new->value, text);
    if (!wheel_pos) {
        wheel_pos = new;
        new->next = new;
        new->prev = new;
        return (true);
    }
    new->next = wheel_pos;
    new->prev = wheel_pos->prev;
    wheel_pos->prev = new;
    new->prev->next = new;
    wheel_pos = new;
    return (true);
} /* add_to_wheel */


/*===========================================================*/
static boolean  add_to_template( text, kind )
    char    *text;  /* IN */
    int     kind;   /* IN */
/*- - - - - - - - - - - - - - - - - - - - - - - - - - - - - - - - - - - - - - -
Purpose:
    Add a word to the circular list of template words. Each word must
```

belong to exactly one of the following grammatical categories:

```
        constant
        <noun>
        <verb>
        <adjective>
        <adverb>
```

Parameters:
     text   text of word to add; this is IGNORED if
              kind != IS_A_CONSTANT
     kind   flag (one of the IS_A_xxx defines) that tells
              which grammatical category this word belongs to;
              zero indicates a constant word that can never be
              replaced by a word from the word wheel
     Sets global template_position template_pos and updates
     pointers in the template list.
- -*/

```c
{
    template_word    *new, *end;
    void             *malloc();

    if (!(new = (template_word *)malloc(sizeof(template_word)))) {
        printf("out of memory\n");
        return (false);
    }
    if (kind == IS_A_CONSTANT) {
        new->category = IS_A_CONSTANT;
        strcpy(new->value, text);
    }
    else if (kind == IS_A_NOUN) {
        new->category = IS_A_NOUN;
        strcpy(new->value, " <noun>");
    }
    else if (kind == IS_A_VERB) {
        new->category = IS_A_VERB;
        strcpy(new->value, " <verb>");
    }
    else if (kind == IS_A_ADJECTIVE) {
        new->category = IS_A_ADJECTIVE;
        strcpy(new->value, " <adjective>");
    }
    else if (kind == IS_A_ADVERB) {
        new->category = IS_A_ADVERB;
        strcpy(new->value, " <adverb>");
    }
    else {
        printf( "unknown kind %d of template word: %s\n",
```

```
                    kind, text);
        free(new);
        return (false);
    }
    if (!template_pos.word) {
        template_pos.word = new;
        new->next = new;
        return (true);
    }
    for (   end = template_pos.word;
            end->next != template_pos.word;
            end = end->next )
        ;
    new->next = template_pos.word;
    end->next = new;
    template_pos.word = new;
    return (true);
} /* add_to_template */


/*================================================================*/
static void     display()
/*- - - - - - - - - - - - - - - - - - - - - - - - - - - - - - - - - -
Purpose:
    Provides a very crude user interface for the grammar game.
    Relies principally upon gotoxy(x,y), a THINK C function that
    moves the cursor on the screen to the given (x, y) character
    position; (0,0) is the top left corner.

    The big arrow that points to the template has already been
    drawn by init_display(), and doesn't need refreshing, so it's
    ignored in display().

    All output is in ASCII. All input is from the keyboard.
Parameters:
    none, but uses global template_position display_pos
- - - - - - - - - - - - - - - - - - - - - - - - - - - - - - - - - - - -*/
{
    int             total, i, len;
    template_word   *t_word;
    char            buf[CHARS_DISPLAYED+1];

    gotoxy(0,0);
    /* display about CHARS_DISPLAYED characters of the template: */
    strcpy(buf, &(display_pos.word->value[display_pos.ch]));
    for ( total = strlen(display_pos.word->value) - display_pos.ch,
        t_word = display_pos.word->next;
            ; ) {
        len = strlen(t_word->value);
```

```
                if (total + len >= CHARS_DISPLAYED)
                    break;
                strcat(buf, t_word->value);
                total += len;
                t_word = t_word->next;
            }
        for (i = 0; total < CHARS_DISPLAYED; total++, i++)
                buf[total] = t_word->value[i];
        buf[total] = '\0';
        printf("%s", buf);
        gotoxy(0,2);
        /* display the "big arrow" simply by telling what word of
            the template it currently points to: */
        printf( "%s%s\rTEMPLATE -> %s",
                blanks, blanks, template_pos.word->value);
        /* display word which is currently at the top of the wheel: */
        gotoxy(0, 4);
        printf("%s\r%s", blanks, wheel_pos->value);
    } /* display */
```

CHAPTER 14
Extending an Interpreter with Code Modules

In this chapter, we want to design and implement a mechanism for passing information between a certain kind of interpreter and "plug-in" object code modules. These code modules can be invoked in place of built-in interpreter statements. We're doing this so we can have both flexibility and speedy execution. The flexibility comes from using an interpreter, and the speedy execution comes from using precompiled code modules.

OVERVIEW OF RELATED PROBLEMS

Before looking at interpreter code modules, we will briefly consider some generalizations of the problem. We'll focus our interest in the following three stages:

1. In the most general sense, we are interested in tips on using the "built-ins plus" method of program organization. This method organizes large programs as a set of basic built-in entities plus a facility for adding user-defined custom extensions.
2. More specifically, we are interested in adding custom extensions to one kind of "built-ins plus" program: special-purpose interpreters. These are interpreters whose purpose is to execute powerful statements interactively in various orders with various parameter values.
3. Most specifically, we are interested in one kind of custom extension to these interpreters: code modules that can be "plugged in" and used instead of functionally

equivalent but less flexible built-in statements. Code modules are self-contained pieces of relocatable object code that can be loaded and executed from an interpreter; an interpreter and a code module communicate by way of parameters that are passed when the module is invoked.

Let's start by considering the "built-ins plus" method of program organization. There are many examples, but two are likely to be familiar to most C programmers: the emacs text editor and the UNIX™ shells (the Bourne shell, csh, or any other command interpreter will serve as an example). Both emacs and shells provide a set of basic built-in operations plus facilities for adding custom extensions.

For instance, emacs has the basic operations "move down one line" and "insert from buffer at current position" built in. Emacs can be customized by defining virtually any sequence of basic operations as a "macro." To be very specific, suppose we're editing a file that contains a list of C source filenames with one name per line:

```
cm_test_module.c
cm_interpreter.c
ent.c
match.c
graph.c
failure.c
```

We could define a macro M as "insert from buffer, then move down to beginning of next line." Grep is a UNIX tool that searches files for instances of a given string. By placing the cursor at the top of the file, placing "grep bug" in the insertion buffer, and invoking M six times, for instance, we could produce this file:

```
grep bug cm_test_module.c
grep bug cm_interpreter.c
grep bug ent.c
grep bug match.c
grep bug graph.c
grep bug failure.c
```

We've now changed a list of filenames into a sequence of commands that will find all instances of "bug" in the listed files.

M and similar editing operations are too rare to justify building them directly into emacs. But it's very tedious if we have to repeat the same simple steps over and over and over again to get our editing done. Since M and similar operations are easily defined in terms of simple built-in operations, we shouldn't just ignore them. Instead, we support them by way of macros. This is an excellent solution, because it allows users to avoid tedium without making emacs unreasonably large by building in scores of rarely used operations.

A UNIX shell or any other command interpreter provides a second example of the "built-ins plus" methodology. Typical built-in shell operations repeat the previous command, read and write shell variables, and redirect I/O. In other command interpreters, built-ins are used to list the files in a directory, delete files, and copy files. But most of the commands invoked by command interpreters are customized extensions. Examples include tools like grep, sort, the C compiler, and (coming full circle here) emacs. Many such tools are installed at the same time as part of the "standard" release that includes the command interpreter, but they are custom extensions nonetheless.

In the best designs, all custom extensions have equal opportunity to perform. For instance, the main difference a UNIX shell sees between emacs and some editor written last weekend by Hacketa Lot is the filename of the executable code. The shell is just as happy to pass control to Hacketa's editor as it is to hand the reins to emacs (this is one reason for the memory protection provided by memory management chips and logical addressing!). Likewise, emacs is just as happy to execute a macro that changes "gas" to "petrol" and "color" to "colour" as it is to execute one that (almost) changes C code to Pascal.

Giving all extensions equal opportunity to perform means two things in practice. First, all extensions have equal access to the main program's internals. Second, no knowledge of particular extensions is built into the main program. Treating extensions equally is one of the marks of a useful "built-ins plus" program, and it will be one of our top-level goals.

Now let's move a stage closer to our specific problem by focusing on a particular kind of "built-ins plus" program: interpreters of languages that contain powerful special-purpose statements. This kind of interpreter is useful whenever expensive operations need to be run interactively. But what do we mean by "expensive" and "interactively"?

More to the point, why should we use an interpreter at all? Using an interpreter directly means learning a programming language, and there had better be a good reason if we're making customers do that! Instead of an interpreter, why not provide an application that zips through the special-purpose operations without bothering the user until the work is done? Or, if more control is needed, why not provide a menu-driven interface? To answer these questions, we need a better idea of what the interpreter does. So let's explain what we mean by executing "expensive" operations "interactively."

By "expensive operations," we mean statements that do significant work. They might accomplish this work by performing extensive calculations, by driving special-purpose hardware, or by doing both. For instance, pretend we have an interpreted language PIXELBASIC that is essentially BASIC extended to support computer graphics. Three statements in this imaginary language illustrate different ways to accomplish significant work.

1. The PIXELBASIC "filter" statement performs extensive calculations to filter an image, but it doesn't use any special hardware.
2. The "record" statement drives videotape recording hardware but doesn't do much calculation.
3. The "render" statement makes extensive calculations and also drives special hardware, since it produces an image by doing numerous shading calculations inside a special "pixel-crunching" engine.

PIXELBASIC or any other useful interpreted language would provide looping and conditional and I/O statements to make it easier to change the order in which "render" or other statements are executed. Special data types like "pixel" and "timecode" would also be useful. But the heart of a special-purpose interpreted language lies inside its individually powerful statements. These are the statements like "filter," "record," and "render" that get the expensive operations done.

By running operations "interactively," we mean that users get feedback quickly. We're talking about operations that take seconds, not hours to complete. This in turn allows the responsibility for further progress on the task to pass back and forth from user to interpreter many times during any given session. In other words, the user and the interpreter interact to get the job done.

Interpreters are useful when we need to try different parameters and orders of operation because we can't say whether a result is "right"; we can only say whether it's the "best" result so far. Computer graphics is a good example. There are hundreds or thousands of variations on any but the simplest rendered image which differ from each other in subtle but important ways. Users need to be able to change the parameters passed to the render statement, view the results, and vary the values and try again.

Trying out different parameters and orders is also useful if there are different ways to get virtually the same result, because one execution order or set of parameter values might be much faster than another but still give essentially the same results. Finally, the interactivity an interpreter provides is especially important during development, when we don't have enough experience to know yet what the default parameters and orders of execution ought to be.

In all these situations, an interpreter is clearly preferable to a compiled program that provides few or no choices about the parameters and order of execution of special-purpose operations. In fact, when a rigid application is used where an interpreter is what's really needed, the application often tries to become an interpreter. It begins to utilize command line switches or crude menus or some other scheme to restore to the user some of the flexibility an interpreter provides naturally.

A canned application is a bad alternative to an interpreter, even if it has menus. However, a menu system could be built on top of the interpreter to allow easy access to the most critical parameters and provide reasonable default values for the others. If this were done well, most users would never need to program directly in the interpreted language. What's more, if the menu system produced a program in the interpreted language, users who needed to change parameters unavailable from a menu could do so by editing the program before it was interpreted. It would be a bad idea to do away with the interpreter altogether, though, because of the flexibility we'd lose.

DESCRIPTION OF OUR PARTICULAR PROBLEM

Having considered "built-ins plus" programs in general and interpreters of powerful special-purpose statements in particular, let us now turn to the problem we want to solve in this chapter. We want to design and implement a method for passing information between the interpreter and our code modules. Several questions come to mind immediately. As we have in other chapters, we'll list all the unanswered questions together, even though they arise piecemeal.

BOX 14-1: Unanswered questions.

---

1. What are the tradeoffs involved in using code modules instead of building functionally equivalent statements into the interpreter?
2. What information do we need to pass from the interpreter to code modules? What information is passed back from code modules to the interpreter?
3. What guarantees are made by the interpreter that the information passed between the interpreter and the code modules is valid?
4. What restrictions must be placed on the source and object code used to create code modules?
5. What exactly does a code module prototype look like? What are the rules governing prototype syntax and semantics?
6. What exactly are the syntax and semantics of the code module launcher statement?
7. What are some of the typical function and internal variable addresses that need to be put in the parameter blocks along with the gathered code module parameters?
8. What exactly does a parameter block look like?

Question 1 asks about the tradeoffs between using code modules and built-in statements. Before we can decide what the tradeoffs are, we need a better description of the differences between built-in statements and code modules. A very general description of what an interpreter does to interpret a special-purpose statement is shown in Figure 14-1.

Actually, the same things are done for general-purpose statements like FOR or IF as for special-purpose statements, but the "execution" step in such cases normally includes interpretation of additional statements. Since we're concentrating on individually powerful statements, we will restrict ourselves to the case where there is no such recursion. In other words, one code module cannot directly invoke another.

If no code modules are used, all the actions shown in Figure 14-1 take place in built-in statements, so all results are computed by the interpreter proper. If there are code modules, however, the processing is divided between the interpreter and the code modules as shown.

While we're talking about what code performs what, we should make it clear that code modules are not implemented in the interpreted language. They are implemented in C or some other compiled language, just as the interpreter is, because they do so many calculations. Interpreters are no match for compilers when it comes to optimizing object code. And we need optimized code to get the performance we want, unless our code modules do only simple calculations to drive some special hardware.

Now consider the "parameter gathering" shown in Figure 14-1. This produces the interpreter equivalent of a compiled function's parameter block. For instance, suppose we have this PIXELBASIC statement in the middle of a FOR loop:

```
record 2*time% status%
```

This statement means "record the image at position $2*time\%$ on the videotape; zero *status%* if the record works, and put the nonzero error code in *status%* if the record fails."

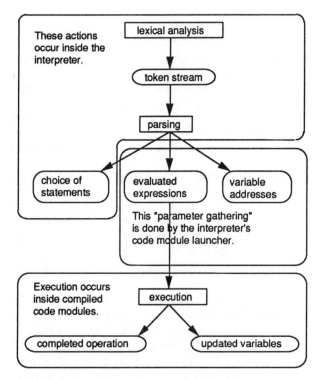

FIGURE 14-1: The sequence of actions and their results during interpretation of a special-purpose statement.

Like regular BASIC, PIXELBASIC uses the character at the end of a variable's name to specify the variable's data type; '%' means "integer." To do its job, the code that implements *record* must have the current value of 2*time% and the *address* of status%. The "evaluated expressions" mentioned in Figure 14-1 include expressions like 2*time%, which need to be evaluated before a statement can proceed. Likewise, "variable addresses" in Figure 14-1 refers to the fact that statements sometimes need the address of a variable such as *status%* so they can update its value.

Notice that every built-in statement has to gather its own parameters. Only the statement knows which parameters are values and which are variables (addresses). For instance, in the statement below, only the code inside *obscure* knows if the address of *x%* should be passed, or the current value of *x%* should be passed:

```
obscure x%
```

Code module parameters must be gathered, too, but we can put the gathering code in one place instead of scattering it throughout the code modules. If there are more than, say, ten statements, this becomes a significant savings. Scattering the gathering code amongst built-in statements means writing similar code to gather each statement's parameters. Maintaining all these slightly different versions is tedious and dangerous. The duplication also wastes code space, making the interpreter bigger than it needs to be.

We'll consolidate the parameter gathering code by adding a special statement to the interpreted language whose purpose is launching code modules. This "launch" statement will do the following:

1. Evaluate expressions and obtain variable addresses.
2. Put the results of step 1 someplace the code module can find them.
3. Invoke the code module, passing it the results of step 1.

But the launch statement can gather code module parameters only if it has some way to know what each code module expects by way of parameters, and some way to tell which code module is being launched. We'll just use the name of the file that contains the object code to identify code modules to the launcher. Code modules can only be "plug-in" if they aren't linked into the interpreter, so we'll need that filename anyway to load the object code into memory at some point.

The launch statement also needs "prototypes" that describe each code module's parameters. From the code module implementer's point of view (as opposed to the launch statement implementer's point of view), prototyping will be easy. In ANSI C, Pascal, Ada, and plenty of other languages prototyping amounts to providing a calling sequence and a mode for each parameter. Of the languages mentioned, Ada provides the most complete set of modes: in, out, and in-out. These modes mean just what they sound like. "In" parameters are passed by value, like the parameter $2*time\%$ in this record statement:

```
record 2*time% status%
```

All expressions are passed as "in" parameters—it's impossible to pass the address of an expression. Even if an actual "in" parameter happens to be a variable, the statement cannot change the variable's value, because it doesn't know the variable's address. The address is unavailable because C (and most other languages that allow recursion) pass an "in" parameter by evaluating the expression that defines its value and putting a copy of the answer on the stack.

"Out" and "in-out" parameters, by contrast, are passed as addresses. C does not distinguish between these modes. The difference is that the value of an "out" parameter that comes into a function is ignored inside the function. That is, "out" parameters are used only to pass data out of a function, while "in-out" parameters pass one value in and carry another one (or the same one) back out. In the record statement above, *status%* is an "out" parameter.

We have enough detail now to decide what some of the tradeoffs are between code modules and built-in statements. Suppose the launch statement is implemented and specifying a code module's prototype is easy. Then adding code modules is easier than adding statements for several reasons:

1. Changing a code module's parameter list is easier than changing a built-in statement's, because all we have to do is change the code module's prototype and the parameter accesses inside the module. The unchanged launcher will gather the new set of

parameters just as it gathered the earlier parameters. To change a built-in statement's parameters, we have to change the accesses and the statement's parameter gathering code as well.

2. Since parameter gathering is handled by the launcher, the level of interpreter-specific knowledge required to write a code module is less than that needed to write a built-in statement. This makes it easier to distribute the interpreter implementation work among several programmers. In other words, it's possible to make one programmer responsible for the interpreter proper, while as many other programmers as necessary work on the code modules. People can write code modules without knowing how the interpreter works internally.

3. The turnaround time between changes to a code module is shorter than it is between changes to a built-in statement because the interpreter doesn't have to be relinked.

On the other hand, built-ins are linked into the interpreter, but code modules are not. This means the built-in statements automatically have access to global variables and system functions and library functions that code modules do not. However, code modules execute in the interpreter's address space, so we can pass all these addresses explicitly to code modules when we pass in the gathered parameters.

This brings us to question 2. Via the launcher, the interpreter has to pass the following to each code module:

gathered parameters (values and addresses, as appropriate)
addresses of any functions or globals the code module needs but does not have because it isn't linked into the interpreter

Variables that are used inside the interpreter but are not directly available in the interpreted language will be called "internal variables." The FILE pointers used for standard and error output are typical internal variables; another example would be a global that controls the level of debugging. In the following statement, *time%* and *status%* are not internal variables, because they are accessible to programs written in the interpreted language:

```
record 2*time% status%
```

This means that the launcher passes code modules the addresses of two kinds of variables: "out" and "in-out" parameters, and internal variables.

Question 3 asks what guarantees the interpreter will make about the information it passes code modules. At first glance, the answer is "none"—how can the interpreter make sure the right values or variables are passed? Only the programmer who writes the launched code module knows what parameter values are acceptable.

However, the launcher does know from the prototype what type of parameters to expect, how many to expect, and what their modes are. The launcher can guarantee, for instance, that a code module whose prototype demands one floating point variable as an "in" parameter never gets passed the addresses of two integer variables.

Moving on to question 4 about restrictions on code modules, the main thing to keep in mind is that the code module is not linked into the interpreter. This means it has to be loaded into memory by the interpreter at some logical address that is unknown ahead of time and that varies from load to load anyway. So, for instance, the code module cannot have any absolute addresses in it. All jumps and variable references have either to be relative to the program counter or to use addresses passed in from the interpreter. In other words, the object code must be "relocatable."

Programs like the interpreter, by contrast, typically have the entry point to their code at logical address 0x0000. So every time the command interpreter jumps to the start of main(), it is jumping to the same logical address. It's easier for a compiler or linker to generate addresses if the code segment always starts at the same logical address. The result of all this is that most compilers have to be told to generate relocatable code, and some simply won't, even if you ask them politely.

The other main restriction on object code modules has already been mentioned: They can only invoke external functions or access variables whose addresses have been passed to them by the interpreter's launch statement.

We have enough background now to design our code module-interpreter interface, so let's get started.

TOP-LEVEL GOALS

Several of these goals have already been mentioned, but we'll list them all here for easy reference:

All code modules have equal access to the interpreter's internals.

No knowledge of particular code modules is built into the interpreter.

The code module launcher will pass gathered parameters (values and addresses) to the code module being launched.

The code module launcher will also pass the addresses of any functions or globals the code module needs but does not have because it isn't linked into the interpreter.

The launcher will not invoke a code module unless the data types, modes, and number of actual parameters supplied matches the code module's prototype.

Changing a code module's prototype should be relatively easy. In particular, it should not require any changes to the code module launcher unless a new data type is being added to the interpreted language.

GUIDING EXAMPLES

Based on our efforts so far, the following would seem to be a good set of fundamental characteristics of code modules:

the number of formal parameters (zero is a possibility)

the formal parameter modes (in, out, in-out)

the formal parameter data types

whether the code module needs function addresses passed in by the launcher

whether the code module accesses internal interpreter variables (recall that these are
variables other than those corresponding to the module's actual parameters)

We can cover these characteristics pretty completely with just a few well-chosen
examples. In the PIXELBASIC statements below, we follow the convention that integer
variables end in '%,' floating point variables end in '!,' and string variables end in '$.' Our
guiding example code module invocations are as follows:

```
launch "no_parms"
launch "one_int_parm_in" a_in%
launch "two_int_parms_out" a_out% b_out%
launch "one_each_type_in" a_in% b_in! c_in$
launch "one_int_each_mode" a_in% b_out% c_in_out%
launch "calls_fopen_writes_global" a_in%
```

These code module names are mainly self-explanatory, but *calls_fopen_writes_global*
deserves a brief note. This module has to be passed three items: the current value of actual
parameter *a_in%*, the address of standard function *fopen()*, and the address of an internal
interpreter global variable.

ABSTRACT DATA TYPE DESCRIPTION

Now we're ready to complete the abstract data type description. It should go quickly because
we need to deal with only one parameter block at a time.

**What name does this particular collection of data elements go by, that is, what
abstract data type are we concerned with?** The data elements are code module
parameter blocks.

What is the geometry of the collection? There isn't any geometry to speak of. The
collection contains at most one element at a time. There doesn't need to be a stack of
parameter blocks because one code module cannot directly invoke another. Likewise, there
is no need for a list or tree or other arrangement to organize parameter blocks because only
one code module is invoked at a time. The basic sequence of operations for interpreting a
launch statement is always this:

1. Gather the parameters, verifying their number, data types, and modes against the
   code module's prototype.
2. Allocate and fill a parameter block with the gathered parameters and the addresses
   of functions or internal interpreter variables.
3. Load the module's object code into memory if necessary.

4. Invoke the code module, passing it the parameter block.
5. Free the parameter block.
6. Interpret the next statement.

What relations hold between the data elements in the collection? There's never more than one parameter block in the collection at a time, so there are no relations between data elements. Likewise, there are no other collections, unless we want to talk about other interpreters, which we don't.

What are the properties of each position in the geometry, with respect to the operators, and with respect to elements in other positions? There's no geometry, so there are no positions within the geometry.

What are the operators? We need three operators: allocate and fill a parameter block, deallocate a parameter block, and pretty-print the contents of a parameter block for debugging.

What are the restrictions on membership in the collection? Aside from the fact that we have only one parameter block in the collection at a time, the main restriction on membership is the need to match actual parameters against the code module's prototype.

What is the meaning of each element in the collection? Parameter blocks have two components: the gathered actual parameters, and the additional addresses of functions and internal interpreter variables. Like the object code itself, the parameter block must be relocatable—it must have the same meaning no matter where it is in memory. We don't know where the code will be because it's loaded at interpreter run-time. We don't know where the parameter block will be because it is allocated when the module is launched.

The gathered actual parameters for a given code module may differ from one invocation of the module to the next, but we will probably send the same list of function addresses and internal variables to each code module. This is easiest, and safest as well, since there's no prototype to make sure we send the right functions and internal variables to each module; prototypes only check gathered parameters.

ATTEMPT ONE

Several points are still vague; they give rise to questions 5 through 8. We'll start with question 5 about code module prototypes. It would be nice if a prototype looked like an invocation of the code module. Prototypes in other languages follow this convention, but is it possible in our interpreted language?

Let's compare the information present in an invocation with what we need to supply in a prototype. A prototype has to provide the launch statement with the code module's name and the type and mode of each of its parameters. We can tell the code module name and the data type of each parameter from the invocation, but we can't tell the mode.

We can tell parameter types from an invocation because, as we've seen, each variable's type is inherent in its name. Integer names end in '%,' floating point names in '!,' strings in '$,' and so forth. Types are inherent in names because PIXELBASIC variables are not formally declared. We never write something like *int a;*. Instead, variables are created (i.e., allocated and entered in the symbol table) the first time they're encountered. The data type of a variable has to be inherent in its name so that a PIXELBASIC interpreter can tell from the name how much memory to allocate for the variable.

As far as parameter data types are concerned, then, a code module prototype can have the same syntax as an invocation of the module. The invocation also tells us the number of parameters and their positions. But the invocation does not tell us parameter modes, except that expressions must be matched to "in" parameters. And if a variable is an actual parameter, we don't know from the invocation whether it matches an "in," "out," or "in-out" formal parameter.

So the syntax for a prototype has to be an extension of the syntax for an invocation. These are a few of the many possibilities:

```
1. proto "one_int_each_mode" in:a% out:b% in_out:c%
2. proto "one_int_each_mode" ->a% <-b% <->c%
3. proto "one_int_each_mode" >a% <b% *c%
4. proto "one_int_each_mode" >a% b%> <c%>
5. proto "one_int_each_mode" a% *b% *c%
```

Notice that the '*' syntax in example 5 doesn't distinguish between "out" and "in-out" parameters; it is analagous to C's '&' operator. The distinction between "out" and "in-out" is difficult to enforce in a compiler, since it means the compiler has to make sure the function doesn't treat an "out" variable as an "in-out" variable by reading from it before it has written to it.

Moreover, the distinction between "out" and "in-out" parameters is impossible to enforce in a code module, because the body of the code module is written in a language other than the one being interpreted. The interpreter knows something about the type of parameters the module wants, but it has no way to know what happens to those parameters inside the module. So the choice between "out" and "in-out" for a code module parameter is actually commentary, not enforced semantics.

The '*' syntax in example 5 is preferable for three reasons. First, it doesn't imply a distinction between "out" and "in-out" parameters; we don't want to imply that we're enforcing something we're not, and commentary that isn't right inside the code tends to be out of date and therefore misleading. Second, the syntax is easy to remember because it looks like C. Third, the syntax uses only one character.

This third reason requires some explanation. Since we don't want to implement a whole interpreter here, we'll use a simple trick to make lexical analysis trivial. In our toy PIXELBASIC interpreter, there will be a one-to-one match between characters and tokens. Numeric and string constants will be the only exceptions.

For instance, a typical code module prototype will look like this:

```
proto "one_int_each_mode" a% *b% *c%
```

This means the object code is stored in a file named "one_int_each_mode," and the module expects three parameters. Each parameter is an integer. The first is an "in" parameter and the other two are "out" or "in-out" parameters; the proto statement doesn't tell us whether the values passed in via $b\%$ and $c\%$ are actually used, only that values can be passed out via $b\%$ and $c\%$. The parameters do *not* have to be named "a," "b," and "c" in an actual invocation:

```
launch "one_int_each_mode" 2*i% row% col%
```

Having decided why the '•' syntax is preferable, we're now free to abandon it, and that's just what we'll do. All variables in the toy interpreter that we've actually implemented are passed by address. That is, all parameters are "out" parameters. This was done for two reasons. First, it's easier to implement. Prototype syntax is simpler, and parameter gathering is easier, and there's no danger of confusing parameter modes inside a code module. Second, we have to trust the code modules anyway, so there's little security to be gained by passing fewer addresses. The only increase in safety comes if we don't pass the code modules any addresses at all, and that makes them almost useless.

The example above of a launch statement does much to answer question 6 about the launcher statement's syntax and semantics. But let's be a bit more precise. A launch statement has the following syntax:

launch <code module filename> <code module actual parameters>

<code module filename> is the name of the file that contains the relocatable object code. <code module actual parameters> is a possibly empty list of parameters, each of which follows this syntax:

<name><data type>

The <name> is one character in (a..z, A..Z). The <data type> is one of '%,' '!' or '$,' indicating integer, real, and string respectively. Parameters are always "out" or "in-out."

A constant value or the value from an expression can only be passed by assigning it to a variable and then passing the variable's address. For instance, this is illegal:

```
launch "one_int_each_mode" x% 27 -1
```

Instead, we have to do something like this:

```
y% = 27
z% = -1
launch "one_int_each_mode" x% y% z%
```

All formal and actual parameter data types must match; the following is illegal because the parameters are supposed to be integers, not strings or reals:

```
launch "one_int_each_mode" s$ r! s!
```

We could relax this restriction to do some automatic type conversion if we wish, but that doesn't change the general purpose of a prototype, which is to do as much as possible to make sure the code module is passed the right parameters.

Question 7 points out the major weakness of using code modules as opposed to built-in statements: It's harder with code modules to get at the standard library functions we're accustomed to using. These functions are linked into the interpreter but not into the code modules, so their addresses must be explicitly passed during each module launch. For instance, the launch statement has to pass the following addresses for a code module to use typical UNIX stream I/O, memory management, and string manipulation:

```
char    *stdin;
char    *stdout;
char    *stderr;
int     printf();
int     fprintf();
int     scanf();
int     fscanf();
FILE    *fopen();
int     fclose();
int     fread();
int     fwrite();
int     fflush();
void    *malloc();
int     free();
char    *strcat();
char    *strcpy();
int     strcmp();
int     strlen();
```

It's not that we can't pass these addresses. We can. But we had better be sure that the mechanism we use allows room for growth (preferably unlimited growth), because there's no way to predict up front what functions code modules will need to call years from now.

We can pass the addresses of internal interpreter variables the same way we pass the standard functions. Three examples of such variables come to mind; there might well be some others, too:

a global interpreter error status
a global set of interpreter debugging flags
UNIX's stdin, stdout and stderr stream buffers

Question 8 asks what a parameter block looks like. The answer is "something like Figure 14-2." Notice in that figure that the list of standard functions and internal variable addresses is accessed through one level of indirection. This allows us to add new addresses to the list as we please without affecting code modules created before the list was changed. The offsets used by such modules are still correct, so code modules don't even need to be recompiled when another standard function or internal variable address is added. Notice, however, that it would be very bad indeed to use a new code module with an old copy of the interpreter that hasn't set up the addresses the new module uses.

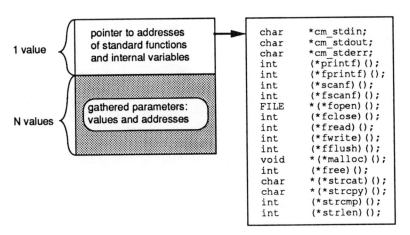

```
             char    *cm_stdin;
             char    *cm_stdout;
             char    *cm_stderr;
             int     (*printf)();
             int     (*fprintf)();
             int     (*scanf)();
             int     (*fscanf)();
             FILE    *(*fopen)();
             int     (*fclose)();
             int     (*fread)();
             int     (*fwrite)();
             int     (*fflush)();
             void    *(*malloc)();
             int     (*free)();
             char    *(*strcat)();
             char    *(*strcpy)();
             int     (*strcmp)();
             int     (*strlen)();
```

FIGURE 14-2: Structure of a code module parameter block. In the toy interpreter, "in" parameters are not implemented, so the gathered parameters contain only variable addresses, not values and addresses.

The typedefs that correspond to Figure 14-2 are as follows:

```
/* code module (hence "cm") parameter block: */
/* Note that cm_parm_block.parms is actually N values long—it's
   allocated dynamically to hold parameters; int was used for
   convenience (it is often the same size as a machine word),
   NOT to indicate that all parameters are integers—they aren't. */
typedef struct {
   cm_fcns    *fcns;
   int         parms[1];    /* actually N values */
}   cm_parm_block;
/* add new addresses at the end of this list as they are needed: */
typedef struct {
   char *cm_stdin;
   char *cm_stdout;
   char *cm_stderr;
   int  (*printf)();
   int  (*fprintf)();
   int  (*scanf)();
   int  (*fscanf)();
   FILE *(*fopen)();
   int  (*fclose)();
   int  (*fread)();
   int  (*fwrite)();
   int  (*fflush)();
   void *(*malloc)();
   int  (*free)();
   char *(*strcat)();
```

```
        char * (*strcpy) () ;
        int   (*strcmp) () ;
        int   (*strlen) () ;
} cm_fcns;
```

Notice that the members of struct *cm_fcns* are all named the same as the function or internal variable whose address they hold, except for *cm_stdin*, *cm_stdout*, and *cm_stderr*. These hold the addresses of standard UNIX stream buffers *stdin*, *stdout*, and *stderr*, but the names had to be changed because *stdin*, *stdout*, and *stderr* are actually #defines. The same names are used wherever possible to make the function calls inside the code module look familiar:

```
code_module_main ( parm_block )
   cm_parm_block   *parm_block;
{
   (* (parm_block->fcns->printf)) ("Hello, world!\n");
   return (0);
} /* code_module_main */
```

Notice also that the size of a particular *cm_parm_block.parms* is not necessarily $1*sizeof(int)$. The comment by *cm_parm_block.parms* is more accurate than the typedef in this instance. The amount of space actually allocated for *cm_parm_block.parms* depends on the number of parameters the code module's prototype says it has, and what data types the parameters are. Examples are shown in the listings.

Before we look at the code, please note that there are some differences in statement syntax between the toy interpreted language that is actually implemented here and the more powerful and general interpreted language that we've described above:

"In" and "in-out" parameters are not implemented—everything is passed by address.
Expressions are not implemented.
The syntax for assignment statements is awkward (or LISP-like, if you prefer that characterization).
Statements are abbreviated: "l" for "launch," "p" for "proto," and so on.

But the main parts of the general case discussed above—prototypes and launchable code modules with parameters—are implemented.

Code modules are a very powerful way to extend programs. They provide the flexibility of an interpreter without sacrificing the optimized object code produced by a compiler. The toy interpreter implemented here would actually be as powerful as any interpreter if we added expression evaluation, a few general-purpose statements like IF and WHILE, and a good assortment of code modules.

LISTING: code_modules.h

```
/*------------------------------------------------
                     code_modules.h
------------------------------------------------*/
```

```
/*===================================================================
Purpose:
    Typedefs for relocatable, dynamically loaded object code
    modules.
--------------------------------------------------------------*/
#ifndef _CODE_MODULES_H_
#define _CODE_MODULES_H_

#include <stdio.h> /* for FILE */

/* add new addresses AT THE END of this list as they are needed: */
typedef struct {
    FILE    *cm_stdin;
    FILE    *cm_stdout;
    FILE    *cm_stderr;
    int     (*printf)();
    int     (*fprintf)();
    int     (*scanf)();
    int     (*fscanf)();
    FILE    *(*fopen)();
    int     (*fclose)();
    int     (*fread)();
    int     (*fwrite)();
    int     (*fflush)();
    void    *(*malloc)();
    int     (*free)();
    char    *(*strcat)();
    char    *(*strcpy)();
    int     (*strcmp)();
    int     (*strlen)();
}   cm_fcns;

/* code module (hence "cm") parameter block: */
typedef struct {
    cm_fcns     *fcns;
    void        *parms[1];  /* actually N values long */
}   cm_parm_block;

#endif _CODE_MODULES_H_
```

LISTING: cm_test_module.c

```
/*--------------------------------------------------------------
                        cm_test_module.c
--------------------------------------------------------------*/

/*===================================================================
```

```
Purpose:
    This file provides an object code module that can be invoked
    by the toy interpreter in cm_interpreter.c.

    This code was compiled under THINK's LightspeedC® on a
    Macintosh™ SE. The module was built as a code resource with
    these attributes: preloaded, locked, protected. The actual
    executable code starts in the resource file after the standard
    16 byte header prepended by THINK. Their Mactraps library
    can be used, but wasn't needed for this example.

    WARNING: The parts of this source marked by "THINK" inside
    comments are very specific to THINK's LightspeedC Macintosh
    environment.
--------------------------------------------------------*/
#include "code_modules.h"
#include <SetUpA4.h> /* THINK */


static  char    buf[] = "This is NEAT!";


/*================================================================*/
main( parm_block )
    cm_parm_block    *parm_block;
/*------------------------------------------------------
Purpose:
    Exercise the toy interpreter's launch statement. Prints the
    the value of one actual parameter, sets another, opens and
    writes and closes a file, and returns status 0.
Parameters:
    The prototype should look like this:
        p cm_test x% r!
    x%'s value is printed, and r! is set to 1.2345.
-------------------------------------------------------*/
{
    cm_fcns *fcns;
    int     i;
    FILE    *fp;
    Handle  hnd;

    RememberA0(); /* THINK */
    SetUpA4();    /* THINK */
    /* Now we see the kind of code that could be any code
       module, THINK C or not, Macintosh or not: */
    fcns = parm_block->fcns;
    (*fcns->printf)("%s First parm = %d\n",
                    buf,
                    *((int *)(parm_block->parms[0])));
    fp = (*fcns->fopen)("cm_did_it", "w");
```

```
    if (fp) {
        (*fcns->fwrite) (buf, sizeof(buf), 1, fp);
        (*fcns->fclose) (fp);
    }
    *((float *) (parm_block->parms[1])) = 1.2345;
    RestoreA4(); /* THINK */
    return (0);
} /* main */
```

LISTING: cm_interpreter.c

```
/*---------------------------------------------
                    cm_interpreter.c
-----------------------------------------------*/


/*===============================================================
Purpose:
    This file provides a toy interpreter as a testbed to exercise
    object code modules; the testbed driver is main().

    This code was compiled under THINK's LightspeedC® on a
    Macintosh™ SE.

    WARNING: The parts of this source marked by "THINK" in comments
    are very specific to THINK's LightspeedC Macintosh environment.
-----------------------------------------------*/
#include <stdio.h>
#include <Storage.h>
#include <boolean.h>
#include "code_modules.h"

/* functions the interpreter makes available to code modules: */
extern int   printf();
extern int   fprintf();
extern int   scanf();
extern int   fscanf();
extern FILE *fopen();
extern int   fclose();
extern int   fread();
extern int   fwrite();
extern int   fflush();
extern void *malloc();
extern int   free();
extern char *strcat();
extern char *strcpy();
extern int   strcmp();
```

```
extern int  strlen();

/* functions used to load THINK C code resources on a Macintosh: */
extern pascal int       OpenResFile();
extern pascal void      CloseResFile();
extern pascal Handle    GetNamedResource();
extern pascal void      LoadResource();
extern pascal int       ResError();

/* DEFINES: */
/* status codes: */
#define CM_OK                   0
#define CM_ERR                  1
/* offset of executable code inside a THINK C code resource file: */
#define CM_THINK_CODE_OFFSET    16
#define CM_MAX_PARMS            10 /* max # of code module parameters */
#define CM_MAX_STATEMENT_LEN    64
#define CM_MAX_FILENAME_LEN     256

/* TYPEDEFS: */
/* type used to represent variables and constants: */
typedef struct cm_varb {
    struct cm_varb  *next;
    char            name;   /* variable's name (just 1 char) */
    char            type;   /* % = int, ! = float, $ = string */
    union {
        int     int_val;
        float   float_val;
        char    *string_val;
    } u;                    /* variable's value */
}   cm_varb;

/* type used to represent code module prototype: */
typedef struct cm_prototype{
    struct cm_prototype *next;
    char                *name;      /* code module's name */
    char                parms[CM_MAX_PARMS+1];
    /* parms holds one type definition character */
    /* ('%', '!', or '$') per parameter + '\0' string terminator */
}   cm_prototype;

/* GLOBALS: */
static cm_prototype *cm_protos = NULL;  /* prototypes user makes */
static char         cm_input_text[CM_MAX_STATEMENT_LEN];
/* standard arguments passed by the interpreter to every code module: */
static cm_parm_block    *std_cm_args = NULL;
static cm_varb      *cm_varbs = NULL;   /* variables user makes */
static char         cm_code_dir[CM_MAX_FILENAME_LEN];
```

```
static char              cm_module_name[CM_MAX_FILENAME_LEN];

/*===============================================================*/
main()
/*----------------------------------------------
Purpose:
     This is a toy interpreter that recognizes these statements:

          prototype:  tells the interpreter what parameters to pass
                      a code module
          launch:     checks the actual parameter types against the
                      code module's prototype, builds a parameter
                      block, and invokes the code module
          assignment: assigns a value to an integer, floating point
                      or string variable; creates the variable and
                      initializes it to 0, 0.0 or " " if it doesn't
                      already exist; this statement is the ONLY way
                      to create a variable
          display:    prints the current value of a variable
          quit:       exit the interpreter

     To make lexical analysis easy, all tokens except constant values
     are one character long. That is, statement and variable names
     are each one character long—"p" for "prototype," "l" for
     "launch," etc.
     A typical program is shown below on the left; the comments shown
     on the right are not part of the program:

     p "cm_test" a% *b!  prototype module "cm_test" to have one
                         integer "in" parameter and one floating
                         point "out" parameter
     a x% 27             create integer variable x, assign 27 to it
     a r! 1.1            create floating point variable r and assign
                         1.1 to it
     l "cm_test" x% r!   launch code module "cm_test," passing it
                         a pointer to the current value of x% (27)
                         and a pointer to the variable r!
     d x%                print the current value of x% (still 27)
     d r!                print the current value of r! (depends on
                         what code module r! did)
     q                   quit

     Note also that the only white space character handled is
     blank (' '), and strings are not quoted.
Parameters:
     none—input is read from stdin and sent to stdout
----------------------------------------------*/
{
```

```
        boolean     cm_init();
        void        cm_read_statement(),
                    cm_assign(),
                    cm_display(),
                    cm_launch(),
                    cm_proto(),
                    cm_clean_up();

    if (!cm_init()) {
        printf("main: failed to initialize interpreter\n");
        return (CM_ERR);
    }
    while (true) {
        cm_read_statement();
        if (cm_input_text[0] == 'a') {
            cm_assign();
        }
        else if (cm_input_text[0] == 'd') {
            cm_display();
        }
        else if (cm_input_text[0] == 'l') {
            cm_launch();
        }
        else if (cm_input_text[0] == 'p') {
            cm_proto();
        }
        else if (cm_input_text[0] == 'q') {
            printf("Quitting...\n");
            cm_clean_up();
            return (CM_OK);
        }
        else {
            printf("Unknown statement\n");
        }
    }
} /* main */


/*================================================================*/
static boolean  cm_init()
/*-------------------------------------------------------

Purpose:
    Initialize the interpreter.
Parameters:
    global cm_parm_block *std_cm_args is set to point to a newly
    allocated and initialized parameter block
--------------------------------------------------------*/
{
    cm_parm_block   *cm_init_args();
```

```c
    if ((!std_cm_args) && !(std_cm_args = cm_init_args())) {
        printf("cm_init: init standard parameter block failed\n");
        return (false);
    }
    strcpy(cm_code_dir, "dizzie:"); /* JWLO's THINK disk */
    return (true);
} /* cm_init */

/*===============================================================*/
static cm_parm_block    *cm_init_args()
/*-----------------------------------------------------
Purpose:
    Allocate and initialize standard code module parameter block.
Parameters:
    Returns pointer to initialized block if successful, else NULL
-------------------------------------------------------*/
{
    cm_parm_block    *new_parm_block;
    cm_fcns          *new_fcns;
    void             *calloc(); /* malloc() then fill w/ zeroes */

    /* use calloc() to allocate new parm block and initialize
       it to NULLs: */
    if (!(new_parm_block = (cm_parm_block *)calloc(
            1,
            sizeof(cm_parm_block) + sizeof(long)*CM_MAX_PARMS))) {
        printf("cm_init_args: out of memory\n");
        return (NULL);
    }
    if (!(new_parm_block->fcns = (cm_fcns *)calloc(
            1,
            sizeof(cm_fcns)))) {
        printf("cm_init_args: out of memory\n");
        cfree(new_parm_block);
        return (NULL);
    }
    new_fcns = new_parm_block->fcns;
    new_fcns->cm_stdin  = stdin;
    new_fcns->cm_stdout = stdout;
    new_fcns->cm_stderr = stderr;
    new_fcns->printf    = printf;
    new_fcns->fprintf   = fprintf;
    new_fcns->scanf     = scanf;
    new_fcns->fscanf    = fscanf;
    new_fcns->fopen     = fopen;
    new_fcns->fclose    = fclose;
    new_fcns->fread     = fread;
    new_fcns->fwrite    = fwrite;
```

```
        new_fcns->fflush    = fflush;
        new_fcns->malloc    = malloc;
        new_fcns->free      = free;
        new_fcns->strcat    = strcat;
        new_fcns->strcpy    = strcpy;
        new_fcns->strcmp    = strcmp;
        new_fcns->strlen    = strlen;
        return (new_parm_block);
} /* cm_init_args */


/*================================================================*/
static void cm_clean_up()
/*------------------------------------------------
Purpose:
    Free allocated memory, close opened files, etc.
Parameters:
    All globals that point to allocated memory:
        std_cm_args
        cm_protos
        cm_varbs
-----------------------------------------------*/
{
    cm_prototype *nxt_proto, *zap_proto;
    cm_varb      *nxt_varb, *zap_varb;

    free(std_cm_args->fcns);
    free(std_cm_args);
    for (nxt_proto = cm_protos; nxt_proto; ) {
        zap_proto = nxt_proto;
        nxt_proto = nxt_proto->next;
        free(zap_proto->name);
        free(zap_proto);
    }
    for (nxt_varb = cm_varbs; nxt_varb; ) {
        zap_varb = nxt_varb;
        nxt_varb = nxt_varb->next;
        if (nxt_varb->type == '$')
            free(nxt_varb->u.string_val);
        free(zap_varb);
    }
    return;
} /* cm_clean_up */


/*================================================================*/
static void cm_read_statement()
/*------------------------------------------------
Purpose:
    Read the next statement to be interpreted.
```

```
Parameters:
    global char cm_input_text holds the ASCII text read;
    always returns true
---------------------------------------------*/
{
    char    *gets();

    printf("\n>");
    gets(cm_input_text);
    return;
} /* cm_read_statement */


/*===============================================================*/
static cm_varb  *cm_find_make_varb( typed_name )
    char    *typed_name;    /* IN */
/*---------------------------------------------
Purpose:
    Create variable if it doesn't exist, and initialize it.
    Return pointer to internal variable description if variable
    already exists.
Parameters:
    typed_name  holds a three-character string; first char is
                variable's name, second is its type, third is null
                (string terminator)
---------------------------------------------*/
{
    cm_varb     *varb_desc,
                *cm_find_varb(),
                *cm_make_varb();

    /* see if this is one of the variables that already exist */
    if (varb_desc = cm_find_varb(typed_name))
        return (varb_desc);
    /* didn't find it; make it and add it to the end of the list */
    return (cm_make_varb(typed_name));
} /* cm_find_make_varb */


/*===============================================================*/
static cm_varb  *cm_find_varb( typed_name )
    char    *typed_name;    /* IN */
/*---------------------------------------------
Purpose:
    Try to find a variable. Return pointer to internal variable
    description if found, NULL otherwise.
Parameters:
    typed_name  holds a three-character string; first char is
                variable's name, second is its type, third is null
    global cm_varb *cm_varbs points to list of variable descriptions
```

```
-----------------------------------------------*/
{
    cm_varb      *nxt;

    if (!typed_name)
        return (NULL);
    for (   nxt = cm_varbs;
            nxt &&
                ((nxt->name != typed_name[0]) ||
                 (nxt->type != typed_name[1])    ) ;
            nxt = nxt->next )
        ;
    return (nxt);
} /* cm_find_varb */

/*==============================================================*/
static cm_varb  *cm_make_varb( typed_name )
    char    *typed_name;     /* IN */
/*----------------------------------------------------------
Purpose:
    Create variable, initialize it, add to end of list.
Parameters:
    typed_name  holds a three-character string; first char is
                variable's name, second is its type, third is null
    global cm_varb *cm_varbs points to list of variable descriptions
-----------------------------------------------*/
{
    char        *strsave();
    cm_varb     *new, *nxt;
    void        *calloc(); /* malloc() then fill with zeroes */

    if (!typed_name)
        return (NULL);
    if (!(new = (cm_varb *)calloc(1, sizeof(cm_varb)))) {
        printf("cm_make_varb: out of memory\n");
        return (NULL);
    }
    new->next = NULL;
    new->name = typed_name[0];
    new->type = typed_name[1];
    if (new->type == '%') {
        new->u.int_val = 0;
    }
    else if (new->type == '!') {
        new->u.float_val = 0.0;
    }
    else if (new->type == '$') {
        if (!(new->u.string_val = strsave(" "))) {
```

```
                printf("cm_make_varb: out of memory\n");
                free(new);
                return (NULL);
            }
        }
        else {
            printf("cm_make_varb: unknown data type\n");
            free(new);
            return (NULL);
        }
        /* add to end of list */
        if (!cm_varbs) {
            cm_varbs = new;
        }
        else {
            for (nxt = cm_varbs; nxt->next; nxt = nxt->next)
                ;
            nxt->next = new;
        }
        return (new);
    } /* cm_make_varb */


/*================================================================*/
static void cm_assign()
/*------------------------------------------------------------

Purpose:
    Create variable if it doesn't exist, and assign value to it.
    No type conversion is done. An assignment statement is the only
    way to create a variable.
Parameters:
    global char cm_input_text should hold an assignment statement
        that looks like one of these:
            a x% 27
            a r! 0.33
            a s$ this is working
    global cm_varb *cm_varbs points to the list of variables
        created so far
----------------------------------------------------------------*/
{
    /* varb[3]: variable name (1 char) + type char + NULL */
    char        varb[3],
                *strsave();
    cm_varb     *cm_find_make_varb(),
                *varb_desc;
    int         i;
    int         int_val;
    float       float_val;
    char        *string_val;
```

```
        /* skip leading 'a' and extract variable name */
        for (i = 2; cm_input_text[i] == ' '; i++)
            ;
        varb[0] = cm_input_text[i++]; /* variable's name */
        varb[1] = cm_input_text[i++]; /* variable's type */
        varb[2] = '\0';
        if (varb[1] == '%') {
            sscanf(cm_input_text+i,"%d", &int_val);
        }
        else if (varb[1] == '!') {
            sscanf(cm_input_text+i,"%f", &float_val);
        }
        else if (varb[1] == '$') {
            for (; cm_input_text[i] == ' '; i++)
                ;
            string_val = cm_input_text+i;
        }
        else {
            printf("cm_assign: unknown data type\n");
            return;
        }
        if (!(varb_desc = cm_find_make_varb(varb))) {
            printf("cm_assign: couldn't find or create variable\n");
            return;
        }
        if (varb[1] == '%') {
            varb_desc->u.int_val = int_val;
        }
        else if (varb[1] == '!') {
            varb_desc->u.float_val = float_val;
        }
        else if (varb[1] == '$') {
            if (varb_desc->u.string_val)
                free(varb_desc->u.string_val);
            if (!(varb_desc->u.string_val = strsave(string_val))) {
                printf("cm_assign: out of memory\n");
                return;
            }
        }
    return;
} /* cm_assign */


/*=============================================================*/
static void cm_display()
/*-------------------------------------------------------------
Purpose:
    Display the current value of a variable in the proper format.
Parameters:
```

```
        global char cm_input_text should hold a display statement that
            looks like one of these:
                d x%
                d r!
                d s$
        global cm_varb *cm_varbs points to list of variable descriptions
------------------------------------------------------------*/
{
    /* varb[3]: variable name (1 char) + type char + NULL */
    char        varb[3];
    int         i;
    cm_varb     *varb_desc,
                *cm_find_varb();

    /* skip leading 'd' and extract variable name */
    for (i = 2; cm_input_text[i] == ' '; i++)
        ;
    varb[0] = cm_input_text[i++]; /* variable's name */
    varb[1] = cm_input_text[i++]; /* variable's type */
    varb[2] = '\0';
    if (!(varb_desc = cm_find_varb(varb))) {
        printf("cm_display: variable %s does not exist\n", varb);
        return;
    }
    if (varb_desc->type == '%') {
        printf("%s = %d\n", varb, varb_desc->u.int_val);
    }
    else if (varb_desc->type == '!') {
        printf("%s = %f\n", varb, varb_desc->u.float_val);
    }
    else if (varb_desc->type == '$') {
        printf("%s = %s\n", varb, varb_desc->u.string_val);
    }
    else {
        printf("cm_display: unknown data type used internally!\n");
        return;
    }
    return;
} /* cm_display */


/*===============================================================*/
static void cm_launch()
/*-------------------------------------------------------------
Purpose:
    Validate the actual parameters passed by comparing them to the
    code module's prototype, gather the parameters into a block,
    and invoke the code module.
Parameters:
```

```
    global char cm_input_text should hold a launch statement that
        looks something like this:
            l cm_test x% r!
        Notice that the module name is not quoted, and all actual
        parameters are variables, whether they're "in" or "out";
        all actual parameters are passed by address as "out"
        parameters.
    ---------------------------------------------------------*/
{
    char            module_name[CM_MAX_STATEMENT_LEN],
                    varb[3];
    int             i, j, parm, res;
    int             (*code)();
    void            *cm_load_module();
    cm_varb         *varb_desc,
                    *cm_find_varb();
    cm_prototype    *proto_desc,
                    *cm_find_proto();

    /* skip leading 'l' and extract code module name */
    for (i = 2; cm_input_text[i] == ' '; i++)
        ;
    for (   j = 0;
            cm_input_text[i] && cm_input_text[i] != ' ';
            i++, j++) {
        module_name[j] = cm_input_text[i];
    }
    module_name[j] = '\0';
    if (!(proto_desc = cm_find_proto(module_name))) {
        printf( "cm_launch: no prototype defined yet for %s\n",
                module_name);
        return;
    }
    if (!(code = cm_load_module(module_name))) {
        printf("cm_launch: failed to load object code\n");
        return;
    }
    /* gather parameters */
    for (parm = 0; cm_input_text[i] && (parm < CM_MAX_PARMS); ) {
        for ( ; cm_input_text[i] && cm_input_text[i] == ' '; i++)
            ;
        if (!cm_input_text[i])
            break;
        varb[0] = cm_input_text[i++]; /* variable name */
        varb[1] = cm_input_text[i++]; /* variable type */
        varb[2] = '\0';
        if (!(varb_desc = cm_find_varb(varb))) {
```

```
                printf("cm_launch: couldn't find variable %s\n", varb);
                return;
        }
        if (varb[1] != proto_desc->parms[parm]) {
                printf("cm_launch: parameters don't match prototype\n");
                return;
        }
        std_cm_args->parms[parm++] = &varb_desc->u;
        if (parm > CM_MAX_PARMS) {
                printf( "cm_launch: %s has too many parameters\n",
                        module_name);
                return;
        }
    }
    if (parm != strlen(proto_desc->parms)) {
        printf("cm_launch: wrong number of parameters\n");
        return;
    }
    /* this is the statement the rest of the program was written
       to support—invoke that code module!: */
    res = (*code)(std_cm_args);
    if (res != 0)
        printf("cm_launch: code module returned error = %d\n", res);
    return;
} /* cm_launch */


/*================================================================*/
static void     *cm_load_module( name ) /* very THINK-specific */
    char    *name;  /* IN */
/*----------------------------------------------------------------
Purpose:
    Load object code into memory. ALL IMPLEMENTATION-DEPENDENT
    INFO NEEDED FOR LOADING RELOCATABLE CODE INTO MEMORY SHOULD
    BE IN THIS FUNCTION. Don't worry if it looks like magic. The
    same sort of thing can be done on other systems. The hardest
    part is getting a compiler to generate relocatable code, not
    getting that code loaded into memory.
Parameters:
    name    file containing module's object code.
    This implementation uses code resources created by the THINK C
    Macintosh development system. The resources are loaded by name;
    the resource name is the same as the file name. Also, resource
    attribute flags were set to make modules locked, preloaded and
    protected, so use of LoadResource(), HLock(), and HUnlock() is
    not required. The code resource type is INCM ("interpreter's
    code module"). Code modules live in the directory specified
    by global cm_code_dir[].
```

```
--------------------------------------------------*/
{
    int            resfilrefnum;
    Handle         codehandle;
    ResType        coderestype = 0x494e434d; /* "INCM" */

    /* prepend name of directory that contains code modules */
    sprintf(cm_module_name,"%s%s", cm_code_dir, name);
    /* convert C string to Pascal String to make Macintosh happy */
    CtoPstr(cm_module_name);
    resfilrefnum = OpenResFile(cm_module_name);
    if (resfilrefnum == -1) {
        printf( "cm_load_module: OpenResFile %s failed, err = %d\n",
                name, ResError());
        return (NULL);
    }
    /* we made resource name and file name identical */
    strcpy(cm_module_name, name);
    CtoPstr(cm_module_name);
    codehandle = GetNamedResource(coderestype, cm_module_name);
    if (!codehandle) {
        CloseResFile(resfilrefnum);
        printf("cm_load_module: GetNamedResource %s failed", name);
        printf(", err = %d\n", ResError());
        return (NULL);
    }
    if (!(*codehandle)) {
        CloseResFile(resfilrefnum);
        printf("cm_load_module: code resource not loaded\n");
        return (NULL);
    }
    /* the executable code starts after the THINK C code
       resource header */
    return (*codehandle + CM_THINK_CODE_OFFSET);
} /* cm_load_module */

/*==================================================================*/
static void cm_proto()
/*------------------------------------------------
Purpose:
    Create a code module's prototype.
Parameters:
    global char cm_input_text should hold a proto statement that
        looks something like this:
            p cm_test x% r!
        Notice that the module name is not quoted, and all formal
        parameters are variables, whether they're "in" or "out";
```

```
              all actual parameters are passed by address as "out"
              parameters.
          global cm_proto *cm_protos points to the list of prototypes
              created so far
-------------------------------------------------*/
{
     char              module_name[CM_MAX_STATEMENT_LEN],
                       type,
                       *strsave();
     int               i, j, parm;
     cm_prototype      *nxt, *new,
                       *cm_find_proto();
     void              *calloc(); /* malloc() then zero new memory */

     /* skip leading 'p' and extract code module name */
     for (i = 2; cm_input_text[i] == ' '; i++)
         ;
     for (   j = 0;
             cm_input_text[i] && cm_input_text[i] != ' ';
             i++, j++) {
         module_name[j] = cm_input_text[i];
     }
     module_name[j] = '\0';
     /* see if a prototype already exists; for now, bail out if
        it does */
     if (cm_find_proto(module_name)) {
         printf( "cm_proto: prototype for %s already exists\n",
                 module_name);
         return;
     }
     if (!(new = (cm_prototype *)calloc(1, sizeof(cm_prototype)))) {
         printf("cm_proto: out of memory\n");
         return;
     }
     /* calloc nulled out new->next and new->parms[] */
     /* gather parameters */
     for (parm = 0; cm_input_text[i] && (parm < CM_MAX_PARMS); ) {
         for ( ; cm_input_text[i] && cm_input_text[i] == ' '; i++)
             ;
         if (!cm_input_text[i])
             break;
         i++; /* skip 1-character variable name */
         type = cm_input_text[i++]; /* variable type */
         if ((type != '%') && (type != '!') && (type != '$')) {
             printf("cm_proto: %c is an unknown data type\n", type);
             free(new);
             return;
```

```
            }
            new->parms[parm++] = type;
            if (parm > CM_MAX_PARMS) {
                printf( "cm_proto: %s has too many parameters\n",
                        module_name);
                free(new);
                return;
            }
        }
    new->parms[parm] = '\0';
    if (!(new->name = strsave(module_name))) {
        printf("cm_proto: out of memory\n");
        free(new);
        return;
    }
    new->next = cm_protos;
    cm_protos = new;
    /* for debugging, display the prototypes defined so far: */
    for (   nxt = cm_protos;
            nxt;
            nxt = nxt->next) {
        printf("PROTO: %s %s\n", nxt->name, nxt->parms);
    }
    return;
} /* cm_proto */


/*================================================================*/
static cm_prototype *cm_find_proto( module_name )
    char        *module_name;    /* IN */
/*------------------------------------------------
Purpose:
    Try to find a prototype. Return pointer to internal prototype
    description if found, NULL otherwise.
Parameters:
    module_name holds name of code module whose prototype is sought
    global cm_prototype *cm_protos points to list of prototype
                descriptions
--------------------------------------------------*/
{
    cm_prototype *nxt;

    if (!module_name)
        return (NULL);
    for (   nxt = cm_protos;
            nxt && strcmp(module_name, nxt->name);
            nxt = nxt->next)
        ;
    return (nxt);
} /* cm_find_proto */
```

CHAPTER 15
Partitioning a Simulator's Event List

PROBLEM DESCRIPTION

A simple but useful way to view a simulation program is summarized by the following pseudocode:

```
static events    *event_list = NULL;

main()
{
   initialization, including calls on generate_event() to
     create initial event list;
   while (more events) {
     execute_event();
   }
} /* main */

generate_event( ?? )
{
   read some data file or determine in some other way what each event
     is, and when it's supposed to occur (in simulation-time,
     not in real-world wall clock time);
   put_event(??);—add the event to the global event list
} /* generate_event */

execute_event()
```

```
{
  next = get_event();—get next event from front of global list
  if (no next event)
    return;
  do whatever is needed to make the event "happen"—update the
    display, add side-effect events to the global list, update
    statistics, etc.
} /* execute_event */
```

In other words, a simulator is essentially two routines and a list of events. The routines are *generate_event()* and *execute_event()*. The events are listed in order, according to the time at which they should be executed. *Generate_event()* creates new events and inserts them in the appropriate place in the list. *Execute_event()* executes the events in order by updating data values, changing the screen display, and calling *generate_event()* to add side-effect events to the list. Time inside the simulated world jumps forward unevenly as *execute_event()* moves from the current event to the next one. Simulated time stops and the simulation is finished when the event list has been emptied.

Incidentally, notice that the events are kept in a list, not a queue. *Execute_event()* always removes events from the front of the list, but *generate_event* may add them in the middle as well as at the end. Remember this, because simulator event lists are also known as "priority queues," in spite of the fact that they are not really queues, that is, they are not FIFOs.

In this chapter, we don't care what we're simulating, or what events cause other events as side effects, or what the screen display looks like. We are concerned instead with the very specific problem of how best to insert new events in the list of events. The *put_event()* routine that *generate_event()* uses to insert a new element in the ordered event list will be called frequently; the simulator only runs as long as there are more events to process. Event insertion could be very expensive if we aren't smart about it, because the global event list might contain hundreds or thousands of elements. We must partition the event list somehow. It's just too slow to traverse a typical list of several thousand elements from front to back until we find the right insertion point.

There are a number of efficient solutions. As mentioned, the event list is an example of a priority queue, a data structure on which considerable research has been done. Brown (1988), for instance, describes a "calendar queue" which partitions a priority queue in the same sort of way a desk calendar partitions a year. In this chapter we will pursue an alternative solution. Our solution has not been rigorously compared to the calendar queue or other priority queue models, but I believe it would compare favorably to calendar queues if the number of events in the list vacillates often and widely during a simulation. No formal comparison was made because our main purpose is to explore the use of ADTDs and the other parts of the Plan, not to write a production simulator.

There is a psychological reason to optimize simulators more than other programs. Even if the simulation doesn't claim to be real-time, people will expect better performance from a simulator than they would, say, from a program that does a post-mortem analysis of the simulator's output. This expectation is not logical, but it is quite real. People expect better performance just because the simulator is a simulator. The amount of time required to run a simulation is always compared to the time it would take to perform the simulated process in the real world. People are usually unhappy with a simulator that is slower than the process being simulated, unless that process is extremely expensive or dangerous.

TOP-LEVEL GOALS

We have one top-level goal: Make the event insertion routine as fast as possible. Because this is a book on C, we won't take the final essential step here of translating the insertion routine into assembly language. However, we will try to keep the routine simple so that translating it into assembly is as painless as possible.

GUIDING EXAMPLES

The fundamental characteristic of interest is how many events there are in the list. If there are only a few events, under 100 say, simply traversing the list to find the insertion point is acceptable. Assuming a more-or-less uniform random distribution of events, our average worst case insertion requires traversing half the list, that is, chasing 50 pointers.

Suppose, however, there are 1,000 elements, or 10,000. In these cases we need to partition the event list, so we can start our traversal from somewhere closer to the insertion point than the front of the list. Notice that deletion does not require partitioning, because events are always taken from the front of the list by *execute_event()*. The difference between event list insertion and deletion is illustrated in Figure 15-1.

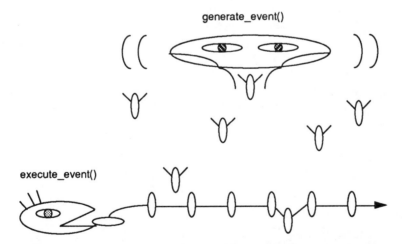

FIGURE 15-1: The difference between event list insertion and deletion. Events are inserted more or less randomly throughout the list, but they can be deleted only from the front of the list.

The only reasonable way to partition the event list is to keep pointers into it; each pointer points to an event sublist. But how should we generate, organize, and update these pointers? We need an ADTD.

ABSTRACT DATA TYPE DESCRIPTION

What name does this particular collection of data elements go by, that is, what abstract data type are we concerned with? The data elements of our collection either point into the event list or point to something that points to something, and so on, that points to an event. Since the purpose of these data elements is to partition the event list into manageable sublists, we'll call the elements of our collection "partitioners."

What is the geometry of the collection? In other words, how do we organize the partitioners to give us the fastest access into the event list? If there aren't too many events, we don't need the partitioners at all. But we're assuming there are enough events to require partitioning. The simplest thing to do is to put the partitioners in a list that parallels the event list, as shown in Figure 15-2.

To simplify things so we can concentrate on geometry, we've assumed that time advances by integer units. The events in Figure 15-2 are labeled by the time at which they are to occur. The times are always in increasing order, but some values might be skipped, as shown. Duplicate times are possible, since the simulation model might allow more than one event to occur at a given time. Internally, of course, any simulator running on hardware that has only one CPU will execute only one simulated event at a time.

How much does using the parallel list geometry shown in Figure 15-2 save us during our event list insertions? That is, suppose we start our traversal with the partitioner list and move to the event list only when we have to instead of simply starting at the front of the event list. How many fewer pointers do we have to chase than we would if there were no partitioner list? All our estimates will be rough, since we can't assume the production simulator event and partitioner lists will be so neatly spaced and interwoven. But an estimate is better than nothing.

Suppose each partitioner points on average to an event sublist of length N, and the event list contains M elements. Accessing the "average" event at position $M/2$ by simply starting at the beginning of the event list requires us to chase $M/2$ pointers. At each position

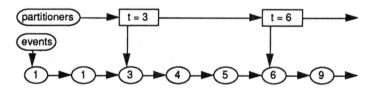

FIGURE 15-2:   Close-up of partitioners organized as a list that parallels the event list. The number inside an event represents the simulation-world time at which the event will occur.

along the way, we have to compare the time of the new event to the time of the event at our current position in the list to make sure we haven't gone down the list too far to insert the new event in order.

Accessing the same event by starting our traversal with the partitioner list requires us to follow $(M/2)/N$ pointers in the partitioner list plus (on average) $N/2$ pointers after we slip down into the event list. We require the same test at each position, in either list, to make sure we haven't passed the insertion point.

For instance, if there are 100 events in the event list, the average value $M/2$ is 50. If we build a partitioner list in which each partitioner points to an event sublist of length $N = 5$, the estimated cost for accessing an average event via the partitioner list is $(M/2)/N + N/2 = 50/5 + 5/2 = 12.5$. Without the partitioner list, the cost is 50, so using the partitioner list is roughly $50/12.5 = 4$ times faster. We can put all this together to write a general formula for the speedup factor gained by using the partitioner list:

M = number of elements in event list
N = average number of events in each partitioner sublist
P = average number of pointers to chase by traversing the partitioner list first =
  $(M/2)/N$ on partitioner list + $N/2$ on event list
E = average number of pointers to chase traversing event list only = $M/2$

(1) K = speedup factor = E/P = $(M/2)/(M/2N + N/2)$ = $NM/(M + NN)$

This formula for the speedup factor confirms our intuition about the parallel lists depicted in Figure 15-2.

If N is 1, sublists are just one element long. This means that there are as many elements in the partitioner list as there are in the event list. The speedup factor is then $M/(M + 1)$, which is less than one—it's actually a slowdown factor! In this case, the partitioner list is a waste of time and memory.

If we hold N constant but increase M, we're keeping the length of a sublist constant while increasing the total number of events. As M grows, the speedup factor tends toward N. It makes sense that chasing partitioner pointers is roughly N times faster than chasing event list pointers, since each partitioner pointer substitutes for N event list pointers. This is except for the sublist, of course, on which we have to chase event pointers to reach the event we're after. But the effort to chase those last few pointers in the sublist shrinks to insignificance compared to the effort spent chasing partitioner pointers as the event list (but not its sublists) grows ever longer.

If we let the sublist grow too large, our speedup factor tends toward one, as shown in Figure 15-3.

Saying that N tends toward M is the same as saying that we're tending toward one partitioner list that contains the entire event list as its sublist. So we don't want sublists too long. But we've already seen that sublists that are too short lead us toward sublists of length one—one partitioner list element per event list element, and we don't want that either.

In spite of all this, Formula 1 confirms that we're better off with the partitioner list than without it. With a little calculus, it can be shown that the optimal sublist length is $N = $ square root of M. For instance, if the event list contains 5,000 elements, optimal $N = $ sqrt(5,000) =

$$\lim_{N \to M} K = \lim_{f \to 1} K, \text{ where } N = fM \text{ for } 0 <= f <= 1$$

$$K = \frac{NM}{M + N^2} = \frac{fM^2}{M + f^2 M^2} \blacktriangleright \frac{M^2}{M + M^2} = \frac{M}{1 + M}$$

$$\text{so } \lim_{f \to 1} K = \frac{M}{1 + M} \longrightarrow 1 \text{ as } M \to \infty$$

FIGURE 15-3: Behavior of parallel list geometry as sublists grow too large.

70.7, yielding a speedup factor $K = 35.3$. Even without sublists of optimal length, however, the improvement can be quite dramatic. We can expect speedup factors somewhere between 10 and 35 for other values of N in the general neighborhood of the optimal value:

$N = 10$:	$10 \cdot 5{,}000/(5{,}000 + 10 \cdot 10)$	$= 9.8$
$N = 50$:	$50 \cdot 5{,}000/(5{,}000 + 50 \cdot 50)$	$= 33.3$
$N = 75$:	$75 \cdot 5{,}000/(5{,}000 + 75 \cdot 75)$	$= 35.3$
$N = 100$:	$100 \cdot 5{,}000/(5{,}000 + 100 \cdot 100)$	$= 33.3$
$N = 500$:	$500 \cdot 5{,}000/(5{,}000 + 500 \cdot 500)$	$= 9.8$

However, Formula 1 says nothing about other ways to partition the event list. We should consider other geometries if only because of the problem illustrated in Figure 15-3. The partitioner list grows linearly as the number of events grows. If the partitioner list grows too long, we'll need to partition it! We don't have unlimited memory, and layering partitioner lists on top of each other may not be the best way to use that memory.

There must be some alternative to adding partitioner lists of partitioner lists, until we have a pile N levels deep of increasingly longer partitioner lists with the event list at the bottom. Actually, such a triangular pile of lists looks very much like a tree that has pointers from sibling to sibling as well as pointers from parent to child. So let's see what happens if our ADT's geometry is a partitioner tree like the one shown in Figure 15-5.

Let's try to determine how much faster event list accesses are if we use the partitioner tree shown in Figure 15-5 instead of the partitioner list in Figures 15-2 and 15-4. We'll make several simplifying assumptions:

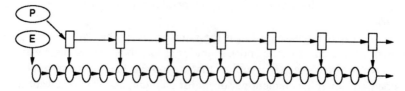

FIGURE 15-4: A more global view of the partitioner and event lists shown in Figure 15-2. Notice that traversal of partitioner list P could become slow enough to require giving P its own partitioner list, just as P was provided to avoid unecessary traversal of events in list E.

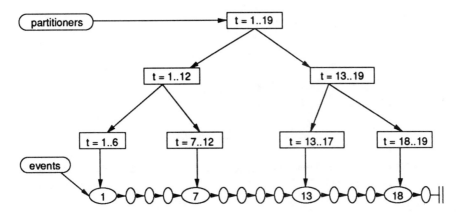

FIGURE 15-5:   A small partitioner tree. Each event contains the simulation-world time at which it will be executed, but these times are shown only for the first event in each sublist in order to save space in the figure.

Event list accesses are more or less uniformly distributed.

Accesses are random in the sense that they don't proceed from front to back or in any other order that might influence our design.

The partitioner tree is binary and perfectly balanced.

The average length of an event sublist pointed to by a partitioner tree leaf node is N.

To reach the event list from the root of the partitioner tree, we have to chase D pointers, where D = the depth of the partitioner tree. Once we reach the event list, we have to chase an average of $N/2$ pointers to reach the position at which the new event will be inserted. If the event list contains M elements, the leaf level of the partitioner tree contains M/N nodes. The partitioner tree level above that contains $M/2N$ nodes, the one above that $M/4N$, and so on, until we reach the root.

It's actually more complicated than this. On the one hand, M/N isn't necessarily a power of two. But on the other hand, the tree is binary and perfectly balanced, so the number of leaf nodes must be a power of two. We're just after an estimate, so we'll assume that M/N is in fact a power of two. This means that M equals N times two to the power D, where D is the partitioner tree's depth. A tree that has just one node, the root, is zero levels deep. A tree with two leaves is one level deep, and so on. Another illustration of the relationship between M, N, and D is provided in Figure 15-6.

For event lists like the one in Figure 15-6, which have a length M equal to the average sublist length N times two to the depth D, we can easily figure the event list access cost. We have to chase D pointers through the partitioner tree and then chase an average of $N/2$ pointers through the appropriate event sublist. In other words:

M = number of elements in event list
N = average number of events in each partitioner sublist
P = average number of pointers to chase by traversing the partitioner tree first
  = D in partitioner tree + $N/2$ on event list = $\log_2(M/N) + N/2$

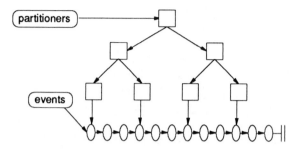

FIGURE 15-6:　A partitioner tree in which depth $D = 2$, average event sublist length $N = 3$, and total number of events $M = N * 2^D = 12$.

E = average number of pointers to chase traversing event list only = $M/2$

(2)　　K = speedup factor = E/P = $(M/2)/(D + N/2)$ = $M/(2*\log_2(M/N) + N)$

The main point to notice about Formula 2 is that its denominator grows much more slowly than Formula 1's denominator as M increases. The fact that the partitioner tree is more efficient than the partitioner list is reflected in the two formulas. The denominator in Formula 1 is linear in M, so it grows faster than the denominator in Formula 2, which is logarithmic in M. This makes the speedup factor for a partitioner list decrease faster than the speedup factor for a partitioner tree as we add more events.

A little calculus shows us that $N = \ln(2)/2 = 2.9$ is the optimal sublist length for a partitioner tree. Sublists can't have 2.9 elements, but taking $N = 3$ yields a speedup factor $K = 204.6$, which is much better than anything we saw using partitioner lists. Even when sublists are not of optimal length, speedup factors are much better with a partitioner tree than with a partitioner list. For instance, compare the speedup factors for an event list of length $M = 5,000$:

	Partitioner List	Partitioner Tree
$N = 10$:	9.8	179.0
$N = 50$:	33.3	79.0
$N = 75$:	35.3	57.4
$N = 100$:	33.3	44.9
$N = 500$:	9.8	9.8

As a result of all this, we'll use a partitioner tree, not a partitioner list, as our ADT's geometry.

What relations hold between the data elements in the collection? What relations hold between this collection and other collections? We have the usual relations between tree nodes: child, parent, sibling. The question of relations between this collection and others is moot—there are no other partitioner trees because there is only one tree per event list and just one event list per simulator. However, there is an important relationship between the partitioner tree and itself at different points in time. The tree has to expand to keep event sublists from growing too long when events are added faster than they are executed. Likewise, the tree has to shrink when events are executed and removed from the list faster than new events are added.

What are the properties of each position in the geometry with respect to the operators and with respect to elements in other positions? We have the usual tree positions: root, inner node, and leaf node. We know in a very general way what tree operators we'll need— insertion, deletion, traversal—but we need more details. Since elements are deleted only from the front of the event list, there's a good chance that some tree nodes are different than others as far as deletion is concerned. To find out, we need to decide exactly when nodes should be added and removed in the partitioner tree.

The leftmost partitioner tree leaf node points to the first element in the event list. Since events are deleted from the front of the list, this leaf node must point to a new event after each call to *execute_event()*. The other leaf nodes will always point to the same event before and after *execute_event()*. Or will they? As illustrated by the snapshots in Figure 15-7, each leaf node eventually becomes the leftmost leaf node and then disappears after its event sublist has been executed.

Nodes and branches disappear along the tree's left edge as *execute_event()* runs. New leaf nodes are created as *generate_event()* calls are made, pushing old leaf nodes up into the tree's interior as events are added. If we follow one branch over time, it appears to move from right to left, as shown in Figure 15-8. If we track the motion of two (or more) branches, the partitioner tree appears to "walk" along the time line. So we will use "walking tree" and "partitioner tree" interchangeably from now on.

In fact, there is a shorter and more whimsical name for partitioner trees: "ent." If you've read Tolkien (1965), you'll recall that the Ents are a race of large, strong, deliberate tree shepherds. They resemble the trees they watch over enough for one to say that this ent is a birch and that one an elm. Unlike trees, however, ents can walk. Young ents in particular are excellent walkers; older ents tend to turn inward, root themselves, and turn slowly into things that are very treelike and mobile only when they're very angry. The upshot of all this is that you shouldn't be any more surprised to see "ent" in a piece of code than you would be to see "daemon" or "wizard." It's just one more example of the tradition of whimsical names in programming.

Getting back to the original question about the properties of different geometry positions with respect to the operators, we see that the leftmost leaf node is different from all the other nodes as far as deletion is concerned. This leaves insertion and traversal to investigate. Traversal is easy: The root and leaf nodes are special cases, as they are in any tree.

As far as insertion is concerned, the distinguished positions are the leftmost leaf node and all the other leaf nodes. The leftmost leaf node is special because no events can be inserted in front of the first event. This is a somewhat arbitrary restriction, but it simplifies the simulator and it makes sense to discard events that were supposed to have happened already. The only time we'll allow insertion at the front of the event list is during the first call to *generate_event()*, when the event list is initially empty. Inserting an event in front of an existing first event amounts to letting the simulator move backward in time, and this is generally not a good model of the real world, no matter what you think about the "good old days."

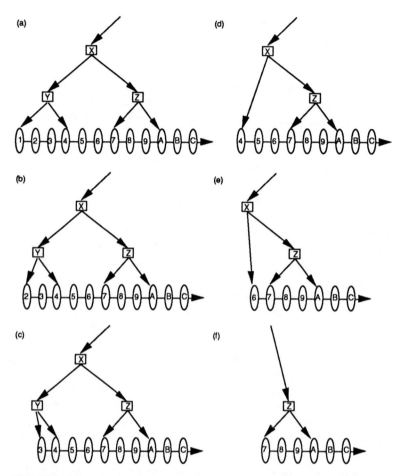

FIGURE 15-7: As events are deleted from the front of the list, the leftmost partitioner tree leaf node is updated. As shown in snapshot (d), the leftmost node is deleted after its event sublist is gone, and a new node becomes the leftmost leaf node.

All leaf nodes occupy distinguished positions because new nodes are created only as children of a current leaf node. We will never insert a node as the parent of an existing node. The insertion algorithm we'll use is illustrated in the snapshots of Figure 15-9. The basic idea is to let a sublist grow until it is twice the desired length and then split it by adding a new leaf node. The left event pointer in the new leaf node points to the first half of the overgrown sublist, and the right event pointer points to the second half.

Instead of waiting until the sublist is twice the desired length, we could split it as soon as it's longer than the desired length. But we can achieve the same effect by changing the desired sublist length.

A more interesting refinement of our splitting criteria is to make the desired sublist

(a)

(b)

(c)

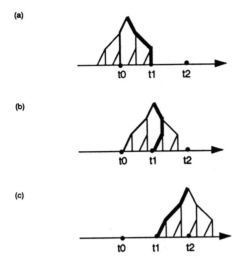

FIGURE 15-8: Three snapshots of a partitioner tree or ent as it "walks" along the time line. Events actually exist only where the tree touches the time line, but t0, t1, and t2 are shown in all three snapshots to make the tree's motion more obvious.

length a function of the current total event list length. As the walking tree grows and shrinks, how should the length of sublists change to minimize the number of pointers we have to chase? This is roughly equivalent to seeking a function $N(M)$ which maximizes the speedup factor K in Formula 2. This can be done with the kind of calculus many colleges require programmers to understand. But don't expect such a function to give perfect results. Formula 2 is based on a perfectly balanced tree, and we've seen from Figures 15-8 and 15-9 that deletion and insertion operations will keep the walking tree almost constantly unbalanced.

What rules does each relation follow? The relation "is a child" is nonreflexive (no node is a child of itself), and antisymmetric (X a child of Y implies Y is not a child of X). If we extend "child" to mean "descendant," we get a relation "is a descendant" that is nonreflexive, antisymmetric, and transitive. "Is a descendant" is a many-to-many relation, while "is a child" is a many-to-one relation.

The relation "is a sibling" might also be called "is at the same depth." This relation is reflexive, symmetric, and transitive. It partitions the tree into layers, with all the nodes at a given depth in the same layer. "Is a sibling" is a many-to-many relation.

What are the operators? We'll be performing typical tree operations, but we don't want to organize our operators with respect to the partitioner tree. That is, we don't want operators like *insert_left_sibling()* and *insert_parent()*.

Instead, we want to support *generate_event()* and *execute_event()*. So we'll need routines to insert an event and delete an event; following the lead of the pseudocode we

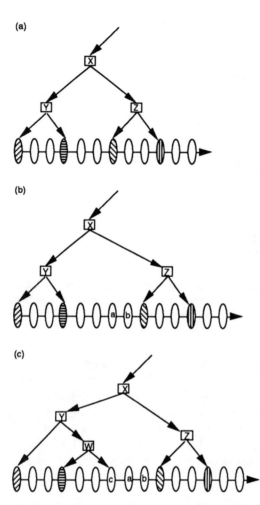

FIGURE 15-9: Snapshots of a walking tree growing as new events are added. In this simplified example, three consecutive insertions added new events to the same sublist, but the algorithm works the same way when consecutive insertion points jump from one sublist to another. Notice the need to distinguish between an event's insertion time and its execution time: Event *c* was inserted after event *a* was in place, but it will be executed before event *a*.

opened the chapter with, we'll call these routines *put_event()* and *get_event()*. *Put_event()* might create partitioner tree nodes as a side effect, but *generate_event()* shouldn't have to worry about that. Likewise, *get_event()* may cause left edge nodes to disappear, and will certainly change an event pointer in the leftmost leaf node, but these changes to the tree are of no direct interest to *execute_event()*.

In addition to *put_event()* and *get_event()*, we'll need a debugging routine that pretty-prints the walking tree and event list. We'll call this operator *dump_ent_events()*, in memory of the ents (walking trees) in Tolkien (1965).

What are the restrictions on membership in the collection? The only restriction on walking tree nodes is that they point, directly or indirectly, to an event sublist. There's no firm upper limit on the number of nodes.

How many collections are allowed by this ADT? We're thinking of one walking tree per event list, and one event list per simulator. So multiple collections are not allowed. We could think of a subtree as a walking tree in its own right if every leaf node in it points to an event sublist. But we haven't seen anything yet that suggests we'll need to deal with subtrees.

ATTEMPT ONE

We have two questions left to answer:

1. What exactly is in a partitioner tree node? Remember that a node may point to other nodes, to event sublists, or to one of each.
2. Figures 15-7 and 15-9 suggest algorithms for *put_event()* and *get_event()*, but they are not detailed enough to code from directly. What do pseudocode versions of these routines look like?

We'll start with question 1. We know that each tree node needs two pointers that point to nodes or to events as the tree walks. In addition, we need a way to navigate down the tree to the correct leaf node. We'll follow the example of Figure 15-5, and put a time in each node. Unlike Figure 15-5, however, we need to store only one time per node. The time in a node is the least of all the times in the events under that node's subtree. The time in the event being inserted will be tested against each node's time to find our way down to the correct sublist.

Finally, we need to keep track of the length of each leaf node's event sublist so we know when to split. Rather than count the sublist each time we add an event, we'll keep a counter in each leaf node. We only need the counters in leaf nodes, but interior nodes will have counters too, since they always start as leaf nodes. We might as well update all the counters so the counter in each interior node gives the total number of events associated with the corresponding subtree. We can use these counters to see how well balanced the tree is.

Before writing the typedef for a walking tree node, we need to decide how to make one pointer point to tree nodes and events at different times. There are two possibilities:

1. Put tree nodes and events together in one typedef using a union.
2. Make the pointers (void *) and cast them appropriately.

We'll use (void *) pointers because it's not very clean to forcibly combine events with tree nodes just to avoid a cast. We can profitably think of the event list as an ADT in its own right, independent of any partitioning scheme that lets us access events more quickly. So our walking tree implementation should be as independent as possible of the event list specifics. Event structs might be nothing more than an index into a fixed set of possibilities:

```
typedef struct event {
    struct event    *next;
    float           time;
```

```
   int                index;
} event;
```

Or an event might actually be a huge collection of linked structures, embedded code modules, and top-secret algorithms. Our walking tree implementation should work equally well in either case with nothing more than a recompilation needed. So putting events and tree nodes together in a union is a bad idea.

We need a way to tell whether the (void *) pointers point at tree nodes or events. Two bitflags will do nicely. So our first try at a typedef for walking tree nodes looks like this:

```
#define ENT_LEFT_POINTS_TO_NODE     1
#define ENT_RIGHT_POINTS_TO_NODE    2

typedef struct {
  void   *left,
         *right;
  float  time;
  int    events; /* sublist length */
  int    flags;
} ent_node;
```

There isn't much room for variation in this typedef, but there are two other places we could put the bitflags if allocating less memory is critical. One possibility is to tuck the bitflags into *ent_node.left*, *ent_node.right*, or both; see the struct trick "Squeezing in Bitflags" (page 395). If both *events* and *ent_nodes* require at least four bytes, aligning both structs requires that the least significant two bits of the pointers be zero. We could use the low two bits of *ent_node.left* or *ent_node.right* to hold the bitflags. We just have to be sure to mask the bitflags out whenever we chase the pointer. Or we could put one bitflag in each pointer:

```
#define ENT_POINTS_TO_NODE  1

typedef struct {
  void   *left,
          right;
  float  time;
  int    events;
} ent_node;

if (current->left & ENT_POINTS_TO_NODE)
  left_node_ptr = (current->left) & ~ENT_POINTS_TO_NODE;
else
  left_event_ptr = (current->left) & ~ENT_POINTS_TO_NODE;
```

The second possibility is to put the bitflags in the two highest bits of *ent_node.events*. This effectively divides by four the limit on the number of events *ent_node.events* can count. In fact, we could completely ignore *ent_node.events* inside interior tree nodes. Then we would easily have two bits free, since we only need enough low-end bits to count the events in one sublist, and the average sublist length is nowhere near 64K:

```
#define ENT_LEFT_POINTS_TO_NODE    0x8000 /* assumes 2-byte int */
#define ENT_RIGHT_POINTS_TO_NODE   0x4000

typedef struct {
  void   *left,
          right;
  float  time;
  int    events;
} ent_node;

if (current->events & ENT_LEFT_POINTS_TO_NODE)
   left_node_ptr = current->left;
else
   left_event_ptr = current->left;
```

Question 2 asks for pseudocode versions of *put_event()* and *get_event()*. We'll start with an algorithm for *put_event()*. Using Figures 15-5, 15-6, 15-7, and 15-9 as guides, we can create a high-level pseudocode version of *put_event()*:

```
/*=============================================================*/
boolean   put_event( data )
   event  *data;  /* IN */
/*---------------------------------------------
Purpose:
        Add a new event to the event list, and update the ent that
        points into the event list as necessary.
Parameters:
   data    pointer to event containing data to add to list;
           put_event() allocates a new event and copies data
           into it
   the global list of events
   the root of the ent tree that partitions the list of events
---------------------------------------------*/
{
   Throw away data if it should have already happened. That is,
      don't put an event in the global list if its time is
      earlier than the time of the current first event;
   Allocate new event struct and initialize it;
   Find the current leftmost leaf node, that is, the ent_node
      which has the first event in one of its sublists;
   Insert the new event in the correct sublist of the current
      leftmost leaf node, creating a child node if the sublist
      needs splitting;
} /* put_event */
```

This pseudocode version of *put_event()* still leaves it unclear how to find the leftmost leaf node. Suppose we try to devise an algorithm based on Figure 15-5. Imagine trying to insert an event with time $t = 8$. We start at the root and have to go left or right at each node until we reach the correct leaf node. How do we decide which way to go at each node? If nodes contain two times, as Figure 15-5 suggests, not one as the current *ent_node* typedef has, then we can look at the nodes below our current position to decide which way to go.

The same idea will work if our tree looks like Figure 15-7, as long as each node contains two times. Notice, however, that the leaf nodes in Figure 15-7 have two event sublists each, while the leaf nodes in Figure 15-5 have only one sublist each. The current *ent_node* typedef has room for two sublist pointers, but just one time field and one sublist length counter. To find our way down the tree to the correct leaf node, we need two times. We also need two counters, since we have two sublists. Finally, since fast access is the whole point of the partition tree, we'll separate flags from pointers to avoid bitmask operations. This means that our *ent_node* typedef needs to be changed to look like this:

```
typedef struct {
  void    *left,
          *right;
  float   left_time,
          right_time;
  int     left_count,
          right_count;
  int     flags;
}   ent_node;
```

We need to make one more change. All the node sublist pointers point to the first (leftmost) event in the sublist. *Get_event()* also takes events from the front (left) of the global event list. We want to devise a way to reach the leftmost leaf node of the ent tree from the root, given an event to insert. But the times in the tree nodes in Figure 15-5 don't reflect this left-handed bias. We see the time of the first element of the left sublist clearly, but Figure 15-5 shows the time of the last, not first, element of each right sublist.

We need the time of the first element of the right sublist, not the last element, if we are to avoid traversing the entire left sublist only to find out that the new event belongs in the right sublist. So we'll disregard Figure 15-5 by making *ent_node.right_time* the time in the right event sublist's leading element, not its final element. The *ent_node* typedef is still the same. Having done this, we can write the routine that will take us to the insertion node, that is, from the ent root down to the leftmost leaf node:

```
/*===================================================================*/
static ent_node      *find_insertion_node( time )
  float    time; /* IN */
/*-------------------------------------------------
Purpose:
  Find the leaf node to insert a new event in the sublist of,
  based on the existing ent and the new event's time. Assumes
```

```
      the ent tree is not empty; that is, that at least one event
      has already been inserted via put_event().
Parameters:
   time    time of event being inserted
   global ent_root, the root of the ent that partitions the
          event list
   Returns pointer to insertion node, or NULL.
-------------------------------------------------*/
{
   ent_node      *next_node;

   next_node = ent_root;
   while (true) {
     if (time >= next_node->right_time) {
        if (next_node->flags & ENT_RIGHT_POINTS_TO_NODE) {
          next_node = next_node->right;
        }
        else {
          break;
        }
     }
     else {
        if (next_node->flags & ENT_LEFT_POINTS_TO_NODE) {
          next_node = next_node->left;
        }
        else {
          break;
        }
     }
   }   /* while not yet at (correct) leaf node */
   return (next_node);
}   /* find_insertion_node */
```

So much for *put_event()*. What about a pseudocode overview of *get_event()*?

```
/*================================================================*/
event        *get_event()
/*------------------------------------------------
Purpose:
   Remove event from the front of the list, but don't deallocate
   it. Update ent as needed.
Parameters:
   the global list of events
   the ent that partitions the event list
   Returns pointer to event that was first in list, or NULL.
-------------------------------------------------*/
{
```

```
    Find the current leftmost leaf node, so we can update the ent
        after removing an event from the front of the global list;
    Unhook the first event from the list, and update the ent:
        If there are more events in the sublist that held the
            leading event, the update is easy—just bump the
            leftmost node's sublist pointer and decrement the
            corresponding sublist size counter;
        If the event was the last one in the sublist, the
            current leftmost node can be removed by attaching
            its other sublist to its parent in place of itself.
            That is, traveling down the tree, we used to have:
```

```
                              [parent]
                                |    |
        [current leftmost node]    [parent's other child]
                      |                      |
            [nonempty sublist] [empty sublist]
```

```
                        After the merge, we'll have:
```

```
                              [parent]
                                |    |
        [nonempty sublist]    [parent's other child]
```

```
    Return a pointer to the still-allocated memory that holds
        the event that was just taken off the front of the
        global event list—the memory must be freed elsewhere,
        by execute_event();
} /* get_event */
```

Notice that we'll need parent pointers to implement *get_event()*. The parent pointer is needed to do the kind of merge described in the pseudocode; this merge is illustrated in Figure 15-7, snapshots (c) and (d). So our typedef gets one more pointer:

```
typedef struct ent_node {
    void            *left,
                    *right;
    float           left_time,
                    right_time;
    int             left_count,
                    right_count;
    int             flags;
    struct ent_node *parent;
}   ent_node;
```

That takes care of all the questions, so we'll go ahead and start coding.

LISTING: ent.c

```
/*------------------------------------------------
                          ent.c
------------------------------------------------*/

/*================================================
Purpose:
    This file provides two routines, put_event() and get_event(),
    which implement an ent. Ents are also known as "walking trees"
    or "partitioner trees". The purpose of an ent is to partition
    a simulator's event list so insertion of new events is as fast
    as possible.

    This code was compiled under THINK's LightspeedC (TM) on a
    Macintosh SE.
------------------------------------------------*/
#include <stdio.h>
#include <Storage.h>
#include <boolean.h>

/* ent_node.flags values: */
#define ENT_LEFT_POINTS_TO_NODE    1
#define ENT_RIGHT_POINTS_TO_NODE   2

/* Tune sublist length for best performance as discussed in text: */
#define ENT_AVG_SUBLIST_LENGTH    3

/* ENT_INITIAL_TIME is greater than all possible event times: */
#define ENT_INITIAL_TIME           10000000.0

#define ENT_DEBUG   /* turn debugging on */

/* type used to represent event list elements; this can be changed
   without breaking put_event() or get_event() (just recompile): */
typedef struct event {
    struct event    *next;
    float           time;   /* Simulation-world time event occurs */
    int             value;  /* This is what we can vary without */
                            /* hurting put_event(), get_event() */
}   event;

/* type used to represent walking tree nodes: */
typedef struct ent_node {
    void            *left,
                    *right;
```

```
    float           left_time,
                    right_time;
    int             left_count,
                    right_count;
    int             flags;
    struct ent_node *parent;
}   ent_node;

static event        *events = NULL;
static ent_node     *ent_root = NULL;
static char         dump_msg[32];    /* used by dump_ent() */
static FILE         *in_fp,          /* program I/O */
                    *out_fp;


#define _ENT_TESTBED_
#ifdef  _ENT_TESTBED_
/*===============================================================*/
main()
/*---------------------------------------------
Purpose:
    Interactively call put_event(), get_event(), and
    dump_ent_events() to add to the event list, delete the
    first event in the list, and dump the list for inspection,
    respectively.
Parameters:
    none—input is read from stdin and sent to stdout
------------------------------------------------------------*/
{
    boolean     put_event();
    event       *get_event(), *to_execute, to_insert;
    void        dump_ent_events(), get_cmd();
    char        cmd = '\0';
    int         junk;

    printf("Event list insertion and deletion test.\n");
    in_fp  = stdin; /* or fopen() something */
    out_fp = stdout;
    get_cmd(in_fp, &cmd);
    while (cmd != 'q') {
        if (cmd == 'p') {
            if (in_fp == stdin)
                printf("time and value of event to put>");
            fscanf( in_fp,
                    "%f %d",
                    &to_insert.time, &to_insert.value);
            if (in_fp == stdin)
                junk = getc(in_fp); /* toss carriage return */
            put_event(&to_insert);
```

```
        }
        else if (cmd == 'g') {
            if (to_execute = get_event()) {
                fprintf(out_fp,
                        "Got event: time = %f value = %d\n",
                        to_execute->time, to_execute->value);
            }
            else {
                fprintf(out_fp, "get_event() failed\n");
            }
        }
        else if (cmd == 'd') {
            dump_ent_events(out_fp);
        }
        else {
            fprintf(out_fp, "\nillegal command\n");
        }
        get_cmd(in_fp, &cmd);
    }
    if (in_fp != stdin)
        fclose(in_fp);
    if (out_fp != stdout)
        fclose(out_fp);
} /* main */
#ifdef _ENT_TESTBED_

/*===============================================================*/
static void     get_cmd( fp, cmd )
    FILE    *fp;     /* IN */
    char    *cmd;    /* OUT */
/*---------------------------------------------------------------
Purpose:
    Read a one-character command from the user or from a data file.
Parameters:
    fp        stream to read from
    cmd       command read from user or data file
------------------------------------------------------------------*/
{
    int ch;

    if (in_fp == stdin) {
        printf("Legal Commands:\n");
        printf("   d: display event list and partitioner tree\n");
        printf("   g: get the first event from the event list\n");
        printf("   p: put a new event in the event list\n");
        printf("   q: QUIT\n");
        printf("command>");
    }
```

```
        ch = getc(fp);
        *cmd = (char)ch;
        ch = getc(fp); /* throw away carriage return */
        if (in_fp == stdin) {
            printf("\n");
        }
    }   /* get_cmd */


/*================================================================*/
boolean     put_event( data )
    event   *data;  /* IN */
/*------------------------------------------------------------
Purpose:
    Add a new event to the event list, and update the ent that
    points into the event list as necessary.
Parameters:
    data    pointer to event containing data to add to list;
            put_event() allocates a new event and copies data
            into it
    global event *events—the global list of events
    global ent_node *ent_root—root of the ent that partitions
            the global list of events
-----------------------------------------------------------*/
{
    event       *new_event;
    ent_node    *new_ent_node(),
                *insertion_node, *find_insertion_node();
    void        dump_ent_node();
    boolean     add_to_sublist();
    void        *malloc();
#ifdef ENT_DEBUG
    boolean     event_list_ok();
#endif ENT_DEBUG

    /* VALIDATE parameters: */
    if (!data)
        return (false);
    /* throw away events that should have already happened: */
    if (events && (data->time < events->time)) {
        fprintf(out_fp,
                "put_event(): can't put %f; current time = %f\n",
                data->time, events->time);
        return (false);
    }
    /* ALLOCATE new event and initialize it: */
    if (!(new_event = (event *)malloc(sizeof(event)))) {
        fprintf(out_fp, "put_event(): out of memory\n");
        return (false);
```

```
        }
    new_event->time  = data->time;
    new_event->value = data->value;
    /* FIND the insertion point: */
    if (!ent_root) { /* this is the first event ever */
        if (!(ent_root = new_ent_node(new_event, NULL))) {
            return (false);
        }
        events = new_event;
        new_event->next = NULL;
        return (true);
    }
    /* It's not the first event; chase thru an existing ent to
       find the insertion point for new_event: */
    if (!(insertion_node = find_insertion_node(data->time))) {
        return (false);
    }
    /* INSERT the new event in the correct sublist of the
       insertion node; create a new node if the sublist needs
       splitting: */
    if (!add_to_sublist(insertion_node, new_event)) {
        return (false);
    }
#ifdef ENT_DEBUG
    return (event_list_ok());
#else
    return (true);
#endif ENT_DEBUG
} /* put_event */


/*================================================================*/
static ent_node       *find_insertion_node( time )
    float   time; /* IN */
/*----------------------------------------------------------------
Purpose:
    Find the leaf node to insert a new event in the sublist of, based
    on the existing ent and the new event's time. Assumes the ent
    tree is not empty; that is, that at least one event has already
    put inserted via put_event().
Parameters:
    time     time of event being inserted
    global ent_node *ent_root - root of the ent that partitions
             the global list of events
    Returns pointer to insertion node, or NULL.
----------------------------------------------------------------*/
{
    ent_node     *next_node;
```

```
        if (!ent_root)
            return (NULL);
    next_node = ent_root;
    while (true) {
        if (time >= next_node->right_time) {
            if (next_node->flags & ENT_RIGHT_POINTS_TO_NODE) {
                if (!(next_node->right)) {
                    return (NULL);
                }
                next_node = next_node->right;
            }
            else {
                break;
            }
        }
        else {
            if (next_node->flags & ENT_LEFT_POINTS_TO_NODE) {
                if (!(next_node->left)) {
                    return (NULL);
                }
                next_node = next_node->left;
            }
            else {
                break;
            }
        }
    }   /* while not yet at (correct) leaf node */
    return (next_node);
}   /* find_insertion_node */


/*===============================================================*/
static boolean      add_to_sublist( node, to_add )
    ent_node    *node;        /* IN */
    event       *to_add;      /* IN */
/*---------------------------------------------------------------
Purpose:
    Add event to node's sublist. Add_to_sublist() chooses the
    correct sublist, creates a new child leaf node if necessary,
    and updates the node's counters.
Parameters:
    node        node to add event to sublist of
    to_add      event to add
-----------------------------------------------------------------*/
{
    boolean     result, insert_or_split();
    ent_node    *next_node;
    event       *next_event;
```

```
if (!(node->flags & ENT_RIGHT_POINTS_TO_NODE) &&
    (to_add->time >= node->right_time) &&
    (node->right_count > 0)) {
    /* add to right sublist */
    return (insert_or_split(node,
                            &node->right,
                            &node->right_count,
                            &node->right_time,
                            &node->flags,
                            ENT_RIGHT_POINTS_TO_NODE,
                            to_add));
}
else if (!(node->flags & ENT_LEFT_POINTS_TO_NODE) &&
    (to_add->time >= node->left_time) &&
    (node->left_count > 0)) {
    /* add to left sublist */
    return (insert_or_split(node,
                            &node->left,
                            &node->left_count,
                            &node->left_time,
                            &node->flags,
                            ENT_LEFT_POINTS_TO_NODE,
                            to_add));
}
else if (!(node->flags & ENT_RIGHT_POINTS_TO_NODE) &&
    (node->right_count == 0)) {
    /* add to right sublist */
    result = insert_or_split(node,
                            &node->right,
                            &node->right_count,
                            &node->right_time,
                            &node->flags,
                            ENT_RIGHT_POINTS_TO_NODE,
                            to_add);
    if (!result) {
        return (false);
    }
    if (!(node->flags & ENT_LEFT_POINTS_TO_NODE)) {
        next_node = node;
    }
    else {
        for (   next_node = (ent_node *)node->left;
                next_node->flags & ENT_RIGHT_POINTS_TO_NODE;
                next_node = (ent_node *)next_node->right )
            ;
    }
    for (   next_event = (event *)next_node->right;
```

```
                         next_event->next;
                         next_event = next_event->next )
                    ;
                next_event->next = to_add;
                return (true);
            }
            else {
                fprintf(out_fp,
                        "add_to_sublist() failed, time = %f\n",
                        to_add->time);
                return (false);
            }
        }   /* add_to_sublist */


        /*================================================================*/
        static boolean      insert_or_split( node, sublist, count, time,
                                                flags, side, to_add )
            ent_node    *node;      /* IN */
            void        **sublist;  /* IN, OUT */
            int         *count;     /* IN, OUT */
            float       *time;      /* IN, OUT */
            int         *flags;     /* IN, OUT */
            int         side;       /* IN */
            event       *to_add;    /* IN */
        /*---------------------------------------------
        Purpose:
            Insert event in sublist if list is short enough. Otherwise,
            split the sublist by creating a new child leaf node, and then
            insert the event in the new node.
        Parameters:
            node        address of node; sublist, count, and the other
                        pointers are needed even though we have node
                        because we want to use insert_or_split() on either
                        the left or the right
            sublist     address of pointer to sublist to insert event in
            count       address of sublist length counter
            time        address of time stored in node (same as time in
                        first sublist event)
            flags       address of flags that tell whether sublist points
                        to an event sublist or to an ent_node
            side        one of the ENT_xxx_POINTS_TO_NODE flag values
            to_add      event to insert
        --------------------------------------------------------------*/
        {
            ent_node    *new_node, *new_ent_node();
            event       *next_event;
            int         i;
```

```
if (*flags & side) {
    fprintf(out_fp,
            "insert_or_split(): NODE (not EVENT sublist)\n");
    return (false);
}
if (*count == 0) {
    *sublist = (void *)to_add;
    *count   = 1;
    *time    = to_add->time;
    /* implicitly set *flags &= ~side; */
    to_add->next = NULL;
    return (true);
}
if (*count < 2*ENT_AVG_SUBLIST_LENGTH) {
    /* don't have to split sublist */
    for (   next_event = (event *)(*sublist), i = 1;
            ((i < *count) &&
                (next_event->next)    &&
                (next_event->next->time < to_add->time));
            next_event = next_event->next, i++ )
        ;
    to_add->next = next_event->next;
    next_event->next = to_add;
    (*count)++;
    return (true);
}
else {
    /* split sublist */
    for (   next_event = (event *)(*sublist), i = 1;
            i <= ENT_AVG_SUBLIST_LENGTH;
            next_event = next_event->next, i++ )
        ;
    if (!(new_node = new_ent_node(NULL, node))) {
        return (false);
    }
    /* new_ent_node() already set flags to "left and right
       are event pointers" */
    new_node->left        = *sublist;
    new_node->left_count  = ENT_AVG_SUBLIST_LENGTH;
    new_node->left_time   = ((event *)(*sublist))->time;
    new_node->right       = (void *)next_event;
    new_node->right_count = *count - ENT_AVG_SUBLIST_LENGTH;
    new_node->right_time  = next_event->time;
    *sublist = (void *)new_node;
    *flags |= side;
    return (add_to_sublist(new_node, to_add));
}
```

```
}    /* insert_or_split */

/*===============================================================*/
static ent_node    *new_ent_node( e, parent )
    event        *e;        /* IN */
    ent_node    *parent;    /* IN */
/*-----------------------------------------------------------
Purpose:
    Allocate and initialize a new ent tree node. New nodes are only
    inserted as leaves, so new_ent_node() accepts a pointer to an
    event that will be inserted as the new node's left sublist.
    It is still the caller's responsibility to insert the event
    e in the event list; new_ent_node() only sets the new node's
    pointers, not the pointers in the event list.
Parameters:
    e        event to add, or NULL if caller will handle sublist
             creation
    parent   pointer to parent of this node
    Returns pointer to new node, or NULL.
-----------------------------------------------------------*/
{
    ent_node    *new;
    void        *malloc();

    if (!(new = (ent_node *)malloc(sizeof(ent_node)))) {
        fprintf(out_fp, "new_event_node(): out of memory\n");
        return (NULL);
    }
    if (e) {
        new->left       = (void *)e;
        new->left_time  = e->time;
        new->left_count = 1;
    }
    else {
        new->left       = NULL;
        new->left_time  = ENT_INITIAL_TIME;
        new->left_count = 0;
    }
    new->right       = NULL;
    new->right_time  = ENT_INITIAL_TIME;
    new->right_count = 0;
    /* set bitflags to "left and right point at events": */
    new->flags       = 0;
    new->parent      = parent;
    return (new);
}    /* new_ent_node */


/*===============================================================*/
```

```
static boolean   event_list_ok()
/*-------------------------------------------------
Purpose:
    For debugging, look for problems caused by bugs in put_event().
Parameters:
    global event *events—the global list of events
    global ent_node *ent_root—root of the ent that partitions
            the global list of events
-------------------------------------------------*/
{
    event    *next_event;

    /* run the event list, making sure order was maintained */
    for (   next_event = events;
            next_event;
            next_event = next_event->next) {
        if ((next_event->next) &&
            (next_event->time > next_event->next->time)) {
            fprintf(out_fp,
                    "BUG: EVENTS OUT OF ORDER: 0x%08lx and next\n",
                    next_event);
        }
    }
}   /* event_list_ok */


/*==============================================================*/
event        *get_event()
/*-------------------------------------------------
Purpose:
    Remove event from the front of the list, but don't deallocate
    it. Update ent as needed.
Parameters:
    global event *events—the global list of events
    global ent_node *ent_root—root of the ent that partitions
            the global list of events
    Returns pointer to event that was first in list, or NULL.
-------------------------------------------------*/
{
    event        *result;
    ent_node     *old_left, *find_insertion_node();
    boolean      zap_unused_nodes(), merge_node();

    if (!events || !ent_root)
        return (NULL);
    /* get pointer to current leftmost leaf node: */
    if (!(old_left = find_insertion_node(events->time))) {
        return (NULL);
    }
```

```
        if (!(old_left->flags & ENT_LEFT_POINTS_TO_NODE) &&
            (old_left->left_count > 0)) {
            /* remove from left sublist */
            if (old_left->left_count == 1) {
                /* delete ent_nodes that are no longer needed: */
                if (old_left->right) {
                    old_left->left_count = 0;
                    old_left->left_time  = ENT_INITIAL_TIME;
                    old_left->left       = NULL;
                    if (!merge_node(old_left)) {
                        return (NULL);
                    }
                }
            }
            else {
                old_left->left =
                            (void *) (((event *) (old_left->left))->next);
                old_left->left_time = ((event *) (old_left->left))->time;
                (old_left->left_count)-;
            }
        }
        else if (!(old_left->flags & ENT_RIGHT_POINTS_TO_NODE) &&
            (old_left->right_count > 0)) {
            /* remove from right sublist */
            if (old_left->right_count == 1) {
                /* delete ent_nodes that are no longer needed: */
                if (old_left->left) {
                    old_left->right_count = 0;
                    old_left->right_time  = ENT_INITIAL_TIME;
                    old_left->right       = NULL;
                    if (!merge_node(old_left)) {
                        return (NULL);
                    }
                }
            }
            else {
                old_left->right =
                            (void *) (((event *) (old_left->right))->next);
                old_left->right_time =
                            ((event *) (old_left->right))->time;
                (old_left->right_count)-;
            }
        }
        else {
            return (NULL);
        }
        result = events;
        events = events->next;
```

```
    if (!events) {
        if (!merge_node(old_left)) {
            return (NULL);
        }
        if ((ent_root->flags & ENT_LEFT_POINTS_TO_NODE) ||
            (ent_root->flags & ENT_RIGHT_POINTS_TO_NODE)   ) {
            return (NULL);
        }
        free(ent_root);
        ent_root = NULL;
    }
    return (result);
} /* get_event */


/*===============================================================*/
static boolean  merge_node( leaf )
    ent_node    *leaf;  /* IN */
/*-----------------------------------------------
Purpose:
    Merge node with parent. This is necessary when get_event()
    removes the last event in a sublist, so only one of leaf->left
    and leaf->right is in use.
Parameters:
    leaf    node to merge upward
------------------------------------------------*/
{
    if (leaf->parent) {
        if (leaf->parent->left == leaf) {
            leaf->parent->left = leaf->right;
            leaf->parent->left_count = leaf->right_count;
            leaf->parent->left_time = leaf->right_time;
            if (leaf->flags & ENT_RIGHT_POINTS_TO_NODE) {
                leaf->parent->flags |= ENT_LEFT_POINTS_TO_NODE;
                ((ent_node *)(leaf->right))->parent = leaf->parent;
            }
            else {
                leaf->parent->flags &= ~ENT_LEFT_POINTS_TO_NODE;
            }
        }
        else if (leaf->parent->right == leaf) {
            leaf->parent->right = leaf->right;
            leaf->parent->right_count = leaf->right_count;
            leaf->parent->right_time = leaf->right_time;
            if (leaf->flags & ENT_RIGHT_POINTS_TO_NODE) {
                leaf->parent->flags |= ENT_RIGHT_POINTS_TO_NODE;
                ((ent_node *)(leaf->right))->parent = leaf->parent;
            }
```

```
                else {
                    leaf->parent->flags &= ~ENT_RIGHT_POINTS_TO_NODE;
                }
            }
            else {
                return (false);
            }
            free(leaf);
        }
    return (true);
} /* merge_node */

/*================================================================*/
void        dump_ent_events(fp)
    FILE    *fp;    /* IN */
/*- - - - - - - - - - - - - - - - - - - - - - - - - - - - - - -
Purpose:
    Pretty-print the entire ent and event list for debugging.
Parameters:
    fp        stream to print to
    global event *events—the global list of events
    global ent_node *ent_root—root of the ent that partitions
              the global list of events
- - - - - - - - - - - - - - - - - - - - - - - - - - - - - - - - -*/
{
    void        dump_ent(),
                dump_event();
    event       *next_event;

    if (!ent_root) {
        fprintf(fp, "No ent.\n");
    }
    if (!events) {
        fprintf(fp, "No events.\n");
    }
    if (!ent_root || !events) {
        return;
    }
    fprintf(fp, "************** EVENT LIST: **************\n");
    for (   next_event = events;
            next_event;
            next_event = next_event->next) {
        dump_event(fp, next_event);
    }
    fprintf(fp, "++++++++++++++++ ENT: ++++++++++++++++++++\n");
    dump_ent(fp, ent_root);
}   /* dump_ent_events */
```

```
/*================================================================*/
static void      dump_event(fp, data)
    FILE      *fp;    /* IN */
    event     *data;  /* IN */
/*--------------------------------------------------------
Purpose:
    Pretty-print an event for debugging.
Parameters:
    fp        stream to print to
    data      non-NULL pointer to event to print
------------------------------------------------------*/
{
    fprintf(fp, "EVENT @ 0x%08lx: time = %f, ", data, data->time);
    fprintf(fp, "value = %d, ", data->value);
    fprintf(fp, "next = 0x%08lx\n", data->next);
}    /* dump_event */


/*================================================================*/
static void      dump_ent(fp, data)
    FILE          *fp;    /* IN */
    ent_node      *data;  /* IN */
/*--------------------------------------------------------
Purpose:
    Pretty-print an ent node for debugging, then recursively print
    its left and right subtrees.
Parameters:
    fp        stream to print to
    data      non-NULL pointer to root of subtree to print
------------------------------------------------------*/
{
    void      dump_ent_node();

    dump_ent_node(fp, data);
    if (data->flags & ENT_LEFT_POINTS_TO_NODE)
        dump_ent(fp, data->left);
    if (data->flags & ENT_RIGHT_POINTS_TO_NODE)
        dump_ent(fp, data->right);
}    /* dump_ent */


/*================================================================*/
static void      dump_ent_node(fp, data)
    FILE          *fp;    /* IN */
    ent_node      *data;  /* IN */
/*--------------------------------------------------------
Purpose:
    Pretty-print an ent node for debugging.
Parameters:
```

```
    fp      stream to print to
    data    non-NULL pointer to root of node to print
------------------------------------------------*/
{
    event   *next_event;
    int     i;

    if (data->flags & ENT_LEFT_POINTS_TO_NODE)
        strcpy(dump_msg, "LEFT *NODE ");
    else
        strcpy(dump_msg, "LEFT *EVENT ");
    if (data->flags & ENT_RIGHT_POINTS_TO_NODE)
        strcat(dump_msg, "RIGHT *NODE ");
    else
        strcat(dump_msg, "RIGHT *EVENT ");
    fprintf(fp,
            "ENT NODE @ 0x%08lx: %s, parent = 0x%08lx\n",
            data, dump_msg, data->parent );
    fprintf(fp,
            "left_time = %f, left_count = %d, left = 0x%08lx\n",
            data->left_time, data->left_count, data->left);
    fprintf(fp,
            "right_time = %f, right_count = %d, right = 0x%08lx\n",
            data->right_time, data->right_count, data->right);
    if (!(data->flags & ENT_LEFT_POINTS_TO_NODE)) {
        fprintf(fp,
                "left sublist:\n");
        for (   next_event = (event *)data->left, i = 1;
                (i <= data->left_count) && next_event;
                next_event = next_event->next, i++ ) {
            dump_event(fp, next_event);
        }
    }
    if (!(data->flags & ENT_RIGHT_POINTS_TO_NODE)) {
        fprintf(fp,
                "right sublist:\n");
        for (   next_event = (event *)data->right, i = 1;
                (i <= data->right_count) && next_event;
                next_event = next_event->next, i++ ) {
            dump_event(fp, next_event);
        }
    }
}   /* dump_ent_node */
```

CHAPTER 16
Matching String Patterns

STARTING THE PLAN WITH AN ALGORITHM

In our earlier examples, the algorithms used fell more or less directly out of the work done to write the data structures. This allowed us to concentrate on data structure design and implementation without worrying much about the other equally important half of any program: algorithm design and implementation. In practice, this separation of data structures and algorithms is not always feasible. It's not at all unusual to specify a particular algorithm up front, in which case we have to write the data structures to fit the algorithm.

In this chapter we'll do exactly that: specify an algorithm for string pattern matching and design data structures that support the algorithm. To be precise, we'll write a program that scans any file of ASCII text and locates all instances of some set of predetermined keywords.

With slight modifications, this program could be used for many purposes. For instance, suppose the text file contains a bibliography, and suppose the program combines search results according to a boolean expression of keywords. Then we have a tool we can use to find the titles we're interested in. For instance, we could list every title containing either "struct" or "programming," or every title containing both "C" and "advanced."

We'll still follow the Plan, starting with top-level goals and guiding examples as usual. However, we'll find that writing a useful ADTD is easier when we're given an algorithm up front. The gap between a pseudocode algorithm and an ADTD is much smaller than the gap between a general problem description and an ADTD. We don't have to guess what

```
match( text )
    characters  text;    /* IN */
{
    state = 0;
    for (each character ch in text) {
        while (goto_func(state, ch) == FAIL) {
            state = failure_func(state);
        }
        state = goto_func(state, ch);
        if (output_func(state) != EMPTY) {
            printf( "Keyword: %s at %d\n",
                output_func(state), position of ch in text);
        }
    }
} /* match */
```

FIGURE 16-1: The heart of the pattern matching engine. The three functions *goto_func()*, *failure_func()*, and *output_func()* are built by the other parts of the algorithm, shown in Figures 16-2 and 16-3.

operators the abstract data type will need, because we can determine these from the algorithms. Algorithms also tend to suggest particular data type geometries—recursion suggests trees or stacks, a fixed number of data elements suggests arrays, sorting suggests ordered lists or trees, and so on.

The string pattern matching algorithm we'll use comes from Aho and Corasick (1975). Readers who are particularly interested in pattern matching should also consult Wirth (1984) for another algorithm that may be more efficient for longer texts than the one in Aho and Corasick (1975). Readers familiar with Modula-2 might also be interested in an earlier implementation of the pattern matcher in Ogilvie (1985).

The pattern matching algorithm consists of three parts, which are shown in Figures 16-1, 16-2, and 16-3. To make life a little easier, the pseudocode given in Aho and Corasick (1975) has been rewritten in a pseudocode that resembles C.

The pattern matcher algorithm defines a class of finite state machines (FSMs). A given execution of the pattern matcher runs one particular FSM. The goto and failure functions control state transitions and thereby define a particular FSM. Changing the keyword list or the set of legal text characters results in different goto and failure functions, so we get a different FSM. The goto and failure functions are rebuilt for each new set of keywords or legal text characters as is the output function that "recognizes" keywords by printing them as they are found.

For instance, suppose the legal input text is restricted to characters in {A..Z}, and the keywords are "AT," "PAT," "ALP," and "ATOP." The corresponding state machine is illustrated in Figure 16-4. Let's watch this FSM in action as we feed it the string "LOOK AT PAT ATOP AN ALP."

Look at Figure 16-4(a). The long bold arrow leaving state 0 means we begin this transition in state 0. State 0 is the "starting" state—the FSM always begins in state 0. Leaving

```
enter( key_word )
   characters  key_word;    /* IN */
{
   state = 0;
   j = 0;
   while (goto_func(state, key_word[j]) != FAIL) {
      state = goto_func(state, key_word[j]);
      j++;
   }
   for (p = j; key_word[p]; p++) {
      new_state++;
      goto_func(state, key_word[p]) = new_state;
      state = new_state;
   }
   output_func(state) = key_word;
} /* enter */

build_goto_func( text, key_words )
   characters  text;        /* IN */
   words       key_words;   /* IN */
{
   for (all states state) {
      output_func(state) = EMPTY;
      for (each character ch that could appear in text) {
         goto_func(state, ch) = FAIL;
      }
   }
   new_state = 0;
   for (each key_word in key_words) {
      enter(key_word);
   }
   for (each character ch that could appear in text) {
      if (goto_func(0, ch) == FAIL) {
         goto_func(0, ch) = 0;
      }
   }
} /* build_goto_func */
```

FIGURE 16-2: Construction of the goto function; *build_goto_func()* also begins construction of the output function.

state 0, we see the character 'L' as our first input; this is indicated in Figure 16-4(a) by the arrow placed over the first 'L' in "LOOK AT PAT ATOP AN ALP." 'L' is in the set ~{A,P} (every character except 'A' or 'P'), so we make the transition indicated, back to state 0. Our state after the transition is indicated in the figure by a short bold arrow pointing into the destination, which is state 0 in this case. We repeat the trip—state 0 to state 0—for the next four characters, since 'O,' 'O,' 'K,' and blank are all in ~{A,P}.

```
build_failure_func( text )
  characters  text;    /* IN */
{
  init_queue();
  for (each character ch that could appear in text) {
    s = goto_func(0, ch);
    if (s != 0) {
      enqueue(s);
      failure_func(s) = 0;
    }
  }
  while (queue is not empty) {
    r = dequeue();
    for (each character ch that could appear in text) {
      s = goto_func(r, ch);
      if (s != FAIL) {
        enqueue(s);
        state = failure_func(r);
        while (goto_func(state, ch) == FAIL) {
          state = failure_func(state);
        }
        failure_func(s) = goto_func(state, ch);
        output_func(s) += output_func(failure_func(s));
      }
    }
  }
} /* build_failure_func */
```

FIGURE 16-3: Construction of the failure function; *build_failure_func()* also finishes construction of the output function.

Figure 16-4(b) shows the first step in a recognition of the keyword "AT." We leave state 0, see 'A' as input, and make the transition to state 1. 'T' is the next character, so in Figure 16-4(c), we continue by leaving state 1 for state 2. If the next character were 'O' instead of blank, we would move from state 2 to state 8. Instead, Figure 16-4(d) shows us moving back to state 0.

In the graph in Figure 16-4, there is no transition out of state 2 except on 'O,' and we saw a blank after "LOOK AT," not an 'O.' So how did we know to go from state 2 to state 0 if no transition was shown? We used the failure function shown in Figure 16-5. The failure function is invoked whenever the graph fails to provide a transition from a given state for a given input character. *Failure_func(2)* == 0, so we move to state 0. From there we'll accept the blank and make the transition back to state 0, because blank is in ~{A, P}.

Moving on to Figure 16-4(e), we find ourselves in state 5, having gotten there by way of states 0, 3, and 4 as we took blank, 'P,' 'A,' and 'T' as input characters. From state 5, we invoke *output_func()* to tell the user we've found keywords "PAT" and "AT." The output function for the FSM in Figure 16-4 is shown in Figure 16-6. Notice that more than one

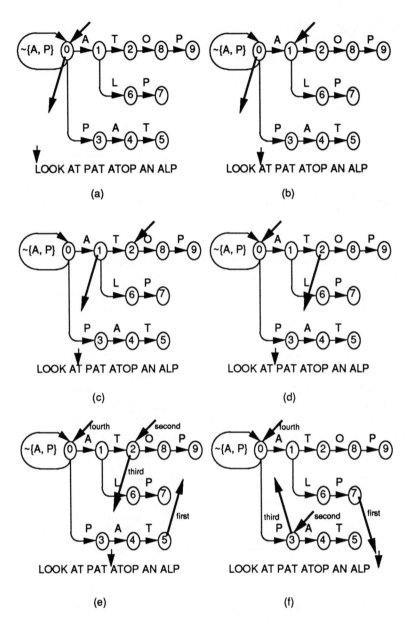

FIGURE 16-4: A pattern matching FSM in action.

keyword can be recognized in a given state. This is necessary because one keyword ("AT") can be a substring of another ("PAT").

There are no transitions from state 5, so processing any input, including the blank after "LOOK AT PAT," requires the failure function. Figure 16-5 shows that *failure_func(5)* ==

Current State	New State on Failure
1	0
2	0
3	0
4	1
5	2
6	0
7	3
8	0
9	3

FIGURE 16-5: Failure function for the FSM shown in Figure 16-4.

2, so Figure 16-4(e) shows us moving to state 2. But there are no transitions on blank out of state 2, so we move to *failure_func(2)* == state 0. There is a transition out of (and back into) state 0 on blank, so we're moving again.

Figure 16-4(f) shows that end-of-file (EOF) is treated like any other character as far as state transitions are concerned. We are in state 7, and we've just informed the user that "ALP" was recognized, as the output function in Figure 16-6 requires. There are no transitions from state 7 on any character, much less on EOF, so we turn to the failure function in Figure 16-5. *Failure_func(7)* == 3. We didn't go back to state 0 from state 7 because the 'P' that ends "ALP" might be the start of "PAT." But it isn't—the only transition out of state 3 is on 'A,' not EOF. So we turn to the failure function again. *Failure_func(3)* == 0, so we go to state 0. There is a transition on EOF out of state 0 (we must be sure to include EOF in ~{A,P}), so the EOF is processed. Since the EOF also marks the end of the text, our processing of "LOOK AT PAT ATOP AN ALP" is complete.

TOP-LEVEL GOALS

Our main goal is to implement the given pattern matcher algorithm. Since we expect to put our code in a library that finds many uses, we want it to be portable. Since pattern matching involves searches, we also want speedy execution. This means there is a potential for

State	Output (Keywords Recognized)
2	{AT}
5	{PAT, AT}
7	{ALP}
9	{ATOP}

FIGURE 16-6: Output function for the FSM shown in Figure 16-4.

conflict—it can be very tough to get both portability and fast execution. If we have to decide, we'll favor portability, but only as long as the implementation runs fast enough to be worth porting.

GUIDING EXAMPLES

Our main guiding example, of course, will be the pseudocode in Figures 16-1, 16-2, and 16-3. But we'll also need some examples of data to feed the pattern matcher. What are the fundamental characteristics of string matching problems? Well, we want to be able to find embedded substrings. We should try a set of keywords in which one keyword is a substring of another. It might also be wise to have two keywords match in the first few characters and then diverge.

To be perfectly honest, this is actually the point at which I generated Figure 16-4. I referred to it earlier in order to explain FSM transition graphs, failure functions, and so on. But Figure 16-4 also shows our guiding example of data to feed the pattern matcher. The text is "LOOK AT PAT ATOP AN ALP," and the keywords are "AT," "PAT," "ATOP," and "ALP." If we do things right, we will find "AT" three times ("LOOK **AT** **P**AT **AT**OP AN ALP"), "PAT" once, "ALP" once, and "ATOP" once. We don't want the FSM to recognize partial matches; looking for "AT" should not yield "ALP," because only the 'A' in "AT" is matched.

ABSTRACT DATA TYPE DESCRIPTION

Let's take a closer look now at the pattern matching algorithm in Figures 16-1, 16-2, and 16-3. Notice that the pseudocode avoids declaring *text* as an array of characters. *Text* is a sequence of characters all right, but we don't want to pin down implementation details yet. For instance, we might read *text* from a file, implementing the pseudocode

```
for (each character ch in text) {
```

as

```
for (ch = getc(fp); ch != EOF; ch = getc(fp)) {
```

Notice also that *goto_func()*, *failure_func()*, and *output_func()* appear on both sides of assignment statements! Thus, the following pseudocode must be implemented in some way that changes the value that *output_func()* returns:

```
output_func(state) = key_word;
```

Something similar must be also be done for *goto_func()* and *failure_func()*. This is most easily supported in C by splitting each of these three functions into two parts: a data structure which can be modified to change the values the function returns, and the function proper, which simply accesses the data structure.

Wait a minute. So far we have goto, failure, and output functions that are actually a combination of functions and data. We have a transition graph. We have three pieces of pseudocode. We've referred to finite state machines. How do all these things relate to each other?

Figure 16-7 shows how all these pieces fit together. For instance, an FSM consists of three functions: goto, failure, and output. Each of these functions in turn consists of a data structure and some access code. To avoid repeating later a diagram that is almost identical to Figure 16-7, I've pretended I'm a clairvoyant and provided the actual names of the functions' data structures: "transition graph," "list of 2-states," and "list of states and sets of strings." We'll see soon enough where these data structures come from. The match function that Figure 16-7 refers to is the main body of the pattern matcher, shown earlier in Figure 16-1.

While we're taking inventory, let's try to decide what abstract data types we'll need. We need a transition graph like the one shown in Figure 16-4 to guide *goto_func()*. We need a *failure_func()* like the one in Figure 16-5. We also need a set of strings to support an *output_func()* like the one in Figure 16-6. Finally, Figure 16-3 refers to a queue of states, so we'll need one of those. In other words, we actually need four ADTDs.

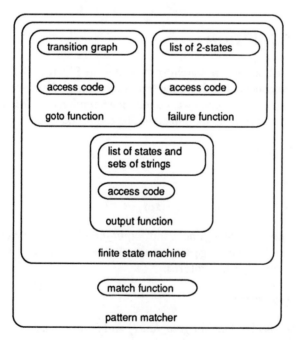

FIGURE 16-7: How the various entities discussed so far fit together to make the pattern matcher.

Transition Graph Abstract Data Type

What is the geometry of this abstract data type? Figure 16-4 will work as a sketch of the transition graph abstract data type, even though different keywords or legal text characters would result in a different graph. State 0 is a special position, because it's the "starting" state, the initial state from which the sequence of transitions always begins for any given text.

What relations hold between the elements of the collection? The transition graph can be viewed as a set of triplets <From_State, To_State, Input_Character>. For instance, Figure 16-4 could be represented as <0,0,B>, <0,0,C>, <0,1,A>, <1,2,T>, <1,6,L>, and a number of other triplets. These triplets define a relation.

In general, there's not much we can say about this relation. It doesn't need to be reflexive or symmetric or transitive, although in some cases it might be. States 0 and 1 in Figure 16-4 both have transitions to more than one state each, so the triplet relation can be one-to-many. But it would be one-to-one if the keywords had no shared characters. This relation is hard to pin down with the ADTD questions we've been using. However, we have the pseudocode, so to implement the type we might not need to know when the relation is one-to-one, when it is reflexive, and so forth.

What are the operators? We need two operators: one to build the transition graph and one to read it. The builder is *build_goto_func()* in Figure 16-2 (plus the *enter()* function that *build_goto_func()* calls). The operator to read the transition graph has the same calling sequence as Figure 16-1's *goto_func()*. Given From_State and Input_Character, it has to find a matching triplet <From_State, X, Input_Character> and return X.

What are the restrictions on membership in the collection? Membership in the transition graph is completely determined by two things: the set of legal text characters and the set of keywords. Changing the set of legal text characters typically changes the set of transitions from state 0 back to itself. Changing the set of keywords causes even greater differences in the graph.

There is no inherent limit on the number of members. It's not obvious, but the algorithm used to build the transition graph guarantees that there are never two transitions out of a state for the same character. That is, triplets like <1,2,K> and <1,4,K> cannot coexist in the same transition graph. If they did, and we saw a 'K' in state 1, we wouldn't know whether to go to state 2 or state 4.

The transition graph data type is closely linked to the next type we'll describe, the failure function.

Failure Function Abstract Data Type

What is the geometry of this abstract data type? Figure 16-5 will serve as a sketch of the failure function. Or, if you prefer, you can think of the failure function as a set of pairs of integers: <From_State, To_State>. As in any set, there are no special positions. What about relations? If we use the integer pairs as the definition of a relation, it's a good bet that the relation is never reflexive, symmetric, or transitive. (I'll leave the reasoning behind this guess to you; think about cycles in the FSM).

What are the operators? As with the transition graph, we need only two operators: a builder and a reader. The builder is *build_failure_func()* in Figure 16-3. The reader has the same calling sequence as *failure_func()* in Figure 16-1.

What are the restrictions on membership in the collection? The <From_State, To_State> pairs are specified by the algorithm in Figure 16-3. There will be exactly one pair for each From_State in [1..however many states there are]. Notice from Figure 16-4 that there is a transition out of 0 for every legal text character, so state 0 does not need an entry in the failure function. For this reason, state 0 is sometimes called a "catchall" state.

Set of Strings Function Abstract Data Type

What is the geometry of this abstract data type? Figure 16-6 will serve as our sketch of a stringset function type. Notice that this is not just a list of stringsets, but a function of stringsets. Each stringset is associated with an integer. The integer is the state, and the strings are the keywords the machine recognizes when it reaches that state. Thus, we could imagine a relation of pairs <State, Stringset>. As with the other data types, there's not much we can say about this relation as far as reflexivity and similar properties are concerned. There are no special positions in this type's geometry.

What are the operators? Once again, we need a builder and a reader. The *output_func()* builder is not explicit in the pattern matching algorithm; output function construction begins in Figure 16-2 and is finished in Figure 16-3. This makes an abstract data type description a bit awkward, but as long as the <State, Stringset> pairs are correct for the associated *goto_func()* and *failure_func()*, that awkwardness has no real impact. The reader operator has the same calling sequence as *output_func()* in Figure 16-1.

What are the restrictions on membership in the collection? As with the other ADTs above, the only restriction is that the data elements (<State, Stringset> pairs in this case) be generated by the pattern matching algorithm.

Queue of States Abstract Data Type

This is a regular queue (a FIFO, in other words). The collection of ADTDs in the Framework section contains a description of another kind of queue (the so-called "lumpy" queue; see page 344), so we won't bother with a detailed description here. Suffice it to say that we need two operators: *enqueue()* and *dequeue()*, and that queue elements (states) are simply integer values. Now let's try to implement these four data types.

ATTEMPT ONE

We'll start with the transition graph implementation. Two possibilities present themselves right away: triplets and adjacency lists.

In the description of the transition graph abstract data type, we viewed the graph as a set of triplets <From_State, To_State, Input_Character>. It's easy to translate this triplet into a typedef. From_State and To_State are ints, and Character is (surprise!) a char:

```
typedef struct {
   int  from,
        to;
   char input;
}   triplet;
```

This typedef raises two issues:

1. Where do we put all these transitions? In an array? Or do we add a pointer and keep the triplet structs in a list?
2. Is there a more efficient way to represent all the transitions from state 0 back to itself?

Before we try to answer these questions, let's see what questions the other graph implementation raises. Maybe we'll be lucky, and adjacency lists will be obviously better than triplets. An adjacency list representation of Figure 16-4's transition graph is shown in Figure 16-8.

To create an adjacency list representation like the one shown in Figure 16-8, we first allocate an array with as many elements as there are states in the transition graph. Then we build a list of adjacent states for each state. A state K is adjacent to state J if we can travel directly from J to K in the transition graph. The necessary structures are quite straightforward:

```
typedef struct adjacency {
  struct adjacency *next;
  int             dest;   /* destination state */
  char            input;  /* make transition on this char */
} adjacency;

static adjacency    *my_graph[MAX_STATES];
```

But this solution raises its own questions:

3. How many states are there? More importantly, at what point do we know how many there are? This influences how we allocate memory; see the design guideline "When to Allocate Lists and Arrays" (page 357). Can we simply allocate an array at compile-time, as we did with *my_graph* above? Or do we have to allocate it dynamically? Maybe even that won't work, and we'll have to use a list like the one shown in Figure 16-9 instead of the array shown in Figure 16-8.
4. What about all those transitions from state 0 back to itself? How are they represented in the adjacency list?

Both implementation possibilities—triplets and adjacency lists—actually raise the

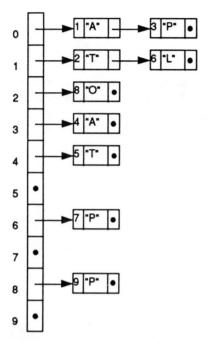

FIGURE 16-8: The transition graph from Figure 16-4 represented as an array of adjacency lists.

same two issues. First, we need to find the point at which the number of states in the transition graph becomes known so we can decide when to allocate structs. Second, we need to decide how to represent the large number of transitions from state 0 back to itself.

When is the number of transition graph states known? We need to know so we can choose between arrays and linked lists. This problem is discussed in the design guideline "When to Allocate Lists and Arrays" (page 357). Look at the pattern matcher algorithm. In Figure 16-2, the goto function is constructed. That is, the transition graph is built. This means we don't know at compile-time how many states the graph has. We don't even know the number at initialization-time, unless you consider building the goto function part of the initialization. I don't, because the goto function must be rebuilt for each new set of keywords, and programs should probably be able to process more than one set of keywords per execution.

The point is, there's no easy way to tell how many states are needed without actually building the graph. So we'll have to use a list. We can't just allocate an array, either at compile-time or during program initialization. If we decide to use triplets, we'll need a list of them. If we choose an adjacency list representation, we'll go with Figure 16-9, not with Figure 16-8. So much for questions 1 and 3.

What about questions 2 and 4? Isn't there some efficient way to represent all those transitions from state 0 to itself? State 0 has transitions back to itself for every character that

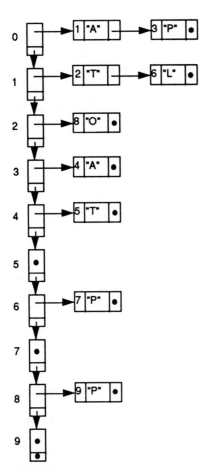

FIGURE 16-9: The transition graph from Figure 16-4 represented as a list of adjacency lists.

might appear in the text, except those relatively few that begin keywords. Simply adding triplets or adjacency list elements to represent all those transitions seems unnecessarily expensive.

However, the goto function will be the transition graph plus some access code, as shown in Figure 16-7. We don't have to represent all the transitions from state 0 to itself explicitly in the graph, whether we use triplets or adjacency lists or something else. We can add "virtual" transitions to the graph. We'll make the access code assume that any transition leaving state 0 returns to state 0 unless the graph explicitly says otherwise:

```
goto_func( state, input )
  int  state;  /* IN */
```

```
      char input;   /* IN */
{
   if (state == 0) {
      if (there is a transition from state 0 on input)
         return (destination of transition);
      else
         return (0); /* "virtual" transition back to state 0 */
   }
   else {
      if (there is a transition from state on input)
         return (destination of transition);
      else
         return (FAIL);
   }
} /* goto_func */
```

We still need to choose between adjacency lists and triplets. Which representation uses memory more efficiently? In an adjacency list, the "from" state is not repeated for each "to" state. For instance, state 1 has two transitions leaving it, so it would require two triplets: <1,2,T> and <1,6,L>, with the "from" state, state 1, repeated in each. By contrast, the adjacency list for state 1 in Figure 16-9 shows that we need only one integer per "from" state, no matter how many transitions leave the state. Therefore adjacency lists look like a better choice.

However, some of the adjacency lists in both Figure 16-8 and Figure 16-9 are empty. In fact, every keyword's ending state (states 5, 7, and 9 in our example) will have no transitions out of it, and so will generate an empty adjacency list. Of course, we don't have to add headers for empty lists. When we build the list of adjacency lists, we won't put in a new header until we have a need for it. So adjacency lists do indeed require less memory than triplets.

Access times are better for adjacency lists, too. We don't have to traverse all preceding adjacency lists to get to the one we want. We will have to traverse all preceding triplets, however, to reach the triplet we want.

For instance, suppose we want to find the adjacency list element that represents the transition out of state 3 on 'A.' In Figure 16-9, we start at the head of state 0's adjacency list, move to the head of state 1's list (without traversing state 0's list), move to the head of 2's list, and then to the head of 3's list. Then we follow state 3's list until we find the character 'A.' At that point we can report that *goto_func(3, 'A')* == 4. Altogether, then, we had to chase four pointers.

By contrast, suppose we want to find the triplet that represents the transition out of state 3 on 'A.' All the triplets are in one long list, so we have to traverse the following triplets to find the one we want: <0,1,A>, <0,3,P>, <1,2,T>, <1,6,L>, <2,8,O>, <3,4,A>. It takes one more pointer than it did for an adjacency list. Adjacency lists look even better if the sublists we skip are longer, that is, if states tend to have many transitions coming out of them.

Of course, we could organize the triplets into sublists. But if we did, we would essentially have a list of adjacency lists! Organizing a long list into a list of shorter lists to save traversal time is not a new idea. Hashing is one way to do this; Chapter 15, "Partitioning a

Simulator's Event List," provides another example. Since adjacency lists are faster and use less memory than triplets, we'll use the adjacency list scheme shown in Figure 16-9 to represent the transition graph.

We know enough now to start coding the transition graph into C. But we'll hold off until we're sure we can get equally precise and implementable representations for the other abstract data types.

The next abstract data type to implement is the failure function. Figures 16-5 and 16-9 taken together suggest an acceptable representation: a list of integer pairs:

```
typedef struct {
    struct two_states    *next;
    int                  from,
                         to;
} two_states;
```

Figure 16-10 shows the list that corresponds to the failure function in Figure 16-5.

The third abstract data type to implement is the stringset function used by *output_func()*. If we pass *output_func()* a state, it should return a (possibly empty) set of strings, namely, the keywords that are recognized when we reach that state. Figure 16-11 shows an implementation that is suggested by Figure 16-6 and the various linked structures we've been considering. In particular, Figure 16-11 bears a strong resemblance to the list of adjacency lists shown in Figure 16-9. This is because both figures show a list of lists.

Notice that Figure 16-11 shows some wasted memory—the keyword "AT" and the struct that point to it are stored twice, once for state 2 and once for state 5. We can avoid this if we use a representation like the one shown in Figure 16-12. In Figure 16-12, the stringsets have been implemented separately from the output function. It is the responsibility of the stringset implementation to avoid wasting memory.

Figure 16-12's approach makes the program more modular, which is nice. But we can get the modularity without using the exact representation shown in Figure 16-12. In fact, we could draw a line separating Figure 16-11 just like the line in Figure 16-12. And that, in fact, is just what we'll do.

Unless a great deal of memory is used otherwise to hold duplicate keyword strings, the representation in Figure 16-12 is just too complex to be worth the effort. For instance, how do we know when we can free the memory held by the string "AT"? We need reference counts, or back pointers, or some other way to tell when it's safe to free "AT." Otherwise, dangling pointers are sure to occur. Also, how do we know whether a string already has memory allocated for it or not? Do we really want to search all existing sets before allocating

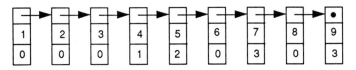

FIGURE 16-10:   The failure function of Figure 16-5 represented as a list of *two_states* structs.

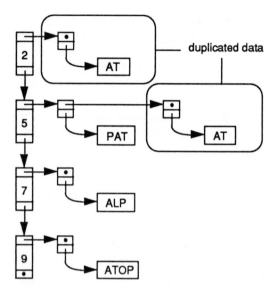

FIGURE 16-11:   A representation of the output function shown in Figure 16-6.

three bytes to hold a null-terminated "AT"? I think not. The memory savings is not worth the effort, so we'll use Figure 16-11 (modified to make stringsets independent of the output function) as our guide, not Figure 16-12.

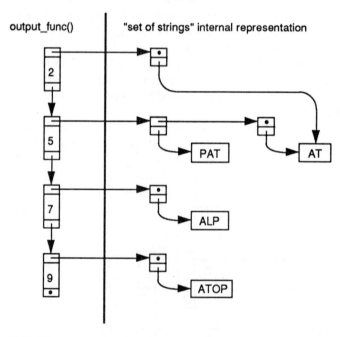

FIGURE 16-12:   A possible alternative to the representation in Figure 16-11.

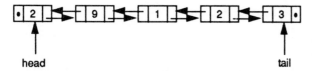

FIGURE 16-13: A queue of states.

This seems like a good place to stop and take inventory of what we've done and what we have left to do. We decided that four abstract data types were needed to support the pattern matching algorithms. Of these, we have a good idea how to implement three. Transition graphs will be represented as adjacency lists like the one shown in Figure 16-9. The failure function will be represented by a list of *two_states*, as shown in Figure 16-10. And the stringset function will be implemented using a list of stringsets and states, as shown in Figure 16-11.

This leaves the queue of states data type. When do we find out how big the queue has to be? That is, can we represent it using an array, or do we need discrete structs linked in a list? The queue is used in Figure 16-3's algorithm, after the transition graph has been constructed by the algorithm in Figure 16-2. So we know how many states are in the transition graph by the time the queue is needed. This does not mean, however, that we know how many elements the queue might need to hold, because a state may be enqueued more than once. So we need a linked list queue implementation like the one shown in Figure 16-13.

Now we are ready to start coding. We have clear goals, guiding examples and ADTDs. We have implementation plans for each abstract data type in the form of detailed figures, or typedefs ,or both. And we have the pattern matching algorithms in Figures 16-1, 2, and 3. By this point in the book, the relationship between top-level goals, guiding examples, and ADTDs on the one hand, and coding on the other should be clear. Also, we have pseudocode to guide us. So I'm just going to present the implementation, rather than examine the critical functions individually as we have in earlier examples.

LISTING: match.h

```
/*---------------------------------------------
                    match.h
-----------------------------------------------*/


/*=============================================================
Purpose:
    This file supplies typedefs and defines for the various
    component files of the string pattern matcher.
-----------------------------------------------*/
#ifndef _MATCH_H_
#define _MATCH_H_
```

```
#include <boolean.h> /* for convenience */

/* status codes: */
#define STAT_OK      0
#define STAT_ERROR  -1   /* any value illegal for a state will do */

#endif  _MATCH_H_
```

LISTING: stringsets.h

```
/*--------------------------------------------
                    stringsets.h
------------------------------------------*/

/*============================================
Purpose:
    This file supplies typedefs for the library of routines that
    deal with sets of strings.

    This code was compiled under THINK's LightspeedC® on a
    Macintosh™ SE.
------------------------------------------*/
#ifndef _STRINGSETS_H_
#define _STRINGSETS_H_

typedef struct ss_elem {
    struct ss_elem  *next;
    char            *value;
} ss_elem;

typedef ss_elem *stringset;

#endif _STRINGSETS_H_
```

LISTING: match.c

```
/*--------------------------------------------
                    match.c
------------------------------------------*/

/*============================================
Purpose:
    This is the main body of the string pattern matcher example.
    Functionality breaks down by files like this:
```

```
        main body (see Figures 16-1,16-2,16-3):   match.c
        adjacency list representation of graph:   graph.c
        failure function:                         failure.c
        output function:                          output.c
        stringsets used by output function:       stringsets.h,
                                                  stringsets.c
        queue of states:                          queue.c
        status codes, other global miscellany:    match.h

    This code was compiled under THINK's LightspeedC (TM) on a
    Macintosh SE.
------------------------------------------------------*/
#include "match.h"
#include <stdio.h>

static boolean  initializing; /* see goto_func() */
static int      new_state;     /* see build_goto_func(), enter() */

/* build_goto_func(), build_failure_func() use these defines: */
#define LO_CHAR     ' '
#define HI_CHAR     '~'


/*================================================================*/
main()
/*-----------------------------------------------

Purpose:
    String pattern matcher.
Parameters:
    none, but sets global boolean initializing
------------------------------------------------------*/
{
    FILE    *fp, *fopen();
    char    fname[1024];
    void    build_goto_func(), build_failure_func(), match();

    printf("String Pattern Matcher\n");
    printf("\tText file name> ");
    scanf("%s", fname);
    if (!(fp = fopen(fname, "r"))) {
        printf("\ncouldn't open file %s\n", fname);
        return;
    }
    build_goto_func();
    build_failure_func();
    match(fp);
    fclose(fp);
} /* main */
```

```
/*================================================================*/
void    match( fp )
    FILE    *fp;    /* IN */
/*------------------------------------------------

Purpose:
    Implementation of string pattern matcher in text. See
    Figure 16-1.
Parameters:
    fp      open text file to scan for keywords
---------------------------------------------------*/
{
    int     state;
    char    input;

    state = 0;
    for (input = fgetc(fp); input != EOF; input = fgetc(fp)) {
        while (goto_func(state, input) == STAT_ERROR) {
            state = ff_eval(state);
        }
        state = goto_func(state, input);
        of_print_state(stdout, state);
    }
} /* match */


/*================================================================*/
static int      goto_func( state, input )
    int     state;  /* IN */
    char    input;  /* IN */
/*------------------------------------------------

Purpose:
    Given a current state and an input state, return the destination
    state for the appropriate transition.
Parameters:
    state   current state
    input   input character seen in current state
    Returns state transition is made to, or STAT_ERROR.
---------------------------------------------------*/
{
    int     dest;

    dest = g_eval(state, input);
    if (dest == STAT_ERROR) {
        if ((state == 0) && (!initializing)) {
            return (0);
        }
        else {
            return (STAT_ERROR);
        }
```

```
    }
    else {
        return (dest);
    }
} /* goto_func */

/*================================================================*/
static int      enter( key )
    char    *key;   /* IN */
/*--------------------------------------------------
Purpose:
    Add graph transitions based on current graph and characters
    in keyword.
Parameters:
    key     keyword to add
    Also uses global int new_state.
    Returns STAT_OK or STAT_ERROR.
--------------------------------------------------*/
{
    int     state, j, p;

    state = 0;
    j = 0;
    while (key[j] && (goto_func(state, key[j]) != STAT_ERROR)) {
        state = goto_func(state, key[j]);
        j++;
    }
    for (p = j; key[p]; p++) {
        new_state++;
        if (g_add(state, new_state, key[p])) {
            printf("\nenter(%s) failed\n", key);
            return (STAT_ERROR);
        }
        state = new_state;
    }
    return (of_add(state, key));
} /* enter */

/*================================================================*/
static void     build_goto_func()
/*--------------------------------------------------
Purpose:
    Corresponds to Figure 16-2 in the text. Assumes any printable
    ASCII character might appear in the text. Reads keywords
    interactively.
Parameters:
    none, but uses global int new_state
--------------------------------------------------*/
```

```
{
    char    buf[128], ch;

    initializing = true;
    /* no loop needed to set output_func(), goto_func() to
       fail initially—it's built into their data structures
       and access code, including the global initializing */
    new_state = 0;
    printf("keyword ('.' to quit)> ");
    scanf("%s", buf);
    for ( ; buf[0] != '.'; ) {
        if (enter(buf)) {
            printf("\nenter keyword %s failed\n", buf);
            return;
        }
        printf("keyword ('.' to quit)> ");
        scanf("%s", buf);
    }
    for (ch = LO_CHAR; ch <= HI_CHAR; ch++) {
        if (goto_func(0, ch) == STAT_ERROR) {
            g_add(0, 0, ch);
        }
    }
} /* build_goto_func */

/*================================================================*/
static void    build_failure_func()
/*------------------------------------------------------
Purpose:
    Corresponds to Figure 16-3 in the text. Assumes any printable
    ASCII character might appear in the text.
Parameters:
    none
------------------------------------------------------*/
{
    char    ch;
    int     state, r, s;

    /* no queue initialization needed; skip to next part: */
    for (ch = LO_CHAR; ch <= HI_CHAR; ch++) {
        s = goto_func(0, ch);
        if (s != 0) {
            if (q_enqueue(s)) {
                printf("\nenqueue(%d) failed\n", s);
                return;
            }
            if (ff_set(s,0)) {
                printf("\nff_set(%d,0) failed\n", s);
```

```
                    return;
              }
          }
      }
      for (r = q_dequeue(); r != STAT_ERROR; r = q_dequeue()) {
          for (ch = LO_CHAR; ch <= HI_CHAR; ch++) {
              s = goto_func(r, ch);
              if (s != STAT_ERROR) {
                  if (q_enqueue(s)) {
                      printf("\nenqueue(%d) failed\n", s);
                      return;
                  }
                  state = ff_eval(r);
                  while (goto_func(state, ch) == STAT_ERROR) {
                      state = ff_eval(state);
                  }
                  if (ff_set(s, goto_func(state, ch))) {
                      printf( "\nff_set(%d,goto(%d,%c)) failed\n",
                              s, state, ch);
                      return;
                  }
                  if (of_union(s, ff_eval(s))) {
                      printf( "\nof_union(%d,ff_eval(%d)) failed\n",
                              s, s);
                      return;
                  }
              }
          }
      }
      initializing = false;
} /* build_failure_func */
```

LISTING: graph.c

```
/*------------------------------------------------
                    graph.c
-------------------------------------------------*/

/*================================================================
Purpose:
    This file supplies the string pattern matcher with functions
    to do the following:

        add transition to graph:              g_add()
        find destination state, given current
        state & input:                        g_eval()
```

```
          print graph's adjacency lists:          g_print()

    No initialization routine is needed.

    This code was compiled under THINK's LightspeedC® on a
    Macintosh™ SE.
------------------------------------------------------*/
#include "match.h"
#include <stdio.h>

/* graph is represented as a list of adjacency lists (see text),
   that is, as a list of adj_headers, each of which has a list
   of adj_elems hanging off it: */

typedef struct adj_header {
    struct adj_header    *next;
    struct adj_elem      *list;
    int                  state;
} adj_header;

typedef struct adj_elem {
    struct adj_elem      *next;
    int                  state;
    char                 input;
} adj_elem;

/* We only need this file to support one graph (compare with
   stringsets.c): */
static adj_header    *g = NULL;

#ifdef _GRAPH_TESTBED_
/*==============================================================*/
main()
/*---------------------------------------------

Purpose:
    Exercise the graph functions.
Parameters:
    none
------------------------------------------------------*/
{
    char    ch, input;
    int     from, to;
    void    g_print();

    for (ch = 'p'; ; ) {
        printf("\nGraph testbed:\n");
        printf("\t(a)dd transition to graph\n");
        printf("\t(e)valuate - find dest from state and input\n");
```

```
            printf("\t(p)rint list of adjacency lists\n");
            printf("\t(q)uit\n");
            ch = getc(stdin);
            if (ch == 'a') {
                printf("from> ");
                scanf("%d", &from);
                printf("to> ");
                scanf("%d", &to);
                ch = getc(stdin); /* toss carriage return */
                printf("input char> ");
                scanf("%c", &input);
                if (g_add(from, to, input))
                    printf("Failed to add transition to graph\n");
            }
            else if (ch == 'e') {
                printf("from> ");
                scanf("%d", &from);
                ch = getc(stdin); /* toss carriage return */
                printf("input char> ");
                scanf("%c", &input);
                to = g_eval(from, input);
                printf("\ng_eval(%d, %c) == %d\n", from, input, to);
            }
            else if (ch == 'p') {
                g_print(stdout);
            }
            else if (ch == 'q') {
                return;
            }
            else {
                printf("unknown command\n");
            }
            ch = getc(stdin); /* toss away carriage return */
    }
} /* main */
#endif _GRAPH_TESTBED_


/*=================================================================*/
void    g_print( fp )
    FILE    *fp;    /* IN */
/*---------------------------------------------------

Purpose:
    Pretty-print the graph's internal representation.
Parameters:
    fp      open file to print to
--------------------------------------------------*/
{
    adj_header  *nxt_header;
```

```
        adj_elem    *nxt_elem;
        int         i;

        fprintf(fp, "\nGRAPH:");
        for (   nxt_header = g;
                nxt_header;
                nxt_header = nxt_header->next) {
            fprintf(fp, "\n\tstate %d:", nxt_header->state);
            for (   nxt_elem = nxt_header->list, i = 0;
                    nxt_elem;
                    nxt_elem = nxt_elem->next)   {
                if ((i++ % 4) == 0)
                    fprintf(fp, "\n\t\t");
                fprintf(fp,
                        "-> %d on %c ",
                        nxt_elem->state,
                        nxt_elem->input);
            }
        }
        fprintf(fp, "\n");
} /* g_print */

/*=================================================================*/
int     g_eval( from, input )
    int     from;   /* IN */
    char    input;  /* IN */
/*---------------------------------------------
Purpose:
    Given a current state and an input state, return the destination
    state for the appropriate transition.
Parameters:
    from    current state
    input   input character seen in current state
    Returns state transition is made to, or STAT_ERROR.
---------------------------------------------*/
{
    adj_header  *nxt_header;
    adj_elem    *nxt_elem;

    for (   nxt_header = g;
            nxt_header && (nxt_header->state != from);
            nxt_header = nxt_header->next)
        ;
    if (!nxt_header)
        return (STAT_ERROR);
    for (   nxt_elem = nxt_header->list;
            nxt_elem && (nxt_elem->input != input);
            nxt_elem = nxt_elem->next)
```

```
            ;
        if (!nxt_elem)
            return (STAT_ERROR);
        return (nxt_elem->state);
    } /* g_eval */


/*===============================================================*/
int     g_add( from, to, input )
    int     from,           /* IN */
            to;             /* IN */
    char    input;          /* IN */
/*---------------------------------------------
Purpose:
    Add a new transition to the graph.
Parameters:
    from,
    to,
    input   add a transition from state <from>, to state <to>, on
            seeing input character <input>
    Returns STAT_OK or STAT_ERROR.
----------------------------------------------*/
{
    adj_header  *new_header;
    adj_elem    *new_elem;
    void        *malloc();

    for (new_header = g; new_header; new_header = new_header->next) {
        if (new_header->state == from)
            break;
    }
    if (!new_header) {
        if (! (new_header =
                    (adj_header *)malloc(sizeof(adj_header)))) {
            printf("out of memory\n");
            return (STAT_ERROR);
        }
        new_header->state = from;
        new_header->next  = g;
        new_header->list  = NULL;
        g = new_header;
    }
    for (   new_elem = new_header->list;
            new_elem;
            new_elem = new_elem->next) {
        if ((new_elem->state == to) && (new_elem->input == input))
            return (STAT_OK);
    }
    if (!new_elem) {
```

```
        if (!(new_elem = (adj_elem *)malloc(sizeof(adj_elem)))) {
            printf("out of memory\n");
            return (STAT_ERROR);
        }
        new_elem->state = to;
        new_elem->input = input;
        new_elem->next  = new_header->list;
        new_header->list = new_elem;
    }
    return (STAT_OK);
} /* g_add */
```

LISTING: failure.c

```
/*--------------------------------------------------------
                        failure.c
---------------------------------------------------------*/

/*========================================================
Purpose:
    This file supplies the string pattern matcher with functions
    to do the following:

        set values in the failure function:   ff_set()
        evalute the failure function:          ff_eval()
        print the failure function structure:  ff_print()

    This code was compiled under THINK's LightspeedC® on a
    Macintosh™ SE.
---------------------------------------------------------*/
#include "match.h"
#include <stdio.h>

typedef struct two_states {
    struct two_states   *next;
    int                 from,
                        to;
} two_states;

/* We only need this file to support one failure function
   (compare with stringsets.c): */
static two_states   *ff = NULL;

#ifdef _FAILURE_TESTBED_
/*========================================================*/
main()
```

```
/*---------------------------------------------
Purpose:
    Exercise the failure function.
Parameters:
    none
-------------------------------------------*/
{
    char    ch;
    int     from, to;
    void    ff_print();

    for (ch = 'p'; ; ) {
        printf("\nFailure function testbed:\n");
        printf("\t(e)valuate failure_func(<from>)\n");
        printf("\t(p)rint failure function\n");
        printf("\t(q)uit\n");
        printf("\t(s)et <from, to> pair in failure function\n");
        ch = getc(stdin);
        if (ch == 'e') {
            printf("from> ");
            scanf("%d", &from);
            to = ff_eval(from);
            printf("failure_func(%d) == %d\n", from, to);
        }
        else if (ch == 'p') {
            ff_print(stdout);
        }
        else if (ch == 'q') {
            return;
        }
        else if (ch == 's') {
            printf("from> ");
            scanf("%d", &from);
            printf("to> ");
            scanf("%d", &to);
            if (ff_set(from, to)) {
                printf("FAILED to set failure function\n");
            }
        }
        else {
            printf("unknown command\n");
        }
        ch = getc(stdin); /* toss away carriage return */
    }
} /* main */
#endif _FAILURE_TESTBED_


/*==============================================================*/
```

```
void    ff_print( fp )
    FILE    *fp;    /* IN */
/*-------------------------------------------
Purpose:
    Pretty-print the failure function's internal representation.
Parameters:
    fp      open file to print to
-------------------------------------------*/
{
    two_states  *nxt;

    fprintf(fp, "\nFAILURE FUNCTION:\n");
    fprintf(fp, "\tFrom\tTo\n");
    for (nxt = ff; nxt; nxt = nxt->next) {
        fprintf(fp, "\t%d\t\t%d\n", nxt->from, nxt->to);
    }
    fprintf(fp, "\n");
} /* ff_print */


/*===============================================================*/
int     ff_eval( from )
    int     from;   /* IN */
/*-------------------------------------------
Purpose:
    Evaluate the failure function.
Parameters:
    from    state to find failure function of
-------------------------------------------*/
{
    two_states  *nxt;

    for (nxt = ff; nxt; nxt = nxt->next) {
        if (nxt->from == from) {
            return (nxt->to);
        }
    }
    return (STAT_ERROR);
} /* ff_eval */


/*===============================================================*/
int     ff_set( from, to )
    int     from;   /* IN */
    int     to;     /* IN */
/*-------------------------------------------
Purpose:
    Change the failure function's definition. If from already had
    an associated value, it is overwritten by to.
Parameters:
```

```
            from,
            to        new pair to add to failure function; after this,
                      ff_eval(from) == to
            Returns STAT_OK or STAT_ERROR.
--------------------------------------------------------*/
{
    two_states  *new;
    void        *malloc();

    /* look for a two_states with right value of from: */
    for (new = ff; new; new = new->next) {
        if (new->from == from) { /* overwrite */
            new->to = to;
            return (STAT_OK);
        }
    }
    /* must create a two_states which has right value of from: */
    if (!(new = (two_states *)malloc(sizeof(two_states)))) {
        printf("Out of memory\n");
        return (STAT_ERROR);
    }
    new->from = from;
    new->to   = to;
    new->next = ff;
    ff = new;
    return (STAT_OK);
} /* ff_set */
```

LISTING: output.c

```
/*-------------------------------------------------
                     output.c
------------------------------------------------*/

/*==================================================================
Purpose:
    This file supplies the string pattern matcher with functions
    to do the following:

        set values in the output function:    of_add(),
                                               of_union()
        print the output function structure:   of_print(),
                                               of_print_state()


    No initialization routine is needed.
```

This code was compiled under THINK's LightspeedC® on a
Macintosh™ SE.

```
--------------------------------------------------*/
#include "match.h"
#include "stringsets.h"
#include <stdio.h>

typedef struct of_elem {
    struct of_elem  *next;
    int             state;
    stringset       value;
} of_elem;

/* We only need this file to support one output function
   (compare with stringsets.c): */
static of_elem      *of = NULL;

#ifdef _OUTPUT_TESTBED_
/*================================================================*/
main()
/*--------------------------------------------------
Purpose:
    Exercise the output function.
Parameters:
    none
--------------------------------------------------*/
{
    char    ch, buf[128];
    int     state, one, two;
    void    of_print(), of_print_state();

    for (ch = 'p'; ; ) {
        printf("\nOutput function testbed:\n");
        printf("\t(a)dd <state, keyword> to output function\n");
        printf("\t(e)valuate output_func(<state>)\n");
        printf("\t(p)rint output function\n");
        printf("\t(q)uit\n");
        printf("\t(u)nion: output_func(<one>) += ");
        printf("output_func(<two>)\n");
        ch = getc(stdin);
        if (ch == 'a') {
            printf("state> ");
            scanf("%d", &state);
            printf("keyword> ");
            scanf("%s", buf);
            if (of_add(state, buf))
                printf("Failed to add to output function\n");
        }
```

```
            else if (ch == 'e') {
                printf("state> ");
                scanf("%d", &state);
                of_print_state(stdout, state);
            }
            else if (ch == 'p') {
                of_print(stdout);
            }
            else if (ch == 'q') {
                return;
            }
            else if (ch == 'u') {
                printf("destination state> ");
                scanf("%d", &one);
                printf("state to add to %d> ", one);
                scanf("%d", &two);
                if (of_union(one, two)) {
                    printf("FAILED to form output function union\n");
                }
            }
            else {
                printf("unknown command\n");
            }
            ch = getc(stdin); /* toss away carriage return */
    }
} /* main */
#endif _OUTPUT_TESTBED_

/*================================================================*/
void    of_print( fp )
    FILE    *fp;    /* IN */
/*-------------------------------------------------
Purpose:
    Pretty-print the output function's internal representation.
Parameters:
    fp      open file to print to
----------------------------------------------*/
{
    of_elem     *nxt;
    void        ss_print();

#ifdef _OUTPUT_TESTBED_
    fprintf(fp, "\nOUTPUT FUNCTION:");
#endif _OUTPUT_TESTBED_
    for (nxt = of; nxt; nxt = nxt->next) {
        fprintf(fp, "\n\tState %d", nxt->state);
        ss_print(fp, nxt->value);
    }
```

```
        fprintf(fp, "\n");
} /* of_print */

/*==============================================================*/
void    of_print_state( fp, state )
    FILE    *fp;    /* IN */
    int     state;  /* IN */
/*----------------------------------------------------------
Purpose:
    Print the keywords associated with output function's state.
Parameters:
    fp      open file to print to
    state   state to evaluate output function at
----------------------------------------------------------*/
{
    of_elem     *nxt;
    void        ss_print();

    for (nxt = of; nxt; nxt = nxt->next) {
        if (nxt->state == state) {
            ss_print(fp, nxt->value);
            return;
        }
    }
    return;
} /* of_print_state */

/*==============================================================*/
int     of_add( state, keyword )
    int     state;      /* IN */
    char    *keyword;   /* IN */
/*----------------------------------------------------------
Purpose:
    Associate keyword with state in the output function.
Parameters:
    state,
    keyword new pair to add to output function; after this,
            of_print_state(state) will print keyword, and whatever
            other keywords were previously associated with state
    Returns STAT_OK or STAT_ERROR.
----------------------------------------------------------*/
{
    of_elem     *new;
    void        *malloc();
    stringset   ss_new();

    for (new = of; new; new = new->next) {
        if (new->state == state)
```

```
                  return (ss_add(&new->value, keyword));
    }
    /* create new state struct to hang set of keywords from */
    if (!(new = (of_elem *)malloc(sizeof(of_elem)))) {
        printf("out of memory\n");
        return (STAT_ERROR);
    }
    new->state = state;
    new->value = ss_new();
    new->next  = of;
    of = new;
    return (ss_add(&new->value, keyword));
} /* of_add */


/*==============================================================*/
int     of_union( dest, added )
    int     dest,           /* IN, OUT */
            added;          /* IN */
/*-----------------------------------------------------------

Purpose:
    Add all the keywords associated with one state in the output
    function to the set of keywords associated with another state.
Parameters:
    dest,
    added   output_func(dest) += output_func(added)
    Returns STAT_OK or STAT_ERROR.
------------------------------------------------------------*/
{
    of_elem     *dest_elem, *added_elem;
    void        *malloc();
    stringset   ss_new();

    if (dest == added) /* {dest} = {dest} + {dest} */
        return (STAT_OK);
    for (   dest_elem = of;
            dest_elem && (dest_elem->state != dest);
            dest_elem = dest_elem->next )
        ;
    for (   added_elem = of;
            added_elem && (added_elem->state != added);
            added_elem = added_elem->next )
        ;
    if (!dest_elem && !added_elem) /* {} = {} + {} */
        return (STAT_OK);
    if (dest_elem && !added_elem)  /* {dest} = {dest} + {} */
        return (STAT_OK);
    /* at this point, we know added_elem is not {} */
    if (!dest_elem) { /* create */
```

```
        if (!(dest_elem = (of_elem *)malloc(sizeof(of_elem)))) {
            printf("out of memory\n");
            return (STAT_ERROR);
        }
        dest_elem->state = dest;
        dest_elem->value = ss_new();
        dest_elem->next  = of;
        of = dest_elem;
    }
    return (ss_union(&dest_elem->value, added_elem->value));
} /* of_union */
```

LISTING: stringsets.c

```
/*----------------------------------------------------
                    stringsets.c
-----------------------------------------------------*/

/*====================================================================
Purpose:
    This file supplies functions to do the following:

        create a new (empty) set of strings:  ss_new()
        add a string to a set:                 ss_add()
        form the union of two string sets:     ss_union()
        print a set of strings:                ss_print()

    This code was compiled under THINK's LightspeedC® on a
    Macintosh™ SE.
-------------------------------------------------------*/
#include "match.h"
#include "stringsets.h"
#include <stdio.h>

/* We need this file to support many sets of strings (compare with
   queue.c, failure.c). */

#ifdef _SS_TESTBED_
/*==================================================================*/
main()
/*----------------------------------------------------
Purpose:
    Exercise the stringset library.
Parameters:
    none
-------------------------------------------------------*/
```

```
{
    char        ch, buf[128], AorB();
    stringset   set_A, set_B, ss_new();
    void        ss_print();

    set_A = ss_new();   /* ss_new() never fails */
    set_B = ss_new();
    for (ch = 'p'; ; ) {
        printf("\Stringsets testbed:\n");
        printf("\t(a)dd string to set A or set B\n");
        printf("\t(p)rint stringsets A and B\n");
        printf("\t(q)uit\n");
        printf("\t(u)nion of stringsets A and B\n");
        ch = getc(stdin);
        if (ch == 'a') {
            printf("value> ");
            scanf("%s", buf);
            printf("set to add value to (A or B)> ");
            ch = AorB();
            if (ch == 'A') {
                if (ss_add(&set_A, buf))
                    printf("Failed to add string to set\n");
            }
            else {
                if (ss_add(&set_B, buf))
                    printf("Failed to add string to set\n");
            }
        }
        else if (ch == 'p') {
            printf("\nset A: ");
            ss_print(stdout, set_A);
            printf(" set B: ");
            ss_print(stdout, set_B);
            printf("\n");
        }
        else if (ch == 'q') {
            return;
        }
        else if (ch == 'u') {
            printf("make which set the union of the ");
            printf("two sets (A or B)> ");
            ch = AorB();
            if (ch == 'A')
                ss_union(&set_A, set_B);
            else
                ss_union(&set_B, set_A);
        }
        else {
```

```
                    printf("unknown command\n");
            }
            ch = getc(stdin); /* toss away carriage return */
    }
} /* main */
#endif _SS_TESTBED_

/*================================================================*/
stringset   ss_new()
/*------------------------------------------------
Purpose:
    Create a new stringset. This call MUST be made before a set is
    passed to ss_add() or other functions.
Parameters:
    Always returns NULL, and always succeeds. This is a rare
    sort of function—when it succeeds, it returns NULL!
------------------------------------------------------------*/
{
    return (NULL);
} /* ss_new */


/*================================================================*/
int     ss_add( set, val )
    stringset   *set;   /* IN, OUT */
    char        *val;   /* IN */
/*-------------------------------------------------------
Purpose:
    Add a string to the set. Does not add duplicates (this is a
    set, not a bag).
Parameters:
    set     originally from ss_new()
    val     null-terminated string to add to set; case counts
    Returns STAT_OK or STAT_ERROR.
------------------------------------------------------------*/
{
    ss_elem *new;
    void    *malloc();

    if (!val)
        return (STAT_OK);
    /* check for duplicates */
    for (new = *set; new; new = new->next) {
        if (!strcmp(val, new->value))
            return (STAT_OK);
    }
    /* add it */
    if (!(new = (ss_elem *)malloc(sizeof(ss_elem)))) {
        printf("out of memory\n");
```

```
            return (STAT_ERROR);
        }
        if (!(new->value = malloc(strlen(val) + 1))) {
            printf("out of memory\n");
            free(new);
            return (STAT_ERROR);
        }
        strcpy(new->value, val);
        new->next = *set;
        *set = new;
        return (STAT_OK);
} /* ss_add */


/*================================================================*/
void    ss_print( fp, set )
    FILE        *fp;       /* IN */
    stringset   set;       /* IN */
/*----------------------------------------------------------------
Purpose:
    Print the current set contents (values only, no addresses).
Parameters:
    fp      open file to print to
    set     originally from ss_new()
------------------------------------------------------------------*/
{
    ss_elem     *nxt;
    boolean     first = true;

    fprintf(fp, "{");
    for (nxt = set; nxt; nxt = nxt->next) {
        if (first)
            first = false;
        else
            fprintf(fp, ", ");
        fprintf(fp, "%s", nxt->value);
    }
    fprintf(fp, "}");
} /* ss_print */


/*================================================================*/
int     ss_union( dest, added )
    stringset   *dest,      /* IN, OUT */
                added;      /* IN */
/*----------------------------------------------------------------
Purpose:
    Form the union of two stringsets.
Parameters:
    dest,
```

```
            added    both originally from ss_new();
                     dest becomes the union of dest and added
        Returns STAT_OK or STAT_ERROR
----------------------------------------------------------*/
{
    ss_elem      *nxt;

    for (nxt = added; nxt; nxt = nxt->next) {
        if (ss_add(dest, nxt->value) == STAT_ERROR)
            return (STAT_ERROR);
    }
    return (STAT_OK);
} /* ss_union */


/*================================================================*/
static char     AorB()
/*--------------------------------------------------------
Purpose:
    Get a response of 'A' or 'B' from the user.
Parameters:
    none
    Returns 'A' or 'B'.
----------------------------------------------------------*/
{
    char     res = '\0';

    while ((res != 'A') && (res != 'B')) {
        res = getc(stdin);
        if ((res != '\n') && (res != 'A') && (res != 'B'))
            printf("\nmust be set A or set B\n");
    }
    return (res);
} /* AorB */
```

LISTING: queue.c

```
/*--------------------------------------------------------
                        queue.c
----------------------------------------------------------*/

/*================================================================
Purpose:
    This file supplies the string pattern matcher with functions
    to do the following:

        add a state to the queue:              q_enqueue()
```

```
        remove a state from the queue:        q_dequeue()
        print the queue:                      q_print()

    No initialization function is needed; all it would do is
    NULL the head and tail pointers, and that's done already.

    This code was compiled under THINK's LightspeedC® on a
    Macintosh™ SE.
--------------------------------------------------------*/
#include "match.h"
#include <stdio.h>

typedef struct q_elem {
    struct q_elem    *next,
                     *prev;    /* next points toward the tail */
    int              value;
} q_elem;

/* We only need this file to support one queue of states
   (compare with stringsets.c): */
static q_elem    *head = NULL,
                 *tail = NULL;

#ifdef _Q_TESTBED_
/*===========================================================*/
main()
/*------------------------------------------------
Purpose:
    Exercise the queue.
Parameters:
    none
--------------------------------------------------------*/
{
    char    ch;
    int     val;
    void    q_print();

    for (ch = 'p'; ; ) {
        printf("\Queue of States testbed:\n");
        printf("\t(d)equeue value\n");
        printf("\t(e)nqueue value\n");
        printf("\t(p)rint queue\n");
        printf("\t(q)uit\n");
        ch = getc(stdin);
        if (ch == 'd') {
            val = q_dequeue();
            printf("Dequeued %d\n", val);
        }
```

```
            else if (ch == 'e') {
                printf("value> ");
                scanf("%d", &val);
                if (q_enqueue(val))
                    printf("Enqueue failed\n");
            }
            else if (ch == 'p') {
                q_print();
            }
            else if (ch == 'q') {
                return;
            }
            else {
                printf("unknown command\n");
            }
            ch = getc(stdin); /* toss away carriage return */
        }
} /* main */
#endif _Q_TESTBED_


/*===============================================================*/
int     q_enqueue( val )
    int val;    /* IN */
/*-------------------------------------------------

Purpose:
    Allocate a new queue element, set its value, add it at the
    tail of the queue.
Parameters:
    val     value to enqueue
    Returns STAT_ERROR or STAT_OK.
-------------------------------------------------------*/
{
    q_elem  *new;
    void    *malloc();

    if (!(new = (q_elem *)malloc(sizeof(q_elem)))) {
        printf("out of memory\n");
        return (STAT_ERROR);
    }
    new->value = val;
    if (!tail) {
        head = new;
        tail = new;
        new->next = NULL;
        new->prev = NULL;
    }
    else {
        tail->next = new;
        new->next  = NULL;
```

```
        new->prev  = tail;
        tail = new;
    }
    return (STAT_OK);
} /* q_enqueue */


/*===============================================================*/
int     q_dequeue()
/*---------------------------------------------
Purpose:
    Remove the element from the head of the queue, free its
    memory, and return its value. Returns STAT_ERROR if the queue
    is empty.
Parameters:
    none
------------------------------------------------*/
{
    int     val;
    q_elem  *decap; /* points to chopped-off head of queue */

    if (!head)
        return (STAT_ERROR);
    val = head->value;
    decap = head;
    if (tail == head)
        tail = NULL;
    head = head->next;
    if (head)
        head->prev = NULL;
    free(decap);
    return (val);
} /* q_dequeue */


/*===============================================================*/
void    q_print()
/*---------------------------------------------
Purpose:
    Print the current queue contents (values only, no addresses).
Parameters:
    none
------------------------------------------------*/
{
    q_elem  *nxt;

    printf("\nQUEUE:\n");
    for (nxt = head; nxt; nxt = nxt->next)
        printf("<%d>", nxt->value);
    printf("\n");
} /* q_print */
```

CHAPTER 17
Simulating Petri Nets

STARTING THE PLAN WITH A DATA MODEL

Figure 17-1 illustrates some of the different starting points for solving a programming problem. In most of our earlier examples, we started with an English description of the problem. We then developed top-level goals, guiding examples, abstract data types, and

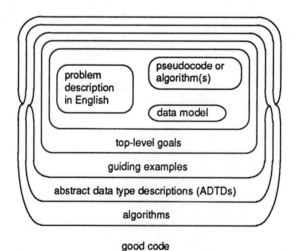

FIGURE 17-1: Three starting points for a journey to good code, and some steps along the way. The twists reflect the fact that algorithms are created before ADTDs in some cases and after in others.

292

algorithms on our way to satisfactory implementations. In the previous chapter, however, we started with an algorithm for a pattern matcher and went on from there.

In this chapter, we'll start with a "data model" that describes Petri nets. Data model is a general term that includes just about any useful way of describing data organization and processing. The abstract data types we've been working with are just one kind of data model. There are many other useful ways to describe data, including the Petri net description which we'll look at shortly.

First, however, there is a basic question to answer. If this Petri net description is so useful, do we still need an ADTD? Why not just use the data model we're given? The answer is yes, we do need an ADTD. We can generate part, but not all, of our ADTD by translating the Petri net description. There are several good reasons to translate other data models to ADTDs:

1. Mismatches between the given data model and our usual description of abstract data types might reveal weaknesses in our ADTD. We may be able to minimize the weaknesses of our ADTD framework by expanding it or refining it.
2. In spite of reason 1, we have a high degree of confidence in ADTDs. Previous examples have shown that writing an ADTD helps prevent us from overlooking anything major. We might not have this security with other data models.
3. In fact, other data models may have been devised for quite different purposes. We have confidence in ADTDs because we've seen how they provide the kind of answers we need to create good code. Other data models might favor other tasks. For instance, a mathematical model is good for proofs and not so good for suggesting implementation possibilities.

Before we look at the Petri net data model, I should mention why Petri nets are worth knowing about. They have been used to simulate concurrent processes, operating systems, network and other communication protocols, FORTRAN compiler optimization, electric circuits, problems in control theory, and the American legal system. Peterson (1977) provides an introduction to Petri nets and a survey of their use. Figure 17-1 shows a simple Petri net. Petri nets have four basic elements: places, transitions, arcs, and tokens. Figure 17-2(a) shows a Petri net with three places (labeled P0, P1, and P2), two transitions (T0, T1), two tokens (shown as black dots in P0 and P1), and five arcs which connect various places and transitions.

Tokens move in a Petri net when a transition "fires." To fire, a transition must be "enabled," A transition is enabled when each place with an arc leading into the transition has a token. In Figure 17-2(a), transition T0 is enabled. However, a transition does not necessarily fire as soon as it is enabled. It waits a finite random amount of time first.

If, for instance, several transitions are enabled, they may fire in any order. The order in which transitions fire is not necessarily the same as the order in which they were enabled. There may be any finite time lag between the firing of two enabled transitions, or between the enabling of a transition and its firing. These lags are one reason why Petri nets make good models of concurrent processes (and legal processes!).

When a transition fires, all the tokens disappear from the places leading into it. Then each place on the other side of the transition gets a token (that is, each place that has an arc

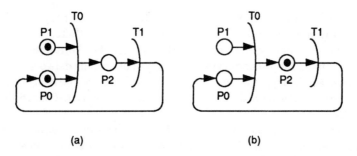

FIGURE 17-2: A Petri net in action. In (a), transition T0 is enabled. (b) shows the net after T0 has fired; now T1 is enabled.

coming into it from the transition). As Figure 17-2(b) shows, the number of tokens is not necessarily conserved. If the place receiving the token already contains a token, we think of overwriting that token, not of adding a token. Or we could think of leaving the token that is already there right where it is, since tokens are indistinguishable from each other.

In implementation terms, a place's token is a boolean (true or false), not a counter (0,1,2,3 . . .). Of course, we could augment our Petri net data model to keep track of the number of tokens in each place, but there's no need for that at present. We'll keep the possibility in mind, but for now we'll do the simpler case where tokens are booleans, not counters.

Readers who are familiar with mathematical probability will be asking what sort of distribution the randomness in transition firings fits. Poisson? Normal? Exponential? The answer is "Whatever you want." The code actually implemented uses a uniformly distributed *random()* function, but other choices might be better. It depends on what we model.

For instance, the net in Figure 17-2 can be interpreted as a simple model of eggnog consumption (I'm writing this two days before Christmas). We assign "meaning" to the places and transitions as follows:

P0: I have some eggnog
P1: I want to drink some eggnog
T0: I drink all the eggnog
P2: I need some more eggnog
T1: I buy some eggnog

Notice that places correspond to conditions, and transitions correspond to events. Thus, Figure 17-2(a) means "I have some eggnog and I want to drink it." After T0 fires, I've satisfied my desire by drinking all the eggnog. Now P2 holds, that is, I need some more eggnog. Apparently, eggnog is free, because P2 is the only condition that must be satisfied for T1 to fire. After T1 fires, I've bought more eggnog, so P0 holds. P1, however, does not hold. I have no further desire for eggnog, so T0 will never fire, that is, I'm not going to drink any more eggnog.

At first glance, Petri nets look a lot like finite state machines (FSMs). Compare, for instance, Figure 17-2 with Figure 16-4 in Chapter 16, "Matching String Patterns." Petri net places correspond more or less to FSM states.

But there are some important differences between Petri nets and FSMs. Petri net arcs go from a place to a transition or from a transition to a place. FSM arcs (which are called "transitions" just to make life harder) go from state to state. Petri net tokens are similar to an FSM's current state in that they move from place to place. But there can be only one current state in an FSM, whereas a Petri net may have many tokens, or one, or none.

Moreover, to get an FSM running and keep it running, we must provide both a starting state and some stream of input. Which transition is made at any point depends on the FSM's current state and the input it receives. When there's no more input, the FSM stops. Petri nets, by contrast, need only a starting token placement. Once that is provided, nets either run for a while and then quit, or they run indefinitely. Either way, they have no need for input to keep them going. We could augment a net to expect input when certain token configurations occur, but this is not necessary, and it is a change in the data model.

The correspondence between Petri nets and FSMs, such as it is, looks like this:

Petri net	Finite State Machine
place	state
token	current state (sort of)
arc	state-to-state transition (sort of)
transition	———

The biggest difference between Petri nets and FSMs is that Petri nets are not deterministic. A finite state machine is deterministic. If you start it in the same state and feed it the same input sequence each time, it will move through the same sequence of states each time it runs, no matter how many times you run it. By contrast, a Petri net may run differently this time than last time, even though we started with tokens in the same places each time.

TOP-LEVEL GOALS

Petri nets are best described with pictures. However, graphic interfaces are notoriously unportable. So our first goal is to make a clean interface between the "heart" of the Petri net simulator and the code used to display simulation results. Some programmers would argue that such a separation is always a good idea. I won't disagree, or agree. I'll just point out that making this separation a conscious decision implies that we've given at least a bit of thought to the tradeoffs between modularity and other goals such as speedy execution. Our concern here is data structures, not graphics.

A second goal is flexibility. We've already mentioned two ways to augment Petri nets—allowing more than one token per place, and accepting input in specified token configurations. Other changes to the data model are probably worth thinking about as well. So we want to allow as many useful changes in the ADTD as we can with minimal redesign and recoding.

GUIDING EXAMPLES

Figure 17-2 falls short as a guiding example for at least two reasons. First, it doesn't run forever. The token in place P1 will never be replenished once transition T0 has fired. We want an example of a net that runs indefinitely, as well as an example of one that grinds to a halt after some finite number of firings. Second, Figure 17-2 has no place with multiple incoming or outgoing arcs. For these reasons, our guiding example will be the net shown in Figure 17-3, not the one in Figure 17-2.

Notice that different starting configurations can greatly affect a Petri net's behavior. If the net starts in either of the configurations shown in Figure 17-3(a) or 17-3(b), it will keep going indefinitely. However, if we start with just one token, placed as shown in Figure 17-3(c), the net will stop after transition T2 fires. Places P1 and P2 will never be replenished, so no more transitions will be enabled, however long we wait.

Figure 17-3 does not cover all the possibilities, of course. For instance, it has no place with multiple outgoing arcs. But it's good enough to start with. We'll take these for our fundamental characteristics:

runs indefinitely
has a place with multiple incoming arcs

We've ignored "has a place with multiple outgoing arcs." Which characteristics are fundamental is likely to vary from one application of Petri nets to another, so this is not as arbitrary as it appears. Since we're not trying to model anything in particular with our nets, we have greater freedom in our choice of guiding examples.

ABSTRACT DATA TYPE DESCRIPTION

The first thing to do is take inventory of our Petri net data model and see what ADTD questions it answers.

What is the geometry of this abstract data type? Figure 17-3 will serve as our sketch of the Petri net abstract data type. From an ADTD point of view, each place in the net is a position in the type's geometry. There are two kinds of position: those that contain a token when the simulation begins and those that do not.

What relations hold between the elements of the collection? Viewing the places, transitions, arcs, and tokens as a relation doesn't help much. We cannot say whether or not such a relation is reflexive, symmetric, transitive, one-to-one, one-to-many.

What are the semantics of the elements? In other words, how do we interpret particular snapshots of the collections as its elements change? We can break the issue of semantics into two parts. First, there is the question of interpreting the simulation to gain insight into the process the net is modeling. This aspect of net semantics depends on what

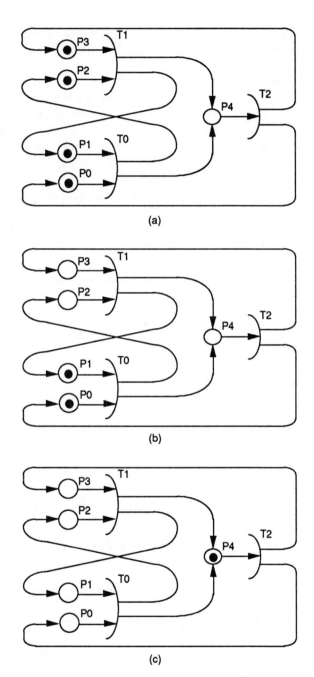

FIGURE 17-3:   Three starting configurations for the Petri net which is our guiding example.

is being modeled and what net components correspond to what real-world entities. Since we're not modeling anything specific here, we can't say anything specific about this aspect of the semantics.

A second aspect of Petri net semantics is limited strictly to the operation of the net. We have already discussed this. For instance, if tokens are present in all places leading to a transition, it means the transition is enabled. As another example, suppose the net is like the one shown in Figure 17-2. Every path that tokens can take through the net includes a transition that only fires once because a place leading into the transition can never be replenished once its token is gone. That means the net will not run indefinitely.

What are the operators? The data model we started with is silent on this question. But we can answer it ourselves. Suppose we have an empty Petri net—no places, arcs, transitions, or tokens defined yet. What operators do we need to build a working net? The most obvious answer is to provide one builder for each type of net component:

```
/*================================================================*/
int     add_place( name )
    characters  name;   /* IN */
/*----------------------------------------------------------
Purpose:
    Add a new place.
Parameters:
    name    name of the new place
----------------------------------------------------------*/


/*================================================================*/
int     add_token( place_name )
    characters  place_name; /* IN */
/*----------------------------------------------------------
Purpose:
    Add a token to an existing place.This is a no-op if the place
    already has a token.
Parameters:
    place_name  name of the place that gets the token
----------------------------------------------------------*/


/*================================================================*/
int     add_transition( name )
    characters  name;   /* IN */
/*----------------------------------------------------------
Purpose:
    Add a new transition.
Parameters:
    name    name of the new transition
----------------------------------------------------------*/
```

```
/*===============================================================*/
int     add_arc( from, to )
    characters  from;      /* IN */
    characters  to;        /* IN */
/*---------------------------------------------------------------
Purpose:
    Add a new arc. This is a no-op if the arc already exists. Also
    enforces restrictions on arc placement. For instance, from
    and to can be a place name and a transition name, or a
    transition name and a place name, but they cannot both be
    places or both be transitions.
Parameters:
    from    name of the place or transition the arc leaves
    to      name of the place or transition the arc enters
---------------------------------------------------------------*/
```

The net shown in Figure 17-2(a) could be built using these operators with the following sequence of calls:

```
add_place("P0");
add_place("P1");
add_place("P2");
add_token("P0");
add_token("P1");
add_transition("T0");
add_transition("T1");
add_arc("P0,""T0");
add_arc("P1,""T0");
add_arc("T0,""P2");
add_arc("P2,""T1");
add_arc("T1,""P0");
```

This seems awkward, and not just because it uses component names where numbers would do. The operators above don't reflect the interaction between Petri net components. Omitting one call would be easy, and potentially disastrous. We need a group of operators that make mistakes harder.

To devise a new group of net-builders, let's focus on the most important element of the net and then think of the other components in terms of their relationship with the chosen element. Transitions are where all the action (and all the delay) occur, so let's write a set of operator calling sequences that focus on transitions:

```
/*===============================================================*/
int     add_transition( input_places, output_places, transition )
    integer_set input_places;   /* IN */
    integer_set output_places;  /* IN */
    integer     transition;     /* IN */
```

```
/*-----------------------------------------------------
Purpose:
    Add a new transition.
Parameters:
    input_places    set of IDs of places that send an arc into
                    the new transition
    output_places   set of IDs of places that receive an arc from
                    the new transition
    transition      ID of the new transition
-----------------------------------------------------*/


/*=====================================================*/
int     add_tokens ( places )
    integer_set places;      /* IN */
/*-----------------------------------------------------
Purpose:
    Add a token to each of the places indicated; the places
    should already exist.This is a no-op if a place already
    has a token.
Parameters:
    places  set of IDs of the places that get a token
-----------------------------------------------------*/


/*=====================================================*/
integer_set     set ( ID1, ID2, ID3,... )
    integer ID1;    /* IN */
    integer ID2;    /* IN */
    integer ID3;    /* IN */
    ...
/*-----------------------------------------------------
Purpose:
    Create a set containing the indicated IDs. Note variable
    number of parameters.
Parameters:
    IDn     elements of the new set
-----------------------------------------------------*/
```

The net shown in Figure 17-2(a) could be built with these new operators as follows:

```
add_transition(set(0,1), set(2), 0);
add_transition(set(2),    set(0), 1);
add_tokens(set(0,1));
```

This is much better. Even if we count the nested *set()* calls, there are fewer calls to make. But even if there were more calls, this group of calls is preferable because it is organized in a way that makes it easy to see what's happening. The calling sequences reflect the semantic relationships between net elements.

Also, the initial token placement can always be done with one call to *add_tokens()* and one call to *set()*. The earlier group of operators required one call per token to initially load the net. Since a net large enough to model some real-world process might well require hundreds of initial tokens, it is much easier to install the initial tokens with our current operators.

To be perfectly honest, there is some sleight-of-hand going on here. We have glossed over the fact that *set()* takes a variable number of parameters. If this were not the case, our operators would be much more awkward. We would need either different *set()* operators for each number of parameters, or separate calls on *set()* to add each element. Neither choice works as well as passing *set()* a variable number of parameters, but using separate calls is particularly error-prone:

```
/* different set() functions for different number of parameters: */
add_transition(set_2(0,1),  set_1(2),  0);
add_transition(set_1(2),    set_1(0),  1);
add_tokens(set_2(0,1));


/* one call per element to build a set: */
int_set tmp_set_A, tmp_set_B;

init_set(&tmp_set_A);
add_to_set(&tmp_set_A, 0);
add_to_set(&tmp_set_A, 1);
init_set(&tmp_set_B);
add_to_set(&tmp_set_B, 2);
add_transition(tmp_set_A, tmp_set_B, 0);
init_set(&tmp_set_A);
add_to_set(&tmp_set_A, 2);
init_set(&tmp_set_B);
add_to_set(&tmp_set_B, 0);
add_transition(tmp_set_A, tmp_set_B, 1);
init_set(&tmp_set_A);
add_to_set(&tmp_set_A, 0);
add_to_set(&tmp_set_A, 1);
add_tokens(tmp_set_A);
```

We have a problem—two problems, actually. First, can we assume it is possible to implement a function that has a variable number of parameters? Second, should we even be talking about implementation? After all, ADTDs are supposed to be implementation-independent.

We'll deal with the last issue first. We have hit upon one of the few aspects of ADTDs that are language-dependent, or at least dependent upon certain facilities being available in the language. I can think only of three such dependencies, but there may be others.

1. Many ADTDs implicitly assume that the implementation language supports pointers and dynamic memory allocation. Many of our ADTD sketches show discrete structures linked together in a tree, for instance, or some sort of list or list of lists.

Yes, we could try to do the same thing with large arrays by using indices instead of pointers, but it's just not the same. Try it sometime if you don't believe this.

2. Every ADTD assumes that certain basic types are available in the language, and that these types can be combined somehow. At a minimum, the implementation language should support integers, floating point numbers, strings, and (as mentioned above) pointers. It should also include some facility (like structs in C or records in Pascal) that can be used to combine different types.

3. The Petri net ADTD will assume that the implementation language supports functions that have a variable number of parameters. Every C compiler I've used supported this facility, if only because *printf()* uses it.

In other words, the rule against implementation-dependent ADTDs has a few loopholes. This does not mean we should stop trying to separate ADTD and implementation details. It just means there are a few well-defined instances in which it is foolish or impossible to do so.

Now back to the main problem *set()* raises. Is it safe to assume we can implement a function that has a variable number of parameters? The best way to a sure answer is to figure out how to implement such a function. Kernighan and Ritchie (1978) discuss functions with a variable number of arguments. They present two ways to implement these functions:

1. The first parameter must always be present, and it must provide the function body with some way to tell which other parameters were actually supplied. This is what the format string in *printf()* does, for instance. When all the parameters are of the same type, another technique is to make the first parameter a count, which tells how many additional parameters to expect.

2. If the parameters are of known types (not the case with *printf()*), a NULL or some other special value can be passed as the last parameter. When the body of the function reaches this marker, it knows there are no further parameters.

We don't have to choose between these possibilities just yet. For now, it is sufficient to know we can implement a *set()* function that takes a variable number of parameters.

So much for operators to build the Petri net with. What about other operators? We'll need some way to display the net after each transition fires so that we can watch the simulation in progress:

```
/*================================================================*/
void    display()
/*------------------------------------------------
Purpose:
    Displays the Petri net. This is extremely unportable code,
    unless it does no graphics.
Parameters:
    none
------------------------------------------------*/
```

Finally, we might want various statistics kept during the simulation. Statistics being statistics, there is a wide range of possibilities, but we'll keep it simple. We'll just keep track of how many times each transition has fired:

```
/*==============================================================*/
void    statistics( transition )
    int     transition;     /* IN */
/*--------------------------------------------------
Purpose:
    Prints the number of times transition has fired.
Parameters:
    transition  which transition's statistics to print
--------------------------------------------------*/
```

What are the restrictions on membership in the collection? There are no obvious restrictions on transitions, except that they cannot be "sinks" (no outgoing arcs) or "sources" (no incoming arcs). There is no predetermined limit on the number of transitions or places or arcs; the only numeric limit is that there cannot be more tokens than places.

What are the rules governing multiple collections? Proper subsets of the net can certainly be viewed as nets in their own right; depending on what the net is modeling, this might be a very useful thing to do. However, the "subnets" would have to be separate as far as token travel was concerned, so tokens could neither leave nor enter a subnet. We won't bother with subnets here because we're not modeling anything in particular.

In summary, the Petri net data model we started with matched the ADTD quite well. The main exception was the original model's lack of any explicit operators. By translating the data model into an ADTD, we have remedied this problem. Now we know enough to start implementation.

ATTEMPT ONE

Several questions raise themselves right away. As usual, we'll collect all the unanswered questions up front.

BOX 17-1:   Unanswered questions.

1. How do we implement transitions as data structures?
2. How do we represent tokens, places, and arcs?
3. How do we implement the *integer_set* type referred to in the ADTD operators?
4. How do we make transitions fire?

The first three questions are closely related. The *add_transition()* calling sequence we decided on implies a transition structure that looks something like this:

```
typedef struct {
    int_set     in;
    int_set     out;
    int         ID;
} transition;
```

But this leads to question 3. How do we implement *int_set*, that is, sets of integers? The design guideline "Implementing Sets" (page 373) suggests we should use an array of bits. We meet the criterion put forth in that guideline: Set elements are closely spaced integers (assuming we insist on numbering places consecutively 0,1,2,3...).

Next we have to decide whether to set a compile-time limit on the number of set elements. Limiting the number of set elements means limiting the number of places in the net. If we do impose a limit at compile-time, the typedefs are straightforward:

```
#define BITS_PER_WORD     16
#define WORDS_PER_SET     4
#define MAX_PLACES        (WORDS_PER_SET*BITS_PER_WORD)
typedef struct {
    int     elements[WORDS_PER_SET];
} int_set;

typedef struct {
    int_set     in;
    int_set     out;
    int         ID;
} transition;
```

Or we could eliminate typedef *int_set* entirely:

```
typedef struct {
    int         in[WORDS_PER_SET];
    int         out[WORDS_PER_SET];
    int         ID;
} transition;
```

Either way, the set operators are simple enough to be implemented as macros:

```
#define set_is_member(n, set)   \
        ((0x1 << ((n) % BITS_PER_WORD)) & set[(n)/BITS_PER_WORD])

#define set_insert(n, set)  \
        set[(n)/BITS_PER_WORD] |= (0x1 << ((n) % BITS_PER_WORD))

#define set_delete(n, set)  \
        set[(n)/BITS_PER_WORD] &= ~(0x1 << ((n) % BITS_PER_WORD))
```

However, if we can't allocate the bit arrays at compile-time, life becomes much harder. We don't know at compile-time how big *int_sets* are, so we can't use them directly in any typedefs. Instead, we use pointers to *int_sets*. We have to be sure to initialize all these pointers properly, so they're either NULL or pointing to *int_sets*. C++ initializers would come in handy here, but we'll make do:

```
typedef struct {
    int     *in;
    int     *out;
    int     ID;
} transitions;

#define BITS_PER_WORD    16

/* globals: */
int     max_places    = 0;
int     words_per_set = 0;

void    init()
{
    ...
    scanf("%d", &max_places);
    words_per_set = (max_places + BITS_PER_WORD - 1)/BITS_PER_WORD;
    ...
} /* init */

int     add_transition( input_places, output_places, transition )
    int_set input_places;    /* IN */
    int_set output_places;   /* IN */
    int     transition;      /* IN */
{
    transition  *new;
    void        *malloc(), calloc();
    ...
    if (!(new = (transition *)malloc(sizeof(transition)))) {
        printf("Out of memory\n");
        return (FAILED);
    }
    /* calloc() allocates memory and zeroes it: */
    if (!(new->in = (int *)calloc(words_per_set, sizeof(int)))) {
        printf("Out of memory\n");
        free(new);
        return (FAILED);
    }
    if (!(new->out = (int *)calloc(words_per_set, sizeof(int)))) {
        printf("Out of memory\n");
        free(new->in);
        free(new);
```

```
        return (FAILED);
    }
    ...
} /* add_transition */
```

If we use this version of *int_sets* and decide to change later to a different implementation, it could be painful because this "pointer to array of bits" representation is embedded throughout the code.

Another potential problem with this version is that now the set operators can cause addressing errors. We haven't changed the operators, but now the arrays they reference are allocated at initialization-time. If we skip an allocation, *set_is_member()* and the other macros will crash because they chase a pointer that is inadvertently NULL or garbage.

So what does this representation do for us that the compile-time allocation does not, other than make the code more complex? It lets users determine the upper bound on set size, that is, on the number of places a net can contain. This is not as friendly as letting the user simply enter as many places as she wants, but it is better than imposing a hard limit at compile-time.

Or is it? Maybe we could set an upper limit that no one was likely to hit. Let's decide precisely how much memory we need. If we need one bit per element, we can figure out the storage needed to hold all the sets for all the transitions in a net as follows:

```
# bytes needed to hold sets of places =
    (2 sets per transition) * (N transitions) * (max_places+7) /8
```

Storage requirements for three nets are shown below. The first is a very large net. The second is large enough for many uses. Notice that it has twice as many places as transitions; Figures 17-2 and 17-3 suggested that proportion. The third net is our guiding example shown in Figure 17-3.

bytes	no. of transitions	max no. of places	comment
256K	1024	1024	very large net
8K	256	512	large net
6	3	5	guiding example from Figure 17-3

It looks like trying to set a large compile-time limit on set size may waste a lot of space. For this reason, we'll use the more complicated but more flexible second implementation, in which sets are allocated at initialization-time. By the way, an examination of the tradeoffs between these different set implementations led to the design guideline "Implementing Sets" (page 373). It's worth your time to look at that guideline now.

We now have representations of transitions, places, and arcs. They are implemented by way of the transition typedef we saw earlier:

```
typedef struct {
    int     *in;  /* set of input places  */
```

```
    int     *out; /* set of output places */
    int     ID;   /* this transition's ID */
} transitions;
```

What about tokens? Well, each place either has a token or it doesn't. We can use one *int_set* to keep track of the entire net's tokens. If element *N* is in the set (that is, if bit *N* of the *int_set*'s array of bits is 1), then place *N* contains a token; otherwise, it does not. Notice that this works only if:

> every token is identical to every other token
> each place contains at most one token

Luckily for us, both these conditions are met, because we decided they would be!

The only unanswered question left is how to make transitions fire. Remember, the net is indeterminate. Transitions fire at random once they're enabled. We need a loop like this:

```
while (true) {
    next = (pick a transition ID at random);
    if (next is enabled) {
        fire(next);
        display(current net and tokens);
    }
}
```

But how do we generate random transition IDs? How do we tell if a transition is enabled? How do we fire it? Let's take these questions one at a time.

We can generate transition IDs by scaling a random number generator that returns a value in [0.0 .. 1.0]:

```
rand_trans = (int) ((random() * (hi_trans-lo_trans)) + lo_trans);
```

This is actually a more general formula than we need—*lo_trans* is always zero because transitions are numbered 0,1,2 . . . .

Good random number generators are not obvious, but this problem has been studied at length. We'll follow the suggestions in Park and Miller (1988). Their article discusses various problems to avoid when using random number generators and presents "guaranteed" implementations of the familiar "modulus" randomizer:

```
f(z) = az mod m
```

We can tell quite easily if a transition is enabled. We have two sets:

> current, the set of all places that currently contain a token
> a particular transition's set of input places (*transition.in*)

If the set of input places is a subset of the current places with tokens, then the transition is enabled. Otherwise, it is not enabled.

We can also fire the transition quite easily. We simply remove its input places from current and add its output places to current. That is, its input places no longer have tokens, and its output places do.

ATTEMPT TWO

Several improvements on our first attempt have been made in the actual code. The implementation of sets has been broken out into a separate module, which is listed after the design guideline "Implementing Sets." Instead of ints, bitsets are implemented as arrays of chars, since that's more portable. We also added minimal error checking to our macro operators (insert, delete, and test for membership).

A *next* pointer was added to our typedef of *transition*, so we can keep all the transitions together in a list. Incidentally, this is not necessarily an ordered list. Strictly speaking, it's a linked-list implementation of a "set of transitions" abstract data type. No transition statistics are kept.

We slightly modified our formula for mapping *random()* values in [0.0 ..1.0], in order to improve the odds of generating the ID of the last transition added. See the comment above function *rand_trans()* for the details.

The main loop is a little smarter about exiting the simulation than the original version. We keep track of the number of transition firings and quit the simulation after a user-supplied maximum is reached. Something like this is necessary because some Petri nets will run forever. We also check for nets that have come to a halt because no transitions are enabled, and we exit the simulation if that happens.

The code gets around the problem of implementing functions like *set()* which have a variable number of parameters, by using *bs_read()* to interactively read a set's elements. It also uses *bs_print()* to print the set of places that currently have tokens instead of a graphic *display()* function. Drawing an arbitrary Petri net is not a straightforward problem. Writing portable code to draw the net is even harder, and graphic display is not our concern here, in any case. So a simple ASCII pretty-printer (*bs_print()*) is used instead.

LISTING: petri.c

```
/*-----------------------------------------------
                       petri.c
-----------------------------------------------*/


/*===============================================================
Purpose:
    Main body of Petri net simulator (uses bitsets.c, random.c).
    This code was compiled under THINK's LightspeedC (TM) on a
    Macintosh SE.
-----------------------------------------------------------*/
```

```c
#include <stdio.h>
#include "bitsets.h"

typedef struct transition {
    struct transition    *next;
    bs_type              in,      /* set of input places */
                         out;     /* set of output places */
    int                  ID;      /* transition's ID (0..N) */
} transition;

static transition    *all_trans = NULL; /* all defined transitions */
static int           hi_trans  = 0;     /* ID of newest transition */
#define LO_TRANS     0                  /* lowest transition ID */

static bs_type   current; /* set of places that contain tokens now */
static bs_type   empty;   /* treated as a constant (empty set {}) */

static int       max_places;    /* to initialize bitset library */
static int       max_firings;   /* to avoid infinite simulation */

#define _AUTO_TEST_

/*================================================================*/
main()
/*-------------------------------------------------
Purpose:
    Simulate a Petri net. The user interactively enters the
    transitions that define the net as sets of input- and
    output-places; the user also enters the set of places that initially
contain tokens.* Sets are implemented as bitsets,
    using the code that follows the design guideline "Implementing
    Sets." Then the simulation runs until either

        1. no more transitions are enabled, or
        2. the maximum number of firings allowed has been reached

    Simulation results are, unfortunately, NOT presented
    graphically. Instead, the new set of places that contain
    tokens is printed after each transition firing.

    *Instead of entering the net and initial token placement
    interactively, it is also possible to generate a program
    that automatically builds a particular net, with tokens.
    This can be done by defining _AUTO_TEST_ and recompiling.
Parameters:
    none
    ---------------------------------------------------*/
{
```

```
int     trans, failures, i, firings;
boolean found, intro_inited(), enabled();
void    fire(), bs_print();

if (!intro_inited())
    return;
for (firings = 0; firings < max_firings; ) {
    trans = rand_trans(); /* pick a transition at random */
    if (enabled(trans)) {
        firings++;
        fire(trans);
        printf( "\nFired transition %d, now tokens are in: ",
                trans);
        bs_print(current);
        failures = 0;
    }
    else { /* check every so often to see if no more transitions
              are enabled; how often to check is arbitrary: */
        if (++failures > hi_trans) {
            for (   found = false, i = 0;
                    (i <= hi_trans) && !found;
                    i++ ) {
                if (enabled(i))
                    found = true;
            }
            if (!found) {
                printf("\nNo more enabled transitions\n");
                return;
            }
        }
    }
}
printf("\nReached max number of transition firings allowed\n");
} /* main */


/*===============================================================*/
static boolean  intro_inited()
/*---------------------------------------------------------------
Purpose:
    Initialize the Petri net simulator. Prints appropriate error
    message on failure.
Parameters:
    none
-----------------------------------------------------------------*/
{
    bs_type bs_new();
    void    bs_read();
    boolean bs_inited(), read_trans();
```

```
        printf("\nPetri net simulator\n");
#ifdef _AUTO_TEST_
        max_firings = 30;
        max_places  = 5;
#else
        printf("\tmaximum number of times to fire transitions> ");
        scanf("%d", &max_firings);
        printf("\tmaximum number of places in the net> ");
        scanf("%d", &max_places);
#endif _AUTO_TEST_
        if (!bs_inited(max_places)) {
            printf("\nFailed to initialize bitsets library\n");
            return (false);
        }
        if (!(current = bs_new())) {
            printf("\nFailed to create current state bitset\n");
            return (false);
        }
        if (!(empty = bs_new())) {
            printf("\nFailed to create empty bitset {}\n");
            return (false);
        }
        if (!read_trans())
            return (false);
#ifdef _AUTO_TEST_
        bs_insert(0, current);
        bs_insert(1, current);
#else
        printf("\nWhich places initially contain tokens> ");
        bs_read(current);
#endif _AUTO_TEST_
        return (true);
} /* intro_inited */


/*================================================================*/
static boolean  read_trans()
/*----------------------------------------------------------------

Purpose:
    Obtain (from user or hard-coded _AUTO_TEST_) definitions of
    the Petri net's transitions. From the user's point of view,
    a transition is a set of input places (numbered 0..max_places)
    and a set of output places (same range). Prints appropriate
    error message on failure.
Parameters:
    none
----------------------------------------------------------------*/
{
    transition  *new, *new_trans();
```

```
        void        add_trans(), bs_read();
        boolean     bs_equal();

        hi_trans = 0;
#ifdef _AUTO_TEST_
    new = new_trans(); /* skip error checks during auto test */
    bs_insert(0, new->in);
    bs_insert(1, new->in);
    bs_insert(2, new->out);
    bs_insert(4, new->out);
    new->ID = hi_trans++;
    add_trans(new);

    new = new_trans();
    bs_insert(2, new->in);
    bs_insert(3, new->in);
    bs_insert(1, new->out);
    bs_insert(4, new->out);
    new->ID = hi_trans++;
    add_trans(new);

    new = new_trans();
    bs_insert(4, new->in);
    bs_insert(0, new->out);
    bs_insert(3, new->out);
    new->ID = hi_trans++;
    add_trans(new);

    goto read_trans_ok;
#else
    printf("\nEnter transitions now; terminate transitions by\n");
    printf("entering an empty {} input or output set. Terminate\n");
    printf("entry of each set's elements by entering an illegal\n");
    printf("set member (a value outside 0..%d.\n", max_places-1);
    for ( ; ; ) {
        if (!(new = new_trans())) {
            printf("\ncould not allocate new transition\n");
            return (false);
        }
        printf("input places> ");
        bs_read(new->in);
        if (bs_equal(new->in, empty))
            goto read_trans_ok;
        printf("output places> ");
        bs_read(new->out);
        if (bs_equal(new->out, empty))
            goto read_trans_ok;
        new->ID = hi_trans++;
```

```
            add_trans(new);
        }
#endif _AUTO_TEST_
read_trans_ok:
    hi_trans--;
    return (true);
} /* read_trans */


/*================================================================*/
static void    add_trans( new )
    transition *new;    /* IN */
/*------------------------------------------------------
Purpose:
    Add transition to global list headed by all_trans.
Parameters:
    new     a completely defined transition
----------------------------------------------------------*/
{
    new->next = all_trans;
    all_trans = new;
} /* add_trans */


/*================================================================*/
static transition    *new_trans()
/*------------------------------------------------------
Purpose:
    Allocate a new transition, including its two bitsets.
Parameters:
    none
    Returns NULL on failure.
----------------------------------------------------------*/
{
    transition  *new;
    void        *malloc();
    bs_type     bs_new();

    if (!(new = (transition *)malloc(sizeof(transition)))) {
        printf("out of memory\n");
        return (NULL);
    }
    if (!(new->in = bs_new())) {
        printf("couldn't create new bitset\n");
        return (NULL);
    }
    if (!(new->out = bs_new())) {
        printf("couldn't create new bitset\n");
        return (NULL);
    }
```

```
        return (new);
} /* new_trans */


/*================================================================*/
static boolean  enabled( trans )
    int     trans;  /* IN */
/*--------------------------------------------------------------
Purpose:
    See whether a transition is enabled, that is, whether each of
    its input places contains a token.
Parameters:
    trans   transition's ID
---------------------------------------------------------------*/
{
    transition  *nxt;
    boolean     bs_subset();

    for (   nxt = all_trans;
            nxt && (nxt->ID != trans);
            nxt = nxt->next )
        ;
    if (!nxt) {
        printf("internal inconsistency #1 (trans %d)\n", trans);
        return (false);
    }
    return (bs_subset(nxt->in, current));
} /* enabled */


/*================================================================*/
static void     fire( trans )
    int     trans;  /* IN */
/*--------------------------------------------------------------
Purpose:
    Fire a transition, that is, remove the token from each of its
    input places and add a token to each of its output places.
Parameters:
    trans   transition's ID
---------------------------------------------------------------*/
{
    transition  *nxt;
    void        bs_remove(), bs_union();

    for (   nxt = all_trans;
            nxt && (nxt->ID != trans);
            nxt = nxt->next )
        ;
    if (!nxt) {
        printf("internal inconsistency #2 (trans %d)\n", trans);
```

```
        return;
    }
    bs_remove(current, nxt->in);
    bs_union(current, nxt->out);
} /* fire */


/*================================================================*/
static int      rand_trans()
/*-------------------------------------------------------

Purpose:
    Generate a random transition ID in the range 0..hi_trans.
    Notice that we actually generate one in 0..hi_trans+1 and
    then map results >= hi_trans to hi_trans. This is because
    otherwise hi_trans is returned much less often than the other
    values. Without this fix, we have to get a perfect 1.0 from
    random() to return hi_trans, while all the other trans
    values correspond to a range of random() values.
Parameters:
    none
----------------------------------------------------------*/
{
    double  random();
    int     res;

    res = ((int)((random()*(hi_trans - LO_TRANS + 1)) + LO_TRANS));
    if (res > hi_trans)
        res = hi_trans;
    return (res);
} /* rand_trans */
```

LISTING: random.c

```
/*---------------------------------------------------
                    random.c
----------------------------------------------------*/


/*================================================================
Purpose:
    Provides an excellent random number generator.
    This code was compiled under THINK's LightspeedC® on a
    Macintosh™ SE.
----------------------------------------------------*/


static double   seed = 1.2345;

#define RND_A   16807.0
```

```
#define RND_M    2147483647.0
#define RND_Q    127773.0          /* RND_M / RND_A */
#define RND_R    2836.0            /* RND_M % RND_A */


/*================================================================*/
double      random()
/*------------------------------------------------
Purpose:
    Returns random numbers generated according to implementation
    given in:

    Park, S.K., K.W. Miller, "Random Number Generators: Good Ones
    Are Hard to Find," Communications of the ACM, Volume 31,
    Number 10, October 1988, pp. 1192-1201.

    The general algorithm is:

        random(z) = az mod m = (RND_A*z) % RND_M

    This implementation works when max long value > 16807, and
    doubles are represented with a 32-bit or larger mantissa
    (including the sign bit).
Parameters:
    none; seed is a global
------------------------------------------------------*/
{
    double  lo, hi, test;

    hi = (double)((int)(seed/RND_Q));
    lo = seed - RND_Q*hi;
    test = RND_A*lo - RND_R*hi;
    if (test > 0.0)
        seed = test;
    else
        seed = test + RND_M;
    return (seed/RND_M);
} /* random */
```

CHAPTER 18
Summary

We have seen how the Plan and the Framework provide a good method for designing and implementing data structures, in C or any similar language. "Good" means two things. First, the Plan and the Framework are worth the effort they require, because they are focused and flexible. Second, the Plan and the Framework are good because they have been tested and revised by working programmers and computer scientists.

The Framework and the Plan both focus our attention on critical aspects of data structure design and implementation. They help us solve problems in an order that makes sense, providing both guidance and flexibility. The Plan guides us through goal-setting, selection of critical examples, and abstract data type design to implementation of the most difficult portions of the program; the Framework guides us by making our past experience easily available. The Plan is flexible because we are free to skip or repeat or expand each step as we see fit. The Framework is flexible because it is a framework, that is, a collection of templates and examples that grows as we learn more.

The Plan and the Framework are nothing more (or less) than an organized selection of the programming tips, techniques, folklore, and tools I have encountered as a professional programmer. There is really nothing new in them. They have been used successfully in the past and are very much in use today in a wide variety of forms. Many people try to determine top-level project goals; many people use some form of abstract data type. *Advanced C Struct Programming* simply presents selected "tried-and-true" ideas in a coherent, useful way, and illustrates their use.

We have also seen that the Plan and the Framework are not substitutes for careful and earnest application of our skills as professional programmers. There is no automatic substitute for human experience, for human judgment, or for human effort.

Writing reliable, useful, and commercially viable software is hard for many reasons, but data structure complexity is one of the most critical ongoing programming problems standing between you and success. Using the Plan and the Framework to guide your data structure design and implementation will make you a better programmer, and improve your chance of success. What's more, as a better programmer, you will make better use of these tools. Without a good method like the one in *Advanced C Struct Programming*, you will fail. The choice is up to you.

SECTION THREE

The Framework

CHAPTER 19
Introduction

This section of *Advanced C Struct Programming* contains goals, ADTDs, struct design guidelines, and tricks referred to in the Examples section. It also contains additional examples of these items. The ADTDs provided in the Example chapters are not duplicated here.

This Framework section also contains templates for each of the following kinds of programming knowledge: top-level goals, abstract data type descriptions, struct design guidelines, and struct tricks. To get the most out of the Framework, you should use it as a starting point for your own organized collection of expert tidbits and principles.

Your personal copy of the Framework should grow as your programming expertise grows. Think of the Framework as a database of programming knowledge, and keep it current. For instance, as an exercise, try to summarize a chapter on stacks or lists or trees from an introductory text on data structures by writing the corresponding ADTD. If you have trouble, experiment with different ADTD questions. Summarizing essential information in a compact, useful format is a surprising and pleasant experience.

When you're adding an item to the Framework, you may have trouble deciding whether it is a struct design guideline or a struct trick. The distinction is somewhat arbitrary. In general, however, design guidelines suggest one sort of typedef over another (arrays versus lists, for instance), while the effects of tricks are more local. Guidelines affect basic functionality, while tricks affect convenience or performance.

Speaking of performance, it is important to keep the Framework in context. For instance, you can speed up a typical program more by profiling it and rewriting or assembly-coding the sections where you spend the most time than you can by rearranging typedefs to make pointer offsets zero or using similar struct tricks. Actually, of course, you'll probably want to do both.

The point I'm trying to make is that the Framework is not a substitute for programming expertise. It's a useful way to keep track of part of that expertise. If it works as well for you as it has for me, and I see no reason why it shouldn't, you'll be a big step closer to programming ecstasy. Or at least to a reasonably bug-free simulation thereof.

CHAPTER 20
A Collection of Top-Level Goals

A template for top-level goal descriptions is described below. Please keep the following points in mind while reading goal descriptions:

1. Because top-level goals are so general, most of the discussion in the goal descriptions applies to programming in general, not just to struct design and implementation. Aspects of the goal that pertain strictly to struct design and implementation are discussed in the "Application to C Structs" section of each description.

2. The most commonly perceived conflicts are between memory space and execution time, or between portability and efficiency. But other tradeoffs can be important, too. Watch for unexpected relationships. For instance, porting an application from running in RAM to running strictly in ROM (which can't support a stack) might require us to sacrifice some understandability by avoiding recursion.

3. Only three of the top-level goals mentioned earlier in *Advanced C Struct Programming* are described here, because (a) space is limited, (b) some goals have very little effect on struct design and implementation, and (c) it's easy to expand these goal descriptions and create new ones.

TOP-LEVEL GOAL TEMPLATE

Motivation

This section states the main reasons people give for pursuing (or avoiding) whichever goal is being described.

Likely Champions

These are the people who are most likely to press hard for this particular top-level goal.

When the Goal Is Needed Most

This section lists some circumstances that increase the goal's importance.

Advantages

This section lists the advantages of achieving the goal.

Disadvantages

This section lists the disadvantages of achieving the goal. "Spending time that could have been spent on another goal," and "risking unintended side effects by changing the code to meet this goal" are generally not listed, since they are disadvantages of pursuing any top-level programming goal. This section may also include estimates of the effort required to meet the goal.

Ways to Measure Progress

Most of the goals are achieved a bit at a time, so this section provides suggestions on measuring progress toward the goal.

Likely Trouble Spots

This section lists some of the problems to watch out for as you pursue the goal. It may also list other top-level goals that often conflict with this goal.

Application to C Structs

By their very nature, top-level goals apply not just to C struct design and implementation, but to all aspects of programming. This section applies the ideas presented in the previous sections to the specific problem of writing good C structs.

TOP-LEVEL GOAL: UNDERSTANDABLE CODE

Motivation

Understandable code is easier to debug, easier to modify or enhance or swipe good pieces from, and easier to port. Interestingly, a few programmers believe this is exactly why they should *not* write understandable code. They simply refuse to make their code clear enough to allow another programmer of similar experience to debug or enhance it. The only valid argument against understandable code is specifically against "documenting" code because it takes too much time and space. The question in this case is "how much documentation is enough?" We'll look at different levels of documentation below, but let's deal first with the question of deliberately cryptic code.

The most common argument in favor of cryptic code runs something like this: "When you ask me to document my code, you're asking me to trash my job security. If everyone else can maintain my code, why should my boss keep me around?" More often, they just say "I don't have time!"

It's true that you have good job security if you're the only one who can maintain a critical piece of code. It's also true that one way to be the only person who can maintain a program is to make the source (and your explanations of it) so cryptic that no one else can decipher it. But even if we ignore ethical and aesthetic considerations, there are several practical drawbacks to securing your job by making your code difficult to decipher:

1. You spend effort devising schemes to disguise the source that could have been spent improving your programming skills in other ways. You also spend more time on debugging, enhancing, or revising your code because the code is harder to understand.

2. You may be unable to separate yourself from a messy program when you want to without leaving your job. This is justice in action.

3. "Blackcoding" (as in "blackmailing via cryptic source code") only works once per company. Your manager, having been burned once, will be unlikely to keep you around to make further trouble after most of the fires in your original code are extinguished. What's more, blackcoding might not even work once. If a manager of average experience and programming ability reviews your code and sees how cryptic it is, you will either be required to clarify your code or you will be invited to seek employment elsewhere.

4. You might not be assigned the projects you wanted. Put yourself in your boss's place. Would you rather assign work to a programmer who writes code no one else can maintain, or one who writes code that someone else in the group can assume responsibility for if worst comes to worst and this marvelous person leaves or gets hit by a bus?

Likely Champions

programmers who have been forced to decipher unclear or inconsistently documented code in the past

managers who have had to force programmers to decipher such ugly code

When Understandable Code Is Needed Most

Programmers have access to program source.

Users cannot determine everything they want to know about the expected inputs and outputs, files used, and so forth by running the program or by asking someone.

The program will be used for more than a day or two.

The original programmer will not be maintaining the program.

The program will be the basis for another program later on.

The code will undergo many revisions or customizations.

Pieces of the program's code will be used in other programs.

The program is complex—it uses obscure or clever algorithms, assumes a particular hardware architecture, is not tiny (should be in more than one source file), consumes or produces a lot of data, and so on.

Advantages

Understandability decreases implementation/modification time for large programs.

Understandability makes code easier to debug, port, enhance, or copy good bits from.

Disadvantages

Once you are committed to writing clear code, it's easy to spend time documenting code to a higher level than is appropriate. Too much documentation is just as bad as too little. See the next section, "Ways to Measure Progress," for help in deciding "how clear is clear enough?"

Ways to Measure Progress

Code cannot simply be described as either easy to read or impossible to read; there are different levels of understandability between these extremes. A commitment to clear code is not a promise to write a technical reference and tutorial for every function. It's up to you as programmer to decide what level of understandability your code needs and how best to meet that need. One way to gauge understandability is to use the following scale.

A Code Understandability Scale

Least Understandable: This level of clarity is fine for code that's meant to be used once or twice by whoever wrote it to get something done fast. The code is formatted, it compiles, and it does something useful. The source contains few or no comments, identifiers are of minimal length, and constants are hard-coded. Assumptions about what files are used, what input is expected, and even what the program is supposed to do are not documented.

Minimally Understandable: This level of clarity is fine for programs used only by other programmers who have access to the source, or by the original programmer, or by both. The original programmer understands the code well enough to port it to a machine with a different architecture, say, or to translate it from C into Pascal. The original author could debug or enhance this code, but anyone else would probably need some help.

Very Understandable: In a better world, all the code for all the products on the market would be in this category. Another programmer with similar experience can understand this code well enough to debug or enhance it without the original author sitting by her side.

Dream On: The code is published in paperback and becomes a bestseller worldwide. Strangers ask the original programmer to autograph their listings and that person makes two million dollars a year in hardware endorsements.

To help decide what level of understandability is appropriate, answer the following questions:

Who will run this program, how often, and why?

Who will read this program's source code, how often, and why?

What different environments (machines, operating systems, compilers, debuggers) will this program run in? See page 333 in the description of the top-level goal portability for more details.

How appropriate and useful are each of the following as documentation?

- The original programmer answers questions.
- The program prints prompts and status reports while running.
- The program's source listing can be read.
- References consulted while creating the program can be read.
- The program's technical notes can be read (for instance, see the Programmer's Code Summary described on page 329).
- The program's tutorial or user's reference manual can be read.

Likely Trouble Spots

Some people have very strong opinions about programming style and documentation conventions. Don't let yourself be dragged into a four-hour meeting where people do nothing but argue about tab stop settings! Pick a small set of formats and conventions that work for you and your group, and use them consistently. Inconsistency can be very frustrating. Discard any of the following:

comments that don't match the code

comments that just echo the code (e.g., "x += inc; /* increment x */")

use of a #defined value, *sizeof()*, or enumeration value in some places and (possibly different) hard-coded values in others where one would expect the defined value, the *sizeof()* call, or the enum value again

Consider including the following information in your source:

at the top of each source file:
- the file's name
- the shared purpose of all the code in this file
- a history of global changes to this file, including its creation date and the name of the programmer who started the whole thing

- a description of any variable or function naming conventions
- a list of any books, articles, people, or pieces of code consulted while writing this code, and a list of critical but not obvious assumptions

at the top of each function:

- purpose of the function
- brief descriptions of the incoming and outgoing parameters and return value, if any
- who modified this function and when and why and what they did; the first entry in this history should be something like "JWLO   17 Jan 90   creation"
- any comments on how the function works that might help someone who calls, debugs, or modifies this function
- comments on the function's performance, such as how often you expect it to be called, or how many cycles it takes on average
- suggestions for later improvements to the function
- known bugs (alas, there are such things) and limitations

To understand a program that is large, or is intimately connected to other programs, or is one instance of a class of programs, we often need to know more than we can learn from skimming the source code. And some things are almost never noted in the source, like where the most useful breakpoints are, which parts of the program are very delicate, and how the goals for the program have changed since coding began. In such a case, it is useful to take a day or two after the program is stable and summarize the code for other programmers, and for yourself.

To make this summary easier, an outline of a Programmer's Code Summary (PCS for short) is provided on page 329. Keep in mind that documentation can exist at the following different levels, some of which might not be applicable to a given collection of code:

well-chosen variable, typedef, function, and #define names
comments in the source: next to declarations, inside and at the beginning of functions, and at the top of files
technical notes describing particular aspects of a program
Programmer's Code Summary
user reference manuals
user tutorials

Application to C Structs

The guidelines for writing understandable typedefs are simple:

1. Choose good struct and member names.
2. If there's any doubt about a member's use, add appropriate comments.

But following these guidelines requires some judgment. For instance, there might be doubt about a member's use if it is used different ways in different parts of the program, if it's just there as padding to get the alignment right, if its use isn't clear from its name, or if it's an integer.

Integers are commonly used in four quite different ways:

as numeric values
as non-negative counts or indices
as enumerations
as bitflags

An example of each use of integers follows.

```
/* "NUMERIC" integer: */
typedef struct {
  char *name;
  int  games_won;   /* "numeric" int—might be negative; */
} score; /* for instance, suppose more games */
         /* have been lost than won */

/* "COUNT" integer: */
typedef struct {
  struct foo *first;      /* points to first element */
  int        count;       /* total number of elements (>= 0) */
} foo_set;

/* "ENUMERATION" integer: */
/* alien.home_planet values: */
typedef enum {
  drifter = 0;
  earth   = 1;
  mars    = 2;
  venus   = 3;
  jupiter = 4;
  vulcan  = 5;
} homes;

typedef struct {
  char *name;
  int home_planet; /* values are enumerated above */
} alien;

/* "BITFLAG" integer: */
/* display_char.mode flags: */
#define BOLD          1
#define ITALIC        2
#define UNDERLINED    4
#define FLASHING      8
typedef struct {
```

```
    char value;
    int  mode;  /* bitflags are defined above */
} display_char;
```

PROGRAMMER'S CODE SUMMARY TEMPLATE

Note: It should be left to individual programmers to decide exactly what goes in a Programmer's Code Summary (PCS). The outline below suggests useful information to consider including and a way to organize that information, but final authority (and responsibility) must be left with the programmer who is writing the PCS. The PCS can start as a copy of this outline, with the outline categories turning into titles of text sections, or the programmer can simply look at a hard copy of this outline while writing the PCS in her current word processor of choice. Whatever works best is the way to go.

The PCS is not meant to answer every question about a piece of code, nor is it a substitute for well-written source and good user manuals. It is meant to help transmit from one programmer to another the kind of information that is hard to get from the source or from the manuals. The idea is to help one programmer learn from another's experiences.

You'll notice that the code being described is referred to throughout the PCS as a "program." This is for convenience. The code in question might be a stand-alone application program, but PCSs are also useful in describing libraries, operating system kernels, device drivers, and other pieces of code some people might not think of when they hear the term "program."

Programmer's Code Summary of <Program Name>

Revisions: June 29, 1989   John Ogilvie created this template

I. Understanding This Program
   A. Tell why this PCS was written—some possible reasons follow
      1. The programmer decided a PCS was needed.
      2. The program contains a lot of source.
      3. The program's source is spread over several directories.
      4. The program is intimately connected to other programs.
      5. The program is one example of a particular kind of: program we'll probably see more of in the future, such as diagnostics and device drivers.
   B. Give an overview of *each* product this program is a part of
      1. Diagram the product's functional components in a Functional Module Diagram (FMD); one of the modules in the FMD represents this program.
      2. Describe each path in the FMD that takes data through this program.
      3. List the other programs this program communicates with directly, and the circumstances under which the communication is optional. List the methods of communication—following are some possibilities:
         a. sockets
         b. shared memory
         c. serial or parallel port, modem

    d. data files

    e. spawning each other as a process

C. Give an overview of this program's functionality:

  1. Give an FMD for this program, describing what each module does and listing the source files that implement each module (note that a module is a functional abstraction that may take one or more actual source files to implement).

  2. Describe typical and critical data paths through the FMD; this is a high-level description, not a function call tree.

  3. Describe how the modules communicate with each other—following are some possibilities:

    a. setting global variables directly

    b. setting static variables via function calls

    c. passing data via files

    d. passing data by calling one module's functions in another module

  4. List the other sources of information that are useful in answering questions about this program's functionality and semantics—following are some possibilities:

    a. earlier versions of this PCS

    b. technical notes on specific aspects of this program

    c. engineers or product managers who had a say in the program's specification

D. Summarize the history of this program:

  1. Describe the goals for this program when it was originally planned and contrast them with the current goals for the program—following are some possible goals:

    a. functionality

      i. describe minimal functionality in the original specification versus what's acceptable now

      ii. list changes to this program that were predicted, and whether they were needed after all

      iii. list changes to this program that were not foreseen and how they were handled

    b. schedule constraints

      i. having demos ready

      ii. having the beta test version ready

      iii. having the original product and subsequent releases ready

    c. portability goals

      i. making this program part of other products

      ii. using other hardware

      iii. using other operating systems

      iv. using other window systems

    d. performance goals

      i. taking advantage of special hardware

      ii. performing better than existing products

      iii. executing certain operations quickly

      iv. using less memory

      v. being reliable

      vi. being secure

  2. Describe this program's design phase

    a. List the people mainly responsible for the current design.

    b. List the parts of the program that were hardest to design, and tell why.

    c. List the resources that were useful during this program's design—following
      are some possibilities:
      i. existing programs
      ii. books, articles, technical notes
      iii. people

3. Describe this program's implementation phase
    a. Tell who implemented what, in a broad way, and don't forget critical include
      files and libraries.
    b. List the parts of the program that were hardest to implement, and tell why.
    c. List the resources that were useful during this program's implementation—
      following are some possibilities:
      i. existing programs
      ii. books, articles, technical notes
      iii. people
      iv. operating system, hardware, and software used to develop the program,
         including version numbers
    d. List the parts of the program that are still being implemented, and describe
      their current state.
    e. List the parts of the program's source that have been abandoned, and tell why.
    f. Describe the main resources the current implementation needs at run-time—
      following are some possibilities:
      i. other programs this program communicates with directly
      ii. memory this program needs overall, and any particularly large contiguous
         pieces needed
      iii. particular interface hardware needed, and under what circumstances it
         can be omitted—following are some possibilities:
         (1) keyboard (special function keys?)
         (2) tablet, light pen
         (3) mouse (how many buttons?)
         (4) serial and parallel ports
         (5) speaker
         (6) recording devices
         (7) monitor (color? resolution?)

II. Modifying This Program
   A. Tell which parts of the code are delicate and why.
   B. Tell which parts of the code you are proud of, and why (this serves two purposes—
      it lets the PCS writer brag a bit and it gives other programmers a way to tell what
      the PCS author thinks excellence means).
   C. List the parts of this program that will be hard to port and tell why; keep in mind the
      different types of portability mentioned earlier when discussing this program's
      goals.
   D. Describe the coding conventions followed in the source—following are some
      possibilities:
    1. Naming conventions—following are some possibilities:
      a. standardized abbreviations like "adr" for "address"
      b. prefixes
      c. filename extensions
      d. globals might be named according to some pattern

      e. capitalization, prefixes, and suffixes might be used for flags, constants, macros, conditional compilation target environment names, and other #defines

  2. Preferences for particular standard functions—*fprintf()* over *printf()*, *fopen()* over *open()*, a custom allocation function over *malloc()*, and so forth

  3. Philosophy of error handling; this breaks down further into the following:

      a. List the kinds of functions that pass back a status.

      b. List the kinds of functions that post their status in some global variable.

      c. List the kinds of functions that print error messages to the user, and the format they use—what does the user see?

      d. List the kinds of errors this program can recover from.

      e. List the central functions, if any, that errors trap to (these are good breakpoint candidates).

      f. If certain compiler errors are to be ignored when rebuilding the program, describe them.

E. Describe how to make typical changes to the program (for instance, adding a new system trap, adding a new statement to an interpreter, adding a new data type to a database library).

F. Describe how to run this program's test suite, if it has one.

G. Describe the debugging aids available specifically for this program—following are some possibilities:

  1. formatted struct dumpers (see the discussion in "Top-Level Goal: Debuggable Code," page 341)

  2. conditional compilation to add *printf()* calls or produce other debugging code that doesn't belong in the final product

  3. testbeds (may be quick and dirty code, but can be very useful to a knowledgeable programmer)

  4. central functions every action of a particular type goes through; these include custom routines built around *malloc()*, *exit()*, and so forth, as well as the functions errors trap to

  5. global variables to set the debugging output level or debugging options

H. List the places that are good breakpoints for particular kinds of bugs.

I. List common bugs and tell what causes them and how to fix them—these bugs are probably related to the typical changes to the program that were described above.

TOP-LEVEL GOAL: PORTABLE CODE

Motivation

"Porting" is often used to mean "copy the source code from machine type *A* to machine type *B*, get it to recompile and relink, and you're done." For instance, it's certainly a port to move a Macintosh program to an IBM PC. But this narrow definition of porting doesn't go far enough. There are many other types of "port" as well. Here are a few examples:

from a Macintosh™ 128K to a Macintosh 512K or vice versa (same architecture with more or less memory) from an 8086-based IBM® PC to an 80386-based PC (the target machine's instructions are a superset of the original's)

from BSD UNIX™ to System V UNIX, or to MS-DOS® (lesser or greater differences in the operating system)

from a system with a bit-mapped display to one with a tty-style screen, or from a system with a mouse to one with a tablet (greater or lesser differences in user interface hardware)

from Pascal to C on a given machine (same hardware and operating system, different compilers)

from MPW C to LightspeedC on a Macintosh (different standard header files, different C compilers)

from C code to assembly or microcode (rewrite to take advantage of hardware)

from C code to ROM (initialized statics must be treated as read-only constants)

from running under X-windows to running under the Macintosh's Window Manager (different user interface software)

from running with only *printf()* and an assembly language debugger to running with a source-level debugger (we may be able to rip out many of the debugging hacks now that we can step through the C source code)

from running in batch mode to running interactively

These examples make it clear that porting is more common, and more complex, than just copying code to a new machine and recompiling. We need a more general definition of porting that reflects our daily work better and leads us toward a list of likely trouble spots.

Definition of "Porting"

Porting is the act of reimplementing a program's functionality and performance in a different "environment." The difference between porting and "modifying" or "enhancing" is subjective. One person's port is another's bug fix. Porting often involves simply reproducing a program's essential internal structure in a new environment, but this is not necessarily the case. New algorithms and data structures might also be needed to get the desired effect in the new environment.

A program's environment consists of the items below. Programming caused by a substantial change in any of these items is a port:

CPU, bus size, word size, clock speed, and so on

available memory (both size and type—RAM/ROM, big/little endian, etc.)

operating system

user interface hardware and the program's interface to it

peripheral hardware and the program's interface to it

user interface software (e.g., window systems)

source programming language

compiler, assembler, linker, debugger

standard macros, typedefs, defines, globals, and library routines available for use in the program

coding conventions needed to make the program "fit in"
functionality and performance constraints

Likely Champions

Given the examples and definition above, it's clear that just about everybody who programs or directs programmers is a champion of portability at one time or another, because ports are needed so often.

When Portability Is Needed Most

It's needed anytime a program has to see continued use; see the "Advantages" below.

Advantages

Software and hardware environments change continually and quickly. A program that isn't ported to keep up with a changing environment will fall quickly into disuse. To take an extreme example, there's very little call these days for code that runs under CP/M with a tty-style windowless interface and reads its data from paper tape.

More to the point, if you're reading this book, chances are very good you've been programming long enough to have used a piece of hardware or a language or an operating system that is no longer in demand (or perhaps never was in great demand). Portability will be an important concern as long as our programming environment keeps changing rapidly.

Disadvantages

The classic argument against portability is that it's inefficient. If you can write time-critical sections of a program in assembly or microcode, for instance, you'll generally get faster execution. This is really a special case of the following observations.

Efficacy of Specificity Law

A program is totally useless unless the programmer makes specific assumptions about every aspect of the program's environment and codes according to those assumptions.

Portability Corollary

Grand schemes to write perfect code that will simply need to be recompiled and relinked to run correctly in any new environment are like a porcupine in a balloon factory—they ignore certain critical details.

In other words, we must make specific assumptions about what kind of portability we want, and what we're willing to trade for it. There is no such thing as pure portability; there are just specific kinds of portability, each with its own cost. The price of a particular portability is often efficiency, but sometimes it's increased implementation time. Sometimes it's some other type of portability. Sometimes the price is decreased ease of use or less programming enjoyment.

Let's consider an example. Suppose we want to write an application that runs on both a Macintosh and an IBM PC. We have a spectrum of choices. We could make the program easily portable by giving up efficiency (no assembly code), ease of use (minimal use of QuickDraw, the Window Manager, the mouse, etc.), and some functionality (no networking). In return, we can probably port the program simply by recompiling and relinking. However, a program that's so restricted might not be worth running, much less worth porting.

The other extreme is to keep run-time efficiency, ease of use, and all the functionality at the expense of greatly increased implementation effort. In this case, we tailor the application to each environment, using the Macintosh Window Manager, for instance, and coding critical sections in 68020 assembly. Part of the port is the reimplementation of critical assembly, library, and driver routines on the IBM PC (or vice versa, if we're moving to a Macintosh from an IBM PC).

Different kinds of portability can have very different tradeoffs. As an extreme example, suppose that we want to port our application into ROM and hardware logic. The reason for the port is to make a card someone can slide into a PC and get incredible interactive performance from. Then we have a new set of problems, quite different from those encountered during the Macintosh-to-IBM port. Code size is restricted, we can't write to ROM during execution so recursion is ruled out unless we can find some RAM to use for a calling stack, and so it goes.

In brief, portability costs, but the price is not always best measured in terms of run-time efficiency.

Ways to Measure Progress

There are so many different types of port that it's hard to list all the specific ways to measure porting progress. Keep in mind, however, that measuring progress only by the percent of code that's been recompiled and relinked in the new environment is a mistake. The fact that code compiles and links does not mean it will perform correctly. There are plenty of problems to check for once the link is finished.

For instance, operating systems and run-time libraries in the two environments might contain functions that have the same name (so the linker is satisfied) but behave very differently. The program might run correctly but very slowly because of differences in the amount of memory available, or in the CPU's power or clock speed. Binary data files might not port because bytes are reversed or struct members are aligned differently in memory. Many other problems are possible too, as we'll see in the next section.

Likely Trouble Spots

There's a wide variety of problems to watch out for as we pursue one or another type of portability. A useful way to organize a list of likely trouble spots is to start with a list of common characteristics of ports. One such list is provided below. Some of the problems associated with different characteristics are also listed. This list of potential problems is by no means complete, but it's enough to get us thinking.

Notice that any particular porting effort can involve several of the listed characteristics. Moving a program from a Macintosh to an IBM PC, for instance, involves a new operating system, different user interface hardware, a radically different CPU, and different compilers and linkers. It may or may not involve different RAM availability or rewriting assembly code.

Some Port Characteristics and Associated Trouble Spots

More RAM is available.

Less RAM is available.

Code moves from RAM to ROM.

- Watch out for initialized statics that are given new values elsewhere in the code—writing to ROM is generally a no-op.
- Make sure the RAM and ROM data are put in separate sections by the compiler; ROM data belongs in a read-only "code" section.

Code moves from ROM to RAM.

One machine has a different memory organization than the other.

- One machine may be "big endian" while the other is "little endian." That is, the most significant byte of a word may be at the high address end of the word in one machine and at the low end of the word in the other machine.
- One machine may address 8-bit bytes while another addresses 16-bit words and a third addresses 32-bit words.
- The amount of data or code cache may differ.
- The number of registers needed to hold an address may differ.
- One machine may have an MMU (memory management unit) while the other does not.
- System page size for the MMUs may differ.

The new CPU instruction set is a superset of the old CPU's.

- It may be desirable to rewrite assembly or microcode sections to take advantage of powerful new instructions.

The new CPU is radically different from the old CPU.

- Assembly and microcode sections must be rewritten. This can be tough if there are fewer registers in the new CPU, or powerful instructions are missing, or the size of program-counter-relative jumps is smaller.

The new system provides a different screen, mouse, or other user interface hardware.

- Sampling rates for different mice, trackballs, and tablets can differ substantially.

- Screens may have different resolutions and/or aspect ratios.
- One system may use square pixels while the other does not.
- Screens may use different color standards; in particular, one may be monochrome while the other is color.
- One system may use a touch screen while the other does not.
- One system may use a mouse while the other does not.

Code moves to run under a different operating system.

- Semantically different functions may have the same name.
- One stack may be of fixed size while the other is allocated dynamically.
- Chasing a NULL pointer may be legal on one system (that is, zero is a valid address) while it causes a segmentation violation on the other.
- One operating system may provide a virtual address space while the other provides only physical memory.
- One operating system may provide a *fork()* function to spawn child processes while the other does not.
- Files may be randomly accessible under one operating system but treated only as sequential tapes under the other.
- One system may use memory-mapped IO while the other does not.
- One system's device drivers may use newlines where the other uses carriage returns.

Code moves to run under a different windowing system.

- Functionality may be radically different. For instance, one system may support menus over wireframes or live video while the other does not.
- One system may provide built-in text editing facilities to edit values displayed in a window while the other does not.

The source code changes from one high-level language to another.

- The languages may be relatively close (Pascal to/from C), or not so close (LISP or FORTRAN to C). Some tools are available, but translation can be just as hard as implementing from scratch.
- The languages may use different data formats (e.g., C strings versus Pascal strings).
- Languages other than C do not necessarily use "short-circuit" expression evaluation. In C, evaluating "(next && (next->value < 0))" is possible when next == NULL, because short-circuit evaluation stops as soon as it can (as soon as it sees next == NULL, in this case).
- The order in which function actual parameters are evaluated may differ from one compiler to another.

The source code changes from a high-level language to a low-level one.

- Generating low-level translations is easy if you have a compiler; these translations can then be tailored by hand. The main problem to watch for is the amount of code. It's easy to generate an enormous, unmanageable low-level program from a sweet and small high-level one by tailoring a compiler's translation without adding comments, decent variable names, and so forth.

The source code changes from a low-level language to a high-level one.

- Create appropriate new typedefs.

- Find high-level function calls or create interfaces for the low-level ones that do things like read disk sectors.

The source code changes from one low-level language to another.

- Different assemblers may have different pseudo-ops, and different syntactic philosophies ("opcode <source> <dest>" versus "opcode <dest> <source>," for instance).

Different C compilers are used.

- One compiler may allow casts on the left side of an assignment while the other doesn't.
- One implementation of the C preprocessor may support tricks the other doesn't, such as using /**/ in defines to concatenate strings.
- Struct members may be aligned differently. This can be a problem when code compiled under one scheme is used to read binary data files that use the other compiler's member alignment scheme.
- Short-circuit evaluation of boolean expressions may be the default in one compiler but not in the other.
- The order in which function parameters are evaluated may change.
- Providing extra actual parameters in a function call may have no effect in one environment but be fatal in another.

Different linkers are used.

- One linker may catch duplicate names the other doesn't, allowing two functions of the same name to pass unnoticed. It can be very painful if the wrong function (with the right name) is linked in.
- Libraries may be loaded at run-time on one system but not on another.
  Different floating point formats are used.
- This can be big trouble if the same binary data files must work with both systems.

Different floating point precisions are used.

- A float may be 32 bits on one system and 64 or 80 bits on another.
- One compiler may use "long float" (or something else) to mean what another uses "double" to mean.

Different integer or pointer sizes are used.

- Bitflags may no longer fit in one int.
- Casts between int and pointer types may be allowed on one system but not on another.

Different run-time libraries are used.

- Semantically different functions may have the same name.

Different standard header files are used.

- One system may allow header files to include other headers, while the other system requires every header to be listed explicitly in the C source files that use it. See the struct trick "Nesting Include Files" (page 397).
- Convenient defines may be missing.
- Things may have been moved from one standard header file to another.

Coding conventions change.

- One system's applications may use newlines where the other uses carriage returns.
- One system may check the values returned from functions while the other checks a global variable like UNIX's *errno*.
- One system may use a Pascal-style string representation (one byte containing the string's length followed by 0 to 255 characters) while the other uses C-style representation (null-terminated, arbitrary length).

Performance needs change.

- The program may change from a batch job to an interactive application, so it needs a better user interface and faster execution.
- The program may move from a single-user workstation to a time sliced system, so real time no longer corresponds to CPU time. Also, the program will need to leave system resources in a consistent state and assume that other programs didn't.

Application to C Structs

See the list of "Port Characteristics and Associated Trouble Spots" above.

TOP-LEVEL GOAL: DEBUGGABLE CODE

Motivation

Motivation in this case seems obvious: Who wants to rely on code that hasn't been debugged? Who wants to work with code that's harder to debug than it needs to be?

Likely Champions

Good programmers.
Managers who have been left with the responsibility to maintain half-debugged code.
Stockholders.

In other words, a champion is anybody whose money or reputation is on the line.

When Debuggable Code Is Needed Most

The code is under development.
The code will probably be enhanced or ported.
Something important depends on correct code—for instance, people's lives, a business's reputation, or your job.

Advantages

Debugged code provides a firm foundation for the programming that follows. "Nailing" nasty bugs can be very satisfying.

Disadvantages

Debugging takes time and effort you may prefer to spend in other ways. Tracking down bugs can be very frustrating.

Ways to Measure Progress

Useful code is never guaranteed to be 100 percent bug-free. There are different levels of "debuggedness" for code. It's up to programmers and their managers to decide what level of testing is appropriate. As a rough guide, you can decide which one of these categories you want the code to fall in:

"It doesn't have to be right—it's just an example to show someone the gist of how to do something. In effect, it's pseudocode, not code that's meant to be compiled and used forever the way it is right now."

"If it compiles and runs without crashing and the output isn't obviously wrong, I'm happy."

"I've thought about it, I've stepped through it in the debugger, I've examined the output closely, and I'm satisfied."

"People have been using it for a while now, and it doesn't break very often. There are only eight or nine known bugs."

"It passes an extensive, carefully designed test suite. Everyone here in the group and out at the customer sites has tried to break it, and no one has succeeded."

"It was extensively tested and customers have been using it for years. The last bug was fixed over a year ago, and the code hasn't been touched since."

Likely Trouble Spots

If code is hard to read it will be hard to debug, but code that's easy to read is not necessarily easy to debug. To determine how hard it will be to debug code even if it is easy to read, answer the following:

What restrictions does the debugger put on filenames? On function names?

What symbol generation or tie-in is needed during compilation or linking?

Does the program being debugged think it has exclusive ownership of any resource that the debugger uses (e.g., memory, screen, CPU, or keyboard)?

What struct "dumpers" are available? These are customized functions that pretty-print your struct contents, interpreting bit flags, printing the names of #defined values, choosing the right format for unions, chasing pointers, and so forth.

What kind of test suite is available?

Does the test suite test all those special cases that came to mind while the code was being written?

How complete is the test suite—will it help you make sure fixing one problem hasn't created another one?

How automatic is the program's command input mechanism, that is, how easy is it to make a test suite that runs automatically? In particular, if the program is menu driven, can you write a program that selects menu options and thus drives the program being tested?

What sort of testbed is available to exercise library functions you called but didn't write?

To what degree does adding or enabling debugging code affect the bugs you're chasing? How else does debugging code affect the program's performance? How does use of a debugger affect the program's behavior? For instance, it's very hard to single step through an interrupt handler. As another example, a debugger sometimes cannot be run because there's just not enough memory.

Application to C Structs

The most useful tools for debugging structs are "dumpers." These are routines you write to print out the current values of various structs you've defined. Source-level debuggers will do some of this work for you, but sometimes you need to write dumpers even if you have a good debugger. Dumpers are more than just formatters; they interpret the struct's values in various ways as needed:

1. Dumpers convert bitflags and enumerations to text. For instance, suppose we have the following:

```
/* shuttle.state bitflags */
#define SHUTTLE_FUELED          1
#define SHUTTLE_BOARDED         2
#define SHUTTLE_SECURED_IN_BAY  4
#define SHUTTLE_REPAIRS_DONE     8

typedef struct {
  char *name;
  int  state;
} shuttle;
```

A *shuttle* dumper should print something like this:

```
shuttle struct @ 0x4012a1c0:
  name:  Queenie Marie
  state: SHUTTLE_SECURED_IN_BAY SHUTTLE_REPAIRS_DONE
```

2. As in the shuttle example above, it's a good idea to have the dumpers print struct addresses as well as contents. If you suspect bad pointers, you might also want to print the sum of the struct's address and *sizeof(shuttle)*, so you can easily tell where the struct is supposed to end in memory.

3. Dumpers print union contents in the correct format, according to the union's tag:

```
/* buddy.u_isa enumeration values */
#define ANDROID    1
#define FROID      2
#define HUMAN      3
typedef struct {
  int u_isa;
  union {
    char    *name;          /* u_isa == HUMAN */
    int     part_number;    /* u_isa == ANDROID */
    float   transparency;   /* u_isa == FROID */
  } u;
} buddy;
```

A *buddy* dumper should print something like this:

```
buddy struct @ 0xa882a1c0:
  u_isa:          FROID
  u.transparency: 0.7764
```

Some debuggers will let you invoke a dumper when you need to while stepping through the code. This is very useful, but it usually means a dummy function must be written to make sure the dumpers get linked in. If you can call dumpers directly from the debugger, you don't need any dumper calls in the code. But if the dumpers aren't called anywhere, the linker will probably optimize them out of the executable! So it's often necessary to add a dummy function like the one below to the file that contains the dumpers. Call this function in *main()* or someplace else to force the linker to include the dumper object module in the executable:

```
/* in dumpers.c: */
int dbg_link_in_dumpers()
{
  return (0);
} /* dbg_link_in_dumpers */

/* in main.c: */
main()
{
  ...
  dbg_link_in_dumpers(); /* ensure dumper availability */
  ...
} /* main */
```

CHAPTER 21

A Collection of Abstract Data Types

The template below can serve as the basis of your abstract data type descriptions (ADTDs), but it's very general. You'll need to look at the ADTDs here and in the Examples section to get an idea of which specific questions about geometry and operators will be useful to you.

ADTD TEMPLATE

Conceptual Model

This section gives an overview of the data type, including a sketch of a typical collection of elements.

Relatives

This section lists some abstract data types similar to the one being described, and the differences between them.

Geometry

This section describes the data type's geometry, including any special positions like top of stack. This section also summarizes the relations that hold between data elements.

Operators

This section lists pseudocode function headers for the data type's operators. Each operator's parameters (including type and mode) and semantics are described. This is also where membership restrictions and the number of collections involved become evident.

Notice that operators are specified in an ADTD as C function calling sequences, but the corresponding typedefs and defines are not provided. For instance, the *union()* operator in the Bag ADTD has parameters of type "bag." But this type is not defined in the ADTD. Nor should it be. ADTDs are language-independent. An ADTD is not concerned with whether a bag is implemented as an array or as a linked list or with bitflags. That will be decided in the Struct Design step of the Plan.

ABSTRACT DATA TYPE DESCRIPTION: LUMPY QUEUE

Conceptual Model

A queue is a FIFO, that is, a first-in-first-out list. Elements can only be inserted one at a time at the "tail" of the queue and removed one by one from the "head" of the queue. Elements are removed in the same order in which they were inserted.

All of this is true for lumpy queues, with one important difference. As shown in Figure 21-1, several elements can be inserted at the same time in a lumpy queue. Elements inserted at the same time are neither in front of nor behind each other; they are "side by side." Elements inserted at the same time must be removed together.

Relatives

A *common queue* is a lumpy queue without the lumps—every element is either in front of or behind every other element. No elements of a common queue are side by side, since the elements are always inserted and removed one at a time.

A *stack* is the same as a queue except that elements are inserted ("pushed") and removed ("popped") at the same position ("top of stack") instead of at different positions ("tail of queue," "head of queue"). This makes a stack a LIFO (last-in-first-out list), where a queue is a FIFO.

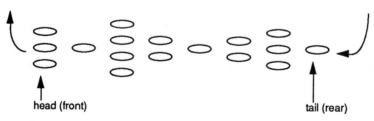

head (front)   tail (rear)

FIGURE 21-1: A typical lumpy queue.

A *lumpy stack* is a stack that allows several elements to be pushed or popped at once. Like lumpy queues, lumpy stacks have a relation "is to the side of."

In a *sorted list*, order is determined by some ordering relation on the values in the list. Elements may be inserted or removed at any position in a sorted list. By contrast, order in a queue depends on the order of calls to the insertion operator. Queue insertions occur only at the tail of the queue and queue removals occur only at the head of the queue.

Geometry

Special Positions

1. *Tail.* All insertions occur here.
2. *Head.* All removals occur here.

Relations Between Elements

1. *Is in front of.* If element A was added before element B, A is in front of B, irrespective of the values held by A and B. This relation is:
   antireflexive—no element is in front of itself
   antisymmetric—if A is in front of B, B is not in front of A
   transitive—if A is in front of B and B is in front of C, then A is in front of C
   In the lumpy queue shown in Figure 21-2, A is in front of B.
2. *Is to the side of.* If element A was added at the same time as element B, A and B are side by side, irrespective of the values held by A and B. This relation is:
   reflexive—every element is to the side of itself
   symmetric—if A is to the side of B, then B is to the side of A
   transitive—if A is to the side of B and B is to the side of C, then A is to the side of C
   "Is to the side of" partitions the collection of queue elements.
   In the lumpy queue shown in Figure 21-3, A, B, and C are to the side of each other. They were added together and must be removed together.

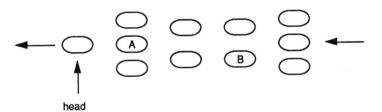

head

FIGURE 21-2:   Another lumpy queue.

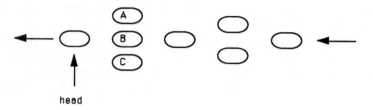

FIGURE 21-3: Yet another lumpy queue.

Operators

```
/*===========================================================*/
int      is_empty( a_queue, empty )
  queue      a_queue;        /* IN */
  boolean    *empty;         /* OUT */
/*-------------------------------------------------
Is_empty() sets empty  true if a_queue  is empty and false otherwise; it
returns status "OK" or "no such queue."
---------------------------------------------------*/


/*===========================================================*/
int      add( elem, a_queue )
  elements elem;             /* IN */
  queue      a_queue;        /* IN, OUT */
/*-------------------------------------------------
Add() adds all the elements in elem to a_queue; it returns
status "OK" or "no such queue."
---------------------------------------------------*/


/*===========================================================*/
int   remove( elem, a_queue )
  elements elem;             /* OUT */
  queue      a_queue;        /* IN, OUT */
/*-------------------------------------------------
Remove() removes the element(s) at the front of a_queue and
copies their values into elem; it returns status "OK" or
"queue empty" or "no such queue."
---------------------------------------------------*/


/*===========================================================*/
int  peek( elem, a_queue )
  elements elem;             /* OUT */
  queue      a_queue;        /* IN */
/*-------------------------------------------------
Peek() copies the values of the element(s) at the front of
```

```
a_queue  into elem without removing them from a_queue; it
returns status "OK" or "queue empty" or "no such queue."
------------------------------------------------*/


/*================================================*/
int     concatenate( head, tail, result )
  queue   head;    /* IN */
  queue   tail;    /* IN */
  queue   result; /* OUT */
/*-------------------------------------------------
Concatenate() creates a new queue result that has all the
elements of head in order followed by all the elements of
tail in order; it returns status "OK" or "both queues empty"
or "no such queue."
------------------------------------------------*/


/*================================================*/
int  merge( one, two, result )
  queue   one;     /* IN */
  queue   two;     /* IN */
  queue   result; /* OUT */
/*-------------------------------------------------
Merge() assumes queue elements are timestamped when they are inserted.
It creates a new queue result that has all the
elements of one and all the elements of two interleaved
depending on their insertion times. That is, if element alpha
is in front of element beta in queue one, alpha will still be
in front of beta in result, but some elements of two might
also be in front of beta. Merge() returns status "OK" or
"both queues empty" or "no such queue,"
------------------------------------------------*/
```

ABSTRACT DATA TYPE DESCRIPTION: BAG

Conceptual Model

Bags have less structure than any other data type. As shown in Figure 21-4, bags have no geometry to speak of, no special positions, and no ordering or other relations between members. Insertion and deletion occur anywhere. From the user's point of view, the elements are just jumbled together like marbles in a bag (hence the name).

Relatives

A *set* is a bag in which duplicate elements are forbidden. In other words, a set is a bag that can only count to one.

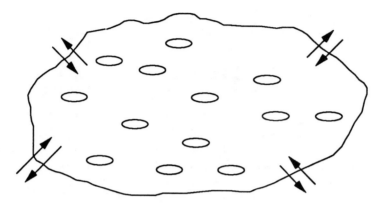

FIGURE 21-4:   A typical bag.

A *biased bag* is a bag with restrictions on the values it can contain.

Geometry

There is no geometry to speak of. Every position in a bag is equivalent to every other. There are no relations between elements, aside from the fact that they're all in the same bag.

Operators

In spite of the fact that bags have so little structure, there is no lack of operators. In addition to the usual insertion and deletion operators, there are all the set operations (union, intersection, etc.), suitably modified to take duplicate elements into account. Traversal of a bag (e.g., to print its contents) requires a bit of thought, since the elements are not ordered. This is done by the *get_next_element()* operator.

```
/*============================================================*/
int  union( one, two, result )
  bag  one,    /* IN */
       two;    /* IN */
  bag  result;/* OUT */
/*- - - - - - - - - - - - - - - - - - - - - - - - - - - - - -
Union() sets result so it contains all the elements in bag
one plus all the elements in bag two; it returns status "OK"
or "no such bag." If an element occurs three times in bag one
and twice in bag two, it will occur five times in result.
- - - - - - - - - - - - - - - - - - - - - - - - - - - - - -*/


/*============================================================*/
```

```
int  intersection( one, two, result )
   bag  one,   /* IN */
        two;   /* IN */
   bag  result;/* OUT */
/*-----------------------------------------
Intersection() sets result so it contains whatever elements
are in both bag one and bag two; it returns status "OK" or
"no such bag." If an element occurs three times in bag one
and twice in bag two, it will occur twice in result.
-------------------------------------------*/


/*========================================================*/
int  symmetric_difference( one, two, result )
   bag  one,   /* IN */
        two;   /* IN */
   bag  result;/* OUT */
/*-----------------------------------------
Symmetric_difference() sets result so it contains one of every
element that is in either bag one or bag two, but not both;
it's an "exclusive or." If an element occurs three times in
bag one and twice in bag two, it will occur once in result.
Symmetric_difference() returns status "OK" or "no such bag."
-------------------------------------------*/


/*========================================================*/
int  is_an_element_of( elem, a_bag, count )
   element  elem;  /* IN */
   bag      a_bag; /* IN */
   int      *count;/* OUT */
/*-----------------------------------------
Is_an_element_of() sets count to the number of times elem is
an element in a_bag; it returns status "OK" or "no such bag."
-------------------------------------------*/


/*========================================================*/
int  is_empty( a_bag, empty )
   bag      a_bag; /* IN */
   boolean  *empty;/* OUT */
/*-----------------------------------------
Is_empty() sets empty true if a_bag is empty and false
otherwise; it returns status "OK" or "no such bag."
-------------------------------------------*/


/*========================================================*/
int  add( elem, a_bag, count )
   element  elem;  /* IN */
   bag      a_bag; /* IN, OUT */
   int      count; /* OUT */
```

```
/*---------------------------------------------
Add() adds count copies of elem to a_bag; it returns status
"OK" or "illegal count" or "no such bag."
--------------------------------------------*/


/*===============================================*/
int  remove( elem, a_bag, count )
   element    elem;   /* IN */
   bag        a_bag;  /* IN, OUT */
   int        count;  /* OUT */
/*---------------------------------------------
Remove() removes up to count copies of elem from a_bag; it
returns status "OK" or "illegal count" or "no such bag" or
"found fewer than count copies and removed them all."
--------------------------------------------*/


/*===============================================*/
int  get_next_element( elem, a_bag, first )
   element    *elem;  /* OUT */
   bag        a_bag;  /* IN */
   boolean    first;  /* IN */
/*---------------------------------------------
Get_next_element() copies the data from the "next" element of
a_bag into elem. If first is true, the data is that of the
"first" element, otherwise the data is that of the next
distinct element after the one whose data was returned by the
previous get_next_element() call. From the caller's point of
view, the "first" and "next" elements are chosen arbitrarily,
since bags have no geometry or element relations to provide
an order. However, every distinct element will have its data
returned exactly once by a sequence of get_next_element()
calls if first is true for the first call and false thereafter;
the last call in the sequence returns status "no more
elements." Get_next_element() returns status "OK" or "no more
elements."
--------------------------------------------*/
```

ABSTRACT DATA TYPE DESCRIPTION: TREE

Conceptual Model

Trees are hard to describe with words. For instance, we can define trees as acyclic connected directional graphs, but even that mouthful doesn't tell the whole story. Pictures, however, clear up most of the questions. Figure 21-5 shows two trees. Figure 21-6 shows some node configurations that are illegal in trees. Figure 21-7 shows two different ways to draw trees.

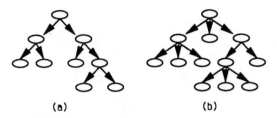

FIGURE 21-5: Some trees. Arrows run from each "parent" node to its "children," if any. The node at the top of each tree is the "root"; it has no parent. Nodes without children are known as "leaf" nodes. (a) shows a binary tree, that is, a tree that has at most two children per parent. (b) shows an N-ary tree, in which a parent may have more than two children.

Notice that Figures 21-5 and 21-7 contain no indications as to where nodes are inserted and removed from the tree. This is not because insertion and deletion positions are unimportant, but simply because the rules differ from tree to tree; this is discussed briefly in the next section.

Relatives

A *list* is a 1-ary tree, that is, a list is a tree in which each node has at most one child.

A *graph* is a tree in which one of the node configurations shown in Figure 21-6 appears, or in which the relation between nodes is "bidirectional" (imagine arrows on both ends of one of the lines in Figure 21-5).

There are many kinds of trees. A common classification is according to the maximum number of children any node can have; this leads to the distinction between *binary* and *N-ary trees*.

We can also classify trees according to the insertion and deletion algorithms used. This leads to *balanced trees* (among other things). "Balance" may mean different things for different trees. We might try to keep the "distance" (i.e., the number of intervening nodes)

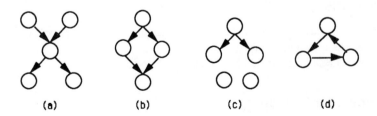

FIGURE 21-6: Some node configurations that are illegal in trees. (a) has two root nodes. (b) has a child with two parents (unlike humans, tree nodes have just one parent; the root node, of course, has no parent). (c) has unattached nodes; in a tree, every node can be reached from the root. (d) has a cycle.

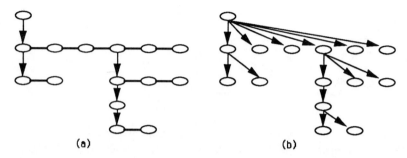

FIGURE 21-7: Two different ways to draw trees. (a) shows the relation "is the parent of" with arrows, and the relation "is a sibling of" with horizontal line segments. (b) shows a more common representation of the same tree using only the relation "is the parent of."

the same from the root to each leaf node. Or we might associate a "weight" with each node and try to make sure that subtrees that have the same number of nodes also have equal weights; a subtree's weight could be the sum or some other combination of the weights of its constituent nodes. Or we could try to make sure that all subtrees whose roots are siblings have equal weight.

A different approach to insertion algorithms leads to *sorted trees*. Sorting requires that some data value be associated with each node. The nodes are inserted so as to keep the values in order when the tree is traversed a particular way. Depth-first and breadth-first are the most popular traversal methods, but by no means the only ones.

There are also many other kinds of trees; see, for instance, the description of *ents* in Chapter 15, "Partitioning a Simulator's Event List." This description of trees is by no means exhaustive, even as a quick overview. Trees and related algorithms for balancing, sorting, and so forth are discussed throughout programming literature. A good place to start is Knuth (1973).

Geometry

Special Positions

1. *Root.* This is the only node that has no parent; there is only one root, and it's always there unless the tree is empty.
2. *Leaf.* Any node that has no children is a leaf node.

Relations Between Elements

1. *Is the parent of.* If node P is one position closer to the root than C, then P is the parent of C. This relation is:

   antireflexive—no node is the parent of itself

   antisymmetric—if P is the parent of C then C is not the parent of P

not transitive, *G* the parent of *P* and *P* the parent of *C* do not imply that *G* is the parent of C. However, the relation "is an ancestor of" is transitive.

The relation "is the parent of" is all we need to have a tree. However, binary or other trees in which the number of children present is important can sometimes benefit from an additional relation, "is a sibling of." The sibling relation is implied by the parental relation: Two nodes are siblings if they have the same parent. The sibling relation partitions the tree nodes since it is reflexive, symmetric, and transitive.

Operators

Two insertion operators are shown below because different trees might use either one or both. Deletion operators might also be needed; they're not shown because they are usually just inverses of the insertion operators. Depending on the tree, different "utility" operators are useful. *Traverse()* takes different forms, but it is almost always needed. Operators like *get_depth()*, *get_weight()*, and *get_child_count()*, on the other hand, are very problem-specific.

```
/*===========================================================*/
tree    make_tree()
/*----------------------------------------------
Makes a new tree that contains no nodes; returns valid tree
ID on success and null tree ID on failure.
-----------------------------------------------*/


/*===========================================================*/
int  insert_by_position(  a_tree,
                          new_node, parent, left_sibling )
   tree    a_tree;      /* IN */
   node    new_node;    /* IN */
   node    parent;      /* IN */
   node    left_sibling; /* IN */
/*----------------------------------------------
Insert_by_position() inserts new_node in a_tree, under parent
and to the right of left_sibling. If parent is NULL_NODE,
then new_node is inserted as a_tree's root. Likewise, if left_sibling is
NULL_NODE, new_node is inserted as parent's leftmost child. This
function returns status "no such tree," "out of memory," or "OK."
Compare this function with insert_by_algorithm().
-----------------------------------------------*/


/*===========================================================*/
int  insert_by_algorithm( a_tree, new_node )
   tree a_tree;        /* IN */
   node new_node;      /* IN */
/*----------------------------------------------
```

Insert_by_algorithm() inserts new_node in a_tree according to some algorithm hard-coded within this function. For instance, we might specify that traversing the tree depth-first and printing some string found in each node produces an alphabetized list. Or we might use an insertion algorithm that keeps the tree balanced by inserting nodes in a way that keeps the depth of sibling subtrees within one of each other. This function returns status "no such tree," "out of memory," or "OK." Compare this function with insert_by_position().
--*/

```
/*==============================================================*/
int      traverse( a_tree, at_each_node )
  tree        a_tree;           /* IN */
  function    at_each_node;     /* IN */
/*-----------------------------------------------
```
Traverse() visits the tree nodes in some order that is determined by traverse()'s code. At each node, the function at_each_node() is invoked; this function has the following calling sequence:

```
int at_each_node( this_node )
  node    this_node;  /* IN */
```

Common traversal methods are depth-first and breadth-first, but others are certainly possible. Traverse() returns status "no such tree" or "OK."
--*/

```
/*==============================================================*/
int      get_weight( subtree, weight )
  node      subtree; /* IN */
  int       *weight; /* OUT */
/*-----------------------------------------------
```
Get_weight() is used in balancing trees; it sets weight to the sum (for instance) of the nodes in the subtree whose root is subtree. Get_weight() returns status "OK."
--*/

```
/*==============================================================*/
int      get_depth( a_node, depth )
  node      a_node; /* IN */
  int       *depth; /* OUT */
/*-----------------------------------------------
```
Get_depth() is used in balancing trees; it sets depth to the distance between a_node and its tree's root. Get_depth() of the root of a tree is zero. Get_depth() returns "no such tree" or "OK" as status values.

```
-------------------------------------------*/

/*==============================================================*/
int     get_child_count ( a_node, count )
  node    a_node;  /* IN */
  int     *count;  /* OUT */
/*---------------------------------------------
Get_child_count() sets count to the number of children a_node
has; it returns status "OK."
-------------------------------------------*/
```

CHAPTER 22

A Collection of C Struct Design Guidelines

These guidelines come into play once we have set priorities for our top-level goals, written down an ADTD, and started coding typedefs. Struct design guidelines deal with functionality, while struct tricks deal with convenience or performance.

DESIGN GUIDELINE TEMPLATE

Key Words and Phrases

This is a brief list of the topics discussed in the design guideline.

Summary

This section summarizes the conclusions of the "Reasoning" section. Three kinds of advice are given:

Do <something>.
Don't do <something>.
Decide <something>, that is, make a conscious choice about particular issues instead of just accepting the first solution that comes to mind.

Reasoning

This section discusses examples that illustrate the conclusions given in the "Summary" section. If the conclusions hold only under particular circumstances, those circumstances are described here.

DESIGN GUIDELINE: WHEN TO ALLOCATE LISTS AND ARRAYS

Key Words and Phrases

The key words and phrases for this particular guideline are arrays, lists, compile-time, initialization-time, run-time, memory allocation, and dynamic allocation.

Summary

Memory allocation is possible at three times: compile-time, initialization-time, and run-time. Programs that use arrays or linked lists will run faster and be less complex if the memory for those structures is allocated at the earliest possible time.

If your program builds a large linked structure in memory and then stores it to disk for later retrieval, a hybrid of initialization and dynamic allocation can be useful.

Note that the design guideline "Avoid Sorted Lists of Arrays" (page 360) discusses a related question, namely when to use arrays and when to use lists and how best to combine them.

Reasoning

The earlier that allocation can be done, the faster and easier it is. Consider an example of each of the three possibilities for allocation.

1. *Compile-time allocation.* This works only for arrays whose size is known at compile-time. The space for such arrays is allocated by the compiler. To be precise, the space is allocated in the program's binary image, probably in a data section. The loader claims the memory from the system when the program is loaded into memory just before it begins executing.

Compile-time allocation requires zero cycles during program execution, so it's like an infinitely fast *malloc()*. There are no pointers to keep track of, so there's no chance of dangling pointers or crashes due to references through an uninitialized or NULL pointer. (Arrays can also be referenced incorrectly, but array indices are easier to keep track of than pointers.) This makes memory that is allocated at compile-time easier to manage than memory that is allocated at other times.

A typical compile-time allocation looks like this:

```
#define MAX_ENTRIES     256
int     my_array[MAX_ENTRIES];
```

2. *Initialization-time allocation.* This works for arrays whose size is unknown at compile-time but can be determined during program initialization. A typical allocation looks like this:

```
int     *my_array = NULL;

boolean init()
{
  ...
  entries_needed = (some calculation to figure out how big
      my_array must be; for instance, my_array's
      size might depend on command line parameters
      or on the first few lines of an input file);
  if (!(my_array = (int *)malloc(entries_needed*sizeof(int)))) {
    printf("Out of memory\n");
    return (false);
  }
  for (i = 0; i < entries_needed; i++) {
    my_array[i] = (an appropriate initial value);
  }
  ...
} /* init */
```

Allocation during program initialization is slower than compile-time allocation because *malloc()* or a similar function must be called. But it is still faster than run-time allocation because we only have to call *malloc()* once. What's more, we might not call *free()* at all—we could let deallocation be done by the operating system when the program exits. Dynamic allocation, by contrast, requires many calls on *malloc()* and *free()* while the program is running.

3. *Run-time or Dynamic allocation.* This works for lists, trees, and other linked structures. Some people use the term "dynamic" for initialization-time allocation as well as run-time allocation, but there are differences. Run-time allocation involves many calls on *malloc()* and *free()*, and it occurs during the heart of the program's calculations. Initialization-time allocation typically involves one *malloc()* call, no *free()* calls, and it occurs before the program has begun its main calculations.

Because many calls on *malloc()* (or a similar function) and *free()* are needed, this is the slowest of the three allocation possibilities. Run-time allocation is also more difficult to manage, because there are more discrete pieces of memory involved, and they are linked by many pointers that can cause all sorts of problems (see Chapter 9, "Protecting a Database During Editing"). However, dynamic allocation is also the most flexible of the three possibilities, and in many cases nothing else will do.

Examples of dynamic allocation can be seen throughout the book; look at Chapter 15, "Partitioning a Simulator's Event List," for instance.

Flexible and Fast Allocation

There is a hybrid of dynamic and initialization-time allocation that deserves mention: loading a block image of contiguous but dynamically linked structures and then resolving their links. This is useful in programs that build databases or other large collections of linked structures dynamically in memory, and then store them to disk for later retrieval back into memory. This hybrid approach provides the flexibility of conventional dynamic allocation and some of the speed of an initialization-time allocation.

The hybrid works as follows. We set MAXSIZE bytes, say, as an upper limit on the size of the database. Then we use *malloc()* or our other regular allocation function to get a contiguous block of memory MAXSIZE bytes long. Our program then allocates the database structs dynamically from this contiguous block using a special function we'll call *my_malloc()*. *My_malloc()* gets memory only from the block of MAXSIZE bytes; when that memory is used up, the program is stuck. It cannot go around *my_malloc()* to get additional memory from the system.

Thus, we have the flexibility to build the database dynamically, but the resulting structs are not spread all over memory. They are all in one big block MAXSIZE bytes long. We can store the database to disk using a single *fwrite()* and load it back into memory with a single *fread()*, so I/O is speeded up.

To load the database back into memory correctly, three steps are required. First, we make one call to *malloc()* for MAXSIZE bytes (instead of one call for each struct in the database, a significant time savings). Then we call *fread()* to read the entire database off disk

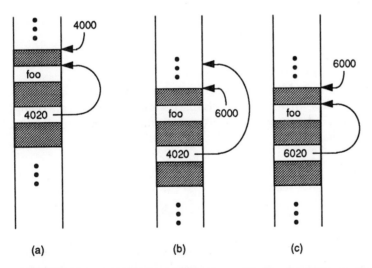

(a)   (b)   (c)

FIGURE 22-1:   (a) shows a database (grey-filled rectangle) in memory right after creation. The database is ready to be stored on disk. (b) shows the same database just after it has been read from disk, before its pointers are resolved. (c) shows the database after the pointers have been resolved.

into the block of MAXSIZE bytes. Finally, we run through the database and resolve the addresses. That is, we make them point where they are supposed to point. All the database structs are still in the same position relative to each other that they were in just after the database was created. So we need to know only three things to resolve all the pointers. We need to know the original starting address of the block, its current starting address, and which values in the database are pointers.

Then all we do is add the difference between the two block starting addresses to each address in the newly loaded database. After this, the database is indistinguishable from one built in memory, as far as database integrity is concerned. This process is illustrated in Figure 22-1. The difference, of course, is that doing one *fread()* and some address resolutions is much faster than allocating all those structs individually. We don't save any time while building the database, but we do save many CPU cycles each time we load the database back into memory.

DESIGN GUIDELINE: AVOID SORTED LISTS OF ARRAYS

Key Words and Phrases

The key words and phrases for this particular guideline are linked list, sorted list, ordered list, array, and hashed list.

Summary

You should not use sorted linked lists of arrays. In other words, avoid structs like the *array_list* shown below. In this example, *flurble* is some data type we are trying to maintain in an ordered list, and the array size doesn't matter much for the discussion that follows, as long as it's bigger than one:

```
typedef struct array_list {
   flurble            data[512];
   struct array_list   *next;
} array_list;
```

Use an array of *flurbles* if you know pretty well how many list elements to expect; otherwise, use a linked list of *flurbles*. Use a classic linked list if hashing *flurbles* is too difficult or if the list is short. Use a hashed array of linked lists if the search time for a single linked list is too great and hashing is feasible.

Reasoning

Suppose there is a data type flurble, and we need to build and maintain a sorted list of *flurble* values. There are two classic data structures we might use: a linked list or an array. Considering combinations of these two leads to four possible data structures:

1. a classic linked list (singly or doubly linked makes little difference for this discussion)
2. an array
3. a linked list of arrays
4. an array of linked lists

Let's consider each structure in turn.

Classic Linked List

Our typedef looks like this:

```
typedef struct element_list {
  struct element_list *next;
  flurble             data;
} element_list;  /* singly linked */
```

or maybe like this:

```
typedef struct element_list {
struct element_list   *next,
                      *prev;
    flurble           data;
} element_list;  /* doubly linked */
```

Here we'll assume a singly linked list; the situation with a doubly linked list is very similar. To get at a particular *flurble* value or to run through the list, we need only one access method—chase the *next* pointer.

Inserting a new *flurble* in order is straightforward. We run through the list to find the appropriate insertion point, allocate a new *element_list* struct, copy the *flurble* value, and fix the pointers. Deleting an element is also straightforward. We fix one or two pointers and free the unlucky element's memory.

There is no wasted data space. That is, memory is allocated to hold a *flurble* value only when we have a new value that needs storage. But there is a heavy order-maintenance overhead per data element. In other words, the ratio of memory words used to keep the list in order to *flurble* values in the list is 1:1.

The list elements are small, so there's no reason to optimize individual elements out for space unless there are many duplicated values. In that case we could still use a linked list, with an added field:

```
typedef struct element_list {
   struct element_list   *next;
   flurble               data;
   int                   count;
} element_list;
```

Each element contains just one *flurble* value, so there's no reason to spend time copying values from one list element to another.

Finally, there is no compile-time limit on the amount of data.

Array

We don't need a typedef; we just declare the array:

```
flurble  data[10000];
```

We only need to worry about one access method—array indexing.

Insertion in order can be a real pain, because we will sometimes need to "slide" values toward the end of the array to make room for a new value in the middle. This is further complicated by the fact that sliding values toward the array's end can push the current end values right out of the array. We can cut down on all this sliding about by initializing the array to some special *null_flurble* constant value and filling it sparsely whenever possible. But if we have to keep the elements in order, we can never eliminate entirely the need to copy elements to new positions.

Deletion from an array is straightforward, unless we want to compact elements afterward. Since we might wish we hadn't compacted them when we try the next insertion, we'll say that deletion just consists of overwriting the *flurble* value with *null_flurble*.

There is potentially a lot of wasted data space. This is because of the hard compile-time limit on the amount of data the array can hold. In fact, use of the array is really appropriate only if

1. We know ahead of time that the number of list elements NumVals satisfies MinVals <= NumVals <= MaxVals, where MinVals and MaxVals are fixed at compile-time.
2. MinVals is close to MaxVals.
3. A classic linked list is inappropriate because the pointers take too much space, or the search time (time spent chasing list *next* pointers) is too great, or the run-time allocation of linked list elements one by one takes too much time.

There is potentially zero order-maintenance overhead per data element in an array. There is no memory allocated for pointers to maintain the list in order. The only memory we must consider as overhead is the array locations we never needed because we declared the array larger than necessary.

The list elements in an array are as small as they can be without data compression, because no pointers are used.

Unfortunately, we do need to copy *flurble* values from one position to another at times to make space for a new value.

Linked List of Arrays

Our typedef is a mixture of arrays and the linked list above:

```
typedef struct array_list {
   struct array_list    *next;
   flurble               data[512];
} array_list;
```

Let's summarize the advantages and disadvantages of a classic linked list and a simple array. The linked list puts no load- or initialization-time limit on the number of list elements and makes insertion easy, but it requires a lot of memory for pointers to keep the list in order and requires allocation time whenever we add a new value. The array imposes a limit on the number of list elements when it is allocated at compile-time or during program initialization. Arrays make insertion expensive, but they require no memory for pointers to keep the list in order and few or no CPU cycles for run-time allocation.

At first glance, a linked list of arrays seems to have the best of both solutions. There's no compile-time limit on the number of list elements because *array_list* structs are allocated at run-time. We do need pointers, but they are few in number relative to the number of list elements; one pointer per 512 elements in the example. We spend some cycles allocating memory at run-time, but we grab space for many *flurble* values at once, so we're much more efficient in this respect than a classic linked list. Unfortunately, the good news ends here.

Running through a list of *flurbles* that's stored in *array_list* structs is complicated by the fact that we have two access methods: chasing pointers and array indexing. This is potentially confusing since we might be using pointers to access the *array_list.data[]* elements as well as the *array_list* structs. But two access methods are manageable if all we need to do is run through the list.

However, new *flurble* values are inserted in arrays, so we have the same old problem of sliding array values around to make room. The problem is not as bad as it could be if all the values were in one huge array instead of distributed in *array_list* structs, but it is still there.

There are also few prospects for efficient deletion of values. We have to choose between two unpleasant possibilities. When an *array_list* struct contains only a few valid *flurble* values, we can accept the fact that the rest of the data space is wasted. This leaves us facing the prospect of a long list of big arrays, with maybe one or two valid *flurble* values sitting alone in each array. Or we can spend time checking neighboring *array_list* structs for unused data space and copying in those few good values so we can empty and free the near-empty *array_list* struct.

In summary, using a linked list of arrays does provide some of the advantages of both linked lists and arrays. But this scheme also has most of the disadvantages of lists and arrays. The main difference is that we get a much wider choice of inefficiencies without changing the typedef! Using a linked list of arrays is not recommended, for the following reasons:

A linked list of arrays does not provide any real advantage over either a classic linked list or a simple array, since it has the main disadvantages of both and no distinct advantages.

A linked list of arrays is much more complicated than the other alternatives.

You can almost always use an array of linked lists instead (this alternative is discussed below).

Array of Linked Lists

Our typedef looks like this:

```
#define HASH_TABLE_SIZE        101 /* prime numbers work best */
typedef struct element_list {
  struct element_list *next;
  flurble              data;
} element_list;  /* singly linked */

typedef struct {
  struct element_list *next;
  int                  count;
} element_list_head;


element_list_head     data[HASH_TABLE_SIZE];
```

For this approach to work, we must have a good hash function. The idea is to separate what would otherwise be one long list into HASH_TABLE_SIZE different linked lists of roughly equal size. The separation is based on the hash function. The hash function takes a particular *element_list*'s *flurble* contents and returns a value i from 0 to HASH_TABLE_SIZE-1. I is used as an index—the *element_list* is sorted into the list pointed to by *data[i].next*.

Devising good hash functions takes practice, but most look something like this:

```
int      hash( f )
  flurble *f;
{
  int      tmp;

  tmp = <some combination of f's member's values>
  return (tmp % HASH_TABLE_SIZE);
} /* hash */
```

Making HASH_TABLE_SIZE a prime number is critical when this "modulo" kind of hash is used. Otherwise, *data[i]* tends to be empty when i is a multiple of a factor of HASH_TABLE_SIZE.

So what are the advantages and disadvantages of an array of lists in comparison with the other three possibilities? Insertion and deletion are almost as easy as with a classic linked list, although the order-maintenance overhead is slightly higher. The biggest disadvantage is the need to find a good hash function. This is usually possible, but tuning the hash function can take a lot of effort.

An array is still the best answer if we know how many values to expect, or if there's no space for pointers, or no time to allocate list elements one by one. But if we were considering an array because the time to chase linked list pointers was too great, then an array of smaller linked lists is worth looking at.

DESIGN GUIDELINE: CONSIDER COPYING DATA TO A BETTER FORMAT

Key Words and Phrases

The key words and phrases for this particular guideline are data format, speedy execution, alternate data representations, copying data, categories of data operations, and data operations occurring in phases.

Summary

There is a tradeoff between the effort required to put data in a convenient form for upcoming operations and the effort saved by doing so. A common practice is to leave data in the same kind of struct for the duration of a program. But sometimes the kind of operations performed on the data come in phases. In this case it may be more efficient to copy the data piece by piece to different structs at the beginning of a new phase, putting the data in a form that is better suited to the upcoming operations.

Reasoning

Typical operations on data fall into general categories like these:

gathering and/or loading
various kinds of processing
- traversing existing elements (chasing pointers)
- reading or writing element data fields (no pointers changed)
- inserting elements
- deleting elements
- storing

Other divisions are certainly possible, since there are roughly as many things you can do to data as there are bits in the universe. The point is not that you should think of data operations in precisely these categories. Rather, the point is that you can divide the operations in your program into some set of categories to determine if data operations come in phases. If operations do come in phases, it may be worthwhile to copy the data to a better format before each phase.

For instance, suppose a set of data passes through two distinct steps: "Fetch 'n Sort" and "Tell Me." During the Fetch 'n Sort phase, the data is read from its source and sorted somehow. During the Tell Me phase, the data is read but never written. The ordering established by the Fetch 'n Sort phase is not changed during the Tell Me phase.

A "flexible" organization is best during the Fetch 'n Sort phase because it makes the sorting easier, and we might not know at compile-time how much data to expect. "Flexible" organizations are dynamically allocated, with the data scattered through memory in many pieces that point to each other. For instance, linked lists and trees are flexible.

We could leave the data in a flexible structure during the Tell Me phase. But it might be more efficient to copy the data to a "rigid" structure in order to speed up Tell Me phase reads. Rigid structures are compact, with few or no pointers. They are allocated at program load-time, or in one big chunk at initialization- run-time. Arrays are rigid.

For instance, suppose we read in and sort a list of employee records to build a linked list. Once all the data is organized in memory, we can dynamically allocate one big array of employee records, copy the data into it, and free the list memory. If we need to read the data frequently after this, the copy is worth the effort because we eliminated many pointers. Access to the data will be faster because we don't need to chase pointers. Also, the memory previously occupied by pointers will be free for other uses.

Whether or not copying the data is actually worth the trouble depends on several things. Of course, we could just implement both solutions and see which one runs faster. Short of that, we can make a pretty good guess as to which route is better by considering the answers to the following questions:

1. How expensive is the copy from the flexible Fetch 'n Sort structure to the rigid Tell Me structure?
2. How limited is memory? The Tell Me structure doesn't need pointers, so it can be smaller. Also, the dynamic Fetch 'n Sort structure may involve entire tree or graph nodes that are used only for sorting and thus don't appear at all in the Tell Me structure. Eliminating these nodes can save memory and cut down access times. Finally, there might not be enough memory to hold both the flexible linked structure and the rigid Tell Me structure, so copying is too slow (because of virtual memory page faults) or impossible (because there's just not enough memory, virtual or physical).
3. How long does it take to dynamically allocate a chunk of memory? The allocation time for the Tell Me struct is probably negligible since it occurs either during program loading or just once at run-time. The flexible Fetch 'n Sort structure, on the other hand, requires many separate allocations.
4. Will we be debugging by dumping memory? The rigid Tell Me structure is more contiguous, so memory dumps are simpler.
5. Do we expect any trouble from using bad pointers or overrunning arrays? The Tell

Me data is not scattered all over memory, so bugs caused when the data is accidentally overwritten are less likely and much easier to track down.

6. One structure may be faster to search than the other. For instance, compare the code generated on your system by

```
for(i = MAX-1; i >= 0; i-)
  zap = data[i].foo;  /* static Tell Me array */
```

with the code generated by

```
for(ptr = data; ptr; ptr = ptr->next)
  zap = ptr->foo;  /* dynamic Fetch 'n Sort list */
```

where we have these declarations:

```
typedef struct test {
  struct test *next;
  int         foo;
} test;
#define MAX    10
static test    data[MAX], *ptr;
```

To make a fair comparison between accessing arrays and chasing pointers, we should use the fastest possible form of each. So the array loop above is written to run backwards because "i– – down to zero" is typically compiled into code that runs faster than the corresponding translation of "i++ up to some limit". This is true when the *i*– – translates into a single decrement-and-skip-on-zero instruction, while the *i*++ translates into an increment followed by a subtraction to do the comparison with the loop's upper limit. Similarly, the *next* pointer is at offset zero into the *test* struct because that typically makes chasing pointers faster.

DESIGN GUIDELINE: REPRESENTING ASCII DATA IN MEMORY

Key Words and Phrases

The key words and phrases for this particular guideline are ASCII data, tables, parsing, tokens, and programming languages.

Summary

If your program reads an ASCII file that contains commands, and there is any chance the commands will change, then think of your program as a language interpreter and act accordingly. Keep a copy of the ASCII commands around for error messages and debugging, but translate the commands and their parameters into tokens for parsing internally.

Reasoning

We can divide program input into ASCII files and everything else. We can further divide ASCII files according to their contents. Some files contain nothing but "pure" data; others contain commands.

For instance, an ASCII file containing nothing but numeric data in some rigid format holds pure data. The program reading the data can simply convert the file's contents to binary as it reads them. Except for flagging illegal values, the program makes the same calculations each time, no matter what the actual data values are. No lexical analysis is needed beyond that provided by *fscanf()*.

Other files, however, contain a sequence of commands as well as some pure data. The easiest way to tell pure data from commands is that different commands cause different parts of the program to execute. Pure data, by contrast, is always put through the same calculation, irrespective of its value. Another test is whether or not you view the data as a program. For instance, if you need some way to put comments in the input so you can explain what certain data values will do, then each of the values you're explaining is a command, not pure data.

Flexibility in any program's input tends to increase as time passes and the program is used more. But change is particularly likely in programs that are already flexible enough to accept commands instead of simply reading in streams of data. It is not a question of whether such a program will change or not. It's a question of how hard it will be to make the changes.

Even if the input command possibilities are extremely simple when viewed as a programming language, it might be worthwhile to treat the input as a language, because it's much easier for a language to grow if you've built in the supporting machinery. This machinery includes lexical analysis, tokens, expression evaluation, flow control, and a division of labor according to a parsing model. That is, there's a switch somewhere based on which language statement is being interpreted. Above all, a language needs an underlying grammar and a carefully designed semantic framework.

Code that processes pure data tends to be organized like this:

```
/* "Pure data" organization: */
fscanf() calls to read entire file of input data;
computations based on input data;
fprintf() calls to output computation results;
```

An interpreter, by contrast, has lexical analysis and parsing stages, so it can deal with a wide variety of input data types and with commands and their parameters:

```
/* "Interpreter" organization: */
until end-of-file or fatal error {
   read an ASCII line containing a command and its parameters;
```

```
do lexical analysis to convert ASCII input into tokens;
switch (first token—it determines command to execute) {
   case COMMAND_1:
      do computations based on COMMAND_1 and its parameters;
      output computation results;
      break;
   case COMMAND_2:
      do computations based on COMMAND_2 and its parameters;
      output computation results;
      break;
   case COMMAND_3:
      do computations based on COMMAND_3 and its parameters;
      output computation results;
      break;
   default:
      printf("unknown command: %s", input seen);
   }
}
```

Changing an established program from the pure data organization to the interpreter organization, or even worse, trying to gain the power and flexibility of the interpreter organization while using a pure data organization is even harder than reaching the end of this sentence. Trust me. If you think your program's input might need the flexibility of a language at some point, structure your program up front as an interpreter.

DESIGN GUIDELINE: RETURNING A SUBLIST

Key Words and Phrases

The keywords and phrases for this particular guideline are linked list, sublist, functions that return a variable number of values, execution time versus memory space, and computation of results versus aggregation of results.

Summary

There are basically two ways for a function to return a variable number of result values:

1. *Successive Computation.* Use a pair of functions—*first()* returns the first value and *next()* returns the rest of the values, one at a time, until *next()* returns NULL or a similar "termination" value.
2. *Aggregation.* Build a list or array of values and return a pointer to it.

Aggregation has several variations, which are discussed below.
Which method or variation is best depends on the following factors:

whether (a) user selections or (b) strictly internal calculations determine the results to be returned

whether (a) the return values are already in memory somewhere and just need to be identified, or (b) new memory must be allocated to hold the results

the amount of memory required by (a) a typical array of return values versus (b) the amount required by adding more pointers or flags to some larger list or array of values already in memory

Reasoning

Figure 22-2 summarizes five ways for functions to return multiple values. We'll discuss them one by one, pointing out their relative pros and cons, and showing how they relate to the factors mentioned in the summary above.

Figure 22-2(a) shows pseudocode examples of the simplest way to return multiple values—make multiple function calls. This is the "successive computation" method mentioned in the Summary; the name refers to the fact that the values returned are computed one at a time. The other four examples in Figure 22-2 illustrate "aggregation" methods—all the values are gathered somehow and then returned with a single function call.

In the pseudocode on the left of Figure 22-2(a), two functions are used. *First_res()* does any necessary initialization and then returns the first value needed. Successive calls to *next_res()* are then used to get the rest of the values. These functions typically update some static variable to keep track of which value to return next. For instance, they might look something like this:

```
static result_struct    *next_result = NULL;
extern result_struct     *possible_results;

result_struct    *first_res()
{
   for ( next_result = possible_results;
         next_result;
         next_result = next_result->next) {
   if (next_result points to a struct we want to return)
        return (next_result);
   }
   return (NULL);
} /* first_res */

result_struct    *next_res()
{
   for (  ; /* pick up where we left off last time */
         next_result;
         next_result = next_result->next) {
   if (next_result points to a struct we want to return)
        return (next_result);
```

```
res = first_res();              res = get_res(NULL);
while (res != NULL) {           while (res != NULL) {
    /* use res, then: */            /* use res, then: */
    res = next_res();               res = get_res(res);
}                               }
```

(a)

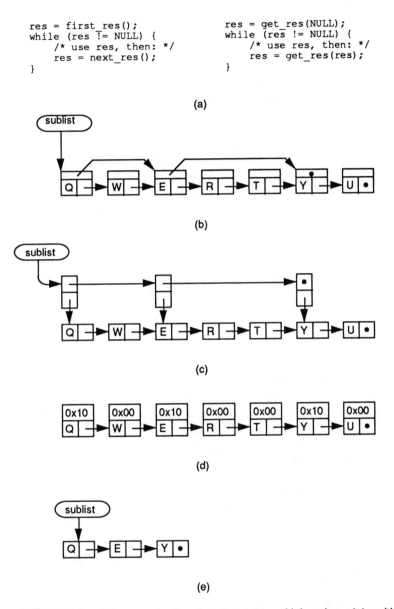

(b)

(c)

(d)

(e)

FIGURE 22-2:   Five ways for functions to return multiple values: (a) multiple function calls; (b) building a sublist of an existing list; (c) building a list of pointers into an existing list; (d) setting flags in an existing list; (e) returning a pointer to a newly created list.

```
    }
    return (NULL);
} /* next_res */
```

The code on the right side of Figure 22-2(a) does essentially the same thing, but the user keeps track of which value was returned last, and *get_res()* uses that parameter to determine what value to return next:

```
result_struct    *get_res( prev )
   result_struct    *prev;  /* IN */
{
   result_struct    *tmp;

   if (!prev) /* start at beginning of list */
     tmp = possible_results;
   else
     tmp = prev;
   for (   ; tmp; tmp = tmp->next) {
     if (tmp points to a struct we want to return)
       return (tmp);
   }
   return (NULL);
} /* get_res */
```

Notice that *get_res()* is vulnerable to mistakes it didn't make; it will fail badly if the wrong value of *prev* is passed in. This is not as great a concern with *first_res()* and *next_res()*, because their state information is tucked safely away in the static variable *next_result*.

In either case, Figure 22-2(a) assumes values are returned one by one. Each return value is used and then discarded before the next value is needed. This is often the case, for instance, when some strictly internal calculations determine the return values. By contrast, aggregates are more likely when user selections are made, or when a particular return value can't be used and discarded because we might need to refer back to it later. The method of Figure 22-2(a) is not useful when we need access to all the return values at once. In that case, one of the aggregating methods shown in the rest of Figure 22-2 would be a better choice.

Figure 22-2(b) shows a sublist of an existing list. In this case, the values we need to return are already in memory; all we need to do is identify them somehow. Let *aggregate()* be the function that returns an aggregate of results. Then *aggregate()* sets up the sublist pointers, and returns a pointer to the first element of the sublist.

In Figure 22-2(b), the sublist pointers are shown above the main list pointers; the sublist contains elements "Q," "E," and "Y." Notice that the sublist skips over elements that were not selected. We need an additional pointer in each element to create the sublist. But if the list elements are large structs, the extra memory for these pointers might easily amount to less than the memory needed to hold new copies of the data (the approach shown in Figure 22-2(e)).

If, on the other hand, sublists tend to be small, so that most of the extra pointers in Figure 22-2(b) are unused most of the time, we might be better off building a list of pointers into the existing list. This approach is shown in Figure 22-2(c). The *aggregate()* function builds a list of pointers and returns a pointer to this list. Once again, the sublist returned contains "Q," "E," and "Y."

One disadvantage of this approach is that we need some way to clean up the list of pointers *aggregate()* allocated. Unlike the method of Figure 22-2(b), Figure 22-2(c) requires a list disposal routine that is separate from the one that we presumably need to have anyway for the "Q," "W," "E," "R," "T," "Y," "U" list.

We could also use a bitflag to indicate selected list elements, as shown in Figure 22-2(d). That is, *aggregate()* runs down the list setting and clearing the correct bit; multiple values are "returned" by virtue of having their "selected" flag set. Thus, elements "Q," "E," and "Y" have their "selected" flag set in the illustration. This takes only one bit per element, if the list elements already contained a set of flags in which one bit was unused. If not, adding a bitflag int to each list element might require much more memory than the method shown in Figure 22-2(e). Notice also that we must now traverse unselected list elements in order to reach selected ones; this was not the case with the methods in Figures 22-2(b) and (c).

Figures 22-2(b), (c), and (d) assumed that the values to return already existed somewhere in memory. Figure 22-2(e) shows a method we can use when the values *aggregate()* returns are not already in memory. *Aggregate()* builds a list of values and returns a pointer to the list. Since we're building the list, rather than identifying elements in an existing list, we allocate memory only for the values being returned. As with Figure 22-2(c), we'll need a corresponding disposal routine to eventually free the memory allocated by *aggregate()*.

In summary, use Figure 22-2(a) when values can be returned, used, and forgotten one by one. Otherwise, use one of the other four methods to return an aggregate of values all at once. Use Figures 22-2(b), (c), or (d) when the values to be returned already exist in memory and simply need to be identified; otherwise, build a new list of values, as shown in Figure 22-2(e). Use Figure 22-2(d) when the existing list's elements already contain bitflags and traversing unselected elements isn't too painful. Use Figure 22-2(b) when the existing list's elements are large, so one more pointer is not significant overhead; otherwise, use Figure 22-2(c).

One final note. Figure 22-2 shows linked lists, but the same reasoning works pretty well for arrays. In fact, returning an array of values that don't already appear in memory is more efficient than returning a list like the one shown in Figure 22-2(e). The choice, of course, depends on what is to be done with the returned values—do we need to add the returned elements to an existing linked list, or can we just keep them in an array?

DESIGN GUIDELINE: IMPLEMENTING SETS

Key Words and Phrases

The keywords and phrases for this particular guideline are sets, bitsets, bitflags, linked lists, bags, compile-time allocation, initialization-time allocation, and dynamic allocation.

Summary

There are basically five ways to implement sets:

1. as a linked list of structs that are allocated dynamically
2. as an array of structs allocated at compile-time
3. as an array of structs allocated at initialization-time
4. as an array of bitflags allocated at compile-time
5. as an array of bitflags allocated at initialization-time

For a discussion of compile-time versus initialization-time allocation, see the design guideline "When to Allocate Lists and Arrays" (page 357).

Which implementation is best depends on a number of factors. The most important factors are

the type of data stored in the set's elements
when (if ever) an upper bound on the number of elements is known

Reasoning

Figure 22-3 summarizes five ways to implement sets. These implementations can be categorized in different ways. For instance, Figures 22-3(a), (b), and (c) are all based on structs, while (d) and (e) are based on bits. This difference corresponds to the type of elements the set will contain. Sets whose elements each contain multiple values cannot easily be implemented using the bit arrays shown in Figures 22-3(d) and (e). Instead, we use one of the collections of structs shown in Figures 22-3(a), (b), or (c).

By contrast, sets that contain integers or other enumerations can be represented efficiently by bit arrays. This includes sets of characters, for instance, or sets containing other values that map easily to a finite closely packed range of integers. The element (corresponding to) N is in the set if and only if the Nth bit in the array is 1. Any bits that are 0 correspond to elements that are not presently in the set, but could be.

The implementations shown in Figure 22-3 can also be categorized according to their time of allocation. Memory for the sets in Figures 22-3(b) and (d) is allocated at compile-time. This implies that an upper limit on the number of set elements is known at compile-time. If, however, there is never a limit on the number of elements, then memory must be allocated whenever a new member is added to the set. This case is illustrated in Figure 22-3(a).

Sometimes the number of elements is limited, but the upper bound can be determined only after the program begins running. The limit might be a command-line parameter, for instance, or it might depend on the contents of a data file. Or it might be input by the user interactively. Implementations to support these cases are suggested by Figures 22-3(c) and (e). The basic idea is to allocate an array (of structs or bits, as appropriate) to hold the largest possible set once the limit is known. In Figure 22-3(a), by contrast, memory is allocated separately for each set element, so there is no upper limit on set size except the amount of memory available on the system.

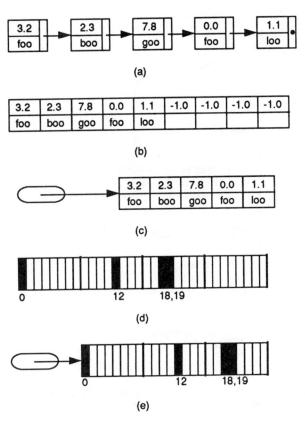

FIGURE 22-3: Five ways to implement sets: (a) linked list of structs; (b) array of structs allocated at compile-time; (c) array of structs allocated at initialization-time; (d) array of bits allocated at compile-time; (e) array of bits allocated at initialization-time.

Figure 22-4 shows how to use these different categorizations to choose between the implementations illustrated in Figure 22-3.

Now that we know from Figure 22-4 how to choose between the implementations, we'll take a brief look at each of them.

Figure 22-3(a) shows a linked list of structs. This implementation is necessary when we need to begin adding elements to a set before we have an upper bound on the number of elements. Since structures are used, set elements can contain more than one value each— we could implement a set of employee records, or legal citations, or graphics windows, for instance.

Of course, we could also implement a set of integers this way, but if we know a bound on the set's size, the implementations shown in Figures 22-3(d) and (e) are much more efficient for most integer sets. The exception is integer sets in which the values span a large range. If the legal values are between zero and one million, for instance, and sets tend to

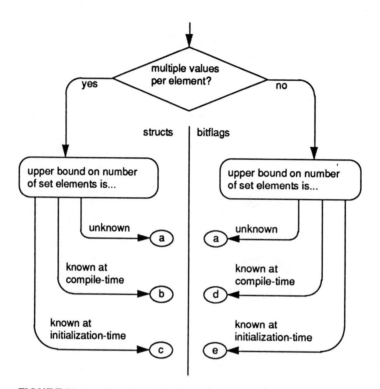

FIGURE 22-4: How to use the kind of data elements in the set, and the point at which an upper bound on the number of set elements becomes known to choose between the implementations illustrated in Figure 22-3.

contain only a few hundred elements, Figure 22-3(a)'s implementation probably requires less memory than the representations in Figures 22-3(d) and (e).

Incidentally, the implementation in Figure 22-3(a) can be used to represent bags as well as sets. A bag is a set that allows duplicate elements; see the bag ADTD on page 347. {1,1,2,3} and {1,2,3} are identical sets, but different bags. Perhaps the easiest definition is that sets are bags that can only count to one. We could implement bags by allowing duplicate structs to be added to the list. Or we could place a counter in each struct in the list.

Figures 22-3(b) and (c) show arrays of structs. These implementations are appropriate when

> set elements contain multiple values, so we can't use the schemes in Figures 22-3(d) or (e)
>
> the number of set elements is bounded before we begin putting elements into the set, so we don't have to use the implementation shown in Figure 22-3(a)

Since the implementations shown in Figures 22-3(b) and (c) use structs, they could also represent bags as well as sets.

If set elements are integers that lie in a relatively small range, the implementations shown in Figures 22-3(d) and (e) require less memory than the other possibilities. The small range requirement means that we know how big the largest possible set is before we add any elements; we allocate one bit for each integer in the range. The range must be small if sets tend to have few elements, or many of the bits will be wasted space, and we're better off with Figure 22-3(a).

Figures 22-3(d) and (e) can also be used for sets of characters and other enumerations that map easily to a small range of integers. These implementations cannot be used to represent bags, because there is only one bit per potential element. There is no way to know how many times a given bit has been turned on, that is, how many times a given value has been added to the set.

A working C library and testbed that implement the approach suggested in Figure 22-3(e) follow this design guideline.

LISTING: bitsets.h

```
/*---------------------------------------------
                  bitsets.h
---------------------------------------------*/

/*=============================================================
Purpose:
    This file supports the bs_xxx library of bitset functions.
-------------------------------------------------------------*/
#ifndef  _BITSETS_H_
#define  _BITSETS_H_

#include <boolean.h> /* for convenience */

/* a bitset is a pointer to an array of chars, with each char used
   as 8 bitflags: */
typedef char    *bs_type;

/* this would be a static in bitsets.c, but the macros below need it: */
#ifdef  _BITSETS_GLOBALS_
int         bs_bits_per_set = 0;
#else
extern int  bs_bits_per_set;
#endif  _BITSETS_GLOBALS_

/* some bit operations that could be reimplemented as functions
   instead of macros if better error-handling becomes more
   important than speed: */
```

```
/* as a function, would be: boolean bs_member(n, set) */
#define bs_member(n, set) \
            ((((n) < bs_bits_per_set) && ((n) >= 0) && set) ? \
            ((1 << ((n) % 8)) & (set)[(n)/8]) : \
            (printf("\nbad bs_member parameter\n") & false) )


/* as a function, would be: void bs_insert(n, set) */
#define bs_insert(n, set) \
            if (((n) < bs_bits_per_set) && ((n) >= 0) && set) \
            (set)[(n)/8] |= (1 << ((n) % 8)); \
        else \
            printf("\nbad bs_insert parameter\n")


/* as a function, would be: void bs_delete(n, set) */
#define bs_delete(n, set) \
            if (((n) < bs_bits_per_set) && ((n) >= 0) && set) \
            (set)[(n)/8] &= ~(1 << ((n) % 8)); \
        else \
            printf("\nbad bs_delete parameter\n")


#endif   _BITSETS_H_
```

LISTING: bitsets.c

```
/*--------------------------------------------
                    bitsets.c
-----------------------------------------------*/


/*============================================================
Purpose:
    This file supplies functions to do the following (macros are
    in bitsets.h):


        initialize the bitset library (call first!):   bs_inited()
        create a new empty bitset:                     bs_new()
        clear a bitset (set it to {}):                 bs_clear()
        MACRO to insert integer in a bitset:           bs_insert()
        MACRO to delete integer from a bitset:         bs_delete()
        MACRO to test for membership in a bitset:      bs_member()
        remove one set from another:                   bs_remove()
        test to see if one set is a subset of another: bs_subset()
        test to see if two sets have the same members: bs_equal()
        make a set the union of itself and another set: bs_union()
        read a set's elements interactively:           bs_read()
        print the current members of a set:            bs_print()
```

Error checking is minimal.

Bitsets are discussed in the design guideline "Implementing Sets."

This code was compiled under THINK's LightspeedC® on a Macintosh™ SE.

```
------------------------------------------*/
#include <stdio.h>
#define _BITSETS_GLOBALS_
#include "bitsets.h"

static int  bs_bytes_per_set = 0;

#define _BITSETS_TESTBED_
#ifdef  _BITSETS_TESTBED_
/*==============================================================*/
main()
/*-------------------------------------------
Purpose:
    Exercise the bitset library.
Parameters:
    none
------------------------------------------*/
{
    bs_type set_A, set_B, bs_new();
    char    ch, toss, AorB();
    int     n, size;
    boolean george, bs_inited(), bs_equal(), bs_subset();
    void    bs_clear(), bs_print(), bs_read(), bs_remove(),
            bs_union();

    printf("\nBitset library testbed:\n");
    printf("\tupper limit of number of elements per set> ");
    scanf("%d", &size);
    toss = getc(stdin); /* toss away carriage return */
    if (!bs_inited(size)) {
        printf("initialization failed\n");
        return;
    }
    else {
        printf("legal set elements are 0..%d\n", size-1);
    }
    if (!(set_A = bs_new())) {
        printf("create set A failed\n");
        return;
    }
```

```
if (!(set_B = bs_new())) {
    printf("create set B failed\n");
    return;
}
for ( ; ; ) {
    printf("\t(c)lear a set\n");
    printf("\t(d)elete integer from a set\n");
    printf("\t(e)quality test between sets A and B\n");
    printf("\t(i)nsert integer in a set\n");
    printf("\t(p)rint sets A and B\n");
    printf("\t(q)uit\n");
    printf("\t(R)ead a set's elements interactively\n");
    printf("\t(r)emove one set from the other\n");
    printf("\t(s)ubset test\n");
    printf("\t(t)est for membership in a set\n");
    printf("\t(u)nion of sets A and B\n");
    ch = getc(stdin);
    if (ch == 'c') {
        printf("set to clear (A or B)> ");
        ch = AorB();
        if (ch == 'A')
            bs_clear(set_A);
        else
            bs_clear(set_B);
    }
    else if (ch == 'd') {
        printf("element to delete>");
        scanf("%d", &n);
        printf("set (A or B)> ");
        ch = AorB();
        if (ch == 'A')
            bs_delete(n, set_A);
        else
            bs_delete(n, set_B);
    }
    else if (ch == 'e') {
        if (bs_equal(set_A, set_B))
            printf("set A IS equal to set B\n");
        else
            printf("set A is NOT equal to set B\n");
    }
    else if (ch == 'i') {
        printf("element to insert>");
        scanf("%d", &n);
        printf("set (A or B)> ");
        ch = AorB();
        if (ch == 'A')
            bs_insert(n, set_A);
```

```
        else
            bs_insert(n, set_B);
}
else if (ch == 'p') {
    printf("\nset A: ");
    bs_print(set_A);
    printf(" set B: ");
    bs_print(set_B);
    printf("\n");
}
else if (ch == 'q') {
    return;
}
else if (ch == 'R') {
    printf("read new values for which set (A or B)> ");
    ch = AorB();
    if (ch == 'A')
        bs_read(set_A);
    else
        bs_read(set_B);
}
else if (ch == 'r') {
    printf("remove from which set (A or B)> ");
    ch = AorB();
    if (ch == 'A')
        bs_remove(set_A, set_B);
    else
        bs_remove(set_B, set_A);
}
else if (ch == 's') {
    printf("see if which set is a subset ");
    printf("of the other (A or B)> ");
    ch = AorB();
    if (ch == 'A') {
        if (bs_subset(set_A, set_B))
            printf("A IS a subset of B\n");
        else
            printf("A is NOT a subset of B\n");
    }
    else {
        if (bs_subset(set_B, set_A))
            printf("B IS a subset of A\n");
        else
            printf("B is NOT a subset of A\n");
    }
}
else if (ch == 't') {
    printf("element to test for>");
```

```
                    scanf ("%d", &n);
                    printf ("set (A or B)> ");
                    ch = AorB();
                    if (ch == 'A')
                        george = bs_member(n, set_A);
                    else
                        george = bs_member(n, set_B);
                    if (george)
                        printf("%d IS a member\n", n);
                    else
                        printf("%d is NOT a member\n", n);
                }
            else if (ch == 'u') {
                printf("make which set the ");
                printf("union of the two sets (A or B)> ");
                ch = AorB();
                if (ch == 'A')
                    bs_union(set_A, set_B);
                else
                    bs_union(set_B, set_A);
            }
            else {
                printf("unknown command\n");
            }
            toss = getc(stdin);
        }
} /* main */
#endif  _BITSETS_TESTBED_


/*================================================================*/
boolean    bs_inited( max )
    int    max;    /* IN */
/*- - - - - - - - - - - - - - - - - - - - - - - - - - - - - - -
Purpose:
    Initialize the bitset library. This MUST be the first bitset
    function (or macro) invoked.
Parameters:
    max    maximum number of elements a bitset can have. Bitsets
           are pointers to arrays of chars (allocated by bs_new())
           so we need to know how big to make those arrays of chars
    Returns true unless max <= 0.
- - - - - - - - - - - - - - - - - - - - - - - - - - - - - - - -*/
{
    if (max <= 0) {
        printf("bs_inited: bitsets with %d elements??\n", max);
        return (false);
    }
    bs_bits_per_set = max;
```

```
        bs_bytes_per_set = (bs_bits_per_set + 7)/8;
        return (true);
} /* bs_inited */


/*===============================================================*/
bs_type     bs_new()
/*-------------------------------------------------------------
Purpose:
    Allocate a new bitset and initialize it to the empty set {}.
Parameters:
    none
    Returns NULL on failure. Uses bs_bits_per_set to see if
    bs_inited() has been called.
-----------------------------------------------------------*/
{
    bs_type new;
    char    *nxt;
    void    *malloc();
    int     i;

    if (bs_bits_per_set == 0) {
        printf("must call bs_inited() first!\n");
        return (NULL);
    }
    if (!(new = (bs_type)malloc(bs_bytes_per_set))) {
        printf("out of memory\n");
        return (NULL);
    }
    for (nxt = (char *)new, i = 0; i < bs_bytes_per_set; i++, nxt++)
        *nxt = '\0';
    return (new);
} /* bs_new */


/*===============================================================*/
void        bs_clear( set )
    bs_type set;     /* IN, OUT */
/*-------------------------------------------------------------
Purpose:
    Clear a set—make it equal to the empty set {}.
Parameters:
    set     set to zap (originally from bs_new())
-----------------------------------------------------------*/
{
    char    *nxt;
    int     i;

    for (nxt = (char *)set, i = 0; i < bs_bytes_per_set; i++, nxt++)
        *nxt = '\0';
```

```
} /* bs_clear */


/*=============================================================*/
boolean      bs_equal( one, two )
    bs_type one;      /* IN */
    bs_type two;      /* IN */
/*-------------------------------------------------------------
Purpose:
    See if two sets have the same members.
Parameters:
    one,
    two     sets to compare (both originally from bs_new())
-------------------------------------------------------------*/
{
    int     i;

    for (i = 0; i < bs_bytes_per_set; i++) {
        if (one[i] != two[i])
            return (false);
    }
    return (true);
} /* bs_equal */


/*=============================================================*/
void         bs_print( set )
    bs_type set;      /* IN */
/*-------------------------------------------------------------
Purpose:
    Pretty-print a set's current members.
Parameters:
    one,
    two     sets to compare (both originally from bs_new())
-------------------------------------------------------------*/
{
    int     i;
    boolean first = true;

    printf("{");
    for (i = 0; i < bs_bits_per_set; i++) {
        if (bs_member(i,set)) {
            if (first)
                first = false;
            else
                printf(", ");
            printf("%d", i);
        }
    }
    printf("}");
```

```
} /* bs_print */

/*===============================================================*/
void        bs_read( set )
    bs_type set;    /* OUT */
/*-------------------------------------------------
Purpose:
    Read a set's members from the user; whatever was in the set
    before is overwritten. To terminate list of members, enter
    one that is out of bounds.
Parameters:
    set     sets to get members of (originally from bs_new())
------------------------------------------------------*/
{
    int     n;
    void    bs_clear();

    bs_clear(set);
    printf("{");
    for ( ; ; ) {
        scanf("%d", &n);
        if ((n < 0) || (n >= bs_bits_per_set)) {
            printf("}");
            return;
        }
        printf(", ");
        bs_insert(n, set);
    }
} /* bs_read */

/*===============================================================*/
void        bs_remove( dest, removed )
    bs_type dest;       /* IN, OUT */
    bs_type removed;    /* IN */
/*-------------------------------------------------
Purpose:
    Remove elements of one set from another set.
Parameters:
    dest,
    removed     sets to use (both originally from bs_new())—
                dest becomes dest minus removed
------------------------------------------------------*/
{
    int     i;

    for (i = 0; i < bs_bytes_per_set; i++)
        dest[i] &= ~(removed[i]);
} /* bs_remove */
```

```
/*=============================================================*/
boolean      bs_subset( sub, super )
    bs_type sub;      /* IN */
    bs_type super;    /* IN */
/*-------------------------------------------------------------
Purpose:
    Check to see if one set is contained in another set. Note
    that the empty set {} is contained in every set.
Parameters:
    sub,
    super    sets to use (both originally from bs_new())—
             returns "sub is a subset of super"
---------------------------------------------------------------*/
{
    int     i;

    for (i = 0; i < bs_bytes_per_set; i++) {
        if ((sub[i] | super[i]) != super[i])
            return (false);
    }
    return (true);
} /* bs_subset */


/*=============================================================*/
void         bs_union( dest, added )
    bs_type dest;     /* IN, OUT */
    bs_type added;    /* IN */
/*-------------------------------------------------------------
Purpose:
    Add the elements of one set to another set.
Parameters:
    dest,
    added    sets to use (both originally from bs_new()) -
             dest becomes dest plus added
---------------------------------------------------------------*/
{
    int     i;

    for (i = 0; i < bs_bytes_per_set; i++)
        dest[i] |= added[i];
} /* bs_union */


/*=============================================================*/
static char     AorB()
/*-------------------------------------------------------------
Purpose:
    Get a response of 'A' or 'B' from the user.
```

```
Parameters:
    none
    Returns 'A' or 'B'.
_____*/

{
    char    res = '\0';

    while ((res != 'A') && (res != 'B')) {
        res = getc(stdin);
        if ((res != '\n') && (res != 'A') && (res != 'B'))
            printf("\nmust be set A or set B\n");
    }
    return (res);
} /* AorB */
```

CHAPTER 23

A Collection of Struct Tricks

This is a collection of tricks to keep in mind during implementation, or when you are going back through code trying to better satisfy some top-level goal (portability, low memory usage, robustness, and so on).

STRUCT TRICK TEMPLATE

Key Words and Phrases

This section gives a short list of topics related to use of the trick.

Tradeoffs

This section lists the pros and cons of using the trick, so you know what you're getting into.

Trick

Additional sections like this demonstrate the particulars of using a trick, and point out why the tradeoffs listed above come into play.

STRUCT TRICK: CHASING POINTERS FASTER

Key Words and Phrases

The key words and phrases for this particular trick are speeding linked list or tree access, chasing pointers, and cutting search time.

Tradeoffs

By using this trick, we have:

probably made *chasing pointers faster*
made it necessary to *recompile*
rearranged the order of struct members but left sizeof(struct) and all code except typedefs unchanged

Trick

Most compilers take advantage of the fact that the offset of the first member of a struct is zero; they generate more efficient references to that member than to the rest of the members. In trees, linked lists, and other structures held together by pointers, pointers are referenced frequently. We can speed up these references by making a pointer the first struct member.

For instance, a linked list of this struct:

```
typedef struct foo_faster {
   struct foo_faster    *next;
   int                  data;      /* data represents all the */
} foo_faster;                      /* other foo_faster members */
```

is usually faster to search than a list of this very similar struct:

```
typedef struct foo {
   int          data;
   struct foo  *next;
} foo;
```

Of course, to be sure how many cycles are actually saved, we have to look at the assembly code produced in each case. This is easy to do with a little program like the one below. Compile this with your C compiler options set so the assembly code is left where you can find it, and then compare accesses to *roo* and *roo_raster*:

```
main()
{
```

```
foo_faster   roo_raster, *rr;
foo          roo, *r;

roo_raster.next = 0xfa5dfa5d; /* "fastfast" */
rr = roo_raster.next;
roo.next = 0x51005100;        /* "slowslow" */
r = roo.next;
} /* main */
```

STRUCT TRICK: VARIABLES IN HEADER FILES

Key Words and Phrases

The key words and phrases for this particular trick are global variables, header file, include file, global initialization, and extern variable.

Tradeoffs

By using this trick, we have:

> made it possible to *declare and initialize global variables* in a header file
> made it possible to *replace extern references* in *.c files by an include
> *maintained* portability, algorithms, and data structures

Trick

Suppose we are writing a library or program that needs some global variables. These variables are referenced in many files, but we would like to declare them all together so that we'll be aware of what's global and why. We could put them in main.c and reference them everywhere else as externs:

```
/* in main.c: */

int  global1 = 0;
char global2 = "howdy dudes";

/* in other_one.c: */

extern int    global1;
extern char   global2[];
```

```
/* in another_other.c: */

extern char    global2[];
```

This approach has the advantage of making it very clear just which globals are used in a given *.c file. But suppose we have 30 or 40 *.c files! Listing the externs explicitly in each of these files makes editing tedious if we decide to add a new global or change a global's definition. We could use a tool like UNIX's awk or sed to make such widespread edits easier.

Or we can use the following trick to declare and initialize our globals in a header file. This allows us to replace the extern list in each *.c file with a single include statement. The *MY_GLOBALS* guard and define guarantee that the variables are allocated once, in main.c, and referenced as externs everywhere else.

```
/* in globals.h: */

#ifndef MY_GLOBALS
#define MY_GLOBALS
int     global1 = 0;                    /* useful comment 1 */
char    global2 = "howdy dudes";  /* useful comment 2 */
#else
extern int      global1;
extern char     global2[];
#endif MY_GLOBALS

/* in main.c: */

#define MY_GLOBALS
#include "globals.h"

/* in other.c, another_other.c: */

#include "globals.h"
```

A similar trick that works when there is no initialization looks like this:

```
/* in globals.h: */

EXTERN   int     global1;

/* in main.c: */

#define EXTERN
#include "globals.h"

/* in other.c, another_other.c: */

#define EXTERN extern
#include "globals.h"
```

STRUCT TRICK: WRITING ENGLISH IN HEX

Key Words and Phrases

The key words and phrases for this particular trick are memory dump, binary dump, hexadecimal, and debugging.

Tradeoffs

By using this trick, we have:

made it easier to *understand hexadecimal memory dumps*

Trick

Binary data is usually hard to interpret because it has no easily apparent structure. It's just a lot of numbers. But it is possible to put helpful "comments" of a sort in the middle of data. We can make hexadecimal dumps easier to understand by inserting English words in the data. Of course, we can only insert words like "DEAD" and "BEEF" that are spelled with hex characters, but even a few easy-to-locate reference points can make a large hex listing much easier to manage.

But surely this is too crude to be useful! After all, symbolic debuggers are available to help us decipher large pieces of data. A good debugger will interpret bit patterns as floats or ints or whatever is appropriate, and display the results according to the typedefs the data is supposed to fit. Even without a debugger, couldn't we always write struct dumpers (see the top-level goal "Debuggable Code," page 341) to pretty-print the data? Why do we need to play hexadecimal spelling games?

The answer is that, unfortunately, debuggers and dumpers are not always available. Sometimes a bug prevents our program, which expects data in a certain format, from loading the data off the disk into memory. Sometimes the data can only be captured by special-purpose hardware that won't run a debugger or dumper; this is often true, for instance, of data packets speeding about on a network.

But a hexadecimal display of the data will virtually always be available. Even low-level diagnostic hardware (for displaying network data packets, for instance) typically displays in hex. The trick is to take advantage of the hexadecimal "alphabet" to put useful markers or messages inside the binary data.

But where do we put these "comments"? Obviously, we can't fiddle with addresses or with values supplied by other pieces of software. However, large blocks of data often contain IDs whose value can be chosen by the programmer. There are many examples; here are three:

1. Unions need tags to tell which of the variants is in use.
2. A database file contains x records of type A followed by y records of type B and z

records of type C. Since x, y, and z vary, special IDs are used to mark the beginning of each new record type. (Yes, there is an alternative. We can place a record count —x, y, and z, respectively—at the beginning of each section. But if we don't want to buffer up all the records so we can count them before we begin writing them to disk, we can use markers to indicate section beginnings.)

3. Data files contain a key that programs use to determine what kind of data the file contains.

In these and other cases where we have some choice about binary values, we can make dumps easier to read by choosing values that are easy to spot in a 40-page listing of hex values. Values like 0xAAAA, 0xABCD and the ever popular null 0x0000 are easy to see, but they're not program-specific. And, to be perfectly honest, they're not as much fun as we could be having. The trick, therefore, is to use the characters that are legal in hex to spell things that can serve as markers or comments in particular programs:

```
int ready  = 0xAB1EBABE; /* able babe */
int bad_id = 0xDEADC0DE; /* dead code */
int spacer = 0xB10BF00D; /* blob food */
```

The program at the end of this trick description generates all possible four-letter hexadecimal English words and acronyms. This is *not* the same as all possible four-character hexadecimal numbers. Since we're trying to spell English words, characters that don't look like a letter of the alphabet aren't used.

Thus, the program generates all possible four-letter hexadecimal numbers that can be written using 'A,' 'B,' 'C,' 'D,' 'E,' 'F,' '1,' '5,' and '0.' The numerals '1,' '5,' and '0' are used because they look like the letters 'L,' 'S,' and 'O,' respectively. Thus, "C01D" spells "COLD." If you prefer, '1' can stand for 'I,' so "D1ED" spells "DIED." In either case, the rest of the numerals aren't used.

Some of the words that can be written in hex this way are listed below.

```
AB1E A150 BABE BA5E BEAD BEEF B1ED B10B B01D CA5E C10D C0A1
C0DA C0DE C01A C01D C001 DEAD DEAF DEA1 DEED D0D0 EE15 E1F5
E15E FACE FADE FA11 FECE FED5 FEED FEE1 FE11 F1AB F0A1 F00D
F001 1AB5 1ACE 1A55 1EAD 1EAF 10B5 10C0 101A 105E 5AAB 5AFE
5A1E 5CAB 5EA1 5EA5 5E1F 5E11 51ED 510B 50DA 501D 501E 5010
0B0E 01DE 01E0 0510
```

```
#include <stdio.h>

static char alphabet[] = "ABCDEF150";
#define WORD_LENGTH      4
static char word[WORD_LENGTH+1];
static int  letter[WORD_LENGTH];
#define WORDS_PER_LINE  12
#define TOTAL_WORDS     (9*9*9*9)
```

```
/* TOTAL_WORDS = strlen(alphabet) to the WORD_LENGTH power */

main()
{
   void   init(), increment();
   int    i,
          twl, /* total words on current line */
          tw;  /* total words all together */

   printf( "\nThis program prints all %d-letter combinations\n",
        WORD_LENGTH);
   printf( "of the following characters: %s\n",
        alphabet);
   init();
   twl = 0;
   for (tw = 0; tw < TOTAL_WORDS; tw++) {
     for (i = 0; i < WORD_LENGTH; i++) {
        word[i] = alphabet[letter[i]];
     }
     increment();
     printf("%s  ", word);
     if (++twl >= WORDS_PER_LINE) {
        twl = 0;
        printf("\n");
     }
   }
   printf("\n");
} /* main */

static void init()
{
   int i;

   for (i = 0; i < WORD_LENGTH; i++)
     letter[i] = 0;
   word[WORD_LENGTH] = '\0';
} /* init */

static void increment()
{
   int i;

   for (i = WORD_LENGTH-1; i >= 0; i-) {
     if (++letter[i] < strlen(alphabet))
        return;
     else
        letter[i] = 0;
   }
} /* increment */
```

STRUCT TRICK: SQUEEZING IN BITFLAGS

Key Words and Phrases

The key words and phrases for this particular trick are minimizing data space, adding bitflags, pointers, counters, and alignment.

Tradeoffs

By using these tricks, we have:

added bitflags that were not there before

preserved sizeof(foo), where foo is the struct with the new bitflags in it

changed any functions that access the struct field containing the new flags

slowed execution in order to extract and insert bits, and also to mask them out when we want to access the rest of the field they are in

decreased portability by making one of these assumptions

- ints have at least as many bits as pointers (trick 1)
- the amount of memory available will never grow (trick 1)
- a particular addressing unit (e.g., bytes) will always be used (trick 2)
- certain structs will always be N-byte aligned (trick 2)

Trick 1

If an int is stored in at least as many bits as a pointer, we can use the high bit(s) of an int variable that counts data structures as bitflags, since these bits are never needed to represent a valid structure count.

For instance, suppose we want to squeeze a bitflag into the following structure:

```
typedef struct {
    int foo_count;  /* counts the number of foo structs we have */
    (some other stuff)
} I_need_flags;
```

If a *foo* struct is four bytes long, then one megabyte of memory can hold at most 256K *foo* structs. Since 256K is 0x40000, 19 bits (ignoring the sign bit since we don't need it to count from zero up) will hold the range of possible *foo* struct counts. If *I_need_flags.foo_count* has more than 19 bits, we can use the extra high-order bits as bitflags. If a *foo* struct is eight bytes long, one megabyte can hold at most 128K structs, and we need only 18 bits for any *foo* struct counter. 16-byte *foos* require one less bit to count, and so forth. Every time *sizeof(foo)* doubles, one more bit is freed in *I_need_flags.foo_count*.

Of course, if ints are only 16 bits long to begin with, *foo* structs will need to be 64 bytes long before we actually free any bits. There is at least one common architecture (8086) in which pointers are longer than ints, so we are losing some portability by assuming that those high-order bits of *I_need_flags.foo_count* will always be available. Also, we have assumed that the amount of memory available will never grow; if it does, some of those high bits may be needed.

To make the *I_need_flags* typedef reflect what we've done, we could change it to use bit fields explicitly:

```
typedef struct {
  unsigned flags     : 13;
  unsigned foo_count : 19;
  (some other stuff)
} I_have_flags;
```

A cleaner and more portable but slightly less efficient solution is to enforce some upper limit on *I_need_flags.foo_count*. In our functions, we make sure we don't overflow that value. This will almost always release more bits for use as flags, since the maximum number of *foos* seen in practice is much lower than the number we'd have if memory were stuffed with *foo* structs.

Trick 2

We can use the low bit(s) of a pointer variable as bitflags if the struct the pointer points to is always aligned on a multi-addressing unit boundary (e.g., 2-, 4-, 8-,... byte boundary on a byte-addressable machine).

For instance, suppose we want to squeeze a bitflag into the following structure:

```
typedef struct {
  struct foo  *foo_pointer;
  (some other stuff)
} I_need_flags;
```

Suppose further that we are on a byte-addressable machine, and the function used to allocate *foo* structs aligns them on word (four-byte) boundaries. Then the low two bits of *I_need_flags.foo_pointer* are always zero, so we can use these bits for flags. We have sacrificed some portability; if we move to a machine whose addressing unit is two bytes instead of one, one of our free low-order bits disappears. There will also be trouble if *foo* structs are no longer aligned on four-byte boundaries.

And, of course, it will take time to mask out the flags when we want to use *I_need_flags.foo_pointer* as a pointer. So we don't want to use this trick (or trick 1) unless adding a separate bitflag int to *I_need_flags* is out of the question. I have seen two examples of this:

1. The struct that needed flags was part of a database stored on disk; to maintain compatibility with existing databases, it was necessary to use unused pointer bits instead of adding a new int to hold bitflags.

2. Memory was allocated in eight-byte chunks, all the padding bytes needed to align the struct on an eight-byte boundary were already in use, and the struct appeared in memory hundreds or even thousands of times; we didn't want to allocate an additional eight bytes per struct just to get one more bit for a tiny but essential flag.

In both these cases, one of the two tricks just described were used. In general, however, adding a new int to the struct is preferable because masking is slow and error-prone.

STRUCK TRICK: NESTING INCLUDE FILES

Key Words and Phrases

The key words and phrases for this particular trick are include files, header files, "_____ redefined" compilation message, and conditional compilation.

Tradeoffs

By using this trick, we have

made it easier to have *header files include each other* so that the relationships between header files are clearer and editing is easier

avoided problems caused by *including the same header file* more than once in a C source code file

essentially *maintained typedefs, functions, and the rest of the code* that comes out of the C preprocessor; the only difference is that the code in header files is more widely accessible after the header files are modified as shown below

Trick

The trick is simple; explaining why it's a useful thing to do is the hard part. The trick is to put header file contents inside a conditional compilation guard like the one using _COMMON_H_ below:

```
/*---------------------------------------------
                    common.h
-----------------------------------------*/
#ifndef _COMMON_H_
#define _COMMON_H_

#define DIMENSION    3
typedef struct {
```

```
    float     x,y,z;
} point;
```

```
#endif _COMMON_H_
```

Now let's see why this trick is useful. When we build a library to be used in some application, we can usually separate the typedefs and defines into three groups, according to where they are used:

1. typedefs and defines used only by the application
2. typedefs and defines used by both the application and the library
3. typedefs and defines used only by the library

A reasonable approach is to put typedefs and defines that are used by both the application and the library in one header file. In the example below, this file is "common.h." The problem arises when we start writing the other header files for the library. Headers like "library_polyhedra.h" and "library_patch.h" in the example below make reference to the typedefs and defines in common.h. So we have two choices for the headers used only by the library:

1. Have library_•••.h include common.h.
2. Have every source file that includes library_•••.h also include common.h.

Why is it worth taking the time to consider both of these choices and any others we can come up with? Because common.h might rely in turn on some other header (perhaps for system typedefs), so the chain of inclusion can be arbitrarily long. Anything that is arbitrarily "long" or "large" or "small" or "slow" or arbitrarily anything else is worth closer examination.

The two choices are illustrated below. The tradeoffs between them are straightforward. Suppose we use the first choice, and ten source •.c files include library_patch.h, which includes common.h. If we need to change library_patch.h so that it includes another header, security.h, we simply add *#include <security.h>* to library_patch.h. We don't have to change anything in the ten •.c files.

The disadvantage of this approach is that the names of the headers included by a given •.c file are not given explicitly in that file. What appears in the •.c file are the root names of potentially large trees of includes. For instance, library_printers.c might include library_patch.h, which includes security.h and common.h. Security.h might in turn include math.h and stdio.h, while common.h includes system.h.

The conditional compilation guard around common.h (*#ifdef _COMMON_H_* ...) is necessary to prevent the preprocessor from including common.h more than once per •.c file. Without the guard, a •.c file that included both library_patch.h and library_polyhedra.h, for instance, would include common.h twice because each of those library headers includes common.h. This double inclusion may cause a compilation error.

If we use the second choice above, a header file never includes another header file. Instead, the list of headers included is given explicitly in the •.c file. We know by looking at library_printers.c that it includes library_patch.h, library_polyhedra.h, security.h, math.h, stdio.h, common.h, and system.h. The disadvantage is clear if we consider what we have to do if library_patch.h suddenly references a new header, security.h, say. We would need to add *#include <security.h>* to every one of the ten *.c files that include library_patch.h.

It's easy to write a little program that takes a *.c file and a list of directory paths (from a Makefile, for instance) as input and produces a list of all the header files the *.c file actually includes. Some C preprocessors have an option to do this. All the program has to do is traverse the inclusion tree by recursively chasing *#include* statements in the *.c and whatever it includes. With this tool, there is no advantage to the second choice above. The first choice is better because it makes the dependencies between header files more explicit, and it makes the editing involved in creating a dependency trivial instead of tedious.

The first of our two choices (the recommended choice) looks like this:

```
/*-------------------------------------------------------
                        common.h
-----------------------------------------------------*/
#ifndef _COMMON_H_
#define _COMMON_H_
#include "system.h"

#define DIMENSION      3
typedef struct {
    float    x,y,z;
} point;

#endif _COMMON_H_

/*-------------------------------------------------------
                        library_polyhedra.h
-----------------------------------------------------*/
#ifndef _LIBRARY_POLYHEDRA_H_
#define _LIBRARY_POLYHEDRA_H_
#include "common.h"

typedef struct triangle_list {
    struct triangle_list    *next;
    point                   data[3];
} triangle_list;

#endif _LIBRARY_POLYHEDRA_H_

/*-------------------------------------------------------
                        library_patch.h
-----------------------------------------------------*/
#ifndef _LIBRARY_PATCH_H_
#define _LIBRARY_PATCH_H_
#include "common.h"

typedef struct patch_list {
```

```
        struct patch_list    *next;
        point                 data[16];
} patch_list;

#endif _LIBRARY_PATCH_H_
```

```
/*----------------------------------------------
                          library_printers.c
-----------------------------------------------*/
#include "library_polyhedra.h"
#include "library_patch.h"

/* This file contains various library functions that work with patches
and polyhedra. */
```

```
/*----------------------------------------------
                       application_build_patches.c
-----------------------------------------------*/
#include <common.h>

/* This part of the application has to know what type point is to build
patches. */
```

The second choice (not recommended, but shown for comparison) looks like this:

```
/*----------------------------------------------
                               common.h
-----------------------------------------------*/
#include "system.h"

#define DIMENSION      3
typedef struct {
    float    x,y,z;
} point;
```

```
/*----------------------------------------------
                          library_polyhedra.h
-----------------------------------------------*/
typedef struct triangle_list {
    struct triangle_list    *next;
    point                    data[3];
} triangle_list;
```

```
/*----------------------------------------------
                            library_patch.h
-----------------------------------------------*/
typedef struct patch_list {
```

```
    struct patch_list    *next;
    point                data[16];
} patch_list;

/*------------------------------------------------
              library_printers.c
-----------------------------------------------*/
#include <security.h>
#include <math.h>
#include <stdio.h>
#include <common.h>
#include <system.h>
#include "library_polyhedra.h"
#include "library_patch.h"

/* This file contains various library functions that work with patches
and polyhedra. */

/*------------------------------------------------
                application_build_patches.c
-----------------------------------------------*/
#include <common.h>

/* This part of the application has to know what type point is to build
patches. */
```

STRUCT TRICK: KEEPING JUST ONE COPY OF DATA

Key Words and Phrases

The key words and phrases for this trick are minimizing data space, eliminating data duplication, and decreasing structure comparison time.

Tradeoffs

By using this trick, we have:

eliminated duplicate copies of some of the data in our program
reduced the size of structs where data was duplicated
reduced the time needed to compare or copy those structs
added a new structure which contains the data that used to exist in several places
changed any functions which access the structs that used to contain the duplicated data
maintained portability

Trick

If the same fields appear in two different typedefs, and those fields often contain the same values in both structs, we can replace the common fields in each typedef with a "data ID." This data ID is either a pointer or an array index. In either case, the data ID tells us where to find the data that used to be stored in both structs.

For instance, suppose we have some structures like these:

```
typedef struct {
   int     A;
   double  B;
   (some other stuff)
   char    C[24];
} type_one;

typedef struct {
   int     A_value;
   char    C[24];
   double  current_B;
   (yet more stuff)
} type_two;
```

Suppose further that *type_one.A* and *type_two.A_value* have the same value at any point in the code where either is used. Likewise, assume *type_one.B* and *type_two.current_B* are interchangeable, as are *type_one.C* and *type_two.C*. If all this is true, we can decrease data space, decrease the time required to compare two structs, and decrease the likelihood of error all at once by reorganizing things as follows:

```
typedef struct {
   int     A;
   double  B;
   char    C[24];
} shared;

struct shared  one_two_share[256];

typedef struct {
   int     shared_id;  /* index into one_two_share[] */
   (some other stuff)
} new_type_one;

typedef struct {
   (yet more stuff)
   int     shared_id;       /* index into one_two_share[] */
} new_type_two;
```

In other words, just one copy of the data is kept. Total data space goes down if the data in the original *type_one* and *type_two* structs was often duplicated. Of course, if a given *shared_id* never appears more than once in *new_type_one* or *new_type_two* structs—that is, the data format was shared but the values were not—we are worse off than before.

Notice that we get the same tradeoffs if we are considering data that is shared between different *type_one* structs (or *type_two* structs), instead of data shared between a *type_one* struct and a *type_two* struct.

Also, note that *shared_id* could be a pointer instead of an array index. In this case, *one_two_shared[]* would be replaced by a linked list of structs something like this (the reference count is useful when memory deallocation time comes):

```
typedef struct shared_list_element {
    struct shared_list_element    *next;
    int                           ref_count; /* reference count */
    int                           A;
    double                        B;
    char                          C[24];
} shared_list_element;
```

Making *one_two_shared* a list gives us roughly the same data space savings as using the array *one_two_shared[]*. The only differences are the usual tradeoffs between using an array and using a linked list; see the design guideline "Avoid Sorted Lists of Arrays" (page 360).

Incidentally, the fact that this trick requires changes in several typedefs causes some people to categorize it as a struct design guideline rather than a struct trick. It's a close call, but I've kept it here with the tricks because the change, extensive though it is, provides better performance, not basic functionality.

GLOSSARY

Note: Terms that arise in abstract data type descriptions (ADTDs) are defined in Chapter 5.

Abstract data type: See **ADTD**.

ADTD: Stands for "Abstract Data Type Description." In general, an abstract data type is a language-independent description of some data structure, including both its geometry and operators. In this book, abstract data types are described by answering some or all of a list of ADTD questions; see Chapter 4, "Creating an Abstract Data Type."

Customer: As used in Chapter 2, "Setting Top-Level Goals," someone who uses a program without having taken part in its development. See also **contributor, programmer**.

Contributor: As used in Chapter 2, "Setting Top-Level Goals," someone other than a programmer who supports the development of a program. Examples include managers of programmers, technical writers, marketing managers, and user group leaders. See also **customer, programmer**.

Framework: Part of the **Plan**; the Framework is a way to organize programming expertise. Knowledge is divided into four increasingly specific categories: **top-level goals, abstract data types, struct design guidelines,** and **struct tricks**. Templates and examples for each category are provided in Section 3 of *Advanced C Struct Programming*. **Guiding examples** are also part of the Framework, but they are program-specific, so no collection is given here. They are, however, described in the Examples section, and in Chapter 3, "Choosing Good Guiding Examples."

Fundamental characteristics: The ways in which the examples we choose to guide program design and implementation differ from each other. Readers with a mathematical bent may think of these **guiding examples** as points in a space of program actions; the fundamental characteristics are the axes that determine the space's coordinate system. See Chapter 3, "Choosing Good Guiding Examples," for more details.

Guiding examples: The **Plan** suggests that program development be guided by an appropriate set of examples of what the program is to do. As discussed in Chapter 3, "Choosing Good Guiding Examples," the examples should be chosen so they cover all critical possibilities but overlap as little as possible. This is achieved by choosing examples according to their **fundamental characteristics**.

Plan: A top-down flexible approach to data structure design and implementation. An overview is given in Chapter 1. Basically, the Plan consists of a sequence of steps to follow and a **Framework** that both summarizes and guides the decisions made along the way. Examples and suggestions are given throughout the book.

Production code: Code that is used (or is good enough to be used) in products sold on the open market. The standards for production code are different than those for debugging code, for instance, or for quick-and-dirty tools. See, for instance, the description of understandable code in Chapter 20, "A Collection of Top-Level Goals."

Programmer: As used in Chapter 2, "Setting Top-Level Goals," someone who actually writes part of the code for a particular program. See also **customer, contributor**. Because of their different perspectives, programmers, customers, and contributors often have different goals for programs, and for the programming process.

Struct design guidelines: Discussions of the tradeoffs involved in choosing one implementation of a given **abstract data type** over another. For instance, when is an array preferable to a linked list as an implementation of a list ADT? See also **struct tricks, Framework**. Examples are given in Chapter 22, "A Collection of Struct Design Guidelines."

Struct tricks: Discussions of implementation tradeoffs that have no direct connection with a particular abstract data type. Examples include how to squeeze in bitflags without requiring additional memory, and how to declare pointers to speed up data access. See also **struct design guidelines, Framework**. Examples are given in Chapter 23, "A Collection of Struct Tricks."

Testbed: A program whose purpose is to invoke (possibly interactively) some set of functions (typically a library) so their functionality and/or performance can be tested. In the Examples section, the testbeds are simply versions of *main()* which optionally (via conditional compilation) invoke the functions that are the real point of the example. See also **test suite**.

Test suite: A set of data that can be automatically or interactively fed to a program. The program may be an actual application, or it may just be a **testbed** that customers will never see.

Top-level goals: Goals that might be desirable for any program, as opposed to functionality requirements for a particular program. Portability, ease of use, and many other top-level goals are discussed in Chapter 2, "Setting Top-Level Goals," and in the **Framework** section.

BIBLIOGRAPHY

Aho, A.V., and M.J. Corasick. 1975. Efficient string matching: an aid to bibliographic search. *Communications of the ACM* 18 (no. 6): 333–340.

Aho, A.V., J.E. Hopcroft, and J.D. Ullman. 1983. *Data structures and algorithms*. Reading, MA: Addison-Wesley, p. 10.

Booch, G. 1983. *Software engineering with ada*. Menle Park, CA: The Benjamin/Cummings Publishing Company.

Brown, R. 1988. Calendar queues: A fast O(1) priority queue implementation for the simulation event set problem. *Communications of the ACM* 31 (no. 1): 1220–1227, 1988. See also Brown, R. 1989. Technical correspondence. *Communications of the ACM* 32 (no. 10):1241–1242.

Cleaveland, J.C. 1986. *An introduction to data types*. Reading, MA: Addison-Wesley.

Kernighan, B.W., and D.M. Ritchie. 1978. *The C programming language*. Englewood Cliffs, NJ: Prentice-Hall.

Knuth, D.E. 1973. *The art of computer programming, vol. I: Fundamental algorithms*. Reading, MA: Addison-Wesley.

Lammers, S. 1986. *Programmers at work, 1st series*. Redmond, WA: Microsoft Press.

Licker, P.S. 1985. *The art of managing software development people*. New York: John Wiley & Sons.

Ogilvie, J.W.L. 1985. *Modula-2 programming*. New York: McGraw-Hill.

Park, S.K., and K.W. Miller. 1988. Random number generators: Good ones are hard to find. *Communications of the ACM* 31 (no. 10): 1192–1201.

Peterson, J. 1977. Petri nets. *Computing Surveys* 9 (no. 3, Sept): 223–252.

Stroustrup, B. 1987. *The C++ programming language*. Reading, MA: Addison-Wesley. p. 213.

Tolkien, J.R.R. 1965. *The lord of the rings*. New York: Ballantine Books.

Wirth, N. 1976. *Algorithms + data structures = programs*. Englewood Cliffs, NJ: Prentice-Hall.

Wirth, N. 1984. Data structures and algorithms. *Scientific American*, Sept. 1984.

INDEX

INDEX TO THE C CODE

Note: This index contains references to all the C source files in *Advanced C Struct Programming*, as well as references to selected typedefs, functions, and macros.

411